Thee Method of Magick Thee Aim of Science
Old TOPI Proverb

*THOSE WHO DO NOT REMEMBER THE PAST
ARE CONDEMNED TO REPEAT IT.*

The words are just confessions of a mask
They say that thoughts have wings
But our wings have been clipped
The words have gotten in the way
And we are just limping forward
Yet instead of trying to find the thoughts behind the mask
The thoughts that really count without the words
We have fallen for the reflection
The reflection of the shadow of civilization
A civilization that knows no honor
And knows no respect
And knows not its desires or true meaning
A lie within a lie within a lie
The time is long past for a new beginning
The caress within the iron glove.
Monte Cazazza

Embrace reality by imagination.
Austin Osman Spare

The specialized sciences of our times are concentrating
on the study of the three constants of life: sexual instinct,
the sentiment of death, and the anguish of space-time.
Salvador Dalí

ASSUME POWER FOCUS.
Old TOPI Proverb

Second Edition Compiled and Edited by Jason Louv 2006 e.v.
First Edition Compiled and Edited by J. A. Rapoza 1994 e.v.
Copyright Genesis Breyer P-Orridge 1994 and 2010 e.v.
Book design: Hazel Hill, Los Angeles CA
Typography consultant: Will Hill, Anglia Ruskin University, Cambridge
Initial illustrations: Sarah Ross, London UK

Published by Feral House
1240 W. Sims Way Suite124
Port Townsend, WA 98368
www.FeralHouse.com
Hardcover isbn 978-1932595390, Dec 2009, one limited edition
ISBN: 978-193259590
Print count - 3rd printing

THEE
Psychick
BIBLE

THEE APOCRYPHAL SCRIPTURES ℣
GENESIS BREYER P-ORRIDGE
AND THEE THIRD MIND ℣
THEE TEMPLE ℣ PSYCHICK YOUTH

DEDICATED TO MY "OTHER HALF"
THEE ANGELIC BEING

LADY JAYE BREYER P-ORRIDGE
1969-2007

S/HE IS (STILL) HER/E

Feral House

Photo by Sheila Rock, 1983

ACKNOWLEDGEMEANTS

Once upon a T.I.M.E. we were wondering "What would happen if a band took its fans seriously and chose to encourage them to explore... ANYTHING?" This book is a result and was thirty y-eras in the constructing. TOPY remains a unique experiment in collective vision and living, warts and all. Not so much a book as a manual of alternative ways of thinking, of being and of CARING/GIVING! "Thee Psychick Bible" is a result of co-operation and shared dreams, hopes and dynamic imagination. To our knowledge, never in the Astory of our worlds cultures, has there ever been such a single-minded, unconditionally dedicated, collective system of focused orgasm within ritualized living and gender RE-EVOLUTIONARY exploration. These objectives are almost indecipherable in our age of blind consumerism, data addiction and inertia as a way of L-if-E. This book is a research documeant of which we are proud to have been primary instigator. A manual of possibilities, AND impossibilities. At the very least a record of our courageous attempts to defeat "control" and seek ways to consciously take command of our behaviour and our identity. An amazing team of Individuals was drawn to our passionate dream. Special gratitude goes to Joe A. Rapoza for having the vision to propose the original edition; Jason Louv who dedicated months of his irreplaceable time to editing the bulk of the contents from thousands of pages and hundreds of documents; Tom Hallewell the "Ultimate Coyote" who founded TOPYN.A.; Monte Cazazza who was, as always, there at the conception; Peter Christopherson for unique guidance; Jean-Pierre Turmel; Benjamin Tischer; Carl Abrahamsson; Malik; Brother Words; Sister Shadows; Caresse and Genesse P-Orridge; Jay Kinney; Caleigh Fisher; Edward ODowd; Bill Breeze; Johnn Balance; Hazel Hill who turned a dream into an authentic classic; Lady Jaye Breyer P-Orridge who insisted this book must be completed and, most of all Adam Parfrey and Jodi Wille. Adam and Jodi demonstrated saintly patience as this brick of wisdoms evolved showing a level of trust and kindness fully in keeping with the One True TOPI Tribe. Thank you ALL and all those unnamed others who made this adventure possible...

Genesis Breyer P-Orridge NYC, 2009

CONTENTS

VII ESSAYS ON INTUITIVE MAGICK

FOREWORD
THE DECONSTRUCTION OF A MAP
OF AN UNKNOWN TERRITORY

Probably no word does better justice to the TOPY phenomenon than "Occulture." Meshing "Occult" with "Culture," there's also a prefixed trace of "Occident" if you will. The defined concept as such was integrated in the inter-TOPY-"lingo" in the late 80s, and then grew to become a readily accepted general term for anything cultural yet decidedly occult/spiritual.

As a more or less unnamed concept, Occulture had already been active in TOPY since day one. The field of research was never ever occultism per se or culture per se, but always consisted of interchangeability where eventually the clear-cut borders were gently erased. Books, pamphlets, newsletters, film and video screenings, record and cassette releases and other manifestations could certainly contain more or less blatant esoteric form or content, but it was in no way a prerequisite. The literal meaning of "occult" (as in "hidden") was given a wider perspective than the merely "magical" one.

Hidden information, forgotten personalities, discarded thoughtforms, untrendy thinkers, eclectic evolutionairies and anachronistic anarchs... Dusting off shelved illuminations from past ages and offering forgotten morsels of human intelligence proved to be a very fertile soil indeed. A Promethean Strikeforce that passed on the torch of enlightenment from the dawn of mankind to our own revolutionary times.

From very early on, there was a heavy focus on the unhampered sharing of information, hidden or otherwise. All one had to do was let one's interests and areas of research be known through newsletters and other channels, and one was certain to receive something of interest. A second-hand book, long out of print. A compendium of xeroxes from someone's equally enthusiastic archive. A cassette tape copy of some recordings never released on record or broadcast on radio. Seeing the global TOPY Network as a precursor to the Internet is not far fetched at all. The first generation developers of "cyberculture" were certainly aware of—and some of them even active in—TOPY and its ideas and ideals.

Culture in itself is usually associated with performing arts, painting, music, literature and many other forms of traditional manifestation. The sphere of culture. But essentially, culture is exactly what the word entails: a culture—a structure or soil that contains the implicit possibility of growth and manifestation of life and, in extension, ideas and information. The merging of sperm and egg and their continued growth as one DNA-programmed entity in a womb is perhaps the clearest and most potent symbol of culture.

Many of the TOPY "Access Points" (regional headquarters) were involved in releasing material for distribution: books, magazines, records, videos and so on. At TOPY SCAN, the Scandinavian section, we focussed at times more on these kinds of activities than on the actual meeting of members or on doing strange rituals together. The more esoteric and magical activity certainly took place too, but quite often these rituals were "cosmic boosters" for the success of, for instance, a new magazine project or a new record. The intimate seeds of individuals were sown in a communal soil for the benefit of occultural manifestations—these becoming, in turn, seeds in their own right, blooming in a more extroverted universe of readers, listeners, art lovers, etc.

On the more distinctly magical level, we organised several workshops in shamanism (meaning here using archaic techniques of, for instance, drumming to induce states of trance used for information gathering on entirely different, higher, levels of consciousness) and Western ceremonial magic. We made treks into the Swedish countryside, stayed up all night and tried (quite successfully) to communicate with hidden aspects of nature and our own minds.

The rituals suggested in *Thee Grey Book* (the main TOPY compendium dealing with magick and philosophy) and other key documents were often the starting point for members wanting to experiment with meditation, traditional methods of ceremonial magic and one's own sexuality in a directed way. Rituals were by no means confined to the individual monthly sigilising process (as recommended in Thee Grey Book), but would develop and grow in organic forms, either individually or with other members.

The status of "Eden" for the actively sigilising men and "Kali" for the women signified an even stronger internal bond. That is, if one wanted to. There were never any demands on Kalis or Edens to do or achieve anything, except possibly to be truer to themselves than they had been up to that point.

What the central TOPY ritual consisted of, at least structurally, was that on the 23rd of each month, at 2300 hours, the dedicated adepts would perform a sigilising ritual in and/or on an artwork designed by themselves specifically for the desired goal. This piece of highly charged talismanic art was then sent in to a TOPY "Station" (bigger and more administrative headquarters than the Access Points). The idea was to "impose" or inspire self discipline and regularity, to unite with other adepts in time, to initiate personal empirical research about ritual magick and, not forgetting, to honor the weird synchronistic concept of the number 23, as "inherited" from TOPY mentors William S. Burroughs and Brion Gysin.

The augmented level of 23 consecutive sent-in "23-sigils" was reached by very few individuals connected to the TOPY EUROPE headquarters. Usually, however, that level of commitment to an experimental (yet communal) goal manifested itself in other ways too (active help with administration, practical assistance, creating original things—texts, images, music for TOPY publications, etc.) and thus quite few people were able to achieve quite a lot.

The structure of "official" TOPY sigilizing combines elements of traditional sexual magic (using the elevated state of mind reached at and before the orgasmic climax to mentally charge a symbol of the desired, of the ideal, and also using the highly vitally charged residual secretions: semen and vaginal fluids), meditational focus, eastern mantric techniques, Austin Osman Spare's development of an individual "alphabet of desire", elements of sacrificial use of blood and saliva as well as other techniques to maximize the experience as such. Not forgetting creating a totally individual-based artwork to act as a "receiving" vessel or talisman for the desired. Thereby integrating art in its most important and primordial function: As a magical and mystical tool to achieve union with higher cosmic levels of mind and to express one's affinity and desires with and to these levels.

Very seldom is this art historic aspect of TOPY considered. The archival collection of contemporary talismanic art, ranging in styles from totally primitive abstractions to very refined draughtsmanship, over sexually explicit collages to mind-bending mixed media paintings and sculptures, is totally unique in every sense of the word. The term "Magical Art" is usually ascribed to totemic objects from Africa or other non-Western areas. And it's usually something having to do with the past. In the case of the TOPY "collection," all the gathered works are indeed

13

contemporary/present, but all bordering on (at least in the very moment of creation) the future.

Another highly interesting aspect of this art is that it is in many ways an anti-art. It's not art made specifically for other people to see, and thereby it doesn't fit in with the contemporary ideals of pleasing an art market. Here we can return to the very orgins of art (cave paintings, etc.). The idea was not to have a glass of wine together with tribal kin in a cosy cave, to self-aggrandize through witty ironic criticisms. The idea was to impose one's will on the world outside your own personal sphere, or that of the tribe. Art as magical evocation. Whether other members or other tribes actually could see or understand what one had inscribed or painted was beside the point.

On an individual level, the experimenting was active and, I would say, radical. As an administrator of TOPY SCAN and, later, TOPY EUROPE, I was fortunate to see and handle European Kalis' and Edens' "23-sigils" in trust (a trust that has been, is and will continue to be honored). I was also involved in a proto-creative dialogue with several members on magical results, effects, breakthroughs, ups and downs of various techniques, etc. Hearing what had worked for others, I empirically assembled and concocted my own "grimoires" and shared my findings with those who had been sharing in their turn. An occultural TOPY concept in genuinely creative action!

There were also magical workings created and performed together. During the international gatherings, so called "Roto-Rites," elaborate and ceremonial workings would be performed for goals that dealt with greater TOPY ideals and visions. At TOPYSCAN and TOPY EUROPE we would not infrequently experiment with sigilising and other kinds of rituals together. Sharing those kinds of intense and electrified physical and emotional moments with others in trust was a real eye-opener to many of those involved, including myself. The creative framework of a uniting crystal-clear goal and of experimental techniques that evoke a previously unfelt emotional charge in the ritual chamber can be quite an empowering setting to be in.

At the era of conception—not an inappropriate symbol in this case—the TOPY network (or Nett Work, as P-Orridge would aptly call it) was tightly interwoven with the musical constellation "Psychick Televison" (PTV).

From 1982 and onwards, PTV in their many guises were missionaries of individual liberty on a seemingly endless tour. TOPY as a living entity was very integrated in PTV and became philosophical fuel not only for the band members but also for those already active or those just curious when the multicoloured Psychick Circus rolled by all over the world.

Some TOPY members "liked" PTV and some did not. What was obvious though, was that the Gesamtkunstwerk-aspect of what seemed to "others" to be just a weird band, was an enormous source of inspiration for most of us. It was possible to do anything. Music was not confined to pop or noise or anything. Neither were the stage presentations, the performances, the artwork for the records limited in any way.

Many of the young people involved in various phases of PTV grew up to be creative and successful artists in their own right. If there's something I think unites all of these people, it's an openmindedness, a creative courage and a spontaneity that in many regards have their origins in the uncompromising Psychick Television—and Temple ov Psychick Youth—kaleidoscope.

What constitutes the essence of all of this? There are so many things that come to mind, but I guess the most quintessential ones are the offering of different possibilities, of alternative options, of alternative routes, of inspiring courage and will, of breaking apart uncomfortable imposed patterns and showing, by example, that it is after all possible to re-assemble the bits in very creative ways.

15

The concepts of "occult," "culture" and even "occulture" become redundant on a higher level. What's here for us all in our apparently finite timeframe is the de-finite possibility to access the in-finite. How and why we as individuals go about this is another story (no less interesting). The first phase and face of TOPY as an experimental "Centrifugal Intelligence Agency" was so fertile it took on a life of its own and thereby touched upon the infinite. Regardless if one's path is that of a hermit or that of an ardent team player, a lot can be learned from this strange manifestation in human history and culture that has, more than any group structure before, taken on the conscious decision to give form and voice (dare I say even direction?) to the Collective Unconscious.

Carl Abrahamsson, a.k.a. "Eden 162," Stockholm, Sweden, 2006

INTRODUCTION
ON THE WAY TO THEE GARDEN

The Psychic Youth sits in a house of cards. Reaches out. It is not hard. Only takes the will to do it. Only takes a small push, to watch the house they have built for you collapse. To peel back the mask of the identity they gave you. And when the house falls, as it must, it is the first Garden we find ourselves in. Unnamed.

To be awake. To be ex-dream.

These are the apocryphal scriptures of Genesis Breyer P-Orridge and Thee Temple ov Psychick Youth, a representation of an eleven-year experiment (1981-1992) that will be remembered as a crucial period in the development of both the rough beast that is magick and of anarchic and artistic responses to the ever-marching and ever-homogenizing process of globalization.

While the story of the music of Genesis Bryeyer P-Orridge, Throbbing Gristle and Psychic Television is relatively well-known, the story of TOPY remains a cipher, hidden behind slogans and propaganda. The activities of the Temple, outside of the memories of those who were there and participated, have been obfuscated, and quite intentionally so—buried like the Dead Sea Scrolls, or perhaps, as William S. Burroughs once wished for some particularly volatile and explosive fragments of his own cut-up writing, wrapped in lead and sunk to the bottom of the ocean, leaving a blank spot in the history of the progression of both modern occulture—a term that the Temple coined—and modern culture itself.

Founded out of the rubble left by the sonic assault that Throbbing Gristle waged on the English public, Psychic TV was originally conceived as the new forum for ex-TG members Genesis P-Orridge along with Alex Fergusson of Alternative TV and later, for a short time only, Peter Christopherson (later to form one half of "archangels of chaos" Coil with the late Geoff Rushton a.k.a Jhon Balance) and occasional cameos by Marc Almond of Soft Cell. The band's original forays, notably the LPs *Force Thee Hand ov Chance* and *Dreams Less Sweet*, under Fergusson's influence, largely drifted away from TG's pulverizing wall of force and into more pop territory, the band becoming a fully-fledged psychedelic rock outfit by the release of *Allegory and Self*.

Set up as a propaganda device for self-directed consciousness expansion by any means necessary, Psychic TV was structured as the public face of

Thee Temple ov Psychick Youth, a widescale experiment in the meltdown of personal assumptions via guiltless sexuality and more formalized "magickal" techniques derived from Austin Osman Spare, Brion Gysin and Aleister Crowley, among others. TOPY, however, was never an explicitly magickal order, drawing equally on the heritage of the radical action groups and experimental microsocieties of the 1960s, such as the Exploding Galaxy group that Genesis had worked with in London, the Diggers of Haight Ashbury, or the COUM Transmissions performance art collective that Genesis founded in 1969 after a series of "flicker" induced visions and voices, later joined by Peter Christopherson and Cosey Fanny Tutti before creating Throbbing Gristle with Chris Carter.

The magick of the Temple wasn't the magick of the Golden Dawn, designed for the stately Victorian manor; it was magick designed for the blank-eyed, TV-flattened, prematurely abyss-dwelling youth of the late Twentieth Century—like the punk kids in Derek Jarman's *Jubilee*, who have never ventured out of the council flats they were born in. Rather than high ceremony, drawing-room intrigue and exalted initiatory ritual, the focus more often than not became simple survival, and defense of the individual vision from a malevolently dehumanizing culture that the Victorians and Modernists, even in their most racist and reactionary moments, could never have foreseen.

The Temple, as its initiates often said, was a ghost… It was, and is, the realization that your daydreams and fantasies, the teachers within you, are the most important teachers of all. A push in the right direction, towards yourself, towards self-integrity, towards your own connection with the deep waters of Spirit. A method of deprogramming instead of programming. The Chapel of Extreme Experience.

KEYS TO THE TEMPLE

1 Sitting in the back of the car at age six watching the trees on the horizon, the setting sun fickering through them. Heart is infinite moment is infinite.

2 Watching strange androgynous singer on television at age twelve, new world, newfound desires, yearning for something more than the human.

3 Strange books with strange symbols. Screaming orgasm at ceiling gives birth to self.

4 First trip, with friends in the woods. Sudden sense of understanding felt in the body. This is paganism: To find the gods within oneself.

5 What do you want to do with your life?

TOPY were the direct inheritors of a century's worth of occult and countercultural "science," and then some, a crustpunk laboratory where radical and, in many cases, previously forgotten ideas were synthesized into a way of life. The cut-up method of William S. Burroughs and Brion Gysin; Gysin and Ian Sommerville's Dreamachine; Austin Spare's sigil method; sexual magick in the vein of Aleister Crowley and Paschal Beverly Randolph; the otherworldly and psychedelic explorations of John Dee, Timothy Leary and John C. Lilly; Count Alfred Korzybski's General Semantics; and the physical and sexual deconditioning of Wilhelm Reich, among many, many other avenues of theory and practice.

19

Over a drink in a pub on Museum Street in London where Crowley and Spare once whiled away lost evenings, Phil Hine, the Tantric scholar and author of many of the primary texts on chaos magick (a school of progressive occult thought that ran largely parallel in timeline and geographical center of development, and often intertwined with, the efforts of TOPY), related a particularly telling story to me. Speaking in very admiring tones of the Temple—and stating that, in his belief, they have still yet to be surpassed for their revolutionary approach to magick—he recounted the tale of a very *serious* Thelemic symposium held somewhere in the Midlands, in which a very *serious* discussion of the theory and practice of Crowleyan sex magick was enjoined by a few TOPY initiates, who, in the name of freedom of information, displayed a video tape of a TOPY sex magick action, only to have the ever-so "transgressive" crowd descend into nervous, schoolboy-ish giggling fits…

The world of "magick" is, nine times out of ten, a world where people can hide their deep-set insecurity and personal damage behind illusion, constructed identities and claims to privileged knowledge, power or spiritual status. A gaudy carnival magic show, conducted with props that have long since begun to disintegrate with age, that seems to function only to distract people from the real magic that is occurring all around them, in every facet of their lives, every day of their lives. While the rituals and magical techniques of the Temple seem overly simplistic in comparison with the loftier Qabalahs, tables of correspondences and secret formulae of "high" magick, they have one thing which high magick quite often forgets: a concrete function.

The TOPY magickal system centered around its unique approach to the "sigil" method—as derived and modernized by the artist Austin Osman Spare, in the early years of the Twentieth Century, from earlier work by Cornelius Agrippa in the Sixteenth. At the same time every month— the twenty-third hour of the twenty-third day—each active sigilizer would create a "Sigil ov Three Liquids." After careful deliberation on something truly wanted and needed in life, each sigilizer would write in detail what they wanted to happen, thereafter anointing the paper with blood, spit, sexual fluids and a clipping of hair. After drying, this would be placed in an envelope and mailed to TOPY World Headquarters, where it would be filed away anonymously under each sigilizer's identity number within the Temple (these archives remain undisturbed at an undisclosed location somewhere in the world).

Each sigilizer aimed to gain control over the only thing over which control is truly possible: one's self. The apparent simplicity of the Sigil ov Three Liquids masks some very deep processes that have been a part of the human experience since prehistorical times, acting on levels of the brain far deeper, and therefore that much more potent, then those we are expected to use as citizens of the "modern" world. Central to an understanding of the TOPY sigil method is the Law of Contagion as observed by Sir James Frazer in *The Golden Bough*—the assumption, common among most "primitive" peoples, that a fragment (or splinter, as P-Orridge says) of something can be used as a magical link to effect its source. Instead of using bits of hair, blood or fingernail to curse or cast love spells on others—the standard, vulgar view of what magick is—initiates of the Temple used links to themselves to affect their own destinies.

DNA forms the best magickal link possible to one's own self, a perfect holographic splinter, containing everything necessary to create yourself anew.

Willingly put in contact with a symbolic representation of intent, a message is produced and directly sent not only to the non-conscious mind but also to the conscious universe which one inhabits. Such is the bewildering, though incredibly effective, realm of sorcery. (These are also the exact principles that the nascent science of Radionics operates on—readers are directed to the research of Duncan Laurie for an in-depth look at the directions this type of "magick" can be taken in.)

Regardless of any supernatural effects experienced in connection with such experiments, a deeper process was initiated—a dialogue begun between each Temple initiate and their "true will," their core reason for existing, that the truly important aspects of life might be fully tuned into and the background static cancelled out as much as possible.

Genesis Breyer P-Orridge has often stated that the primary "teaching" of TOPY was discipline; that is, discipline in focusing on and actualizing the life one actually wants to live, regardless of social pressure or constraint. In that respect a Quentin Crisp might be a more apt symbol of the type of "initiate" the Temple wished to produce than an Israel Regardie. Magick was never the primary goal of TOPY, though the organization is most often remembered as a magickal or paramasonic order; rather, it was one tool to be used in the formulation and execution of a radically new approach to life outside the confines of the mundane. (Though, if it's magick you want, then backwards, sideways, crossways, and loopwise secrets of magick are manifested throughout this text, mirroring the potential of magick to reach through time—as if time were a single, fluid object—to make its point known.)

21

While TOPY conducted its decade-long ritual, Psychick Television worked overtime with a rotating cast of contributors to provide the soundtrack, forming part of an incredibly fertile if often disjointed period in the evolution of the Industrial genre that Throbbing Gristle had spawned. While Coil, Current 93 and Nurse With Wound spent most of the 1980s delving directly into the darkest and most unsavory facets of TG's legacy, Psychic TV (thanks, in large part, to regular consumption of MDMA), moved from an early focus on tribal, wolfpack-style declarations of war on man's sleepwalking state and into a fully psychedelic (or, rather, hyperdelic), Merry Prankster-esque cheerleader squad for sex, drugs and magick. (When PTV toured America in the late Eighties, they brought along a tour bus painted in full hyperdelic drag, on the front of which they painted "Even Futher," slyly upping the ante on the original Merry Pranksters' acid test bus.)

Following a near-breakthrough to major chart success with "Godstar," a hymn to the late Rolling Stone Brian Jones, Psychic TV and TOPY became early adopters and proselytizers of the English rave scene (Genesis Breyer P-Orridge is credited with popularizing the phrase "acid house" after a particularly fortuitous record-shopping trip in Detroit). By 1988 the role of Genesis' primary collaborator had rotated from Alex Fergusson to electronics guru Fred Giannelli, a collaboration which led to Psychic TV's *Jack the Tab, Tekno Acid Beat* and the near-masterpiece *Towards thee Infinite Beat,* a haunting, very personal album centered around passionate diatribes against mankind's innate need for warfare ("Horror House" and "Jigsaw," later to be revisited in live sets on the eves of both wars in the Persian Gulf) and elegies for Brion Gysin ("Bliss") and Ian Curtis of Joy Division, who was slotted to become a full member of Psychic TV at the time of his suicide in 1980 ("I. C. Water"). The entire lyric of "Jigsaw" was a combination of a backwards, a forwards and a combination of backwards, forwards and whispered vocals using writings from various Processean publications. "Bliss", in contrast mixed Scientology speak with the music of Jajouka.

Acid house was the apex of TOPY's efforts, a widescale scene which allowed for the type of ecstatic, transcendental and magickal bliss that Brion Gysin had found in Morocco in the panpipes of the Master Musicians of Jajouka and introduced to Brian Jones shortly before his untimely demise. Consider the twenty-year arc between the release of *Brian Jones Presents the Pipes of Pan at Jajouka* in 1968 and the explosion of the acid house scene in 1988. Bachir Attar, the most recent Master Musician, lived with Genesis and Lady Jaye for a year, collaborating with Thee Majesty and other projects. Music is the most effective medium extant for the communication of emotion, and the deepest expression of the essence of culture. Manipulation or outright destruction of a culture's music has, therefore, been one of the primary strategies of imperial domination. Western music has at times been particularly concerned with the nullification of anything unstructured, sexually open, "savage," "uncivilized," or otherwise concerned with the joy of life or which speaks to the "old" parts of the brain.

Genesis Breyer P-Orridge's mentor Brion Gysin, confronted with the horror of Western cultural and ontological hegemony when a friend visiting him in Morocco tuned a radio to a classical station, tellingly snapped at him to shut it off immediately, shouting that it was "too white!" While involved in the COUM Transmissions performance art collective and the mail art scene in the early 1970s, P-Orridge created collages with the phrase "E Hate Stockhausen" repeated over and over. The mission statement of Throbbing Gristle was to create anti-muzak, and disrupt the control frequencies of civilization by any means necessary; the lessons of TG were reincorporated within Psychic TV and increasingly oriented towards producing transcendental bliss. The Master Musicians of Jajouka provided a template, but it wasn't until 1988 that the stars aligned for Pan, God of Panic, to sound his cry across the world.

The initiates of the Temple ov Psychick Youth, weaned on Jajouka and the Dreamachine, had already habituated themselves to the states of mind that would be produced en masse by acid house, Ecstasy and computer-generated rave visuals, and became the vanguard of this new eruption of delerium. Hence would Bou Jeloud, Pan, Baphomet, be shepherded into public view yet again, and the mask of control slip, just slightly, for a brief few years, for a whole generation. By the time the Criminal Justice Bill was passed in the UK, effectively outlawing raves, the man behind the curtain had already been revealed, control sliced up as if by Burroughs' expertly-targeted scissors…

23

Throughout its eleven-year lifespan, TOPY aimed to transgress— against Church, State, the nuclear family, and reality itself. Of course, transgression against modern culture is often quickly short-circuited, since culture will sooner or later get round to assimilating its "opposition" by mass-producing a watered-down facsimile—not that the authorities take this macro-cultural mechanism into account when dealing with the vanguard of such innovation.

Consider the current mass popularity of body piercing, introduced to TOPY by Alan Oversby, a.k.a. Mr. Sebastian, a former art teacher who had left his position to promote tattooing and piercing in the gay leather and BDSM community in London. That was one of many phenomena that TOPY "culturally engineered" the wider acceptance of. Body piercing is now an adolescent mandate; yet in 1987 Mr. Sebastian (who provided the vocals on "A Message From the Temple," a track on *Force thee Hand ov Chance* that was the initial open call to affiliation with the Temple) was arrested in the UK government raid known as Project Spanner, along with fifteen other men from the BDSM community. He was subsequently charged with assault with actual bodily harm for consensually piercing a man's penis, as well as using anesthetic without a license and sending obscene material (piercing photos) through the mail. This is now a service that is available at relatively low cost in almost every metropolitan area in the Western world. In 1987, though, Mr. Sebastian was considered a threat to society and was sentenced to fifteen years, later suspended to two years. His profession and life were destroyed; he died, broken-hearted, in 1996.

Operation Spanner was only one tragedy of many in a very bleak English political climate. Wars of imperial futility in the Falklands and Libya; nuclear gridlock; proposed concentration camps for AIDS patients; crackdowns on alternative cultures of all shapes and sizes; constant bloodshed over Ireland; environmental degradation; economic hell. America—with the resurgence of the religious right; secret wars; CIA-supported dictators; socially engineered crack panic; and Mutually Assured Destruction—was hardly better. "The Eighties cower before me, and are abased," Aleister Crowley prophesied in *The Book of the Law*, speaking for the Egyptian warrior god Ra-Hoor-Khuit. In such a climate, TOPY was, first and foremost, a survival strategy. If it were to survive—in Margaret Thatcher's England much as in Ronald Reagan's (or, verily, George W. Bush's) America—magick had to defend itself.

24

If, as Mrs. Thatcher famously quipped to *Woman's Own* magazine, "There is no such thing as society," then the Temple sought to prove her wrong *ex nihilo*, both in the UK and abroad. The tribal mindset present in both punk and, later, rave was refined in TOPY's occultural laboratory, providing - for better or worse—a sense of family, belonging, commitment, and self—expression where previously there had been none.

Along with direct predecessors Aleister Crowley and Timothy Leary, Genesis Breyer P-Orridge ranks as one of magick's greatest propagandists, which he has been alternately deified and reviled for, much as Crowley and Leary were. The British authorities and tabloid press were not the only forces with which Genesis and TOPY had to contend; another was the occult "establishment," or, rather, the "Museum of Magick," as Genesis calls them, who were hardly pleased with the mainstreaming of what was previously considered "dangerous" (and certainly privileged) information.

The Ordo Templi Orientis or OTO, a Masonic body founded in Germany in the late Nineteenth Century and later captained and reformulated by Aleister Crowley in the early Twentieth, can be considered the clearest precedent to TOPY, a secret society created as an access point into the world of magick. Neither the OTO nor TOPY were teaching orders, existing instead to foster socialization around occult ideas—halfway points for those interested in the hidden undercurrents of reality, training wheels that, when eventually discarded, would lead the individual either towards more abstruse orders of robed ritualists or, preferably, onto their own two feet and their own personal apotheosis.

Such organizations have been a running theme in Western history. As one slides into internal fighting and decay, another rises to take its place. Genesis has often related to me that during TOPY's heyday, Hymenaeus Beta, then and current Outer Head of the Caliphate OTO, felt that TOPY was truly representing, and doing the work of, the active current that the OTO had mined in the early half of the century, whereas his current job as head of the OTO was more akin to that of a museum curator.

The story of TOPY's last days is, of course, central to the myth it has left. By the early 1990s the group had grown to a strength of nearly 10,000 connected, if not necessarily active, individuals across the globe. In February 1992 Genesis Breyer P-Orridge was notified by telegram—the P-Orridge family were in Kathmandu, Nepal at the time using their PTV income and donations from the wider TOPY Nett Work to feed and clothe Tibettan refugees, beggars and lepers, sometimes as many as 300 daily—that his home and TOPY Station had been raided by Scotland Yard in connection with a trumped-up Satanic abuse charge. On the back of an old Psychic TV video done years earlier by Derek Jarman for Channel 4—ironically the same channel now alleging the abuse—P-Orridge and TOPY were accused of chaining women in the basement of the house in Brighton, impregnating the women, aborting the fetuses and then forcing them to eat the remains. This is ironic for two reasons—the first being that the same story has been regularly used since the Fourth Century to smash pagan groups, since Epiphanius of Salamis accused the Borborite Gnostic

25

sect of the same crime; the second being that the P-Orridges didn't even have a basement.

After choosing exile in California instead of returning to England, where the public was already crying for blood from the scapegoat of the week, Gen made the decision to dissolve TOPY, issuing a final publication—*Thee Green Book*, reprinted for the first time in this book—and a postcard reading, simply, "Changed Priorities Ahead." It had become obvious that TOPY's moment was over; that the mission, which had only ever been meant as a temporary experiment, was over. It had only been Here to Go. Though some splinter groups remained (and remain) intact, continuing to use the TOPY name and logo, the current moved on, leaving what amount to more displays in the Museum of Magick. As TOPY was ending, a new world—of digital media and cyberculture—was being born, one that TOPY had acted as a midwife for. The ritual now complete, the Temple was banished.

While Psychic TV dissolved along with TOPY in the early 1990s, it would go on to reincarnate for the Larry Thrasher-produced *Trip Reset* and, later, in its current touring lineup as PTV3. Baba Larriji also featrures in the Expanded Poetry project co-founded with Bryin Dall, Thee Majesty.

Fifteen years on, we are left with an occult landscape that has been given its shape and direction by the Temple, whether it is publicly acknowledged or not. The vital current, of course, has mutated and evolved once again—not into a physical order this time, but into dispersal across the World Wide Web and mass publishing. While this provides for an incredibly unique period of open access to occult information, one can hardly help but long for the immediacy and community of a physical network in contrast to the endless flamewars, constant degradation of information quality, and terminal loss of context that are the Internet's stock in trade.

The TOPY years represented a period in which magick was resituated in its natural context—as a survival mechanism, in the urban blight of modern civilization just as it was in the dark forests of precivilization. Though there may be nothing here now but the recordings, the recordings are there for all to see, to learn from, to improve upon.

‡

This is one story of the Temple, in one world, in one place and time. The names and the details change each time it recreates itself anew. It learns, it processes, it incorporates and evolves; thickens its own plot. My story is there for all to read, etched in genetic spirals along its supporting columns. Yours is too. Remember this.

Remember Earth from space. Sun goes round as we breathe as one. Human totality breathes in, breathes out. Cars and electric lights, birth and death, sex, disease, running through the long grass at dawn, walking the ox across the steep mountain path, loading the Kalashnikov, spinning the prayer wheels at dusk, laying the child in the grave, singing the old songs. Listen to the sound of our breath from space. A secret name of the divine. The name of a ritual in which we must all take part. A temple space in which we are all assigned office. The office which you remember when you are...

The Temple is eternal, shimmering on the horizon. It is a ghost. It is the specter that answers us at the séance of our most secret desires.

There is one Process and there are many processes.

Jason Louv, Vancouver and New York City, 2006 Era Vulgaris

LETTER TO JEAN-PIERRE TURMEL

Gen
Hackney
London E8
Timefix: 23 April 1982

Dearest Jean-Pierre,

E was watching an American film on TV last week, there was a lively, strangely attractive woman who discovered she had cancer. She got married to her lover, knowing she would die, then gradually she got more and more ill and haggard until she died. E had to switch it off, and cried so much because it reminded me of Danny. It was as if suddenly E had understood everything about that tragedy and my heart fell open and wept.

It was good of you to understand, to predict to yourself, that E needed a silence to develop, rest, re-orient and evolve and plan. To grow used to living with a new, different person. Of course you knew E think from our talks and our theories that TG had to end, and now E am so glad we had thee courage to do it. Now, already, it's like ghosts, talking about characters in a movie E saw, only it doesn't open my heart, or make tears. Indifferent. Purely history, trapped in time, other people's business, other people's news.

29

Butter it's true, just as TG supported thee ghost of COUM Transmissions, so Psychic TV and Psychick Youth will have to accept a ghost of TG, butter that is thee organic evolution of one dream, thee visualization that makes all things possible through a flexing of will, an expression of imagination.

In thee past, even in TG, E have to admit privately that E was interested in, seduced by thee mass media attention, E wanted to be LIKED, to get thee credit we deserved, E enjoyed to be written about, it affirmed my existence because my self-image was weak and paranoid. Thee biggest change now is that genuinely, in my deepest interior E am DISINTERESTED in what anyone thinks about all our future actions and projects. That their opinion might affect our financial or technical resources is of academic practical interest only and if they chicken out and do not support what we really are this time E REALLY don't care. Before, E acted disinterested, E understood that it was a necessary state and stance, butter a private part of me flirted and dreamed in a desire for flattery and security. It is not surprising to me, butter E am sure it would be to many outside observers, just how near to being right back at thee beginning Sleazy & E are now. Our new musick is receiving more coumfused reaction than it deserves. It's just, JUST soundtracks, functional. Butter no one wants to release that, they say, they want MY voice & TG noise. Hah. Butter then we never actually ASKED anyone to release it in thee first place. Assumptions seem one of thee key elements of cultural alchemy & death. If you notice we do not court thee media now, steering clear of instant new roles in relation to TG past. Sleazy & E thought it would be a dangerous tactic to release a record immediately, if ever, or indeed to do anything in public for at least a yera or more. We are asleep, forgotten men whose ghost drifts.

The mass's desires, non-evolution, conservatism, closing doors are still our enemy. We DO understand that. We have put a few suggestions into thee arena in that interview, we do not have to manifest any of them. We have & feel NO obligation. Not to a public, ugh, or past, or to DO anything ever agen. We are free agents. We shall do, simply, what we want when & if it appeals to us at thee time. And no consistency of vision or direction need apply on any level. We desire choice.

30

Sleazy has arrived with Geoff Rushton of Stabmental (formerly), now an initiate of thee Temple. Today E renew his probationary gestures, relive thee pain of birth, trim thee style of ascetic manipulation and eat thee breath of babies.

There is no why… anymore… there is just us…

Approval & disapproval are moral stances that have no place in our vision here. There is no morality. E want to talk to a vision, a destiny, not a public. We would rather have five or six people committed totally to a coherent yet subliminal dream, than anyone at all that is merely a dilettante-ish dabbler in gestures. We are stripping away thee final strips of camouflage and revealing what we always wanted to be and do once and for all, and don't give a fuck what ANYONE thinks, about ANY response or opinion or blocking action. We will do exactly what we want all thee time and concentrate totally upon realization of any & all our FANTASIES AND desires even if we get attacked, persecuted or destroyed. There is nothing else we can do anymore. To be ignored or reviled doesn't matter. We shall be simply what we desire and no more. And anything that appears in opposition is merely a ministration, a service in thee path of focused imagination and will.

Your theories about a new elite human being, we approve and understand. Thee mass is to be manipulated only to our ends, if necessary, butter primarily to be, most simply, ignored and deflected.

Your interest in evidence & deception is interesting. You know in a way, deception works like transparency. We now declare thee exact truth of what we are doing, at last we are honest, yet thee actual effect is a deception because no one is listening to what we say, because they analyze from assumption based upon past assumptions. In fact they never listen to us at all. So they deceive, deception. It is psychic youth that makes us reach coumclusions so in time with each other. Your analysis is so clear...

Our emphasis from now on is as a philosophical, occult movement; a church without orthodoxy or dogma, an elite organization dedicated to coumtinuance of individual choice and options. Discipline of thee self, involvement to whatever degree a person wishes. As little or as much, where what you give equals what you get, where No is as good an answer as Yes, where thought is stimulated so that response is always a mystery. No guaranteed response expected or requested. A truly non-dogmatic, irreligious church. Psychick Youth thee end in itself. Thee Temple a symbol by its very existence, its work, as an agency and provocateur of ideas & imagination expansion. Visualization, concentration make things happen, events are created by dreaming. So we will encourage self-power, our aim is to becoum redundant eventually to each person involved, to constantly trigger and abandon, to becoum obsolete as we succeed. As a person realizes what we mean, they don't need us anymore. We won't want huge numbers of followers, most churches desire, measure their success and importance by thee numbers of followers they have, and by thee number who say YES unquestioningly to everything their LEADERS say. We would rather have six INDIVIDUALS than six million sycophants. We are here to express possibilities and free associations, not to control or restrict anybody. Restrictions are self-imposed for neuroses' sake. We recognize no leaders, we merely implant thee seeds of immortality.

31

Huh, E wrote that, then turned over your page & hit your saying thee problem is not of "leader" butter of masses. YES YES YES. We do understand. It's all inevitable. Right, god it IS uncanny how we coincide, maybe we are each other, or maybe just evidence of what we believe, thee imagination made real. E hate christianism and leftism and suppression and control so much. E feel sick to think of thee masses. We have declared our intent to generate or at least symbologize a new elite made up of leaders only in thee Psychick Youth. An ultra-elite, justified in itself for no other reason than we chose to exist and demonstrate an alternative method of evolutionary change and structure.

Thee Temple is a church of only LEADERS, no followers. A radical step. Even thee Nazis, though they bred an elite of leaders, still wanted to control thee masses, lead them and entangle themselves with them. We want thee leaders alone. Fuck thee sleeping masses. We have no desire to be superior rulers of boring, dull masses of people who we despise. We want JUST leaders. A church full of leaders, only leaders and not leading anyone. Merely co-habiting. A separate existence for OUR satisfaction. Why waste all that time, energy and vision dealing with boring masses of people. We've got better things to do. Enjoying and stimulating ourselves. A self-centered religion instead of a crippling, selfless Christian ideal.

A PERSONAL MESSAGE FROM
THEE TEMPLE OV PSYCHICK YOUTH

We have reached a crisis point.

We are aware that whole areas of our experience of life are missing.

We are faced with a storm of thee fiercest strength known.

*We are faced with the debasement of man to a creature without feelings,
without knowledge and pride of SELF.*

We are faced with dissolution far more complete than death. A New Dark Ages.

*We have been conditioned, encouraged and blackmailed into self-restriction, into a
narrower and narrower perception of ourselves, our importance and our potential.*

All this constitutes a Psychick Attack of thee highest magnitude.

Acceptance is defeat.

*Resistance is dangerous and unpredictable but for those who realize the
totality of defeat, resistance must be thee only option conceivable.*

RIGHT NOW you have these alternatives:

To remain forever part of a sleeping world…

To gradually abandon thee hopes and dreams of childhood…

To be permanently addicted to the drug of the commonplace…

Or, to fight alongside us in thee Temple ov Psychick Youth! A New Way On!

*Thee Temple ov Psychick Youth has been convened in order to act as a catalyst and
focus for the Individual development of all those who wish to reach inwards and
strike out. Maybe you are one of these, already feeling different, dissatisfied, separate
from thee mass around you, instinctive and alert? You are already one of us. The fact
you have this message is a start in itself.*

*Don't think we are going to tell you what to do, what to be. The world is full of
institutions that would be delighted if you thought and did exactly what they*

told you. Thee Temple ov Psychick Youth is not and NEVER WILL BE one of them. We offer no dogmas, and no promises of comfort or easy answers.

You are going to have to find out your Self, we offer only the method of survival as a True Being, we give you back to yourself, we support your Individuality in which the Spirit and Will united burn with passion & pride.

Our function is to direct and support. Work that is needlessly repeated is simply wasteful. Accordingly we will be making public books, manuscripts & other recordings of our progress, in various formats, video and audio. These do not contain meaningless dogma but are examples of our interests & beliefs in action. They are made not as entertainment, but as experience, not the mundane experience of day-to-day routine but of the Spirit & Will triumphant.

Thee grey book

I

hee Temple strives to end personal laziness and engender discipline. To focus the Will on one's true desires, in the belief, gathered from experience, that this maximizes and makes happen all those things that one wants in every area of Life.

Explore daily your deepest desires, fantasies and motives, gradually focusing on what you would like to happen in a perfect world, a perfect situation, taking away all restrictions and practical considerations—what you'd *really* want.

Then decide to try and do it.

The mere visualization of that true goal begins the process that makes it happen.

Clean out the trappings and debris of compromise, of what you've been told is reasonable for a person in your circumstances.

Be clear in admitting your real desires.

Discard all irrelevancies. Ask yourself who you want as friends, if you need or want to work, what you want to eat. Check and re-check everything, deeper and deeper, more and more precisely, to get closer to— and ultimately integrate with—your *real* Self.

Once you are focused on your Self internally, the external aspects of your life will fall into place. They have to.

Skeptics will say they simply don't believe this Psychick process works— but it does.

It is the Key to the Temple.
Genesis Breyer P-Orridge, 1981

We attempt to commune with spirits, to be friends of the Human Spirit.

We care for the infinite significance of the individual spirit and personal moral responsibility, and its development through experience. We believe in the total significance of the individual, discovered through familiarity with the deepest instincts and explorations of destiny outside the traps of time.

We intend to engender moral freedom, spiritual freedom, sexual freedom and personal independence, to insist upon personal choice in all things.

We are endlessly involved in unraveling the intertwined yet separate threads of Fate and Destiny to evolve a magickal system to maximize and enhance each individual's ability to recognize and focus on, thereby making real, that Destiny.

We accept responsibility. Gladly and with excitement and deliberate ignorance of the outcoum.

We revel in mystery and surprise.

We bury ourselves in challenge and dreams.

We embrace all possibilities and impossibilities with joy and excitement.

We accept the true nature of Life, the way the world is. Flexible and shifting, in flux every moment. Shaped by parallel levels that accept contradiction and inconsistency as inviolate qualities that generate mystery and mastery. We direct ourselves wherever we choose to go with joy and abandon.

A New Era of the Magickal interpretation of the World, and existing in it, is couming. An interpretation in terms of Will and Imagination by contact with intuition and instinct.

Do you want to be part of a world of sleeping people?

Do you want to imbibe the drug of the commonplace?
Will you be forever addicted to self-restriction?

Established orthodoxies and dogmas, conditioned interpretations of living, regard the material world as reality whilst pretending to deal with the spirit or existence. They conceive and propagate evolution and thinking as purely physical, their control of our visions as sacrosanct. Religion has been privately altered to work from a position that accepts itself as totally discredited by science. All establishment modes of control and affiliation, both religious and political, rely upon and revolve around unquestioning faith and dogma, unquestioning acceptance of their inalienable right to assume professional responsibility for our actions upon their shoulders. We are told we are weak, incapable of grasping scale, afraid of ourselves and desperate to push responsibility for all events in our lives onto them. We are insistently trained to accept our corporeal existence as hopeless in itself, to becoum subservient to the greater good. We are perpetually conditioned, encouraged and blackmailed into self-restriction, into narrower and narrower perceptions of ourselves, of our own importance, our own potential and our own experience. We are trained to ignore the evidence of our senses and experiences and to feel guilt when we glimpse sense-derived visions of ourselves as free spirits.

39

The voluntary relinquishing of responsibility for our lives and actions is one of the greatest enemies of our times.

Our enemies are flat.

Our enemies are three-dimensional.

Our enemies are continuity and coherence.

Our enemies are restriction and confinement.

Our enemies are guilt and fear.

Our enemies are material.

Our enemies are direction and fact.

Our enemies are Because.

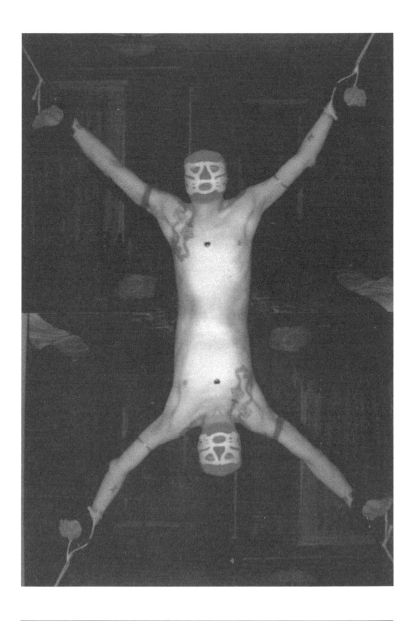

Image by Genesis Breyer P-Orridge

We are not seeking followers, we are seeking collaborators, Individuals for a visionary Psychick alliance. What we suggest next is *not* instruction. It is method—a method which can be used by anyone, alone with friends, regardless of any material or social circumstances; a method to be used by the Individual to break through to their deeper consciousness, where fantasies, ambitions and real wishes reside, the place where all dreams meet. People can most readily identify and relate to dreams that are sexual, and that is the primary reason for our choice of sex as a vehicle for this method to begin with. Our interest is therefore *practical.*

In our experience, although they might deny it, most people never ask themselves what they really want, or they simply say they don't know. But it is only once a person has learned to identify their true desires in an imaginary perfect world, where guilt and retribution are suspended, that they can hope to reach them.

Sex Of all the things people do, at home and in private, usually with close friends, sex alone is subject to extraordinary interference and control from outside forces. This is no accident. They recognize its power. Even if only for a few moments, Individuals can release a power and energy from within that renders any system of society, or regime, meaningless. It is a liberator. Even an Individual in solitary confinement can indulge in it and in their fantasies travel into any situation and possibility unfettered, and, at the moment of orgasm itself, be both blissfully vulnerable and undeniably free, elsewhere, filled by energy.

41

Accordingly, from the moment of birth pressure is exercised upon everyone to limit their release and enjoyment of this power. To limit and restrict the immense potential.

Of course the nature of this pressure varies by place and era. When specific laws becoum unenforceable for a time, more subtle methods are used. Social attitudes, anxiety, guilt, fear of ridicule and failure are all exploited, and diseases that attack only those who indulge in specific sexual activities are introduced. Most give in to this pressure in one way or another, permanently crippling their individual growth.

We believe that it is essential, if we are to survive and progress, that we first recognize, accept and ultimately reach our true sexual desires. This not only satisfies the body and consolidates the spirit but acts as an example for all our sexuality, so it seems crucial to begin at this universally applicable point and develop our awareness from there.

In our culture people have internalized alienating stereotypes that dictate their sexual and social interactions. This makes men agreeable to orders from authority figures and keeps women in line with accepted notions of propriety and authority, and binds up their sexual desire so that they will accept a generally subordinate role to men. The latter is propagated by those who are empowered by the patriarchal lineage which has been handed down through the ages, whose fear of the unknown—in this case women and feminine characteristics—has been countered by a bulwark of dogma which aims at controlling and/or degrading all those forces which they see as a threat to their reign.

By studying the oppression of women through the ages we can see in a nutshell the nature, methods and manifestations of oppression as it is used in any society and in any age against those who are pro-life and expanding. Yet on a broad scale, encompassing both sexes, the repression of sexual instincts functions to make people submissive and inclined to irrational behavior, and thus paralyzes their rebellious potential. On a deeply personal level, where we enter the domain of such energies as might be called "magickal," the effect of such conditioning is no less significant. Psychic energy and sexual energy are different names for the same force. By ridding ourselves of restrictions and the forms of control that have been imposed on us, we can come into our own on more planes than one.

Most Initiates of the Temple believe that there is a power and effect released by an orgasm, focused through Will, that enhances not only the process of Self fulfillment and contentment but also the achievement of creative goals. The strength of this process forces the hand of chance and brings close the objects of your desire.

Ritual Throughout history, man has used ritual to achieve spiritual results from simple physical actions. Recently its use has been limited to established

42

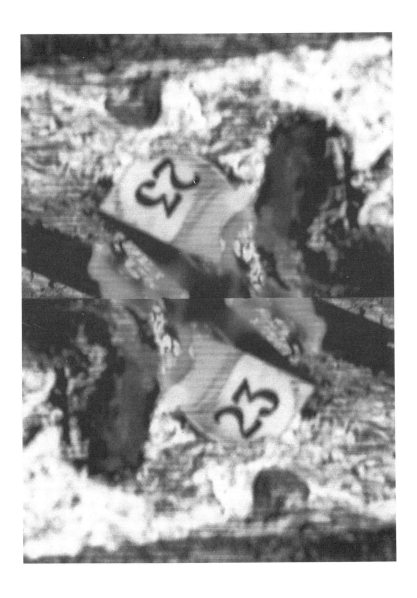

Image by Genesis Breyer P-Orridge

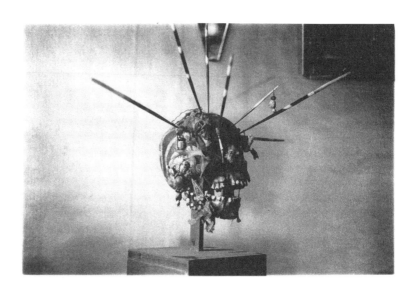

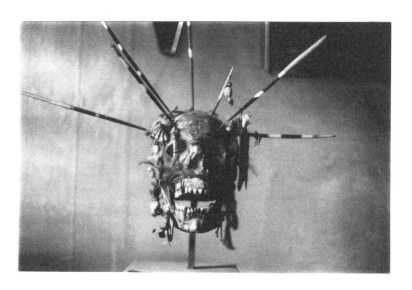

Photos by Peter Christopherson

religious dogmas, and since many if not all of these have fallen into disrepute or have come to be seen as irrelevant, so too has the use of ritual—but its use is far older and far more universal than any organized *church*.

Any ritual is a way of concentrating and focusing those taking part on a particular aim or idea. It is only essential that the techniques employed have meaning and vitality for the participants. Seen without this belief, as many recorded rituals of the past are now, the processes can seem simply ridiculous, and the mechanical repetition of them certainly would be.

Initiates of thee Temple ov Psychick Youth have developed personal methods or rituals not only to strengthen and refine their inner objectives, both sexual and practical, but also to provide a fertile basis for those objectives to grow and becoum real. Although we have no vested interest in others following this example, or contacting the Temple, it is possible that some people will wish to do so. Below are instructions on how to do this. Many people may feel unwilling or unable to put our suggestions into practice, due to the effectiveness of social conditioning. The Temple will only draw Initiates from those who can demonstrate in the manner indicated their resistance to this conditioning, and their commitment to the ideals of the Temple.

45

Thee Sigil Ov Three Liquids This ritual should be performed alone, on the twenty-third of the month, beginning at 23:00 hours, in a place where you will have no interruptions or distractions. Within the limits of what is practical, you should arrange the environment and atmosphere to be as conducive as possible to the execution of this Sigil for yourself.

If at all possible, a candle or candles should be the only source of light.

This Sigil must be performed naked.

One of the aims of the ritual is to concentrate your attention and energy on your most intense sexual fantasy. To do this you must first decide what it is, and write it down on a piece of paper. It should be what you think would generate in you the maximum possible excitement, pleasure and fulfillment, regardless of the identity, sex or age of those who take part with you, alive and guiltless. It is essential to be completely honest with yourself, and not write something because you think it might satisfy other people. Remember that the purpose of the Sigil is to make these things really happen.

Once you have written the fantasy on the piece of paper, you have to make the paper special.

To do this it must be touched by the three liquids of the body—that is, spit, blood and OV, which is the Temple name for the fluids obtained by masturbation, semen from the male and lubrication from the female. For example, first let a few drops of spit fall onto the page, and next a few drops of blood. You must use some kind of sharp and clean instrument to do this. Remember that only a small quantity is required, and you should use your common sense in terms of the method employed and of hygiene both before and after the ritual. Lastly, and in any way that is most pleasurable to you, bring yourself to orgasm and allow the OV to touch the paper. While you are doing this, concentrate not only on the inscribed fantasy, but also on the idea of the Temple and the fact that doing this Sigil is inevitably bringing closer what you really want.

You must then attach a lock of hair from your head and also some of your pubic hair to the paper.

Remember that these two hair types and three liquids may be incorporated on the Sigil Paper in any manner that feels appropriate to the thoughts thereon described. The basic actions outlined above should not be seen as a limitation. Leave the Sigil Paper overnight to dry in a safe place. On the next day send it to the Temple. You do not have to attach your name to the Sigil Paper if you don't want to. All submissions to the Temple will remain at all times absolutely confidential, and will be stored in a locked vault. All applicants who complete this satisfactorily will receive personal encouragement, suggestions and directions for the subsequent month's ritual. Completion of twenty-three such monthly rituals qualifies one as a full Initiate of the Temple.

Note: If you decide to do the Sigil, the responsibility rests entirely with you. You will gain from it, not the Temple. The Temple cannot accept any claims against it, arising from the consequence of the Sigil or any related matters.

The Sigil can only be recommended to those who have reached the legal age of consent in the country in which they live.

In modern society, most people are not able to tolerate concentrated religious thought. This is hardly surprising. Most religious and political groups of the last two centuries have stressed, among other things, the superiority of their leaders and the inferiority of the individual. By now the absurdity of this thinking has become apparent to most people, and a general resistance to any form of religious dogma has developed. There are a number of groups and cult religions that are repeating the old formulas of adoration of their leaders and the relinquishing of the cult's followers of any responsibility for their own lives, but these are in the minority. By and large, people have lost faith in any spiritual teaching whatsoever, and have nothing with which to replace it. If we are to be able to suggest even guidelines in this area, it must be done without dogma and in ways that people will understand.

47

Pleasure has become something which people do not seek after themselves, but instead have presented to them in simulated forms through diverse media, thus building up a frustrating and paradoxical situation where an inherently active form of expression has become a passive pastime, and the results are that expression becomes depression.

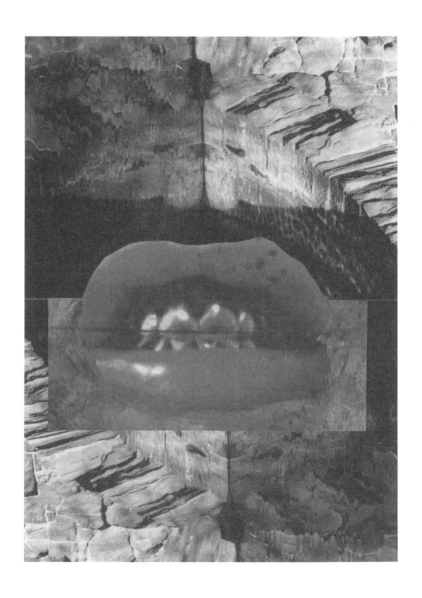

Image by Genesis Breyer P-Orridge

People are constantly being titillated through advertisements and other forms of propaganda by a subtle use of subliminal seduction. Due to the one-sided nature of the affair, the outcome is inevitably frustration. When pleasure's course is inhibited, it has the characteristic of turning into un-pleasure. When, in spite of continual high excitation, a person is not able to experience final gratification, a fear eventually develops - not only of the final gratification, but also of the excitation that precedes it. This will effectively divorce the individual from his or her true feelings and instincts.

A long exposure to Televisualized Reality will have the effect of underlining people's notions about their inadequacy. On an unconscious level, they will have to deal with second-hand traumas and complexes—a task made all the more difficult for the fact that, although the pseudo-experiences achieve their relevance by being linked up with the individual's own experiences, that link is mostly superficial and difficult to trace. Electronic media is man's latest sensory apparatus.

The manipulation and the use made of the sexual instinct through visual media has turned a large portion of people into unknowing fetishists—they are investing sexual energy in images and objects without knowing it, and are thus unable to reclaim and make use of that energy, as the magickal use of a fetish dictates. An essentially magickal act has become vampiric and one-sided. This process breeds a host of scopophiles, people who obtain simulated sexual gratification through the process of watching, where the illusion of active doing is obtained by turning another person into an object which is subjected to a controlling gaze. Scopophilia is, by definition, one of the component instincts of sexuality that exist as drives independently of the erotogenic zones. Indulging in scopophilic activity (and people nowadays hardly seem to have any other choice) can, in the long run, result in an unconscious acceptance of the separation between mind and body, sexuality being denied its natural course. The fragmented world-view that keeps people from drawing the right conclusions and seeking active release from their circumstances is reinforced. Over the last fifty years, TV has been the greatest single factor in the control of the attitudes of the people. Even if it was unintentional, which seems unlikely, the prevailing view of the world as seen by the writers, producers and controllers of TV companies has become the accepted "norm" to which the viewer inevitably compares herself. Of course, the world presented on TV bears little or no relation to reality, and as a consequence the viewer is left not only with a feeling of failure, but also of boredom with the "perfect" world on the screen. Even in the area of news and documentary, those interests that shape and control TV everywhere assume that "the public" cannot cope with the whole truth.

It is our intention to reverse this trend.

We have no desire to ape or emulate the slick perfection and sterile technical quality of traditional professional television. Perfect focus is not perfect content. We deal in implications, exactness of flow and image from a subliminal psychic point of view. It is only by doing this that one can hope to show life as it really is. All media systems devised by man enshrine his own limitations of development and fulfillment, his inner conflicts, his private fears of mortality—yet all media, including TV, are nothing but the decisions of men. Psychic TV will be activist, a positive statement of faith in the capacity of man. To cause things hidden in the dark to appear, and to take the darkness away from them.

Psychic TV is not intended to be a replacement for conventional programming, but rather the first step towards a de-programming, without regard for the preoccupations of commercial TV, or redundant assumptions about entertainment and value. At Psychic TV we accept and exploit the way TV is used by our generation, as raw material to be manipulated by the viewer. Dense enough to be interesting over and over, yet without punch-lines or obvious focal points to become familiar and bored with.

50

The Transmissions we are now producing are intended to be viewed between the hours of midnight and six a.m. We will not be giving any advance indication of the specific content of the Transmissions (rarely are people aware in advance of any momentous occurrence in their lives) but everything will reflect the way the world really is. If they seem to be emphasizing those aspects of life normally suppressed or censored as subversive, contentious, disturbing or too sexual, it is because that suppression is a deliberate attempt to limit the knowledge of the individual. It is our belief that truth and information about anything and everything must be made available in every way possible, if human history is to survive, progress or have any meaning whatsoever.

Genesis Breyer P-Orridge, 1982

A MESSAGE FROM THEE TEMPLE

I To say in day-to-day life that something is "obvious" means, more often than not, that one concedes a note of truth in exchange for a tolerance of the usual hypocrisy and conditioning. You can, for example, make your opposite admit as being obvious that there is no such thing as a theory that is absolutely true; that will not stop them in any way from continuing to brandish their "truths" as before.

Their momentary concession passes by a sordid business in which they buy their future peace of mind. A life without questions.

Hence, there is no higher aim than the *obvious*. It is to approach the closest to a truth which we know to be inaccessible but whose gleam we can see.

The obvious is a protection. Not only does it make people run away, but it also deceives by its vapid commonness, and by the fact that in flat people's minds, whatever is simple cannot be serious.
Jean-Pierre Turmel, 1982

51

II It would be an illusion to think that the Individual can hide all the clues to his Oneness. Their task is therefore to see to it that all the clues are wrongly interpreted. Thus it is that they may seem to indicate a lack of individuality and create a feeling of disappointment rather than curiosity. This tactic gives us space and protection in the traps of time.

An Individual has many personalities or characters in the same time or alternate times (cognitive science supports this).

Most people, little by little, eliminate the personalities considered to be dangerous by their peer group or societal unit, and finally keep only the social personality. They are one-dimensional, *flat* people. But other people, called, paradoxically, "individuals," are always trying to develop all their personalities, even if there is an internal conflict between them. So we can clearly see that the individualist person logically must use "we" to name themselves whilst the person who belongs to the masses must use the "I." The first is multi-dimensional, the second is uni-dimensional.

One of the Temple functions is to encourage and support the development of multi-dimensional individuals. Hence our use of "WE" in our texts. Our enemies are flat.

Jean-Pierre Turmel, 1982

III Our stress on *Self*-discipline is important; it links the internal methods of ritual to our approval and suggestion of other forms of physical discipline to complement the mental and sexual ones. Hence you will often find that Initiates of the Temple will be engaged in such outside activities as marksmanship, martial arts, swimming and so on as an extension of the theory of maintaining and improving one's focus and abilities. The point is not the skill itself, though we appreciate the practical nature, in a society such as ours, of an ability to defend oneself and be fit, but the application, the discipline itself. So one may be poor in terms of results, but excellent in terms of your genuine *application* to a skill that requires thought, co-ordination and a degree of dedication. A synthesis of physical action, thought, reflex and an analysis of both yourself and a target (real and metaphorical).

Genesis Breyer P-Orridge and Kim Klinzer Norris, 1982

FAITH IS FEAR

The first lesson from which all others grow is the simplest. We are mortal. We all die. This is not a morbid wallowing in hopelessness. It is the ability to genuinely coum to terms with our physical transience that liberates us all. Many visionary philosophical systems include the "small death" in their ideas under one name or another. We all die. This realization, truly assimilated, can be turned to positive use, in that it spurs one to action, aware that all time is limited and no life span is certain. Every second counts and must count. This realization can also be used unproductively, crippling an Individual man or woman's search for fulfillment of all their needs and preventing for all their life a complete integration of every aspect of their character and thoughts. The inevitability of death can be

used by outside forces as a weapon to create fear. Religions use this weapon more blatantly than any other suppressive social regulation systems. They use fear of death to justify faith.

Note: Those who escape the traps of religion through a first-stage cynical knowledge of the hypocrisy of modern society, and the emasculation of their individual power to change anything, often seek oblivion from this knowledge—and so they use various drugs (tobacco, alcohol, tranquilizers and opiates like heroin) as a substitute for faith. They want to kill time. Religion wants to side-step time. Both are actions based on fear.

Mankind spends a constant amount of energy in self-preservation. The very phrase "self-preservation" implies a threat of annihilation and is triggered by fear of death. So in a very real sense, fear of death is present behind all normal functioning. It resides permanently in the unconscious, molding our image of ourselves in relation to an inevitable, inexorable crisis of death. Yet fear of death could not be constantly present in our day-to-day conscious mental functioning; this would be an intolerable burden. To behave "normally" the biological organism, the animal man, represses its knowledge of death to acquire comfort. As things are, so they must change—so we are all socially and biologically conditioned to put away our fear of death, yet in a real paradox we become too efficiently oblivious to this fear in our conscious life.

The Temple tries to reconcile all our consciousnesses. To do this it embraces the knowledge of our own inevitable death with courage and uses it to justify action and the proper use of time. In actual fact, none of us know how much time we have, but when we do die it ought to be with Zero Regret. Zero Regret is the magickal state of inner balance and calm acceptance of the mortality of Individuals and the use of Zero Regret to channel all future action. The perfect state is to be sure that no time is wasted, no energy repressed and no fear hidden. In old language, we must experience the small death of literally facing ourselves, and facing the reality of a temporary metabolism—a limit on time. Time can be a tool, a liberator or an oppressor. When we claim time back for ourselves we are at last learning to be free and effective. Control needs time like a junkie needs junk. To escape control we must re-embrace our given time. Initially the human being has no apparent alternative but to succumb to a negative appreciation of death. To feel fear. The brain is genetically programmed for survival and will not allow itself to believe that it shall cease to exist. Thus, as we have already seen, the unconscious mind will seduce the intellect into ignoring logic and fact, a condition bordering upon hopelessness. It will ignore the lessons of experience and observation in favor of an inherited image of existence, and the affect of fear will be repressed. One will immediately becoum vulnerable to a desire for Hope that bypasses a confrontation with unconscious knowledge. Religion thrives upon this. It requires only an act of blind faith in exchange for guaranteed hope and salvation. It denies death and avoids the facts. In short, religion turns away from the truth. The Temple turns towards it. If you face yourself, you face death, and in this way *only you* can re-integrate your entire character and all its levels of consciousness and perception. This cannot be stressed too much or too often.

So, in religion all practical thought must be swept aside in a flood of faith. Answers becoum words, and facts becoum sins. This thing faith is the foundation of all religious thought. So powerful, yet fragile. Faith must be protected. Protected from doubt, protected from questions—it is seen as a constant that will not even tolerate thought. Its causes, its real essence, death, are so entrenched in everyone's mind that it has becoum the basis of every society, and so every society has developed a system to protect it. Dogma. The equation, simplified, goes something like this: Dogma negates thought. Thought is the enemy of faith (therefore the enemy of society). Individual thought patterns are discouraged in order to preserve faith inviolate, to thus preserve society, to preserve the status quo and the vested interests of the keepers of faith and dogma. It is in this web that religion meets politics and they reinforce each other in a web of deceit. Those in power have a personal interest in channeling individual thought down safe, unthreatening avenues geared to the production of materials and services that are to the "benefit" of society, of the "greater good." In other words you sacrifice your time, and your time is your most precious commodity. When you take yourself back it becoums priceless. People are deflected from the theft of their time and trained in how to produce and consume instead of in how to be engaged in their habitat and ideas. Politics organizes, religion directs.

From a child of five to an adult is a short step. From a newborn baby to a child of five is an appalling distance (Tolstoy). Religion invades

55

the child's world. A child without guilt is thus given guilt. A child without fear is thus given fear. The only salvation offered is through faith. Faith, it is suggested, ends death. The price of cheating death through faith is, of course, submission.

People who are not satisfied with this situation, people who want proofs, who wish to develop a system without guilt and fear that absorbs and uses death as a positive and liberating knowledge are discouraged, ridiculed, treated with suspicion and often deliberately misrepresented in the media. They are, after all, a threat to society to some degree. They strike at the core of the trick that controls us, and so in a real sense they are dangerous. Thee Temple ov Psychick Youth is dedicated to the re-acquisition by Individuals of their allotted time. It encourages, it does not discourage. It stands as an example of what is possible. To be involved is to becoum very special.

With the passage of history, society's control over individuals has been so progressively subtle that it has becoum imperceptible, perhaps even genetically inherited. Its very power lies in the fact that even its figureheads and leaders do not know its processes. Control is invisible. Time is invisible. Control is so able to shroud an individual's perception of reality in trivia as to becoum a uniform reality in itself. A reality that cannot ask itself questions. That cannot even formulate a language capable of setting questions that might reveal the truth.

In an age of collapse and transition we must find a language. A way out of the corner donated to us by history. The human brain must develop, becoum the next step in evolution. It is, simply, that we must develop our latent neurological powers or truly die as a race. It is a war for survival. Through experiment, through exploration of these latent powers, by visionary use of science and technology, and by the integration of experience, observation and expression we must revere ourselves.

A reality that cannot face itself becoums an illusion. Cannot be real. We must reject totally the concept and use of faith, that sham. We must emasculate religion. The "universe of magick" is within the mind of mankind. The setting is but illusion even to the thinker. The Temple is committed to building a modern network where people are given back pride in themselves, where destruction becoums a laughable absurdity to

56

a brain aware of its infinite and immeasurable potential. The Temple is committed to triggering the next evolutionary cycle in order to save this flawed but lovable animal man. The Temple is committed to developing a modern, functional and inspiring magickal structure. In engendering at long last the completely integrated and effective Individual. And this network of Individuals is in turn inevitably faced with a task of action to communicate survival and social evolution to others. We are the first truly non-aligned and non-mystical philosophy.

Fear breeds faith. Faith uses fear. Reject faith, reject fear, reject religions and reject dogma. Learn to cherish yourself, appreciate intuition and instinct, learn to love your questions. Value your time. Use mortality to motivate action and a caring, compassionate and concentrated life.
Genesis Breyer P-Orridge with Simon Dwyer, 1980

Temporary temple

II

 ime is an infinite consciousness, often mistakenly named "God." Time is omniscient, omnipresent, neutral. We ourselves are brief physical manifestations measuring our self-importance against time. From time we coum and into *time* we return. It seems that most mystical faiths, occult systems, religions, "God people" beliefs becoum clearer and easier to follow if we substitute thee word time for thee being, entity, almighty adhered to as thee infinite in various group systems. The way ov thee TOPI nomad is to focus upon time itself as thee amorphous consciousness coumtaining all Thistories, Presence and Futures.

Clues In thee black house two voices contradict, each as hybrid as the other. Thee banality ov caring for style reveals a parable ov transient coumuting that revels in trivia. Thee function ov words to devalue vision and emasculate meaning flows through thee digestion ov popular culture. Thee ability ov words to describe no-thing accurately. Time coumvulsing as flesh makes real desire. Thee body focused as a vessel for transmission ov guilt and engrams. Behind thought is a series ov masks that mouth simple platitudes like "E L-OV-E U."

Demand More ov everything for everybody. Money for everyone.

Result Our aim is wakefulness. Our enemy is dreamless sleep. Thee process is thee product.

Title: Temporary Temple
Species: Aural History
Research Project: Cultural Engineering

This event was initiated by thee Grey Organization and John "ZosKia" Gosling on Saturn Day, July 28, 1984. It took place in a derelict circular synagogue in Drayton Park, London, Dis-United Queendom. Psychick Youth volunteers squatted thee venue temporarily. They swept, cleaned, removed trash, sealed broken windows, repaired toilets, and set up a drinks and food area. A TOPI banishing ritual cleansed it ov previous deities and inherited belief systems. Psychick Youth incense was burned and hundreds ov candles were lit. An electricity generator was hired, borrowed video monitors were installed in pyramid banks on thee tiered choral stage and a PA system was rented. Invitations were passed out by hand only, discretely, as small as business cards, dark grey on grey. A secret howl in thee ambient night calling in thee growing pack ov wolves.

On thee night ov thee ritual, several hundred Psychick Youths, and Individuals ov thee Lost Tribe, from thee original first wave ov this movemeant, came out ov thee Shadow. Many are still active in creative and spiritual arenas; others have faded back into their social models, distracted, disillusioned or simply destined. So easy to burn out, lose your nerve and shy away from that leap into thee Abyss, such a loss to miss thee exhilaration ov thee fall into primal darkness, thee original sanctuary before even a sense ov *self.*

There were several police visits. Suspicious. They were told we were making a program about youth in an unspecified future time. Post-apocalypse for Channel 4. A nation's strength lies in its Psychick Youth. It would take hours for them to thoroughly confirm or deny this tale.

If you release an action it will unfold.
Old TOPI proverb

So... it happened. All present agreed. A unique ritual from thee street to thee Temple, from thee mountains to thee ancient stones. A clarity ov purpose, a unity ov intent manifested in a most inappropriate yet absolutely profound situation. Strange, and very special. When an idea ov an occult warrior underground, a chance to fight in thee old ways, using contemporary tools and symbols still seemed powerfully real and potent. Before thee heavy hand ov chance and will was burned with a fire ov betrayal and exhaustion. Yet looking into Them, Now, Next, there is still an unfolding, a scent of those dispersed circling ever nearer thee center once more.

We live, as ever, in a time ov sneering ridicule and Self-abuse. Thee Spew Age entraps thee fearful in thee chamber ov the-rapist, turning thee learning process ov a past into a bondage process ov a present, preventing thee next from ascending. Those who try are seen as weak, those who hide are seen as strong, those who forgive are seen as blocked, those who run are acknowledged as aware, those who care are seen as enemies, those who exploit inner pain are seen as love. Each y-era seems castrated, blinded by thee light, afraid ov thee sanctuary ov night.

Thee imprint Now is *compete*, not *complete*. To refuse is to be punished. Thee word "no" brings wrath, permission is equated with freedom, to explore consciousness remains a blasphemy. An absolute rule ov thee total, internal death ov Self-respect and hope, replaced by a glorification ov self-centeredness. In thee land ov thee inadequate, all are numb.

At two a.m. thee police finally raided. Thee Temporary Temple had already risen in a cone ov flame, and released its energy into all. Material traces and detritus had been erased. Nought butter a few entranced stragglers remained by thee entrance.

This was a mystery playing. There were no pieces ov music within this project, only an ebb and flow ov sound, that tolls ghostly over an era.

Genesis Breyer P-Orridge, November 1987, London / June 1993, California

REVEALED MANIFESTATION

Thee Temporary Temple: A manifestation that revealed and refined many aspects ov thee shamanistic qualities that make up thee pagan nature. Thee destruction ov inhibition and fear brought down upon us as we are brought up. Everyone present was actively colluding in a ridicule ov bourgeois order and a celebration ov thee ecstatic. Those administering sound sources acted merely as catalysts to allow everyone present—themselves included—to becoum part ov a transcendental moameant. Ego forgotten, thee situation transient, butter thee ecstasy and experience fixed in our unconscious forever.

From thee obvious: b-earth to death, all is temporary, seems temporal... butter this is a transitory moameant. This event had no bounds in *time*. We looked in thee mirror ov our *Selves* and our being gathered together and knew release from thee programmed form ov entertainment that we usually receive. We were indeed present at a Temple. At a triumph ov thee flesh. A sacred forbidden place, quite literally, where thee spirit flowed like sexual fluid for our beings... a chantry ov our minds chanting thee same human desire to break thee bounds ov temporality, thee split that serves society's controlling purpose, being a step onto thee path ov magickal practice... revere this night.

Brother Malik, November 1987 TOPY STEEL

LEVELS OF MEANING IN THEE TEMPLE OV PSYCHICK YOUTH

Four Facts

1 Possibility: It is real.
2 Clarity: It is unique.
3 Certainty: It is known.
4 Intimacy: It is immediate.

64

Demystification Demystification means not taking anything for granted, whether that may be your living situation, philosophical point of view or state of mind. We generally don't stop and question ourselves very much about what we are attempting to do. Nevertheless, the beliefs that we hold dear are highly suspect. A belief could be any part of awareness that we simply let operate without attention. There is always a lot of background stuff taking place. When you look at this page, sign your name, walk up a flight of stairs or get into an argument, most of what you are doing is shunted outside of your awareness. Many of the processes that make us go on as we do will never be in our attention for our entire lives. We forget a lot of the past, we are confused about the present and we are ignorant about the future. Demystification means examining all of that. It also means examining why and how we are examining. Examining has a connotation of "operating on" what is being perceived; that we might be trying to reshape reality. Reality might also be trying to reshape us but, ultimately, we don't really have to do anything to maintain the whole thing. We are always stuck in the middle no matter what we do. So demystification means not taking that for granted.

Our tendency is always to be busy. But behind the busyness there is no particular point. Similarly, our tendency is also always to be lazy. We don't make any effort unless we are certain it will be for our benefit, no matter how illogical or self-destructive the action might be. We are impatient but also uncertain. A problem with many "spiritual" disciplines is that we add a layer of abstraction obscuring this basic process. We want to solve the problem, but we are ignoring the fact that it is we who stated it as a problem.

All sorts of things are happening which we may or may not want to have happen. Presumably we want to control the situation such that only things that we want to happen do happen. This is the problem that we perpetually try to solve without ever truly being successful. It is not immediately noticed why this is always the case. We begin to become skeptical of our situation. Usually that is the beginning: doubt. We begin to realize that our way of operating leaves too many loose ends.

You can see this in your living space: it is constantly in a state of progressive disorder from your actions. However, it is also constantly being brought back into order by your actions. Nobody else is doing it except you. It is also the case that it is never in a state of completion. It is never wholly satisfactory. Ritual is seeing this whole process. Your experience is not necessarily a personal commitment, but you cannot extricate yourself from it. So you have to live with that, use that as an inspiration.

Since there is no way out of it we are encouraged to not add to it unnecessarily. This is the process of demystification. We don't actually stay the same, but we begin to divest ourselves—to experience some vulnerability. We can be wrong. It isn't a problem. We can deal with the fact that we have harmed people. We can get beyond the psychological mire. In that way we can know vision, we can see. We can feel, be touched, hear, taste, smell. That could be our guide: just being whatever we are.

Individuality Individuality is an abstraction. You cannot really say that you have experienced individuality. Nevertheless, you cannot really take a holiday from yourself either. Formless, individuality is the foundation of appearances. There is no effort involved in individuality, undivided duality. It is whether you care to notice it or not.

The fact is, we don't really know what we are. We believe we are. We don't really know how this comes about or its fate for that matter, or if there is a fate. Without the crutch of identity, the constant cues that remind us to be something or other, what are we? Being something is inherently unsatisfying, stale yet enticing. We cannot leave it alone. Like mildew, habits build up, and they stick tenaciously to an impenetrable surface.

Individuality is a dead end. It is a hard end. You cannot hope to pose any questions about individuality. At the same time nothing is precluded. Everything is made possible in this empty arena. You cannot even say that you are alone. There is nothing to give up in the end. Discipline is foolishness. Nothing is lost or achieved. However, in this absence, communication becomes possible. There are sensations, thoughts, interactions. Situations arise pristine in precision and clarity, inescapable, a sharp chill, clean and sure in the silence.

Realizing individuality means not dwelling on the mind. What happens happens. Your search looks in the wrong direction precisely because it is a search. By giving up searching, by giving up relief, individuality is immediately apparent. There is no trick to individuality or exclusivity. It is immediately apparent. There is no trick to individuality or exclusivity. It is the ultimate occult teaching, which is available to anyone, anytime. It is shock and familiarity at once. To realize individuality engenders tremendous confidence. You could say that not having anything to hang on to is a tremendous source of energy and inspiration, a quality of panic that makes you continually appreciate what you are.

There is no way to develop individuality. It is a constant. Individuality is neither created nor destroyed. We recognize individuality to various degrees depending on our willingness to do so. Like infinity, individuality is readily recognized but recedes from our grasp, our willingness or unwillingness to relate to individuality being equal. We are forced to come to terms with our snobbery, our lack of generosity, our inhibitions and holding back. There is no other way. We simply wear ourselves out with the whole thing. We are reminded not to take what we are too seriously. Individuality, the essence of ritual, is ultimately no achievement, timelessness in endless change.

Intention Despite its basic simplicity, intention is a very difficult point. It seems to take a lot of work to come to terms with. Normally we build on our experiences. Intention encourages us to work with the experience itself.

Without intention we are only reacting without an overall understanding of the process of our experience. To live intentionally does not mean particularly having a defined plan in place at every moment. Rather it is a state of continual accuracy in all of our actions.

Accuracy comes from two things: clear perception and uninhibited action. These two are linked, and in fact are not really different. Clear perception is receiving without hesitation and uninhibited action is the response: giving back without hesitation. We are acting in experience, not on it.

Hesitation is the perception that your security is being threatened in some way. In order to really give and take you need to give up security and accept the situation you are in as it is. Engaging in outrageous actions, however, is not necessarily giving up security. If you are without expectation, attempting to define yourself in some way is irrelevant. Similarly, without hesitation you can take responsibility for any situation. The normal concern over blame is no longer important. You simply take things at face value. Responsibility also means taking initiative. You do not need to follow precedent. What needs to happen is clear immediately. Frequently the straightforward route causes discomfort. It seems to focus attention on the basis of our anxiety, what we are trying to hide. The effect can be one of a rude awakening. It is necessary to experience our anxiety and discomfort and not try and gloss it over or shovel it under the carpet with technique. For this reason it is necessary not to blame others for our discomfort. Instead we could be grateful that we are being reminded of it. By being reminded of it we are able to work with it. The whole point is to notice it first before doing anything with it. Then one simply learns not to refer to it.

67

Intention lets you get into the groundlessness of your experience. There is no hidden maneuvering or agenda. It is quite simple. You want what you want, but it is not really necessary at the same time. You can drop it because you see that it is groundless.

Intention, obviously, applies in all areas of existence, and not just in ritual. It is what makes "ritual" ritual. Through intention you see that ritual is not necessarily a specific time, place or circumstance but rather your relation with that time, place and circumstance. Intention is not an attempt at gaining control but rather points out the essential needlessness of the game in the first place.

Ritual Without ritual TOPY could not exist. Ritual is much more than working with any specific practice. It enables a complete and coherent response to our experience. Ritual allows us to know the total integration of our experience as it is. It provides a bridge between confusion and certainty.

Ritual must be approached with care. It must be followed through thoroughly and completely. If you are piercing yourself, you know that halfway through you can't say, "Oh, I guess I won't go through with it!" It is the same situation in our daily existence. By not taking care or following through we continually pay the price of haste.

We tend to see problems as being inflicted on us from without. Similarly, we also seek salvation outside of ourselves. Being effectively reciprocal, suffering and relief are intimately linked. Techniques that work tend to make us more aware of our pain and, particularly, our role in it. They show us that looking elsewhere for satisfaction is fruitless. Eventually, we have to take responsibility for the difficulties we experience and not expect to be rescued from them.

To really get into experiences we have to let pleasure and pain happen in their own way. Thus, in order to really get into pleasure we must acknowledge pain. What prevents us from experiencing pleasure is fear— we anticipate pain. Similarly we try to shield ourselves from pain with hope—the anticipation of pleasure. To develop clarity we need to give up our expectations about pain and pleasure in a fundamental way. Otherwise they will constantly lead us astray.

By working with a structured approach we have some way to work with the raw material of our experience. However, adopting a certain approach does not guarantee expected results. We have to take the chance that we are on the wrong track. Because we approach any technique with expectations, we are inevitably going to be disappointed by it. Perhaps the function of technique is not just to be "successful" but also to make us question our motivations and assumptions about it. We are very much a part of the structured approach of technique. That we take a proper approach to technique is vastly more important than any technique we might investigate. With a structured approach, even if the technique is flawed, it should be clear what is going on. Without it, results will be random at best.

Apart from what the source or tradition of the technique brings to the technique, what we bring to the technique consists of two parts:

The first part is a willingness to do the technique. This is a major stumbling block for most of us. We would rather speculate about what we don't know than have to get into it and possibly make a mess.

The second part is that once we have thoroughly worked with the technique we need to evaluate what we are doing. It is necessary to give up the idea of searching for a reward in everything. Not everything works. Whether something works as expected or whether we want to continue with a certain approach is not the important point. Rather we need to clearly see where we are going with it. Otherwise our approach will become superstitious poison.

Working with technique requires both a willingness to surrender as well as critical intellect. Without both of these we are prone to self-deception.

Knowing our role in any success or failure we experience is an important point. Our disappointments are a reminder not to take what we are doing too seriously. If we have taken a wrong approach to a certain technique, we should acknowledge it—we can't blame the chair we tripped over for our sore toe. Similarly, it is not particularly productive to dwell on our success either. We adopt techniques on the basis of other people's experience. Without that experience and generosity we would get nowhere.

Ritual is not limited to technique. Technique is only an entry point, a way to get into experiences. Inevitably technique becomes extraneous. Technique for its own sake is an obstacle. There is always a dan-

69

ger of using what we are doing as a way to emphasize our exclusivity. Although we are always subject to other people's prejudices to some degree, we do not benefit from exaggerating that prejudice. It is not necessary to concern ourselves with whether or not a given situation or tradition fits in with our own or another's preconceptions of what is proper behavior. In actuality we are subject to the same deception and prejudice as anybody else. Without deception we would never have been inspired to work on ourselves in the first place. If everything is OK, why bother? The fact that we want to work on ourselves is just an inevitable part of the process of pain that everybody experiences in one way or another. There is nothing special about that at all. Thus what we are doing, whether it is accepted or not, is not particularly a cause for self absorption or arrogance.

We need to let ritual permeate our whole life. When we are willing to give ourselves to it whole-heartedly, pain and pleasure become an ornament, both personal and ageless. There is nothing mysterious about ritual. By relating with our experience in a straightforward way, ritual is invoked immediately, anytime, anywhere. It is an open invitation.

70   Levels Of Meaning In TOPY The sigil is the result. That is the basic premise. When your whole life becomes ritual, then there is no distinction between procedure and result. Despite its seemingly arbitrary appearance in 1981, TOPY has a highly organized and self-consistent structure. This structure may not be so obvious to the casual observer. In fact, the early documents of TOPY appear to be somewhat incomplete. The purpose of this writing is to attempt to increase the understanding of the underpinnings and implications of TOPY so that individuals who wish to use the methods of intuitive magic may do so with greater clarity of purpose.

Four points seem to make up this whole: ritual, intention, demystification and individuality. These create a self-contained structure of interdependence. Each relies upon the other. From these four points, different links may be inferred.

The goal of sigilization is the coordination and eventual integration of various levels of awareness that are frequently in conflict. We need to connect with other possibilities of awareness apart from the apparently mundane consciousness that we are generally familiar with. That this consciousness is not so straightforward and mundane is the starting point for this natural process of discovery. Much of the process of sigilization could be properly summed up as the development of perspective, We begin to be able to discern the features of different states of awareness. In addition to these intuitively observed states, there is the functional architecture of the brain itself. This has a special significance in the symbolism and structure of TOPY.

Ritual is the concrete expression of experience. It is the foundation of awareness from which the other points are abstracted. Whether we are aware of it or not, we are always working on this level. Much difficulty is caused by the fact that we do not consciously acknowledge this under normal circumstances. Instead of working with our experience in a straightforward way, we invoke superstition and mystification, in many instances without realizing it. Ritual naturally evolves towards intention. Intention represents the state of complete self-acceptance and self-awareness. This state of equanimity is silence. From it the richness of expression is apparent. Ultimately there is no distinction of passivity or activity. One is able to work effortlessly and continually. Intention is the panoramic experience of the process of ritual.

71

Demystification begins with the process of doubt. It is a way of discernment. We need to know *why*. Demystification is the working of ritual over time. We work with ritual to find out. The critical quality of demystification is necessary if we are to develop accurate understanding. Demystification evolves naturally to individuality. Individuality is the primal experience of awareness before perception. It is the basic riddle of experience and the end of all questions. We just have to get into experiences. We cannot hope to codify or prepare them.

Looking at these four points from the perspective of space and time we can see the connection between the timeliness of ritual and the timelessness of intention. From space-time we abstract both process (demystification) and being (individuality). In demystification there is an ongoing sense of working with experience. In individuality there is an ongoing sense of working with experience. In individuality there is a sense of constancy or immutability. These qualities evolve naturally from the experience of ritual. Demystification suggests that situations are knowable. Individuality suggests that they are beyond knowing. Intention, the coordination factor in the puzzle, evolves from the combined intelligence of knowing and not knowing. The fickleness of time and the immutability of space are negated. One is perfectly coordinated in time and space, free in one's expression. Demystification and individuality provide a mirror, the axis of precision, from which the meaning behind the experience is made more apparent. We begin to appreciate our experience more and begin to take more care in how we work with it.

Similarly, ritual and intention provide a mirror of our questions, the axis of openness, in which we know the equality of knowing and not knowing.

The four points of demystification, individuality, ritual and intention form an interdependent and self-referential whole. They do not point to any outside cause for their operation. Thus experience, any experience, is self-contained. We are not particularly under attack or being congratulated by any outside influence. We do not know the final direction of experience. It happens. Being both cause and effect, we work with it as it happens.

Sigilization And The Brain Sigilization is particularly concerned with the control and operation of the limbic system. The limbic system provides the functional ability to experience emotion. It is also important in the formation of long-term memory. It could be thought of as a fulcrum between the cerebral cortex and the autonomic areas of the brain—which, among other things, control sleep and sexual response. The brain, while composed of many sub-systems, is a functional unit. Sigilization is one technique that can reorganize the brain into a more coherent state of function. In the sigil one sees the various functional areas of the brain symbolized:

> Ov: Autonomic brain.
> Blood, Spit: Limbic system.
> The Sigil Paper: Cerebral cortex.

The purpose of the sigil is to connect the cerebral cortex with the "lower" areas of the brain. The coordination of mental and bodily sensations is the primary purpose of the sigil. The limbic system assigns the weights of bodily and mental experiences. That is, it is critical to whether you are aware of a certain aspect of your experience. In various eating disorders, for example, the weight of the bodily sensation of hunger changes to an abnormal level, from being driven from consciousness in anorexia to being the main focus of attention in bulimia. The intended effect of the sigil is to balance the relative weights of mental and bodily sensations, heightening both. The subsequent release provides the impetus for the working of the sigil. While the content of the sigil might be subliminal the medium of sensation that carries the content is not.

The balance of the sigil also follows a horizontal axis in addition to the vertical axis described above:

> Right Hemisphere (Intuition): Inidividuality.
> Left Hemisphere (Planning): Ritual.
> Corpus Callosum (Connection): Demystification.
> Effect of Sigilization (Integration): Intention.

Perhaps the accommodation of desire performed by the sigil is like the sweet taste of an apple. The apple is sweet so that you will eat it and distribute its seed. The apple merely produces seed. The sigil produces balance. If the sigil works then we are encouraged to continue with the process of sigilization, which in turn produces even more balance. Not grasping this point can cause problems. If we try to force situations too much there is a tendency for a backlash to occur. There is nothing mysterious about this. We simply stop paying attention to what we are doing. This negates any positive effect of the sigilization process. By realizing the self-contained, self-actualizing nature of experience, what we mean by ritual, such mistakes will become less frequent.

73

Sigilization is not the only method for working with the basic principles of TOPY. Other methods do apply and can augment or replace the practice of sigilization. The question is in understanding the underlying logic of your situation. You need to decide if sigilization is appropriate. In a way this is impossible to do. To really know what it is, you need to work with it on a practical level. It is very much a personal decision. Success reflects more your willingness to work with your experience than any particular result or reward. That you are rewarded by the process is a side-effect of the process itself. By developing insight, what we want naturally changes. We change and grow as human beings. This naturally encourages us to focus the direction of our energies towards working on ourselves. Will is not, ultimately, what is referred to by the expression "will power." Will is release, the positive expression of energy. You simply let go of that which holds you back. Will is the natural result.

The Emperor's Clothes Self could be said to be the buildup of memory. It is the identity that you are familiar and comfortable with at any given moment. Normally we have two beliefs about the self:

      1 It is distinct.
      2 It is singular.

We have a sense of the self as distinct because we believe that we exist amongst other similar but dissimilar beings. We can say that we are not another because of our experience of "other." The difficulty with "other" is that we never really experience it. We are always involved in our particular point of view. If we suddenly took on another's point of view, there would still be one point of view. We have to admit that "other" exists only as a convention. We use this concept or intuition to navigate around in the world where various perceptions exist in similar or dissimilar states. Without any evidence to distinguish more than one point of view, self is impossible to determine. That self is distinct is a fundamental belief without which the whole experience of self will fall apart. In its stead we have to consider that self and not-self are indistinguishable.

The singularity of self is a theory we create based on our belief in a distinguishable self. By singularity I do not mean a "single" irreducible self but a consistent self-image or set of self-images that occur on a continual basis. This theory of self tries to set up various emotional experiences for itself and then evaluates those experiences for success. The sense of success feeds back into the system as it itself is emotion. Emotion is a sense of energy or change in the system of self. Emotion, however, is not in itself a theory of self and exists interdependently of the self's self-image(s). Ironically, emotions, which provide the means for the creation of self, are also the means of its destruction. Singularity implies permanence, which is in conflict with the capriciousness of emotion.

Working with magick, we need to be realistic and to be willing to discard that which is unnecessary. If we believe magick is the exercise of intention, any reliance on self deception puts us on shaky foundations. If self is indeterminate then we must modify our magickal work to accommodate this fact. The question remains: Isn't magick just irrelevant without the self? Perhaps we need to give it up entirely, to not even start from scratch. Whether this affects our actual practice is another matter. We are reminded of our nonexistence from working with concrete situations. We cannot really abandon the fact that we exist in a concrete, perceptual world.

Working without reference to self cannot occur without a living experience of the ephemeral nature of the self. To accomplish this we need to work with awareness itself in some fundamental way. We have excluded awareness from our working if we rely on a notion of self. Self is any predefined id/entity or goal. If we have a goal whether or not we achieve it will be the same since we have not dared to ask the fundamental question.

Magick that does not invoke the self, search for a "higher" purpose or attempt to solidify itself in achievements is a radically different thing from what most of us might consider to be normal magickal practice. But if we examine what we actually do do in our practice, we can see that this possibility does spontaneously crop up even if it is ignored. Usually we look for the extraordinary to distract us from the fact that we are not really doing anything.

75

If you are dreaming that you are naked, you believe that you are naked but you do not believe that you are dreaming. Working without the self is to see that you are dreaming as well. At least that is the beginning. Knowing that you are dreaming may not change the contents of the dream but it may radically change the character of the dream. By knowing that you are dreaming you are free to give up the idea of being a fixed character in the dream.

While we might feel that we do not have the same freedom in our waking situation (and in a sense the main purpose of magick is to unite the waking and dreaming states) the same possibility applies. It applies because waking in the dream is a state of awareness. Anything we do to invoke it is merely a provocation of awareness. Since awareness applies to any state of mind, since we cannot escape mind for even a second, the same logic applies: We can be in on the joke any time we wish.

Magick without self is both work and play simultaneously, both pain and pleasure. We work directly with the raw materials in this case. TOPY is in a unique position because of our lack of tradition. It is easier to discard any unnecessary accoutrements to our magickal work. Really the whole thing is a question of interpretation. What do you believe you are doing?
Coyote 37

CONSTRUCTING THEE CROSS

Speculations—*About A Few Ambiguous Details* Life is like an investigation, almost a detective story, whose mystery we never manage to unravel. The theories formulated, often invalidated, never turn out to be true (at best we remain hopeful). Their nature is always to be hypothetical and, in the end, simply spiritual points of view.

We should also admit, however, that this is the essence of the pleasure of living. We should never confuse speculation with reality, but on the contrary admit that we are condemned to take our pleasure from that difference.

The Common Denominator Through the medium of Throbbing Gristle, and through that of Psychic TV, and the various texts, Genesis Breyer P-Orridge talks to us of his fascination for the figure "3."

Coming as we do from a Christian culture, we think first of all of the Holy Trinity. But in all times and all places, this number has had preponderant and symbolic value: It can designate the spirit, the soul and the body, or again (still according to the Qabalah) the subject, the verb and the object... For others it represents the phases of existence: birth, growth and death.

For George Dumezil, society itself is tripartite: the priest, the warrior and the producer... Alchemy would take it to have three ways (humid, dry and royal) and astrology, three phases (evolution, culmination and involution).

"Descending"—The title given to the concert, one year after the fact, by Genesis Breyer P-Orridge. Such a delay for reflection can only indicate an extreme significance.

For personal reasons this descent incites me to think of the "fall." It can be seen at the top of the poster made for the concert (cf. the single *Roman P.*), and ineluctably falls back. Those who are under (or who place themselves under) the sign of water are condemned to the cycle of the eternal return. But it must also be noted that the first of June, 1984 (the evening of the concert) happened to be the day following that of Ascension (a religious feast and holiday celebrated in France).

Christ having ascended into the heavens, this "descent" would therefore designate the fall of the fallen angels towards hell and its underworlds...

Who would be surprised? Has not Genesis Breyer P-Orridge already used letter paper decorated with his own portrait representing himself as the devil or Satan? Finally there is the cross with the three horizontal branches, the omnipresent symbol of the group (Psychic TV).

Such crosses are rare and seldom used. The only one that I know of is the "papal cross," whose characteristic is to have a central branch longer than the two others. The one worn by PTV would thus be (the central branch thus being shorter than the two others) an "anti-papal" cross.

The insistence with which this cross is not only reproduced but also highlighted underlines its symbolic importance.

The highlighting culminates with the image of the cross in flames, filmed on video at extreme length. A reference, albeit an obvious one, to the megalomaniac rituals of the KKK (once again the number three), but which should not eclipse the fire itself, a vital and primordial symbol if ever there was one.

If we imagine that the median axis of this cross (the symbol of PTV) divides it into two symmetrical parts, and if we consider only the left part, we see that the figure "3" appears... A peculiarity that logically brings us to consider the right part with equal interest:

The symmetrical equivalent of the figure "3" turns out to be the letter "E."

"E" as in energy, which is what comes to mind first of all. But the symbolism of the letters takes us back to the ancient Gods, to the Greco-Roman mythologies. The "E" designates the goddess Vesta (Hestia in Greek, beginning with the letter Epsilon, corresponding to our "E"). She is fire by principle energy in its purest form.

It is the fire of Hestia that the mystic visionaries feel burning in their bones.
Emmanuel, *Highlights of Ancient Greece*, 1963

By extension she is also the goddess of the home. In the letter "E," onto the vertical line designating the flame, is attached the father for the highest line, the mother for the lowest, and the child for the median.

The family has become the capital theme of the life of Genesis Breyer P-Orridge, as much on the personal level as on that of the public by means of Psychic TV and Thee Temple ov Psychic Youth. (It is not unreasonable to remember the fascination of Genesis Breyer P-Orridge with the Manson family.)

78

As in all other primordial symbols, fire is ambivalent. Its origins are equally as divine as demonic, representing spiritual growth (the rising flame which mounts and illuminates) as much as psychic regression (the underground fire, crawling and consuming). The symmetrical symbol of water is, however, of the same nature, since both have purifying virtues. Do not let us give into the contemporary habits and consider these symmetries as being oppositions; let us rather see them as in the times of the Greco-Roman paganism, as complementary.

The fire in mythology, in another incarnation than that of Vesta, we find associated with Vulcan, which (in agreement with Jean Haab in The Alphabet of the Gods) we shall write as Wulcan, thus associating it with the letter symbol "W." As a preliminary we shall note that this "W" is obtained by a ninety-degree rotation to the left of the letter "E."

Wulcan is the underground fire, that of the forge, close to hell. It therefore indicates metal, which has for all time been associated with the idea of magic. Psychic TV introduces the symbol of metal, essentially in three forms (once again that same number!):

> 1 The knife, obviously a phallic, active instrument inducing the idea of sacrifice. It marks the flesh of the initiate into Thee Temple ov Psychic Youth with three horizontal slashes.

> 2 The bracelets of copper, feminine symbols clasping the wrist (the fist as a symbol of power). Incidentally, copper designates Venus.

> 3 The metal rings used for piercing, as much to decorate as to prevent the open flesh from closing up. This meeting of flesh, sex and metal is in no way surprising for those who know the theories of Jung relating metals to sexual desire, to the libido.

The hidden message of "piercing" is highly troubling and mysterious. What is to be thought of this masculine sex piercing by a ring (the feminine symbol)? A desire for the feminine sex to become "penetrator" and the phallus the "penetrated"? A desire not for castration but for reunification? The theme of fire in itself is unavoidably linked with that of sexuality (the fire obtained by rubbing), sexuality constituting the psychic binder of PTV.

The "W" designating Wulcan, if we take the symmetrical point, or if we make a rotation of ninety degrees to the right of the letter "E," the letter "M" is thus created, which designates Mercury (Hermes). With the "M" we arrive at the ultimate stage of this journey towards the letters presiding over the existence of PTV and its destiny. The most hidden of them in fact turns out to be the most important, its action, although essentially occult, consists in linking the other letters together.

Mercury, the god of messengers, the god of discovery, the god of synthesis. He permits the perfect conciliation between these fundamental themes of metal, water (the liquid element) and fire. Mercury, "the sperm of metals" as it is designated by the Freemason's catechism of 1766 (*The Flaming Star* by Baron de Tschoudy). A liquid metal presiding over all mutations, over the union of all opposites.

79

Mercury the winged god is also the bearer of the Caduceus wand, whose two entwined snakes symbolize the Dionysian synthesis of symmetric principles: good and evil, fire and water, diurnal and nocturnal, masculine and feminine... at last reunited.

[It is Mercury represented (such as Saint Christopher) making Agni the God of fire (for the Indians) cross the water.
It is Hermes, psychopomp accompanying the dead from the world of the living towards that of the shades.

Hermes Trismegistus (thrice great), the founder of alchemy—"he who possesses the three ministries," "he who dominates the body, the soul and the spirit." (Jean Haab, *The Alphabet of the Gods*, 1979)

This alchemical Mercury, sometimes represented in the form of a wolf holding a lamb (the Philosopher's stone) in its mouth...thus bringing us back, in such a forceful way, to this other recurrent theme of PTV.

O Great Mercury of the Wise Ones
In you is unified silver and gold
Drawn from power alive
Mercury, all sun, all moon, triple substance in one
Unity which shows itself to be triple, O sublime Wonder!
Mercury, sulphur and salt
You teach me that in three substances
You are only one.
Marc Antonio Cassellane (Translated from the *italian under the title Light Revealing Itself From the Shadows* by the Baron de Tschoudy, 1766)

80

Finally, Mercury allows us to evoke Venus once again (compare with the text accompanying the PTV single Roman P.)—from the encounter between these two divinities (Hermes and Aphrodite) was born Hermaphroditus, the androgynous, having at the same time the feminine and masculine sexual attributes.

Indifferent to its monstrosity, the hermaphrodite has gradually become a savior who masters conflicts. During the course of the evolution of civilization, the original bisexual being has become the symbol of the unity of the personal-

ity, of the "oneself" in twhich the conflict of constants has managed to calm itself. In this way the original being, already being from the beginning a protection of the unconscious entity, has become the far off goal of the "realization of oneself" of the human essence.
C. G. Jung, *Contribution to the Psychology of the Infant Archetype* (1941)

Mercury, the god of Hermetic Science, but also that of Hermeneutics, the god allowing us to solve the problem of trying to square the circle.
Jean-Pierre Turmel, Rouen, August 15-25, 1985 (Translated by Malcolm Duff)

Thee black book

III

SIGILS: FOR KALI AND EDEN
INTRODUCTION

n thee five yeras since thee first edition ov this booklet was published, thee Temple has grown immeasurably through thee l-ov-e, trust and dedication ov those who care. Thee aim ov this extensively revised edition is to bring this energy we have gained, this l-ov-e we know, this magickal journey we share, to a new and wider circle. We know that those in contact with thee Temple are dedicated to a vision ov a fiercely Individual mode ov life, and it is our deepest desire that this dedication be given every opportunity to find expression in thee face ov thee cynical and reactionary hand ov Control. Thee method could not be simpler, and its potency cannot be denied. Thee Temple seeks to return to thee Individual all that is truly theirs, to awaken thee reality ov dreams, and to crush thee imposed conditioning ov a society scared to look itself in thee mirror, scared to place life ahead ov death.

No matter what difficulties we face from those who would deny us our way, thee Temple will continue to use every means at its disposal to ensure that we are not thwarted. And thee most powerful weapon we have is thee Sigil, thee magickal process by which we charge our dreams and desires, and make manifest their living beauty. It is to thee Sigil that this book is dedicated, and to all those who know.

Everyone who is active in thee Temple, who has freely given their coumitment to its aims, realizes that this is no part-time easy answer that we give. It is a case ov total coumitment; butter there is also no-one in thee Temple who has not found that through this coumitment coums a new and vital energy that makes thee sacrifice an act ov l-ov-e, a way ov living that brings its own reward through thee development ov strength, purpose and freedom from all that denies us our destiny.

Thee TOPY network spans thee Western Hemisphere, its aim is to create an alternative system ov information exchange to counter thee spread ov lies disseminated by thee mass media and thee governments ov Control. And thee growth ov thee network, thee continual development ov new Access Points in thee UK, Europe and America is proof that we are winning. Lines ov coumunication grow stronger daily as we share with each other thee experiences we have gained, thee lessons we have learnt, thee l-ov-e and anger we feel. So it is with thee Sigil. Just as we work to share all that is important to us with you, so by sharing your experiences with us can we all move ahead together as Individuals; not as sheep who follow unthinkingly.

It is always a question ov independence. We are not here to convince thee doubters, to dominate thee weak, to act as crutch or place ov refuge. We are not saviors or dogmatists. Everything that is gained is from within thee Individual, only it was previously asleep. We simply help to awaken thee truth ov desire, and by thee development ov individual thought and responsibility show how it is possible to act on that knowledge.

Our system is functional: that is, it works. And thee result ov this is that we each find our own way, not one dictated to us by others. We remain linked by friendship, not by need; a friendship born ov true understanding and not simply thee freak ov circumstance.

Thee Temple ov Psychick Youth is a network ov Individuals. That is how it should be, and that is thee only requirement.

1 As we have said, Sigils have a functional purpose: they serve as a direct means to make what you want to happen more likely to happen. Butter they are quite different from systems based on faith and false promises. They cannot guarantee anything; they can only help release thee potential that already exists within. And as it is a system for thee Individual there is no right or wrong way—what is right for one person may be entirely inappropriate for another. Therefore thee method is one that must be developed personally, so that thee Sigil as performed by you is something wholly ov your own making, reflecting your own personalities and experiences. We offer only guidance and encouragement, not instructions and rules to obey. We leave those to thee Controllers, thee ones who seek to generate uniformity ov thought, and who strive to create a passive and compliant populace thinking along rigid and conditioned lines, unable to take responsibility for their own lives and actions.

We are sickened by thee negative attitudes ov right and wrong that are promulgated in thee mass media: that if you do this you cannot do that, if you think this you cannot think that. It is a system that destroys thee

Individual; destroys thee ability to think, to question, to force thee hand ov chance; destroys thee will to live according to who you really are and not according to who they say you are. Sigils break down this conditioning, awaken thee possibility ov change and experiment, give back thee joy ov a life rich in experience and challenge.

Sigils are as much about learning as anything else. Not only learning thee method that works for you, butter also learning who it is that you really are, what it is that you really want. A result ov this is that it may take some time before you discover thee method ov working that is best for you, and you may find that thee results ov your Sigils are not as expected. This is not thee result ov getting it wrong, it is thee natural response caused by thee first steps on a road ov discovery. For example, things may not happen in thee order you had expected, or they may take a different form. Thee identity ov thee people involved may be unexpected. Butter if you examine thee results ov your work closely and honestly you will find that these differences—these moves away from thee pre-conceived—reflect thee true aim hidden within thee Sigil, thee underlying qualities ov it. Thee reason for this is that your conscious image is not thee real object ov your desire; thee conscious wish, after all, being subject to thee conditioned responses thee Sigil is designed to break down. Thee results are often more expansive than you could have dreamed, more radical than you would have consciously dared hope. Put simply, what you expect is not always what you really want. And what you think you want is not always what you really want.

Our concern is with thee Individual in thee modern world. Accordingly our methods are designed to meet thee circumstances that prevail today. They are not occult in thee way that word is usually understood, they rely only on thee intuitive use ov that which we already know, directed with purpose. It is a maximization ov thee powers ov thee brain, a joining together ov conscious and unconscious will so that through thee use ov Sigils thee Individual can move towards a desired goal free from thee constraint ov confused ideals and personal contradictions. Unlike much that is called occult, we do not rely on dogma, mystification, references to orthodoxy or thee mimicking ov previously effective butter now redundant rituals, rules and experiences. We believe that thee strength needed is already living in each ov us. It is simply that we need to tune in to thee right channels, see clearly and act on that

87

vision. And that vision must be fiercely personal, not thee dictate ov some other who tries to impose their will on thee Individual, or some corporate view that leaves nothing to chance and tells us that dissent from thee common ground is a sin.

A great deal ov energy is wasted on arguing over thee validity ov much that falls under thee general heading ov "occult"—whether things are real or imagined. Much ov thee evidence to date is confusing, partial or fabricated to meet a given need. This is thee result of research being misdirected, and thee will to understand being compromised. It is better by far to accept "occult" experiences as they occur, to recognize and interpret them personally without trying to fit them into a pre-defined system. Thee Sigil strengthens basic human skills, re-awakens thee intuitive understanding ov thee relationships between events, breaks down linear modes ov thought that offer only tunnel vision and answers that are defined in thee question itself. Thee Temple believes that thee best judge ov truth is experience, combined with an attitude that engenders a discriminating eye hampered neither by prejudice nor fear. Thee Sigil is thee internal working ov thee brain, externalized; thee manifestation ov inclusive will directed outward to positive action.

88

2 In *Thee Grey Book* we discuss thee Sigil ov Three Liquids, which encoumpasses thee essence ov thee practical methods we employ; butter it should be remembered that everything we say is only a guide to further experimentation and not a dictate to be followed in blind faith. Thee Temple is not about instruction, thee giving ov set patterns and modes ov behavior to follow, for that way no-one learns anything, there is no progress, no interchange of ideas and l-ov-e. To slavishly follow ideas set out on a plate is to abdicate responsibility, to lose one's individuality in favor ov an easy, butter doubtlessly wrong, answer.

This may seem hard to those who feel uneasy about how to proceed, who are used to doing just what they are told and no more, butter that is thee point. Thee Temple is about getting rid ov those attitudes which ultimately lead to indifference, getting rid ov thee fear ov experiment and genuine exploration; instead our methods create in thee Individual a precise knowledge ov their own existence, desires and capabilities in thee most creative and positive light possible. And they force thee acceptance ov an attitude ov living that will reflect that knowledge in a direct and practical way. It is only by embracing their individuality that thee Individual can truly coum to thee understanding and fulfillment ov their goals. Anything else is pointless, a waste ov energy, a misdirection ov purpose.

So what we are saying is that while thee basic format is one that can be used by anyone, it is also one that requires absolutely thee direct and personal input of thee Individual to be wholly and perfectly effective. Specific details can and should be arrived at by you. And they can include or exclude anything that we have said: intent is all, as is an ability to focus on thee goal.

Nonetheless, we recognize that guidance can be useful. And neither do we forget that Sigils, in one form or another, have been practiced throughout history. In order to illustrate what we mean, and to encourage your own experimentation, we include here examples from both historical and present-day sources.

Thee following is quoted from a book by Austin Osman Spare (1886-1956):

> *Sigils are used to enable two things to occur.*
>
> *1 Effective communion with unconscious levels.*
> *2 The lodging of a desire or wish at unconscious levels without the conscious mind being involved or aware.*
>
> *My formula and Sigils for sub-conscious activity are a means of inspiration, capacity or genius, and a means of accelerating evolution. An economy of energy and a method of learning by enjoyment.*
>
> *For the construction of Sigils the ordinary alphabet is used. The desire for super-human strength could be formulated as follows:*
>
> *'I desire the strength of nine tigers.*
>
> *In order to Sigilise this desire, put down on a piece of paper all the letters of which the sentence is composed, omitting all repetitions. The resulting sequence of letters, IDESRTHNGOFMY, is then combined and incorporated into your Sigil. (This sequence of letters is*

89

called a glyph.) The wish, thus Sigilised, must then be forgotten; that is to say, the conscious mind must desist from thinking about it at anytime other than the magickal time, for the belief becomes true and vital by striving against it in the consciousness and by giving it (the Sigil) form. Not by the striving of faith.

By virtue of the Sigil you are able to send your desire into the un-conscious (the place where all dreams meet). All desire, whether for pleasure or knowledge that cannot find natural expression, can by Sigils and their formulae findfulfilment via the unconscious.

EXPERIENCE IS BY CONTACT

THE GREAT EXPERIENCE:
SEDUCE THYSELF TO PLEASURE

I AM THE POWER OF MY DESIRE

The energising of such a Sigil must occur at a special time. At the moment of orgasm the wish must be imperatively formulated. It is not in the actual Sigil that the power resides (this is merely the vehicle of the desire) but in the intent with which it is despatched at the moment of exhaustion. Any glyph, personal or traditional, may be used as a Sigil. If personal, it must be the specific vehicle of the desire and designed for no other purpose; if traditional, it must have received a new direction which thereby consecrates it to its secret purpose. Powers of visualisation, and self-discipline and concentra-tion are qualities necessary.

3　Thee following are thee notes ov a current Individual ov thee Temple:

Thee aim ov thee Sigil was to overcoum personality traits ex-hibiting weakness and passivity. E desired thee strength that E knew was within, butter which was hidden. Thee clues as to how to attain this had emerged during earlier work—though they had been unclear at thee time—and in effect amounted to a reclamation ov an earlier state ov being that had been shrouded by years ov continual conditioning. E had been forced to play a role that was not mine. My aim was to reclaim thee power ov my Lion, my sun-sign which E had long rejected. E had thought E was not a Leo.

E began by preparing thee ritual space and gathering objects used in earlier Sigils. Then E set out my intent in words:

Tonight E seek thee root ov my strength.
E draw out that which is there butter hidden.
E call on thee Pride and Grace ov thee Lion.
Thee King ov thee Jungle that strides forth in thee knowledge ov
*   its beauty.*
No more afraid ov its shadow.
No more afraid ov thee mouse.
No more afraid ov fear.
No more afraid ov life.
Tonight E call on thee Lion.
Thee ruler ov my Sun.
E call to thee Lion within, asleep no more.
E call to thee Lion 'Come Forth!'
E command ov thee Lion: 'Come forth!'
E demand ov thee Lion: 'Coum out!'

91

Thee room is calm with thee flicker ov candles, and music plays though E notice it not. E adopt a certain posture to restrict movement and work inwardly, calling on thee Lion within, demanding ov it as a right, not asking meekly. Facing thee challenge head on, E do not flinch or shirk. E build a burning passion inside and direct it towards my goal. Demanding, urging myself to go on, E rock back and forth to summon thee strength. Deeper and deeper E go, disregarding all else. E Will success.

Thee outside is as nothing. E travel to thee plains. E am with thee lions as we hunt and play, kill and eat, and see thee vastness ov thee grasslands, thee sun beating down, thee wind hot on thee face. And we are lords ov our domain. Fearless, without peer. E see through lion eyes, my skull that ov thee beast. E roar inside as thee lion roars, no more asleep, butter awake, prowling; proud and strong.

E force thee issue always, claiming back what is mine. E invoke and

E invoke and E invoke...

And thee call is answered. Thee strength wells up in me and E act with purpose, thee directed force ov will. No more thee passive on-looker, E initiate my action with certainty.

And then E prepare thee Sigil paper, thee record ov what has passed. E begin with a sign ov Leo, butter add in words all thee attributes ov thee Lion that E wish to claim. These words are placed around thee figure ov thee Sun. Thee work is pleasing to me, for it is natural, unforced and has taken on a life ov its own. In thee words, and in my mind, E recall past events: events that might have seemed small butter which E can now see had caused thee lion to sleep so long in its lair. E learn thee reasons for this long sleep, and know that they hold true no more.

Only when E am sure thee paper is coumplete do E anoint it in blood and ov.

E do not always work this way. Sometimes thee preparation is slow, deliberate, thee creation ov a Sigil over several weeks as thee idea grows, takes form inside. And so thee paper becoums a reflection ov many aspects ov my inner self, taking in thee changes, thee intuitive butter not understood thoughts that flit into consciousness. It is a process ov revealing. Only later do thee meanings ov all thee images used becoum clear, especially after the ritual is coumplete. Then E can look back and see thee form ov my weaknesses, thee basis ov my strengths; and use this knowledge to direct my actions. Thus it is that thee unconscious instructs thee conscious, and thee two parts work together in unity ov purpose. With this knowledge E can go about thee practical business ov achieving my goal with an open mind, and eyes that see clearly.

No two Sigils are alike. E change constantly with thee work, so that what seemed unthinkable three months ago is second nature now. And what was important then, and difficult, is now passed by or thee way seems so obvious that E can scarcely believe E once viewed it as a problem. More than anything, that is what E have realized: that Sigils release an incredible power for action. If E were not experienc-

ing it E would not believe it possible. Butter it is, and E know that E will never go back to thee safe life ov conditioned acceptance that flickers like thee dying TV screen from one unchanging day to thee next. Now, every day brings new challenge, new risk, new joy. And E meet it all with relish!

4 This next passage shows a quite different way ov working, and thee effectiveness ov collaboration within thee Temple:

This did not start off as a Sigil. I wanted to set up some objects to photograph. But as we started to lay them out we couldn't help but make it into something more. As soon as intuitive thinking takes over, the frame of mind and atmosphere obviously changes with it. We started to lay out skulls, feathers, bones, dried reptiles, crystals, carved wooden objects... Eden 211 put on some ritualistic music and we lit candles. I started to thread together a rosary, threading on a Psychick cross, half-heartedly counting twenty-three beads on either side, but leaving the other half to chance—hoping numerological as well as neurological magick would be taking place that evening. Eden 211 was burning candles and joss sticks in a round metallic container. He was adding animal fur and photographs, amongst other things, and dripping wax around the edges of the container. The contents looked like our own inner world—and we were in charge. We could blow out the flame. We could use the candle for light, warmth or to burn. The ash may fall off the joss stick, but it doesn't disappear. The wax may drip off the candle, but it just adds to something else. As Eden 211 dripped the wax around the container's edge I thought "ov power"—he was giving the wax in the same way that one releases energy—giving away in order to gain in another way. This is very hard to explain because this was very much intuitive thinking; but it seemed to make sense to both of us when I said it at the time. When I had finished threading the rosary I draped it over the three central skulls, then took two ready-made rosaries and put one around the female carved figure and one around the male, then tied the three rosaries together, therefore linking the male and the female—pandrogyny/equality/oneness—no separation. I could see the dog's silhouette lurking on the landing like a wolf protecting us. She seemed very understanding and wise that night. As the night went on I

93

started to be reassured that I was in control of my life totally, and the most important thing to me is independence. It returned to me that understanding and compassion are very important if people are to respect each other as Individuals. Without these two words privileges start—resulting in bitterness and secrets.

The triangle of barbed wire was speared through the head/eye of one of the skulls. I saw it as being trussed in some way—it was not as independent as it might be; I could relate to it. I took the barbed wire out of its eye so that it was free and placed it on top of the corner of the triangle. To remove it from the triangle of barbed wire would be to separate it from the body's oneness and true will. To separate it would mean an easier existence for now but it would be escapism and result in double trouble eventually. "Those who do not remember the past are condemned to repeat it"... also the law of karma... Throw a boomerang, turn your back and it comes back and hits you on the back of the head. I removed the skull so that it could be removed.

A way of coping and gaining wisdom without getting tied down and knocked down by irrelevancies... Rising above without avoiding issues. I decorated the skull with beads, a Psychick cross and wax that I had burnt onto my hand.

It occurred to me that the human skull in our layout was God—this amused me. Then I realized it was true. The WoMan was and is a god.

I later counted the beads on the rosary and I had put on forty—my Kali number. The Psychick cross made it forty-one. 4+1=5 /2+3=5. Twenty-three is my number. I then saw that the rosary I put around the female belonged to Eden 211 (male) and the rosary I had put around the male was mine (female.)

I finished off my camera film at the end of the Sigil—photo number thirty-six. I turned and looked at the clock, and the minutes said thirty-six. I felt happy again, against all odds. It had been a terrible day but we had made it special. I felt in total control and nobody could touch me unless it was with love.
Notes on Sigils by Kali Four Zero

94

A TOPY ALPHABET OV DESIRE/RISE

A Thee moment ov orgasm is central to thee process. It is special, and all should be done to make it so. Thus we decorate thee moment as we would a jewel, with all manner ov objects and actions that are precious and personal. Like gifts to a lover, we consecrate thee moment in l-ov-e.

B We say to make thee room or space ov work special. We say likewise ov thee interior mood, for so thee one is physical, so thee other is psychick, and our aim is to join thee two to a single purpose.

C In sex, physical self-consciousness is abandoned in favor ov intensified sensual pleasure. In sleep, everyday consciousness is abandoned in favor ov thee unconscious, thee world ov dreams. In Sigils, thee two states meet in a single act, and so is released a special and potent energy. A fertile power ov harmony, transcending thee barriers ov thee conscious/unconscious divide. And so it is that thee Sigil lets forth an energy that cuts through like a flaming sword, overcouming all that stands in its path.

D Intuition and instinct are thee only pointers in everyday consciousness to thee objects and methods from which to construct a potent Sigil. Thee books and lessons are ov thee museum ov thee past—thee future is entirely yours to construct as you will.

E All must coum from experience, and all experience is ov value. It is simply a question ov observation; seeing thee links, and drawing all without exception into thee universe ov magickal intent and action.

F Sex is thee medium for thee magickal act, enacted physically and with direct control ov thee Individual. It generates thee greatest power which, when released, is diverted from its ordinary object and thrust with thee intense force ov will towards thee fulfillment ov desire.

G All must becoum focused to thee single purpose in hand. It is a case ov giving up all pre-conceptions, all inhibitions and preferences, for thee work involves a totality, and anything that gets in thee way ov coumpleteness is as a vestige ov thee past which will remain to trick and trouble thee matter to its detriment. Relinquish all control and prejudice in order to reclaim and master it, redefined it in thee train ov informed desire.

H Sigilization leads to thee realization ov personal truth, and provides thee means with which to express that truth in life.

I E know what E will, and E will what E desire.

J Sigils are thee unity and integration ov Will, Desire and Knowledge. They are thee process by which dreams becoum reality.

K It is certain to us that Sigils, enacted with true determination, and filled with thee perfect strength ov a sincere desire, generate ov their own thee necessary will for success. It is simply a matter ov intent and intensity; thee practice in thee sure knowledge and acceptance ov result.

L Sigils are thee art ov transforming former belief into current knowledge ov thee way ahead. Sigils are thee revealers ov truths, be they hidden or put aside through fear or expedience.

M Thee Sigil is thee declaration ov intent. It awakens thee Individual magickally to thee circumstances ov their life and in this way makes thee focused desire more likely to happen. Sigils are not a way ov guaranteeing success, they can only open thee door for your own action. A Sigil might ensure that an opportunity for what you desire becoums apparent to you, butter you must still act upon that knowledge for thee desire to be fulfilled.

N Without thee physical response thee psychick work is pointless. Be awake, not asleep, to action.

O Thee more Sigils you perform, thee greater thee clarity ov aim you will find within. A cumulative power ov activated will develops, and thee Sigils becoum intensified in direction and effect.

P Thee ritual ov thee Sigil should be enacted to produce a climax ov utmost intensity. At thee moment when thee rising flux ov sexual excitement becoums ungovernable, when thee whole ov physical and mental consciousness undergoes a spasm that takes it beyond thee point ov return, at that moment all must be focused on thee Sigil, thee physical sensation discarded and forgotten.

Q A Sigil can be designed to answer any desire, without limitation or constraint. Thee aim need in no way be sexual. Thee Sigil encompasses all possibility.

R Thee result ov thee Sigil becoums a part ov thee life process. Thus it may not bring obvious results immediately, butter however long it takes you can be certain that if thee desire was true, and thee intent real, you will be moving towards achieving thee desired goal; preparing and passing through all thee necessary stages so that when thee moment is right you will be ready and alive to it.

S As we have said before, thee methods described by TOPY are butter guides to Individual action. As long as thee Sigil contains thee basic element ov focused will, all other details can be varied. Indeed it is essential that thee ritual be one that is reflective ov who you are, and so should be thee result ov personal input intuitively arrived at.

T Although some days and times might have particular significance to an Individual and thee Temple, a potent Sigil can be performed at any time on any day.

U Orgasm during a Sigil can be reached by any method. Alone or with a partner, by masturbation or intercourse, orally or in any other way thee Individual desires. A partner need not be involved in Temple activity to be an effective collaborator.

V Thee act ov making a physical record ov one's Sigil is a useful way ov instructing thee unconscious, and at thee same time ov revealing to consciousness what it is thee unconscious wishes to say. Thus thee process forces thee divided self into Unity, and manifests thee outcoum in thee physical plane.

W Although we strongly recommend thee making ov a Sigil Paper, other methods ov recording may also be incorporated into thee ritual: polaroids, photographs, cassette recordings, drawings (automatic or otherwise), film or video. As with thee Sigil Paper, all these methods should be used in thee ritual to heighten thee intensity ov what it is you do, rather than purely to document thee event. Let intuition and not logic be thee guide in this, and experiment freely without embarrassment or doubt.

6 Because Sigils exploit thee power ov sexual release, dream states and thee unconscious, we believe it essential that all Individuals make an effort to increase their awareness in these areas. One way to do this is to keep a private diary in which to record, in as much detail as possible, all dreams and sexual activity. Thee focus ov attention brought about by doing this will inevitably increase one's sensitivity and Psychick strength, which in turn will strengthen one's Sigils. We also recommend that you keep for yourself a record ov all Sigils, and ov anything you feel happened as a result, or is in some way connected. Again, include as much detail as you can, such as your objective, your feelings and observations, thee quality ov orgasm, fantasies employed and anything else that seems relevant to thee work (no matter how seemingly coincidental) that caught your attention.

7 With thee increased strength ov thee Temple, both in experience and numbers, a considerable amount ov directed energy is being released within a common framework. We know from our own experiences that this combined energy is highly potent, and that it brings individual Sigilizers into close psychick contact in thee knowledge that we are all active, working within thee Temple with a unity ov purpose. Thee recognition ov this—that we are each a part ov a united network ov exchange—serves to further promote individual work and development. It is vital for thee continued growth ov thee Temple to act upon this realization, and to share experiences, ideas and methods.

Thee exchange ov information through active participation in thee network ov Access Points helps each ov us, and provides thee opportunity for positive inter-action. We are all Individuals, butter it is in a modern tribal framework that we progress. We separate ourselves from thee flatness ov everyday life by our choice, and acknowledge our Individuality, and our coumitment to it, and we hold firm thee truth that nothing is beyond our capabilities when we work together. Thee tribe exists everywhere, butter it is invisible to those who don't know how to see. We can use this to our advantage, and promote our ideas and aims through thee subtlest ov means, or by outrage and shock. We can melt away and then appear as we will. We can evade attack by seeing clearly. We can strengthen ourselves with discipline.

Sigils generate thee confidence for coumitment to Individuality by showing each ov us who we are; and that, once known, is something that can never be taken away. They bring thee strength and determination necessary to becoum wholly alive, and thus to accept full responsibility for our own actions. This is thee freedom we strive for. Thee freedom to reject thee dictates ov dogma and fashion in any and every sphere ov life. Thee freedom to be true to our deepest desires. Sigils enable us to overcoum thee debilitating comfort ov habit, to accept new challenge as a friend, to live a life rich in experience and unencumbered by thee negative attitude ov others to change. Life becoums fluid, a continual transformation ov color, energized with magickal purpose.

Inevitably there are as many views about Sigils as there are Individuals working with them, and it is our intention that just as thee Sigil process should remain fluid, reflecting thee Individual, so will this book remain fluid, reflecting thee Temple as it develops and grows. Thee process ov transformation is never coumplete, and whilst this edition can be no more than a snapshot ov thee moment, there is nothing that says we cannot add to thee album. In this way we will draw closer to each other, inter-acting so that we avoid thee dilution ov our efforts that could re-sult from an active/passive split.

Thee Temple is a place for thee active. It is about sharing, working together and for each other. We all have valuable gifts to offer, and personal experi-ences to relate. We are asking, therefore, that you write and tell us ov your ideas and feelings about your Sigil work: how they affect you personally, thee technical process ov working Individually developed, parallels and differenc-es with other methods (both occult and psychological), insights gained from Sigils, both personal and relating to thee wider society and its obsessions. We want your thoughts, essays, criticism, encouragement—in fact, anything that you would like to see in a future expanded edition ov *Thee Black Book*.

Thee Temple's main weapon in overcouming thee insidious hand ov con-trol is our internal exchange ov information, and thee external expansion ov propaganda in thee Information War. It is selfish to keep things to ourselves. By exchanging ideas within thee Temple network we can each develop faster, making thee necessary connections to help remove all un-wanted obstacles. Together we will rise. In strength. In l-ov-e. In unity.

Genesis Breyer P-Orridge (all uncredited parts of *Thee Black Book*), 1983

99

Storming thee psychick barrier

IV

Photo by Perou

FREEDOM OV SALIVATION:
A DISCOURSE ON BEING RADIQUEER...

This G. B. P-O introduction is taken from This Is the Salivation Army *by Scott Treleaven.*
Seek and find.

Our aim is wakefulness—our enemy is dreamless sleep.
Old TOPI proverb

Never forget (and this is hard, especially during adolescence) that you are most certainly not alone—you merely have to signal and find each other. A good place to look is wherever the enforcers of education (an education that decries the learning of how to process thinking by using bogus authority and slight of mind to misdirect you) try to hide from you. For me, discovering the Beats was the first time I knew in my gut that it was possible to live a wildly eccentric, outsider, experimental and bohemian L-if-E (life if evolution... love if energy) no matter what I had been told, indoctrinated or programmed with by the status quo. Not only did I have an epiphany that a L-if-E built upon, and with, creativity enhanced by travel was viable, but I was compelled simultaneously to believe, as a metaphysical by-product, in art as a holy calling, a mission, or quest, that once recognized could never be discarded or abandoned, no matter what the consequences. You cannot forget once you have felt this, and it becomes your duty to serve with honor this campaign as you survive and interact with others of your "army," "tribe" and rogue genetic kind.

2 Next, go looking for these unorthodox, like-minded individuals, have undying faith that they exist and are probably looking for you too. Offer stimulation, speculation, exchange ideas, collaborate, coordinate, share information and theories, recommend sources and names of activators you admire who have come to your attention via media, myth or synchronicity. Nothing is stronger in its anarchic potency and cultural resonance than a pack of previously "lone" wolves. Be prepared to do mundane, tedious and dull tasks to demonstrate to your Self, and those co-operating with you, both your understanding that you are in voluntarily bonded service to a higher calling, *art*, and that your ego and public recognition are not your motive, nor can they nor will they seduce you. Nothing is uglier than a person who actually wants to be rich and famous and thinks those "qualities," those all-consuming contemporary norms, have any actual meaning or value in

terms of human evolution measured against divinity, infinity or the creation of a soul.

3 Then, aware that you have chosen a thankless, endless task (by none-sensus reality standards), due to madness, bad training, neurotic trauma, gender confusion, your parents, your peer group or your parents and peer group, don't ever kid your Self about why you chose to be an artist, writer or otherwise creatively driven being. You have become part of the metaphor, not part of the problem, no matter how under siege I.T. (Imaginary T.I.M.E.) might feel! Having already worked so hard to intersect with, and collaborate with, your contemporaries and any worthy icons you have unearthed that you still respect after initial contact, always keep in mind that no one person, in this post-tech society, can have, or supply, as much inspiration as the sum total of an interacting group, even if that group is primarily a loose knit, ad-hoc collective unable to work together on a daily basis. Just as sampling and cutting-up reality gives us a randomized picture that nevertheless shows us, more accurately than what is immediately apparent, what sense-based material existence looks like; so, too, the interconnecting of two minds will produce as its sum a *third mind* that, by avoiding singular, individuated solo strategies and agendas, preconceptions and blind-spots, is far greater in total, and more relevant in effect in our era than any solitary brain can achieve, no matter how visionary. In order to combat the conceptual and economic programming of conglomerate global alliances, it is an absolute necessity to declare and consolidate liberation, as each one of us conceives it, by shamelessly sharing energy and mutual communication systems (yes, even Xeroxed zines). Know thine enemy. Steal their tactics, raid their resources and turn their weapons of mass media destruction and biological and neurological tyranny back on them.

Nothing short ov a total war.
Old TOPI proverb

4 Finally, in terms of thematic content, decide what really *obsesses* you, *you*. What really turns you on—your deepest (possibly most secret) fetish (sexual, paradoxical, philosophical, political, literal, mechanical, it

really doesn't matter)—and make that central to your work either directly or obliquely, regardless of medium, accepted traditions of talent or any other practical considerations. If you analyze your self effectively, with brutal honesty, this core integrity will charge your work with real individuality, charisma, influence and longevity of power. Surrender to a greater group does not erase self-esteem, ironically. Magickally, it accelerates a flow of matchless integrity into a consciously-constructed personality. (By the way, the most effective tool I can recommend for discovering and directing "True Will" with minimum deviation or self-delusion is the ritual "Sigil" process described in this r-evolutionary manual). Tell your Self that you will make the entire world agree with you, rather than compromise by trying to figure out what the world will like and then agreeing with I.T. in order to please and be pleased. The process is the product, and regardless of how long it takes, one day the clarity of intent permeating your work *will* be recognized and your L-if-E will have purpose. Always and only create based upon the assumption and sincere recognition that you may be so old that you really don't care if they ever "get it," and that it doesn't matter, because the worst thing that can happen is that your physical body dies of starvation or neglect in the meantime.

Genesis Breyer P-Orridge, New York City, 2002

THE SUPREME HOMAGE

What a beautiful legend is that of Danaë—locked up by a father who preferred in this way to save her from men, and whom Zeus sprinkled with a rain of gold to make her fertile. Even more precise is the symbolism of the Rig Veda, in which we may read the following words: *O Lords spray us with the milk of heaven.*

People speak too much about penis envy and not at all about sperm envy. There is something here that is highly suspicious. As if it was impossible to admit that a woman expects a man to give her that which remains feminine in him by its symbolism: the milk of his pleasure. It is most certainly not the only approach possible, but it remains nonetheless an inescapable one.

105

The milk of a man, the sap that she desires, is not only the life but the hope of eternity... lined with fearsome death.

As in the Eucharist—"this is my body, this is my blood"—like a mantis the mistress religiously devours her lover, and by taking and drinking his pleasure makes it her own.

But the ritual becomes incomparably deeper in signification, infinitely more secret, when paradoxically the semen is not ingested but spread, dispersed, sown to the four winds over the loved one's body.

The disappearance, the burying of the sperm in the feminine body (whatever the hole used) is for us somehow directly comprehensible in its symbolism—but when, on the contrary, it is ostensibly shown, everything becomes murky and confusion takes hold of us.

A Strange Muteness The multiplication of pornographic films and their distribution by video has rendered a number of taboos null and void (at least in some circles). The critics in the specialist press now talk without any embarrassment of fellatio, sodomy and other deviant's habits. Everything seems to be normalized.

Nonetheless, a certain territory still resists this popularization, despite the fact that it consists of a theme that is relatively more mentionable than a large number of others (e.g. incest or torture): ejaculation onto women's faces. What a surprising silence—all the more surprising when we consider that, in parallel, it is now almost unthinkable to make a film without consecrating at least one sequence to the theme, so great is the coincidence between its presentation on the screen and the spectator's maximum emotion.

A silence which reveals less a certain prudishness than an incapacity to find the words to express what we feel when confronted with what can be called no less than a mystery.

The ritual has its religious and mystic potential reinforced. The Eucharistic symbolism remains, or rather seems to center and fix itself on that privileged moment of the Elevation.

To be shown is well and truly one of the purposes of every ritual (the Divine must at least be partially unveiled in order for the belief to continue). Man, source of life, is a source that is living. The lover who comes over his beloved renews the gesture of certain primitives masturbating to spray the earth with their seed during the rites of fertility. Woman is the Earth... This perversion brings us back towards this foundational and elementary symbolism.

The Orphic tablets distinguish two types of source: That of Lethe is that of forgetting, of sleep and of death. The second is that of memory, of awakening, of immortality. This ambivalence will always be present in the theme and its symbolism.

In many ancient traditions sperm was considered to have its source in the brain of man. It was seen as directly emanating from his very essence.

Moreover, it is the face that most excellently symbolizes the very essence of the human being, his personality and his spirituality. From that point on, a necessary symbolic order becomes obvious, joining two images: the semen of man and the face of woman.

108

You want to see because it's beautiful... When I see a man come in the air, as if by chance the word that comes to mind is "fuck." It's an expression of triumph. Fucking, it is to come and to go. It's coming in mid-air, coming like children, coming and not wanting to know anything else. It has no importance, since it's outside. It's not giving a fuck, to be exact. And fucking up death and reproduction at the same time is one and the same thing...
Jean-Luc Henning, "The Woman Watcher," from *Obsessions* (1985)

If the sperm symbolizes life, it still contains within it a little the idea of death: expelled by the urinary meatus, the potential ambiguity is great, and many instinctively class it in the category of excrement. Sperm is therefore also dirt, which is not contradictory but complementary, as much as is necessary. Out of this apparent symbolic opposition in fact rises the exacerbation of pleasure. This perversion undeniably allows a certain sadism to be satisfied in a man, and in his partner a certain desire to be sexually humiliated.

The goal here is not to discuss the reasons for these tendencies, only to state that they are in fact satisfied by this ritual.

I read in a book of Kristeva an example of "abjection": as a small girl she cringed with disgust when confronted with the "milk cream" which her father presented her, saying it was abject… The perverse inspires the abject by its "demand for purity."
Daniel Sibony, from Perversions (1987)

The pleasure of the beloved is all the greater for being sprinkled with the sperm of her master, as her disgust was great, beforehand, for this "milk of the paternal dug" which Sibony refers to.

During the development of pornographic films during the '70s, the camera sometimes filmed moments of a rare mystical intensity. The actresses were novices, since they were only beginning the job, but even more so because they had no role models to which they could refer. A certain spontaneity resulted in their reactions or absence of reaction (with the men failures were frequent). Many expressed a certain disgust (which could be in itself exciting for the spectator). But sometimes the sublime occurred when by accident the camera recorded what can only be called a "revelation": at the beginning of the scene the nervousness and a certain anxiety in the actress were clearly perceptible—but when the jet of sperm splashed her face, we were witness to her emotional breakdown, to a complete transformation in her expression, a quasi-spiritual shuddering.

109

Ecstasy… delight… and excitement when she reached a mystical, transcendental state. Eyes popping, mouth open wide, in astonishment, all the muscles going limp and tears of joy sometimes, tears mingling with the white ones of the virile semen. This change from distinct "distaste" to the most obvious "taste" was in itself the most beautiful of spectacles, unreplaceable, one which every man dreams of reading on the face of his beloved.

The look is another fundamental aspect of the feminine desire to visually feast on the spurt of liquid, like the first cry, like the first moment, the first movement. The look also of the man contemplating the woman who offers her features in order to give chaos form. The beloved prints the hollows of her face onto this onctuosity which covers her like a mask, for the formless to become an image. The face is the symbolic matrix of the life and individuality. In order for the ritual to be complete, this had to be seen and the witness to be himself observed.

Supreme Homage Through the humiliation inflicted on her, the lover also honors the one he has taken for his own (in the same way an animal marks out his territory with his secretions), so the beloved becomes his territory.

When a man comes in a woman (whatever the receptacle used) a doubt always subsists: "Would not a hole in some inert but well lubricated material have sufficed to satisfy something which is, after all, rather an animal desire?"

But on the contrary, when he comes on the face of his partner it is an explicit, visible homage he is making to her power of seduction, to her person, to that which is unique in her.

The further we go away from nature, the greater the spiritual part becomes. It shall not be said in vain that perversion is the opposite of bestiality; to limit oneself to the strict framework of reproduction is to deliberately (or unconsciously) opt for that which is animal within us. Morality has turned the tables by stating exactly the opposite—but its strategy, these last years, became different, insidious: rather than to condemn, it integrates little by little every deviation in its own heart. So everything is in peace, opaque in the flat norm. Everything is equal, and the dialogue dies away (for lack of opposition).

Jean-Pierre Turmel, Rouen, January 11, 1987. Translated by Malcolm Duff

THE OUTSIDE HARMS

Should one make one's sexual fantasies come true?

I am tempted to answer that this is the problem of each and every one of us, man and woman alike, and in that so long as there is no "rape" of the other person, all the rules of the game are good to use.

Feminists in search of ideology and morality will retort that the majority of sexual fantasies are masculine ones and that the women who "give themselves up" to such things are in fact manipulated by these two thousand years past of phallic domination, and so on and so on...

So what? In a time where men have come to accept their femininity, why not accept our "male" impulses at the same time without feeling guilty?

Once sexual fantasy has been classed in the red on the scale of moral values, what is there left to do? To be duped into make believe and making love tenderly and only tenderly? (Not to mention romantically, for the romantics, behind their tormented passions hid their sado-maso tendencies!)

What delight there is in becoming aware of certain "perverse" desires and being able to play with them, share them with an accomplice—who is in love to boot!

There are those which are mine, and those which are his: How fantastic a communication it is to tell them one another, and little by little share them, and let the other benefit from them, in such a way as for a dance to come between us. Sometimes, there is a blockage, and I think there is no point in insisting. The important thing in all of this is love.

In the beginning the fantasy of sperm on my face was not one of mine: it was his thing, and little by little, it has become a duet, with a strong undertow of mysticism, a secret shared...

The first picture of sperm on a face I ever had dates to my youth when I read the cartoons of Gotlieb with fervor. "In the charming little wood when we go there we are free" (in Rhaa Lovely) is a revised and corrected version of Tom Thumb, where the poor little children lost in the forest, abandoned by their horrible parents, copy the bright ideas of their brother: the crumbs of bread having been eaten by the birds, there is only one solution left to them without falling into the deepest of despair: to wank together as one man, each with his own hand as is normal: no incestuous pederasty in this tale which is already reaching far enough as an initiation!

The next image, the one which interests us: the spunk of the oldest of the band (which is normal) spurts onto a face—his own.

The question is not to know whether or not he is an early ejaculator (although this can have a certain interest), but rather I shall linger on

111

the drenched face: a comic image to my mind, linked "par excellence" to the joy of "MAS": MASturbatory MASculine...

As I was saying earlier, I do not wish there to be any value judgment between masculine and feminine: they are different, complementary types. They are the basis of life, and these ambivalent things within each one of us are both primordial and essential.

How could I imagine that one day it would be on my own face that the "supreme seed" would spurt, and that it would no longer be in laughter, but an act that would create a profound joy?

Exterior ejaculation is condemned by the church as being an act against nature (I refer to the "Confessor's Manual"):

> *There is another sort of sodomy which consists in carnal union between persons of different sexes, but without the natural recipient: in the behind part, the mouth, between the breasts, the legs or the thighs, etc... This sort of infamy does not fall under the sentences carried out against what is strictly called sodomy, it is no less certain that this act against nature constitutes a great crime.*

This ejaculation is, to my mind, a deeply, highly voluntary act: for a man it is the way of offering to the eyes of another (and to his own) the fruit of his pleasure. The great phallocratic screwer which Bukowski boasts to be does not go so far: when in Women one of his mistresses wants to see him "jerk off his load," he holds himself back, and in the end, due to the woman's fault of course, he has to penetrate her in order to come!

Could it be there is something embarrassing, something too strong which makes it more difficult in having sexual relations to "fuck?" I can state that "seeing" provokes in me an orgasm of a different type: what pleasure there is in being inundated by the fruit of another's pleasure! To eat it, drink it, be covered with it—is this not one form of possession? In a certain way I take the most intimate of him—his masturbation—but I can also feel it on the contrary, as something phallocratic, a necessary hyper-validation of virility (flagrant in pornographic films where this act is very often reproduced).

I do not take, I do not absorb the sperm inside my body, but I give my lover the material image of his power, his domination. Woman watches, eyes in front of his taut sex, cheek against his stomach, no longer existing, for, at that moment, his whole body is cock: a cock stiff with desire, a cock sucked, chewed, licked, caressed, sweet and sour...

But do not let us be mistaken—these acts escape me, and I become myself an object, the object of this desire which satisfies his needs—mouth, breast, lips, fingers, nails, hair, *eyes*—my whole body is at his service. His. Then, suddenly, everything speeds up. We are on another planet. I wet myself even more painfully, vibrate, shiver, desire, feel *him*—"Here it is! It's coming!"—and his sperm spurts forth, trickles over my face in a multi-coloured splash. I drink, lick, he comes again, caress—I am flooded by him, he'll never stop, he is suffocating...

I offer him my sperm-covered face, an expression which I suppose is identical to that of the woman under the shower who splashes herself sensually. Who has never seen the image in an ad or at the cinema of the woman with the smug look, drunk with the contact of the running water—water, the symbol of life, purifying and redeeming? We have all seen her: she represents simple well-being, happiness.

The first image that we have of our well-being and our happiness, is thus this face we have found, the image that complements the mass of our heart.
Françoise Dolto, *Feminine Sexuality*

She is alluding to the child that the mother nourishes and which finds itself against her, reassured, happy with this sight, the famous search for the primitive relation between mother/child, but there is no longer mother nor child: these are two adults who are acting, two adults marked by their childhood, who have kept a taste for play and for certain sensations.

Whatever may be the erogenous place of his partial desires, the object of partial satisfaction of a baby refers to the phallus. For the mouth, it is the erect nipple which takes place and from which spurts milk, while his hands press the bloated, firm form of the maternal breast. For the anus, it is the form of the buttock and faeces [sic]. For the baby boy until the age of twenty-five months, it is the penile erection from which spurts the fountain of urine. Then

113

comes the penile erection for solitary pleasure, while waiting for puberty with the spilling of sperm which concludes erotic erections.
Françoise Dolto, *The Libido is Phallic*

Maternal Milk/Urine/Sperm I think that in the symbolism of love, the playing with milk must be of an intensity comparable with that of sperm—milk being closely linked to the child, the one who has just been born, and the one we keep hidden deep within us, intensely linked to life as well!

It is not the same for urine. "And they piss as I weep over unfaithful women" screams Brel.

It seems that urine is the most often spilled to soil, and even if one may find in it a pleasure of a sexual nature, it is still a waste product (linked to dirt), and does not carry with it so strong a symbolism of life as sperm.

The forces of symbols interlock: All the senses are present within a face: smell, sight, touch, hearing, taste. The whole range of both feelings and sensuality is excited.

114

Behind the face hides the soul, the deepest "me" and the heart, and through its expressions, everything passes: boredom, disgust, pleasure, delight. There can be no question of cheating for an initiate who knows how to read—in short, a lover! A face is not a neutral part of the body, it is a little mirror of the deep within each one of us, a part of the interior which filters out to the exterior—the crack!

As the sperm goes from inside outwards... Some detest this vision of sperm spilled outside of the natural recipient: he who, once let loose in feminine entrails symbolizes life and creation, no longer has the right to be outside, and loses his function, and hence all interest.

I am tempted to make an audacious relation with menstrual blood—blood which is both life and death; life whilst it remains inside, and death when it trickles out. The rotten blood of periods, loaded with the proof of non-fertility, is witness to the uselessness of ovulation. Why does sperm not carry this sense of morbidity with it as it jerks out?

And yet, sperm is more highly considered than blood... we often use the alibi of "dirt" to protect us from blood, yet we use it less when referring to sperm.

Cleanliness which was objected to as an argument against the satisfaction of desire, re-appears afterwards, when it is ordinarily hardly even mentioned in relation to sperm.
F. Edmonde Morin, *The Red Difference*

Is it that blood is stronger in our fears than sperm? There can be no doubt!

Ejaculation onto a face remains a truly symbolic, mysterious act…

…a ritual one?
Chloe, Rouen, October 1987. Translated by Malcolm Duff

Define: con·trol

V

AN OPEN LETTER

To that ignorant and confused part of humanity, not yet aware of "Magick" and "Nature," or the importance of them becoming integrated as soon as possible for the survival of the Human race!

o what thou wilt shall be the whole of the law.

Every Man is a Woman Every Woman is a Man Every Man and Woman is a Star...

"Nature slowly decays" is something you hear quite often. Well, it isn't really so... Nature always evolves, always develops in directions given by the components and forces within it. Nature and the Earth will always exist, be it even in forms of burnt-out lands and hordes of cockroaches. The statement "man's nature slowly decays" is closer to the truth!

Our environment that we need to live and regenerate in IS decaying...

There isn't one single person who can deny this today. It's a sad fact, but even sadder still is the fact that there are people actually opposing human development. There are people violently struggling for their own security and wealth, believing that this will save them and that that's the only one thing that matters...

Well, pardon me if I laugh at you dying of cancer and spit merrily on your graves!

You are despicable and such cowards that you won't even share your dead bodies with the Earth, but put them inside wooden and metal coffins to "protect" them. From what?

What are children taught in school? How to act and behave in a clockwork structure, working in a destructive downward spiral... "Be good and you're welcome to heaven... Sacrifice yourself for the greater good... God knows best... He is omnipotent... You are small and worthless... Just be good and everything will be alright..."

This is feeble, sickly and, most importantly, unnatural morality that we should all help to eradicate. It has no value or justification today, when we should all work together for the restoration of our essential Mother Earth.

There is no god but man. Omnipotency comes from actions that alter the surroundings, mental and physical. If those actions are destructive (for instance, dumping toxic waste into the sea), you'll be sure to get what's coming to you (cancer as a result of toxic groundwater). If those actions are good (for instance, planting trees and flowers), you'll get immediate result (there will be more oxygen in the air). You are the judge, as you are God.

Christianity and its fellow criminal religions Islam and Judaism exist today merely as vehicles of Control, merely as modes of thought to keep people from acting and thinking themselves. Judaism = Christianity = Islam = Communism = Capitalism, etc., etc., and so on, ad infinitum, ad nauseam. Just different words denoting the very same unnatural perversion and illness. Which is the fact that YOU ARE NOT FREE!

When they realize that times and morality have changed, and this time NOT in their favour, they become afraid, like small children who start to scream because their mother says "No," although they are very well able to express themselves. They become ultraparanoid, in need of extreme polarities, a black and white way of regarding the world. And there is violence and death, as always in times of change. Two thousand years ago there was the Roman Empire succumbing to Christianity, in times of war and civil war.

And today? The 23rd pope arrives at Stockholm in the 23rd week of 1989, saluting the Swedish Catholics (Mere thousands. A piss in the ocean...) and praying for peace in the world. At the very same time there is a potential civil war in China, where communist soldiers kill students who think freedom lies in a red and white soft-drink-can. There are train-crashes and pipelines exploding in Russia, corruption having a higher priority than public safety. A religious leader dies and falls out of his coffin into the hands of millions of insecure, and thereby fanatical, followers.

Yes, pray on, old fool, because you may very well need it. There is no Christianity anymore. Sweden has never been a Christian country. You've failed, you are failures, and you are so aggressively neurotic because you know it's true.

Scandinavian mythology has always lived on, through the times of your oppression and contemptuous misunderstanding of Nature and its fantastic forces. The Runes are part of the Scandinavian DNA-structure. Pagan activities have never died, not anywhere, and today it's all coming back to you. A Magickal appreciation of history and Life in thee work for all people's common future.

Theirs is a good definition of a free person, and that's one who is completely honest with her/himself in every situation, and who's thereby working for the procreation of WoMankind. The honesty becomes the medium. The work is the goal itself.

Love is the law, love under will.
Carl Abrahamsson, Thee Temple ov Psychick Youth
Scandinavia 1989, Era Vulgaris-Maximus

LANGUAGE—A WORDLESS SONG

As an outlaw group of Individuals, who are together because we share a thought, a feeling, an association with one another by choice, we must search for the purest expression of that thought, and use it as a common denominator for freedom. Freedom of speech, of love, of will, of roles for ourselves and for all the oppressed in our society.

It seems rare that even a few of us escape the powers and control of society and its peer groups and holders of vested interest. In previous writings and articles published in our monthly documents, "control" and "the trick of time" have been touched upon. The latter we interpret as the false security given to us, often projected as lethargy, by illusory notions of the "future" and "tomorrow," precepts endlessly exploited by all manner of politicians.

To understand the powers and controls of society we must try to understand our society in its purest and impurest forms. How does it control? What are the steps of/to control?

Many steps, and methods are obvious. One is dress, fashion and style. This medium of control has now taken over the bias and purse strings of

121

our own culture, music and acts of celebration. Some try to rebel against this easily defined area in obvious ways. They feel that to dress in filthy clothes, and be filthy, is proof of being radical and is a true rebellion in itself against the filth of our society and its Masonic capitalism. Yet there is nothing easier than to neglect ourselves, knowing it's a simple way to offend our parents, little old ladies and an inherited status quo of behavior. Yet if society has defined acceptability, then to refute it by being its opposite is to accept the original definition. Society wills us to feel no love for ourselves, to hate, to compete, to give up and to be submissive, not proud. Young people have become an oppressed minority, just as blacks and other ethnic minorities have. They are political refugees in their own society. To raise up the banner of apathy and surrender and convince ourselves it is revolution is a laughable non-threat to those who wish us dead. Dead in brain if not in body. So how do we rebel? How do we stand up to society and its latent fascism? And how do we remove the latent fascism that must have infected us all as products of its conditioning?

This is a question with an easy first answer: We rebel and fight. But how do we recognize effective rebellion as opposed to symbolic rebellion? How do we develop our own positive reconstruction from this deconstruction? There's more than meets even the third eye in the games, tricks and territories. We must pinpoint again how society runs, who sets it up, what its ingredients are.

Language—A Songless Speech Language is crucial. We judge and measure so much by it; yet language, to those who can articulate and manipulate it, is merely a game in itself, a word game, played to make their position stronger, to mask their greedy intentions.

For those of us less fortunate, who are awkward and clumsy with our words, though our hearts and minds see clearly enough, we are at their mercy, left to be used and abused. Words to us are foreign; we vibrate to emotions and songs of freedom, the cold accuracy of professionals confuses and controls us against our will, tries to make us servants.

We don't want their dictionary, or their diction, full of words that oppress, that humiliate and control. They use those words to protect their own, their jargon a secretive morse code aimed at maintaining their privilege and social power.

Therefore the first step is for us to understand this common denominator—language—this prime medium of control. It is powerful, power-full. It breaks trusts. It may hurt and kill. It most certainly can control us.

So to break down society, we must break down the ingredients, break down the abilities and methods of the people who communicate through language only to control and confuse. To be even able to dream of changing society and the tenacious grasp of these, people we must change language, its forms and patterns. Chop it up, jumble it around, see what it really does, really says, expose it, reveal its strength, its weakness. We must change the language, the language of promises, contracts, manifestos, advertisements, deputations, mandates, formulas, boundaries, expectations, hopes, treaties, wars, education and justice. People cannot live with a language of right and wrong, black and white, either/or. It does not reflect reality, or life, or how each of us really feels and thinks day-to-day. Language as it stands is designed to result in conflict, and at that moment those who control language step in as experts and control us. Language has to be common to everyone, and to become this language has to be reassessed. Culture has to show people techniques for breaking down the apparent logic of language that follows a line to a conclusion, and develop forms that reflect infinite parallel answers and possibilities, a kaleidoscope with no fixed points or conclusions that therefore describes far more accurately how life feels and how unsure each moment of life can feel, how little can really be planned for or counted on.

123

But is this all fictitious, idealist rubbish? Or is it possible? Can we see ourselves communicating with our feelings, our intuitions, our emotions, our dreams, through a pure deep love for each other and what we feel we could be and should be allowed to try to be? Or have the powers that be so tightly twisted us round their fingers, injecting us with hate, ridicule, cynicism and fear that we are all their robots, falling for all their endless games and sadism, seeing our neighbor as our enemy, accepting that nothing can change, asking what the point is, looking out for number one, despising those who try, needing to be accepted, insecure, guilt ridden, angry where love should be, forever damaging our children, forever willing victims, forever seeing dreams as nightmares and nightmares as normality. Fighting each other with paranoiac intensity instead of those despicable feudal lords that sit smug in that building by the water. No wonder they think we are pathetic scum, fighting what's easiest and nearest to us, ourselves and our kind instead of them. The building they occupy to symbolize their freedom can just as easily be their prison.

The best weapon, the best defense is that which turns your attackers' own energy upon themselves. Language can be reassembled every day in a different way to help free us. Our tiny concrete cages can be our palaces, and their palaces can be their cages.

The key is... what you say... the key is, what you say the key is... the key is, the key is the key... is what you say, is what you say the key is... the key, the key is what you say the key IS...

Kali 5 and Genesis Breyer P-Orridge, London, September 23, 1987

DEFINE "HumanE"
We Are but Serfs Wearing the Emblazoned Shield of a Shoe

Thee essential structure ov our consuming Western Society is still Feudal. Only thee names have been changed to protect thee guilty. In Britain huge estates, whole Islands are still owned by thee descendants ov ruthless invaders and murderers who were paid off for their support in political intrigues and genocides hundreds ov yeras ago. Thee Church and thee Lords were paid in thee land ov those killed for it was cheaper than gold, and could always be stolen agen, and given away as a reward for treachery as often as thee pursuit ov supremacy dictated. Those mere indigenous mortals living on thee land, drawing forth its riches in food or minerals, had no part to play in all this, unless a few symbolic mutilated bodies were required by thee grandiose Lord/Owners. They were Tenants, they were Serfs, they were to all intents and purposes, Slaves. Today, whatever day this is, nineteenth century, twentieth century, twenty-first century, nothing has changed. Most ov thee population are merely seen as a naturally occurring resource, like oil, coal, water, that can be drawn upon for Self-Perpetuation and Self-Aggrandisement by thee present Lord/Owners who have a vested interest in thee administration ov Control and Status Quo. Thee disadvantage of a population seen this way is that they are costly to maintain, to keep in working order and to programme to thee particular skills required by Control. Worst ov all, they occasionally remember they are HumanE Beings, with a right to enlightenment and actually dare to challenge this primitive situation.

DEFINE "HumanE Being"—A Human Being that has, in a conscious process ov thought, seen themselves as individual and capable ov growth beyond thee parameters they have inherited as finite from any given social environment. Thee "E" stands for Enlightenment, Evolution, Energy, Ecstasy, Ecolibrium, Etc…!

NOW! In thee agrarian ages these population resources were useful as farm labourers, they needed knowledge ov thee land, butter little education, and robust health supplied by natural selection, thee weak died. During thee Industrial revolutions these same population resources needed modification. So we see education, health, housing, supplied to ensure an expanding supply ov suitably equipped and useful raw materials. NOW! reprogramming is agen in full force. Control no longer needs healthy, semi-educated, numerically large and pacified resources. In fact they use up far too much food, space, medicine, and TIME. So, our dear Feudal Lords do thee obvious and run down thee services so magnanimously supplied before. These Lords see themselves as superior, separate, chosen to administer Control, and make no mistake, in their heart ov hearts they would rather be rid, once and for all, ov we inferior and outmoded, useless populations. It would be so simple to administer this world if their were hardly any people, and those that were, were quiet, programmed InfoTechs.

BUT, No one Controls Control anymore. It has a parasitic and debilitating L-IF-E all ov its own. Certain very select groups have merely inherited thee almost Priestlike role of its protection and nurturing, even at thee expense ov coumplete extermination of this human race, many with no remembrance ov which came first. Control replicates and expands inexorably in a manner quite exactly like a malignant tumour, or to use a current example, like HIV. Control affects Individual aspirations and potential, our sense ov unity and freedom, our social and ideological compassion in precisely thee same hidden and terminal man-

125

ner that those diseases debilitate and destroy our physical bodies. Control is very much a virus ov thee spirit, it works like HIV diluting our immunity to conditioning and programming. Thee joys, hopes, dreams, visions ov childhood are broken down, reducing our abilities to convince and aspire beyond thee physical manifestation ov L-IF-E. We becoum victims ov a dull immobility imposed on us by this invisible debilitation until we die in Spirit, long before our bodies pass on.

TIME is a Key to thee perception ov this process. Control, Cancer and HIV work through TIME. They are linear problems. Their destructiveness accelerates at an ever-increasing rate until thee termination ov thee host. Control needs TIME also. It hides in social structures like politics, religion, education, technological medicine, mass media, thee family, sexuality, computers. Just like a virus, even like DNA, it exists for its own sake. It relies upon a certain element ov cohesion, thee belief in a rational order, thee inviolate right to a never-ending human history, to an acceptance ov inherited values and measurements. Control relies upon manipulation ov human behaviour. In a word, it relies upon Hopelessness. Science NOW! suspects that DNA does not exist in order to perpetuate US, but rather WE exist in order to perpetuate DNA. That once we have reproduced, or failed to reproduce, thus sending a modified DNA module forward in TIME or being unsuitable vehicles for this function, that this is thee moment when our ageing process really begins, for thee DNA has no further use for our physically manifested host bodies. DNA moves infinitely more effectively through a TIME continuum than we do without any need for reference to thee outside universe ov Society with its petty and pathetic concerns based on a belief in our own absolute immortality against which we measure every Thing. In a conversation with William S. Burroughs in Duke Street, London in 1972, we discussed coum aspects ov Control. More importantly, we concluded that thee most critical question ov this era would be "How do we short-circuit Control?"

We have both chosen different aspects ov an "Under-thee-Counter-Culture" as E dubbed it. Culture in its widest application, inclusive ov behaviour, ritual, exploration ov consciousness, style, art, music, expression ov thee mind, a process ov RE-MINDing our SELF. It seems to me that Culture is an expression ov States ov Mind rooted in thee effects ov behavioural conditioning. Conditioning that begins during gestation, not at thee moment ov b-earth. These states ov Mind becoum a reflection ov States ov Tribe, in other words thee conditioned Self is intended to be a microcosm ov thee State, whether that be anthropologically an enclosed tribal unit in the rainforest, or an amorphous collection on a grand scale like Western country, or thee Soviet Union. Everything is molecular in structure, both at a nano level or at a galactic level. There is good reason to assume that virus like interactions can thus be applied on any scale. If we can release a chaotic virus into thee host State ov Tribe ("Society") then over a period ov TIME thee various coumponent cell structures ov that Host State ov Tribe could break down, short circuiting its synapses in thee form for example ov literature, politics, television, peer group acceptance.

If we see DNA as a language, a carrier ov information, then we also view Culture as a modification ov language that we are also able to read. Culture can thus reveal, describe, measure, and expose Control making thee virus ov Control thee Host, and thee interactions ov consciousness that are one environment, thee virus. Control can from this position be short-circuited. Short circuited by radical Cultural thought and actions. Not by isolated actions, but by a sum total ov integrated imagination, mind, consciousness, enlightenment and communication pointing in every Direction ov Travel simultaneously. This medium "Culture" is what we once called "Art" until it was so corrupted and emasculated that association with its contemporary coumglomerate is cause for shame, not pride. If thee aim is less than to becoum free from physical existence, less than coumfortable co-existence with our planet, less than achievement ov infinite consciousness then it is not "Art" only decoration or diversion. INTENTION IS THEE KEY. Evolution towards Being, towards being HumanE Beings. Thee system ov "AND THEN..?" We find peace, balance, coumpassion—and then...? We becoum dematerialised consciousness, able to diffuse outside thee SPACE limitations ov our physically manifested bodies. No longer a single mentality thee conception ov INDIVIDUAL changes. Just as cells cluster yet are made up ov individual cells, so our mentality will becoum clusters, and memories and information will diffuse without boundaries.

127

What we conceive ov NOW! as an Individual could spread throughout and beyond TIME and SPACE. And then...? We becoum as suprabeings. And then...? And then...? And then...?

Like thee search for HIV, once identified and isolated, thee character ov Control with its invasion ov macro and micro clusters ov molecular L-IF-E becoum visible. Our search within is for methods to break thee preconceptions, modes ov unthinking acceptance, expectations, filial obligations, unnatural clusters and States ov Tribe and constructed behavioural patterns that make us, as organisms, so vulnerable to Control. In our efforts to step outside TIME in order to escape this process we DE-CONSTRUCT to RE-CONSTRUCT. We retain our inherited concept ov what we are told is "reality" and then we discard ALL concepts and definitions irrevocably and constantly reaching a stage ov not-thinking, not-doing.

By applying a non-linear, fragmenting process to every aspect of perception, "reality," society, domesticity, behaviour, philosophy, ideology and morality it is possible to modify and confound Control and wrench away from its manipulation ov behaviour, mind and body thee triad through which it violates Self-Respect. We intend to do damage to thee primary tools ov Control, Guilt and Fear operating within thee same media as Control. We intend to synthesise a system to challenge, decay and render impotent thee virus itself, neutralising it, starving it ov hosts. Not just through music, through writing, or through thee products ov expression, butter by gathering together a loose knit butter coumpassionate Lost Tribe, an experimental Society that exists to detoxify thee behavioural immune system restoring balance, to detoxify thee poisoning ov thee blood ov earth restoring balance, to detoxify information restoring thee possibility ov infinity. We intend to form a Base ov Co-Operations that integrates where Control disintegrates.

A method is a systematic application ov thee fragmenting process to all modes ov inherited belief and behaviour and information processing on a scale that will effect events within and without space-time.

An intention is reclamation ov Self-Determination, Re-Minding one's Self, and Self description by a truly freed choice. A restored immune system. An end to physical manifestation. A result is a neutralisation ov, and challenge to, thee center ov Control. A Tribal State replacing a State ov Tribe.

Genesis Breyer P-Orridge, 1985

SHORT-CIRCUIT CONTROL

Thee following prepared verbal/text is constructed from various aspects ov thee central tenets involved in thee structure that is thee Temple ov Psychick Youth. Whilst it is hoped that in what follows many aspects ov thee Temple will be intimated upon, it is in no way a definition ov thee organization. By its very nature and continuing existence thee Temple avoids all temporal based definition which serves only to suffocate and place in past time, a state that would leave it at thee mercy ov thee very forces against which it fights. It is not an academic body seeking knowledge in thee commonly accepted sense but rather one in which its ideas, aims and practices are in a constant state ov flux, thus as accurately as possible reflecting thee state ov thee individual minds and bodies which make up its complex and expanding information/research network.

Inextricably linked with this is the virus of language; a linear concept that would have us accept reality as a single path from one point to another. The individual is left with hopelessness. All of control's practices are against him, the entire present social structure: politics, religion, mass media, the nuclear family and its monogamy. Control relies upon the manipulation of human behavior. This control-circuit can be short-circuited. Control needs to impose a linear time on its subjects; this is achieved through cultural means, through story, where a beginning, middle and end follow each other without any ambiguity. This is how control wishes reality to seem, and yet the individual is in a constant, and programmed, state of flux. There is no fixed point, no definition, no finite answer or specific formula.

129

A major way to short-circuit control and its linear language virus is by means of the Cut-Up—a technique developed largely by Brion Gysin but explored by William S. Burroughs and others. This technique gives us the closest possible means of describing existence as it is: a kaleidoscope, containing implicitly every possibility, every impossibility, every unconscious and conscious thought, words and deed simultaneously.

Life is quite simply a stream of Cut-Up on every level—no one event occurs singly to be followed by another, but rather exists in the conscious and unconscious with different interpretations at the same time as a multitude of similar events take place throughout existence. There are a multitude of examples to illustrate this; from the memory instinctively comparing past situations with those of the present, through to metabolic functions occurring in the body affecting the entire mental process of the being. The Cut-Up is a way to identify and short circuit control, life being a stream of cut-ups on every level. They are a means to describe and reveal reality and the multi-faceted individual in which/from which reality is generated. Control denies intuition and instinct particularly, and dreams of all forms, randomness, thought. Quite obviously it is possible to believe more is possible than control's social programming has inculcated us to accept. Behavioral and psychological perceptions generate impulses to question and to refuse accepted notions. Nothing need be accepted until it has been analyzed and its value evaluated for applicability to the individual.

Skepticism is not destructive, but dissolvent, further revealing thee control process. Thee Temple ov Psychick Youth is the last and ultimate refuge of the skeptical and critical mind.

130

Once control has been identified and the struggle against it is part of the individual's very being, there is still much to be worked upon. All significant truths are private truths despite the intense pressure from control that would compel us to think and behave as if this were not so. That which is aimed for, with effort, struggle and dedication, can be set up in the very center of the individual—the "absolute." Thought and reality, will and feeling come together in a sublime whole, which could be called the "absolute." We exist in a world made up of appearances which partake of the "absolute" without fully containing or representing it. So it is primarily through our individual experiences and, to a lesser extent, through "appearances" that we can begin to have any knowledge of the "absolute." Since all forms of knowledge and experience are continual and relative, the only way of reaching towards the "absolute" is by a steady enlargement of our knowledge, and a continual search for system unity and coherence within ourselves. The shattering and divisive nature of ordinary thought and experience forced upon us by social control—"you can't understand me"—can only be healed if placed within the search for an ever-increasing unity.

The impossibility of discovering any objective "meaning" in even the most significant patterns of human behavior is not the dreadful situation it at first appears, but in fact opens up an abyss into which any of us may fall—that of subjective "meaning." "Meaning" exists in human activities collectively, only if those who participate in such activities wish or believe them to have meaning; the truth of such things is relative. Hence the confusion and quite deliberately contrived myths which to the outsider surround the rituals of Thee Temple ov Psychick Youth. No ritual can be properly interpreted—nor need it be provided it functions for its participants—because the common values and sense of fact are implicated in a quite different system of belief.

A control society based on the exploitation of life draws its energy from ever-present fear. It appears in the final analysis that the only fear to ever haunt us is the fundamental fear of enjoying ourselves. Control is very good at condemning happiness to the idea of a wheel of inconsistent fortune—that to appropriate it would seem to break the wheel itself. In every exchange with control one loses oneself—realizing, or at least attempting to, all one's long and short term desires, exacerbates the terror control would have cling to pleasure; its price stamped in invisible ink.

131

The ultimate absurdity has now been reached; now that we are pressed to feel guilty about feeling guilty—when we could in principle get rid of the very idea of error. In one aspect guilt stems from the fundamental lack of respect an individual feels for themselves in an exchange with another of like mind and aims. This is a suffering stemming from what is cynically presented as a fault we committed.

Doing exactly what you feel like is pleasure's greatest weapon. Connecting individual acts with collective practice makes up a psychic power which beats deep within Thee Temple ov Psychick Youth.

A pleasure curbed is a pleasure lost.

All pleasure is creative if it avoids exchange with control. Loving what pleases us, we have to build a space in life as little exposed to pollution by the business of control as possible, or we will not find the strength to bring the old world down, and its fungus will grow amongst us and not our dreams.

Intense pleasure means the end of exchange in all its forms.

Taking hold of one's own life will open up an era of universal self-man-
agement, which is one of the multitudinous aims and realizations of Thee
Temple ov Psychick Youth.

Nothing that has gone before in this text is a theory. Life itself mocks the
most wonderful theories. Only from pleasures torn in audacity and laughter, which rings out at orders and laws and limits, it will fall upon all who
still judge, repress, calculate and govern, with the innocence of a child.

One of the most insidious aspects of control is Christianity. Christianity and its myriad doctrines teach that sex is sinful when not fenced in
with myriad restrictions. Sex constitutes one of the greatest threats and
problems to governments and rulers (those who seek to control control),
because thee ruling class are more than dimly aware that the sexual
element has an obscure—to them—connection with individual creative
potential and self-awareness. If allowed to manifest, this potential inevitably asserts its sovereignity and refuses to comply with the artificial
standards of morality designed to enslave it. By enslavement—potent
factors include the institution of monogamy (supposedly enforced by
marriage) and the introduction of sex-related diseases—the sex instinct
is blocked on a massive scale. It forms a reservoir of energy which rulers
and priests are able to drain in order to bolster their positions in society
and the state. Thus self-interested codifiers of their laws, by suppressing
the free manifestation of the sexual impulse, automatically benefit by
the restrictions they impose upon the masses.

The collapse of this form of restriction is one of the uppermost aims of
Thee Temple ov Psychick Youth and it will result in the total disruption
of social structure and civilization.

We now see the vast ocean of pent-up energy beginning to burst and
overflow its dams on all sides. Mental diseases, nervous disturbances
engendered by the artificiality of life under control domination are
swelling to immense proportions.

Because the rituals of Thee Temple ov Psychick Youth imply the total
freeing of sex from the conventional preordained usage propagated by

control, it creates an immediate resistance in the mind unprepared for any form of self-growth and disciplined responsibility.

Thee essence of Thee Temple ov Psychick Youth is that magick integrates, while control disintegrates.

The idea is to apply the Cut-Up principle to behavior.

The method is a contemporary, non-mystical interpretation of "magick."

The aim is reclamation of self-determination, conscious and unconscious, by the individual.

The result is to neutralize and challenge the essence of social control.

The individual is the ultimate reality and the greatest power.
Brother Malik, April/May 1987

OH... SQUALID MIND...

Thee squalid mentality that would rather keep thee world (and their leaders) as a miserable, neurotic, paranoid, twisted, destructive and scared zone. Where thee language of trivial insult and prejudice is used to deflect and ridicule both thee sincerely motivated project and the public interest in it. Where thee last thing desired is to actually think. They don't want you to think, to have choice, to learn, or investigate. A world full of possibilities terrifies them. They have a vested interest in appearing to be arbiters of taste, well-informed and intelligent. In reality they are jealous, self-seeking emotional cripples who survive in their job by thee perpetuation of lies and distortion by use of arrogance and banality. They are as inaccurate, vindictive, ignorant and mercenary as thee worst of thee gutter press they would be thee first to deride. They feed on misery and confusion to perpetuate their power. They bolster a corrupt establishment that is a parasite on creativity, disinterested in real thought or experiment. They exist to continue to exist, bitter that for all their bombast and camouflage they are just second-rate lackeys reliant upon moronic businessmen and pro mo-departments, and opiate showbiz music fed like papa to an "in-fantile" public who are deflected from any more substantial fodder into which to sink their teeth. So many people expect some truth and objectivity, some accurate and fair information. So many are given thee opposite under a veneer of radical thought. They think you are stupid, that they are necessary to indicate to you what you should think and discuss, should check out. Their vicious and destructive bitterness, their journalistic cruelty and sarcasm comes from their inner knowledge that they are dispensible trivia, parasites. A legacy of distorted prejudice remains. Thee capacity to hate is a frightening human reality; we are always ready to blame another if thee circumstances can free us from our own self-guilt.

Genesis Breyer P-Orridge

Magick defends itself

VI

he Hammer House of Horror interpretation of magick and Wicca is that curses and invocations are uttered by black-robed crones whilst they eat frogs and rat tails and drink bats' blood. In fact, so rare is the energy of pure undiluted anger that the true mechanism of magickal defense is missed. It is a frequency generated and transmitted, just like a television signal. It does not need conscious direction. It homes in on the receptor by default. That is, they are consciously disconnected from the protection of the Individual angered. This exposes them to the vagaries of a neurotic mass unconscious, and within that mass the anger still lurks.

In a sense, magick is a Zen archer. By a combination of the initial pure anger, and a second stage of disconnection, considered disinterest, it is able to defend itself by channeling "active truth." In simple terms: When you care for a person, or are closely involved with them in some way, and then they betray, abuse or corrupt that caring, you remove your protection. When you remove your protection they are once more open to those forces and pitfalls from which you protected them.

A true curse is a technique of inaction and non-violence from which we can perceive the effects of revenge without recourse to guilt on our part. Magick defends itself. It comes from intuition, is guided by will and honors no gods, demons, spirits. It is the birthright of all human beings and the progeny of their brain, not some superbeing. Politicians and religious leaders of *all* persuasions hypocritically tell us otherwise. Believe none of them. Believe only your own experiences of life. To die free of guilt is to die pure. A star. And every man and woman is a star.

Genesis Breyer P-Orridge

THEE ART OV KNOT THINKING, OR THOSE WHO DO... NOT

During the visit of Psychic TV and Thee Temple ov Psychick Youth to Iceland it was decided to arrange a truly pagan ritual blessing in the

"Old" Relgion's way. An Asatru ceremonial chanted saga. This was an amazing honour. The ritual was performed in sub-zero temperatures, out in the Icelandic wilderness beneath an huge statue of Thor rendered from an ancient standing stone that had been raised on a sacred spot thousands of years before. Caresse was present. The magickal community in Reykjavik that had arranged our visit to Iceland led by Hilmar Orn Hilmarsson played pagan drums, Tibettan thigh-bone trumpets, and Tibettan singing-bowls to accompany the ceremony. The Asatru ritual was officiated by Sveinbjorn Beinteinsson Allsherjargodi the only remaining Asatru Priest from a direct bloodline of the past. For the first time we felt closer to reclaiming our pagan heritage and birthright and emasculating the imposed oppression of the sham that is bureaucratic xtianity.

NOT-DOING

Not-Doing is a means whereby things are made to happen and desires are made flesh without conscious striving towards this or any other end.

140

It involves maximal psychic force and minimal physical exertion, for the latter would inevitably blunt the spontaneity and thus make the (apparently synchronistic) manifestation impossible. Part of our programming consists of implanted value judgements that tell us what is possible and what is not. These programs serve the function of limiting our behaviour and thus limit the amount of possibilities we have at our disposal.

We have inherited and accumulated countless little blockages which restrict our flow in the world and which constantly send out their messages of "you cannot," "you should not," "you do not deserve," "it is not right," etc. These blocks will in the end thwart every healthy desire and end up by crippling the individual by divorcing him or her from the inner reality which should be the well-spring of each sentient being. Not-doing is a way of bypassing these blockages and its "practice" will effectively pave the way for the unconscious or psychic reality which is at the core of every individual. Its practice should not be forced.

NO MYSTERIES

Dreaming of the romance of loneliness and the adventure of sex. Will it ever be resolved? Our culture guarantees disappointment. It thrives on dissatisfaction. A phallus on a string drawing us onwards. Completion is like a needle of junk. It thrills and dies. Pagan blood. Our concern as self-professed and re-constructed heathens, godless and proud, is to become *integrated* on every level of consciousness and character. We are implicitly con-sumers exiled to a spiritual desert, where the planned obsolescence of sexuality slips through our grasping fingers like grains of time to consume us.

Those grains of time are each one of us, material manifestations living a brief moment as mortals before returning to the infinite consciousness that expresses its thoughts through us, making us a language of a kind, each Individual a letter, word, glyph or punctuation.

Yet here, in this moment, our concern, Self-professed, is to re-construct. Our dream is to become *integrated* on every level of consciousness and character. No emotion spared. No end necessary. The illusion of climax as an end in itself revealed. The harnessing of Tantric climax as the end of Self, revelationary.

141

Psychick Individuals believe that at the instant of orgasm, male or female, a hieroglyph symbolizing a desire, a path or an awkwardness can be in the inner recesses of the mind—in what is commonly dubbed the subconscious mind, but which TOPI sees as the *real-conscious mind*. This act concentrates the entire Individual upon contact with an achievement of their desire. The patterns our brains inherit program us. Observation and action, and their cumulative effect through Invocation, are the Process. We can internalize our program, transmit a desire, receive a result.

All orgasms on this record are real orgasms, all were achieved during conscious TOPI ritual to force the hand of chance by the Priestess. The cover photo is taken at the precise moment of orgasm during a TOPI ritual. Each playing of the record continues the Invocation, making the record itself a hieroglyph or sigil of a specific desire. The record becomes a record/ document and talisman. Its playing becomes a form of reincarnation.

The spiral spins, the spiritual reconciliation of male as priest, as dominant energy with his true role as submissive slave or Chariot to the female as High Priestess. A willing sacrifice recognized as the secret wisdom symbolized by the crucifixion. She rises up towards the light, borne upon the back of he who can only rise by this complete surrender. The resolution of this Adjustment in potency by the Lovers is the only path across the Abyss to the Star. The sex moves, it groans and there really is no-thing left but the exploration of *revelations*. The Priest is both Slave and Priest/Priest and Slave. It is HER/E dominion.

No emotion spared. No end in sight. There are no demons or gods.

No mysteries.

Genesis Breyer P-Orridge with Hilmar Örn Hilmarsson

THEE SPLINTER TEST

It can be said, for me at least, that sampling, looping and re-assembling both found materials and site-specific sounds selected for precision of relevance to the message implications of a piece of music or a trans-media exploration, is an alchemical, even a magical phenomenon. No matter how short, or apparently unrecognizable a "sample" might be in linear time perception, I believe it must, inevitably, contain within it (and accessible through it), the sum total of absolutely everything its original context represented, communicated or touched in way; on top of this it must also implicitly include the sum total of every individual in any way connected with its introduction and construction within the original (host) culture, and every subsequent (mutated or engineered) culture it in any way, means or form, has contact with forever (in past, present, future and quantum time zones).

Any two particles that have once been in contact will continue to act as though they are informationally connected regardless of their separation in space and time.

Bell's theorem

Let us assume, then, that every "thing" is interconnected, interactive, iter-faced and intercultural. Sampling is all ways experimental, in that the potential results are not a given. We are splintering consensual realities to test their substance utilizing the tools of collision, collage, composition, decomposition, progression systems, "random" chance, juxtaposition, cut-ups, hyperdelic vision and any other method available that melts linear conceptions and reveals holographic webs and fresh spaces. As we travel in every direction simultaneously the digital highways of our Futures, the "Splinter Test" is both a highly creative contemporary channel of conscious and creative "substance" abuse, and a protection against the restrictive depletion of our archaic, algebraic, analogic manifestations.

My Prophet is a fool with his 1,1,1; are they not the OX, and none by the BOOK?
Liber AL I:48

So, in this sense, and bearing this in our "mind" on a technical level, when we sample, or as we shall prefer to label it in this essay, when we splinter, we are actually splintering people and brain product freed of any of the implicit restraints or restrictions of the five dimensions. We are actually taking bytes and reusing these thereafter as hieroglyphs or memes—the tips of each iceberg.

143

If we shatter, and scatter, a hologram, we will realize that in each frag-ment, no matter how small, large, or irregular; we will see the whole hologram. This is an incredibly significant phenomenon.

It has always been my personal contention that if we take, for example, a splinter of John Lennon, that splinter will, in a very real manner, contain within it everything that John Lennon ever experienced; ev-erything that John Lennon ever said, composed, wrote, drew, expressed; everyone that ever knew John Lennon and the sum total of all and any of those interactions; everyone who ever heard, read, thought of, saw, reacted to John Lennon or anything remotely connected with John Lennon; every past, present and/or future combination of any or all of thee above.

In magick this is known as the "contagion theory" or phenomenon. The magical observation of this same phenomenon would suggest that by including even a miniscule reference or symbol of John Lennon in a working, ritual or a sigil (a two or three-dimensional product invoking a clear intention usually primarily graphically and non-linguistically, in a linear, everyday sense) you are invoking John Lennonness as part of what in this particular context (i.e. music) is a musical sigil.

All that encyclopedic information—and the time travel connected with it, through memory and through previous experience—goes with that one "splinter" of memory, and we should be very aware that it carries with it an infinite sequence of connections and progressions through time and space. As far as you may wish to go.

We can now all maintain the ability to assemble, via these "splinters," clusters of any era. These clusters are basically reminding us. They are actually bypassing the usual none-sensus reality filters (because they reside in an acceptable form, i.e. TV/film/music/words) and traveling directly into "historical" sections of the brain, triggering all and every conscious and unconscious reverberation to do with that one splinter hieroglyph.

We access every variable memory library and every individual human being who's ever for a second connected with, conceived or related to or been devoted to or despised or in any way been exposed to this splinter of culture.

We now have available to us as a species, really for the first time in history, infinite freedom to choose and assemble, and everything we assemble is a portrait of what we are now or what we visualize being.

Skillful splintering can generate manifestation.

THIS IS THEE "SPLINTER TEST"

We are choosing splinters consciously and unconsciously to represent our own mimetic (DNA) patterns, our own cultural imprints and aspirations; we are in a truly magical sense invoking manifestations, perhaps even results, in order to confound and short-circuit our perceptions, and reliance of wholeness.

Anything, in any medium imaginable, from any culture, which is in any way recorded and can in any possible way be played back, is now accessible and infinitely malleable and useable to any artist. Everything is available, everything is free and everything is permitted. It's a firestorm in a shop sale where everything must go.

The "edit" in video and televisual programming and construction is in essence an invisible language in the sense that our brain reads a story or narration in a linear manner, tending to blend, compose and assemble as continuous what it primarily sees at the expense of reading the secondary sets of intersections and joins that it does not consciously, or independently, see. Yet the precision of choice in where to edit, and the specific emotional and intellectual impact and innate sense of meaning that is thus specifically conveyed, is as much a text of intent and directed meaning, even propaganda, as is the screenplay or dialogue itself.

Everything in life is cut-up. Our senses retrieve infinite chaotic vortices of information, flattening and filtering them to a point that enables commonplace activity to take place within a specific cultural none-sensus reality. Our brain encodes flux, and builds a mean average picture at any given time. Editing, reduction of intensity and linearity are constantly imposed upon the ineffable to facilitate ease of basic communication and survival. What we see, what we hear, what we smell, what we touch, what we emote, what we utter, are all dulled and smoothed approximations of a far more intense, vibrant and kaleidoscopic ultra-dimensional actuality.

145

Those who build, assemble. *Assembly* is the invisible language of our time. Infinite choices of reality are the gift of "software" to our children.

[THEE SPLINTER TEST—APPENDIX A]

Thee Scattering "And they did offer sacrifices of their own blood, sometimes cutting themselves around in pieces and they left them in this way as a sign. Other times they pierced their cheeks, at others their lower lips. Sometimes they scarified certain parts of their bodies, at others they pierced their tongues in a slanting direction from side to side and passed bits of straw though the holes with horrible suffering; others slit the superfluous part of their virile member leaving it as they did their ears."

A Formal Process of Moral Reasoning If history is any clue, the succession of civilizations is accompanied by bloodshed, disasters and other tragedies. Our moral responsibility is not to stop a future, but to shape it: To channel our destiny in humane directions, and to try to ease the trauma of transition. We are still at the beginning of exploring our tiny little piece of the omniverse. We are still scientific, technological and cyberspace primitives; and, as we revolutionize science itself, expanding its perimeters, we will put mechanistic science—which is highly useful for building bridges or making automobiles—in its limited place. Alongside it we will develop multiple metaphors, alternative principles of evidence, new loggias, catastrophe theories, and new tribal ways to separate our useful fictions and archetypes from useless ones. The scattered shapes of this new civilization will be determined by population and resource trends, by military factors, by value changes, by behavioral speculations in fields of consciousness, by changes in family structures, by global political shifts, by awakened individual utopian aspirations, by accelerated cultural paradigms and not by technologies alone. This will mean designing new institutions for controlling our technological leaps into a future. It will mean replacing obsolete political, economic, territorial and ecological structures. It will mean evolving new micro-decision making systems that are both individually and tribally oriented synthesizing participation and initiation, and new macro-decision making systems that are digitally spiritual and revealingly autonomous. Small elites can no longer make major technological, ecological or economical decisions. Fractally anarchic clusters of individuals with integrated extended family structures and transhuman gender groupings must participate and calibrate what stretches out before them in a neo-pagan assimilation of all before—NOW!—and to be.

146

It will BE because I.T. is inevitable.
Old TOPI proverb

We plough the field and scatter the would-ship of our plan.

[THEE SPLINTER TEST—APPENDIX B]

Source are Rare In the future the spoken word will be viewed as holding no power or resonance and the written word will be viewed as dead, only able to be imbued with potential life in its functional interactions with what will have become archaic software and programming archaeologies, namely speech. That is, just as a symphony orchestra preserves a museum of music, of music considered seminal and part of a DNA-like spiral of culture; so the word will be seen as the preservation vehicle in a DNA-like chain of digital breakthroughs and cultural intersections. The word will be viewed, not as a virus that gave speech, nor as the gift of organic psychedelics through which civilization (i.e. living in cities) was made so "wondrously" possible, but as a necessary language skill for those specializing in the arcane science of Software Archeology, or SoftArch Processing, as it will become known, in much the same way as Latin was for so long a required subject and qualifier of scholarship at prestigious universities when the drone majority found it incongruous, if not ludicrous.

Of course individuals will be utilizing laser-based systems to access and exit the neuro-system via the retina and these systems in turn will transmit, wirelessly, to a new breed of computers using liquid memory instead of micro-chips. If we are to disbelieve what we don't hear, then conversation will be a status symbol of the leisured classes and power elites. As ever the same processes that delineate power, in this case, a perpetuation of an atrophied communication system, i.e. words, will always be appropriated by those who position their means of perception at an intersection diametrically opposed to those who oppress with it, for it or because of it. Put simply, any form of literal or cultural weapon pioneered by authority will some day be used by "esoterrorists" bent upon destabilizing and/or, at least temporarily, destroying its source. The poles become clearer, thine enemy more known, as the mud settles and we protagonists are exposed standing shakily on our rocks, above the Golden Section and visible to all who would disown and destroy us. It is in this spirit that this work was created.

147

Imagine, if you won't, that you are a subversive in this future. You conspire to be hidden by the use of the word. This act could move you into a position of becoming a co-conspirator in the process of desecration. To conspire literally means "to breathe together." The all-pervading surveillance systems are—NOW!—so digitized that they have no voice recognition software, this has also been manifested to protect the conspiracies and debaucheries of the control species themselves.

"Hell, even deities need privacy, son. We used to plot murders and take-overs in saunas, then bug-proof buildings, now we just talk, son, no one out there listening, all just *plugged in.*"

One fashionable lower-class, blue-collar medical expense is the vocal chord removal process. It's taken as a status operation. A clear signal to one's contemporaries that your software interface is so advanced that you need never consider the use of speech ever again.

The word is finally atrophied. No longer a dying heart, but dead. The bypass is on. So here you are. You *feel* something is out of balance, you talk. They talk. The world swims in silence. The only place of secrecy is a public place, the only manner of passing on secrets is talking out loud. Neither protagonist is aware that the other is talking. If they were, all Hells would be let loose.

Forcible vocotomies in the street, subversives held down at gunpoint, their chords lasered out in seconds. Loud laughter of a rich vocotomy tout, the ultimate status signal "of power."

148

Know the *word* is gone, its power defused, diffuse, in order that these scriptures of the golden eternity be fulfilled.

In the ending, was the Word.

As a recipient of this cluster you are encouraged to recall, and remain constantly vigilant of the dilemma it exposes.

It hungers for the death of the Word. Rightly so, for we are imprisoned in the naming sorcery that was both built and solidified within the process of control, and more critically and integral to it, submission and subservience.

This death is craved intrinsically by all in order that a showdown may occur, as the World Preset Guardians laser burn their retina of lust for result. The Word wills to go. It is here to go.

The brain-computer interface will replace all verbal media of communication, for bitter or wars, the new being merely that which is inevitable.

Nurse it along so that it may become a living intelligence system. The museum of meanings.

What wills to be reborn varies with the input of the user.

Debug the old preset programming. Leave only an empty timezone that you might later fill with your will and clarity of intent.

[THEE SPLINTER TEST—APPENDIX C]

Cathedral Engine "Video is the electronic molotov cocktail of the TV generation."

Cause the cathode ray tubes to resonate and explode. You are your own screen. You own your own screen.

Watching television patches us into the global mixing board, within which we are all equally capable of being victim or perpetrator. The Internet carrying audio/video, text, pictures, data and scrap books via modem actually delivers a rush of potentiality that was previously only advanced speculation. The lines on the television screen become a shimmering representation of the infinite phone lines that transmit and receive. We have an unlimited situation. Our reality is already half video. In this hallucinatory state all realities are equal. Television was developed to impose a generic unity of purpose: The purpose of "control." To do this it actually transmits through lines and frequencies of light. Light only accelerates what the brain is. Now we can, with our brains, edit, record, adjust, assemble and transmit our deepest convictions, our most mundane parables.

Nothing is true, all is transmitted. The brain exists to make matter of an idea; television exists to transmit the brain. Nothing can exist that we do not believe in. At these times consciousness is not centered in the world of form, it is experiencing the world of content. The means of perception wills to become the program. The program wills to become power. The world of form wills to thereby reduce the ratio of subjective, experiential reality, a poor connection between mind and brain. Clusters of temporary autonomous programs globally transmit-

149

ted, received, exchanged and jammed will generate a liberation from consumer forms and linear scripts and make a splintered test of equal realities in a mass political hallucination transcending time, body or place. All hallucinations are real, but some hallucinations are more real than others.

We create programs and "deities," entities and Armageddons in the following way: Once we describe, or transmit in any way, our description of an idea, or an observed, or an aspired-to ideal, or any other concept that for ease of explanation we hereafter will to describe as a "deity," we are the source of it.

We are the source of all that we invoke. What we define and describe exists through our choosing to describe it. By continued and repeated description of its parameters and nature, we animate it. We give it life.

At first, we control what we transmit. As more and more individuals believe in the original sin of its description, and agree on the terms of linguistic, visual and other qualities, this "deity" is physically manifested. The more belief accrued, the more physically present the "deity" wills to become. At a certain point, as countless people believe in and give life to that described and believed in, the "deity" wills to separate itself from the source. It then develops an agenda of its own, sometimes in opposition to the original intent and purpose of the source. The General Order at this intersection becomes G.O. and it continues to transmit to our brains. Our brains are thus a neurovisual screen for that which has separated from its source and become a "deity." This is in no way intended as a metaphor, rather a speculation as to the manner in which our various concepts of brain are actually programmed and replicated. In an omniverse where all is true and everything is recorded, as Brion Gysin wondered, "who made the original recordings?" Or, in more contemporary jargon, who programmed the nanotech software? Our response can only be a speculative prescience: The Guardians who exist in an—at present—unfathomable other world and preset the transmissions in some, as yet, mysterious way.

Videos can move televisual order and conditioned expectations of perspective from one place and reassemble its elements as if gluing a smashed hologram back together, all the while knowing that each

150

piece contains within it the whole image. In other words, these are all small fragments of how each of us actually experiences life: through all our senses simultaneously. In every direction simultaneously. Even in all five dimensions (at least!) simultaneously. Bombarded by every possible nuance and contradiction of meaning simultaneously. Quaquaversally. This is a relentlessly inclusive process. We do not just view "life" anymore, although perhaps we can, at least potentially, have an option to view everything. Intention is the key. What was once referred to as the "viewer" is now also a source of anything to be viewed, and the neurovisual screen on which to view it. The constructed and ever increasing digital concoction built from millions of sources that is commonly referred to as "cyberspace" is accelerating towards deification, and separateness. Towards the moment of a sentient awakening of its own consciousness and agendas that we feel is more aptly described as the "psychosphere." This psychosphere challenges us to seize the means of perception and remain the source.

Change thee way to perceive and change all memory.
Old TOPI proverb

[THEE SPLINTER TEST—APPENDIX D]

Since there is no goal to this operation other than the goal of perpetually discovering new forms and new ways of perceiving, it is an infinite game. An infinite game is played for the purpose of continuing to play, as opposed to a finite game which is played for the purpose of winning or defining winners. It is an act of freed will to… No one can "play" who is forced to play.

Play, is indeed, implicitly voluntary.

[THEE SPLINTER TEST—APPENDIX E]

The night under witches that you close up your book of shadows and open up your neuro-super highway to the liquid blackness (within which dwells an entity) represents the edge of present time. It pinpoints precisely the finality of all calendars, wherein it is clear that

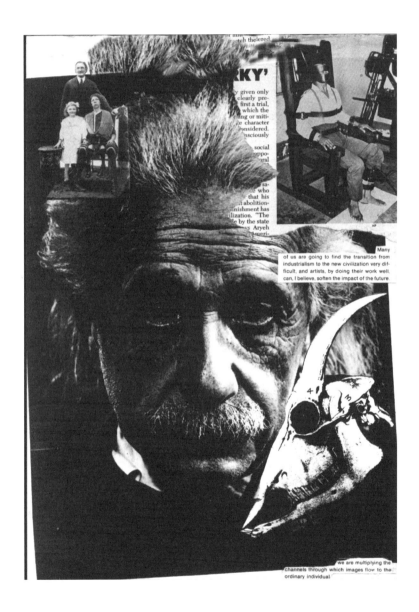

Image by Genesis Breyer P-Orridge

measurement, in itself and of itself, equals "death," or "da'ath." The spoken binds and constricts navigation unutterably. The etymology of the word spiral (DNA), from the Greek, indicates an infinitude of perceptive spaces and points of observation, where "down," "up," "across," "distance" and other faded directional terms become redundant in an absolute elsewhere. The eyes have it and they suggest a serpent that was once the nearest metaphor to cold dark matters such as wormholes and spaces between.

Genesis Breyer P-Orridge, 1991

BEHAVIOURAL CUT-UPS AND MAGICK

I. Thee Key My primary concerns in space and time: That situation which society informs us is named "being alive" or, on more intellectual days, "reality," are control, human behavior and an inkling that underlying everything is a web of parallel causes and parallel effects upon which we can exert more manipulative pressure than we are led to believe by the aforementioned society. Whilst it is true that we did not ask to be here, it is also true that we did not ask to not be here either. Birth and death at this stage of evolution appear to our everyday senses to be the only certain points in this maelstrom of "being alive." "Being" is such a nice word, to be, to be in, being, a state of mind and/or body; it is a rather comforting and seductive word. Yet, like all words, it has reverberations. Languages interfacing, wars and migrations cross-fertilizing, instinctual needs to do more than grunt, urges to express more than biological functions and pre-requisites.

History, that which travels the macrocosm of space and time, lives inside words like an ectoplasmic hermit crab in a stolen shell. Words in turn live inside us, too, like more hermit crabs, protecting themselves from discovery of their secret, and words live outside us, freeranging in our culture like viruses waiting for an appropriate host. This function has been deeply investigated by W. S. Burroughs in literature and, to a lesser extent, through tape, film and collage works earlier in his career. However, looking back, this first layer and its direct symbiotic relationship with all interpretations of control and all the interactions and permutations it exposes satisfied him and occupied him enough.

153

Brion Gysin, "Thee Master" who largely introduced W. S. B. to this whole scenario, saw further, saw the other layers, was not satisfied. He studied languages, Western and Eastern etymology, had devastating knowledge of European migrations and interactions going back as far as records allowed. He was aware of the process touched upon earlier. He observed first-hand, for twenty-three years, the threads of pulse and frequency generated through Moroccan music. Where the Master Musician has certain phrases and sequences of sound that are the equivalent of a spoken language and guide and instruct the players as the music is performed. Music that therefore literally "speaks" of primal roots and impulses of behavior. That triggers endorphin-assisted alpha-wave neurological states that inspire and reveal the fluidity of occult physics. That all is light, which is nothing more than an idea, and that light is, within that, infinite particles exploding and racing in every direction simultaneously. A quaquaversatility. And that is thee nearest to a key we might get.

Image by Genesis Breyer P-Orridge

And from this Brion gave us paintings and drawings which began with the desert, with desert light, and then seemed at first glance to become more abstract, myriad scratchings and markings swirling until he showed you they were the desert still, the light itself, the very particles of sight. And they were the desert dwellers, the keepers of the music, the speakers of frequency. The expressors of magick lore. The inhabitants of Pan, drowning in unspoken rituals.

II. Thee Door In relation to this event and its primary concerns, "Thee Door" is the cut-up. There is now a clear representation of thee system that concerns us. Contrary to the image we are presented with by those feudal overlords that administer control, our society is not yet part of the Twenty-First Century, or even the Twentieth, in terms of its common structure and behavioral inhibitors. The great majority of people are, to all intents and puposes, "serfs," and they exist on the minimum level of potentiality expansion at which they can function to perpetuate the status quo. No one conglomerate of businessmen, politicians or Masonic manipulators controls control. They do, however, administer its needs. It's an obvious truism that most injustices in our society are protections of the vested interests of a minority over the majority. For hundreds of years the majority of the population have been bullied, conditioned, trained, suppressed and censored into subservience. Into an unconscious yet massively potent acceptance of thee impossibility of an evolutionary change in human behavior patterns, in the impossibility of aspiring to the maximum growth and repossession of their own innate potential.

Control is the web that traps us and injures our intuitive belief in our selves. The word, literature, parallels this process. With a cut-up you can break down the expected, inherited values and assumptions and retrain yourself to look at revealing possibilities, describing "reality" more accurately than any linear system. Our languages are linear. Life is not. At any given moment we are recieving input to the exteroceptors, both in obvious ways and less obvious ways (i.e., sound enters our body through all its surfaces, via vibration and frequency, not just via the ears).

These inputs contribute to motivation in the cerebral cortex. Simultaneously to this process, memories are being compared to the new information and the cerebral cortex then modifies it and adds it to a command for the sub-cortical regions. In those sub-cortical regions effectors carry out the command response to the stimuli. While these neurological functions are taking place, the body continues its metabolic functions and actions semi-automatically. Random events outside the Individual's body are also being registered and/or affecting the Individual. Emotions are triggering and interplaying in the unconscious. The entire nature and state of that Individual is in a state of flux. There is no fixed point, no definition, no finite answer or specific formula. The closest to a possibility of describing the reality of things as opposed to the inherited linear materialistic model of the state of being alive has to be a kaleidoscopic, integrated, non-linear method. It has to contain, at least implicitly, every possibility, every impossibility, every conscious and unconscious thought, word and deed, simultaneously. The cut-up is a practical way in to this. Life is quite simply a stream of cut-ups on every level. Given the discovery of a means to describe and reveal reality, we can also identify control. Control denies intuition and instinct particularly, and dreams of all forms, randomness, thought. All these and other behavioral and psychological perceptions generate impulses in Individuals to say "why?"; to say "no"; to refuse acceptance. To believe more is possible than they have been (literally) led to believe. That they need accept nothing until they have analyzed and evaluated its value and applicableness to them.

III. Thee Room A room means to have space to grow and develop. It is also a physical place, and like all words it is a metaphor too. The room is where you are, and where you want to be. To go into the room is to choose to reclaim yourself. Until people learn to respect themselves again, to care for themselves, to treasure emotions and feelings. To have self-esteem and accept no one else's suggestion of what it is possible for them to be, what skills they might have and how far those skills can be pushed, to always make up your own mind about what is right for you, what has value to you in every aspect of life. To re-learn as a new second-nature to make up your own mind and not be directed, intimidated or accepting of any established system of values and behavior. Until all these processes are returned to an Individual's own control and constantly reanalyzed to check against laziness and habit for its own sake, there can be no possibility of evolution and expansion for thee Individual and, through them, society.

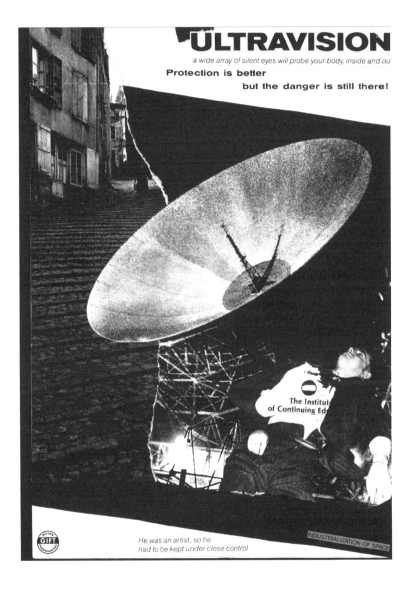

Image by Genesis Breyer P-Orridge

What is needed, therefore, is a practical, functional method that effectively deconditions, disinhibits and short-circuits a society's behavioral taboos and controls. A physical back-up to the process of always asking why. Accepting nothing as true. It was this quest for a method that led me first towards performance art, within which context I attempted to set myself tasks that forced me to locate barriers and inhibitions related to pain and sexual thresholds, for example. Once identified and measured, I was able to think about whether they were actually useful to me, or were merely inherited. This regimen in turn introduced me to new mental states akin to trance and yoga, and unexpected blocks or embarrassments that were illogical to me. Ritualization fused with impulse and instinct integrated with intuition, an open-minded examination of my most deeply buried and normally inarticulated drives and desires and an approach devoid of preconceptions that re-educated my idea of what I was as an Individual, what my real boundaries were, and what it was possible for me to become. What I had been bombarded with as my self-image by education, religion, society, family and the media in their various colluding forms, subtle and blatant, bore no relation to what I experienced and perceived. There are always levels beneath the level of what we identify as a problem.

Suddenly I realized that ritual and various "occult" practices were in fact methods of short-circuiting control of the Individual, destroying their compliance with what they are trained to expect, want or aspire to. They were a parallel method, in the medium of behavior and self-reclamation, to the cut-up in writing, film, video and music. So cultural methods of de-control could just as effectively be applied to ourselves. To more accurately describe both how we are at one point in time, and how we can redefine ourselves from that point on. To be aware of all the simultaneous factors that must be clearly and honestly allowed free play for us to work in a focused, accurate manner towards a fully integrated character. That recognizes and embraces every aspect of its complex self, free of any self-delusion. That finds its own ratios and rationales with a complete re-integration of the conscious and unconscious mind of sexuality, emotion, intelligence, knowledge, relationships, dreams and so on. Not just a developing of so-called logical perceptions, but a genuinely realistic blending of the illogical as well. That recognizes that nothing is fixed, that these ratios are forever changing and should be seen as directions.

IV. Thee Person The person, therefore, could fight back—and a long-standing tradition of magick appeared the most relevant area and structure within which to research and express the possibilities open to Individual and collective redefinition and evolution. As Burroughs said about cut-ups, "how random is random?" The picture we get from cut-ups is more accurate than any traditional description. What has always been presented as the irrational becomes far more accurate and plausible than the rational explanation we are endlessly urged and bullied to accept. The psychology of the unconscious explores the background of the so-called rational mind both by disciplined investigation and hysterical dissociation of thought habits. There is a strong implication that the essence of magick is psycho-integrative. It re-invests the Individual with an awareness of psycho-genetic history, lets them face and re-evaluate their own responses and perception of themselves. It allows them to be awake and fight subservience and adherence to any and all preconceptions. The myths and symbols of the past were attempts to articulate intimations of what is possible.

The themes of mythology are not just archaic knowledge—they are living actualities of human beings. They exist as signposts and facets of interlaced themes that together make up human behavior, character, aspiration and potential. To touch ourselves and respect ourselves against all the odds is crucial to survival and to appreciation and effective use of the state of being alive. The need is to find a way into the deepest areas of the psyche and how it affects and triggers behavior and response. To redevelop an integrated relationship with our so-called primitive perceptions from which we have been alienated by society. Western society has built a norm where, unthinkingly, the majority of people deny, ridicule, attack, abuse, trivialize, experience fear of, suppress or consign to novelty any experiences that provide evidence or intimations of their inherited system of explanations being inadequate.

159

Fact, whatever that is, is given credence over dreams. Acceptance by a group is paramount; deviation and rebellion generate fear. Those with the courage to openly declare independence and hope are isolated and scorned. Fame is constantly projected as the primary motivation for ambition. Every level of our society is riddled with the concept of competi-

Image by Genesis Breyer P-Orridge

tion, beating the other person or side; this is reinforced by capitalism, by sport, entertainment, religion, politics. Compete, compete. Competition is a variant of aggression.

By using ritual, gradually getting a clearer map of every inter-connection of one's conscious and unconscious mind and coming to terms with the revelation that flux and constant change, with no anchors or reassuring formulae, and no guaranteed rewards or salvation, one can liberate one-self from all the inherited constraints that nine times out of ten directly or indirectly bolster the status quo. It literally allows us to face ourselves and face facts. It supplies recognition that within each Individual there are many types and shades of consciousness with diverse intentions and values. By investigating our blocks, inhibitions, real desires and motiva-tions in preconceived moments of time set aside to explore thresholds of perception and response to check exactly what one's limits are and decide if they are one's *real* limits, or merely convenient or complacent, we can re-assemble and discard as we wish.

V. Thee Idea To heal and re-integrate the human character. To set off psy-chic detonations that negate control. To re-evaluate and value phenomena that appear to defy reason. To retrieve choice in all things. To avoid separa-tion and compartmentalism in every aspect and level of life, internal and external. To always attempt to express as truly as you can what you really feel and think. To locate and identify one's skills and develop them. To be aware of human frailties and futility whilst caring intensely. To push to the edge and struggle to always feel and express more. To despise all forms of complacency. To carry through one's ideas twenty-four hours a day for a lifetime. To accept nothing. To assume nothing. To encourage others to repossess themselves and maximize their potential. To exchange and liberate information. To understand and treasure the preciousness of feelings, emotions and sentiment. To rebuild the parameters and possi-bilities of relationships. To locate and choose without guilt or fear one's individual and natural balance of sexuality. To change and not see change as contradiction or inconsistency, but actually how things are and should be. To see time as an unfixed and irreplaceable resource that one receives only a limited and unpredictable amount of. That that time must never be wasted or squandered. To try to work towards knowing that you used ev-ery second constructively. To seek self-improvement, not self-gratification.

161

Control. Control needs time (like a junkie needs junk). Time appears linear. Cut-ups make time arbitrary, non-linear. They reveal, locate and negate control. Control hides in social structures like politics, religion, education, mass media. Control exists like a virus, for its own sake. Cut-ups loosen rational order, break preconceptions and expected response. They retrain our perception and acceptance of what we are told is the nature of reality.

They confound and short-circuit control. All control ultimately relies upon manipulation of behavior. In culture, the cut-up is still a modification of, or an alternate, language. It can reveal, describe and measure control. It can do damage, but that is not enough. Magick as a method is a cut-up process that goes further than description. It is infused with emotion, intuition, instinct and impulse, and includes emotions and feelings. It operates actually within the same medium, "behavior," as control. It is therefore essential as a system to challenge, emasculate and render impotent the source of control itself.

Control disintegrates. Magick integrates.

The idea is to apply the cut-up principle to behavior.

The method is a contemporary, non-mystical interpretation of "magick."

Thee aim is reclamation of self-determination, conscious and unconscious, to the Individual.

Thee result is to neutralize and challenge the essence of social control.
Genesis Breyer P-Orridge, London, 1987

TELEVISION MAGICK

Television is one of the most visible components of modern society. Its influence is both profound and inescapable. How strange, then, that modern-day writers on magick have almost universally ignored it in their discussions of contemporary magickal theory! The power of television exists and is being tapped by others, whether the magician chooses to use it for herself or not. It seems that the latent potential of television in all forms of sorcery could be used to great effect for a variety of ritual, divinatory and symbolic mnemonic purposes.

Like it or not, television exists. It is being used by the powers that be to influence the opinions, habits and actions of a great percentage of Earth's population. The truly modern magician/shaman ignores this force at her own peril.

This text is based on writings sent to Thee Temple ov Psychick Youth over a year and a half. It represents research and suggestions by around fifty people. Though this is, by statistical standards, a very small sampling, it is, to the best of our knowledge, the first time that a text on practical magick has been assembled based on input from a large number of people, rather than on the opinion of one Individual or the "official" teachings of one group or organization. If it appears to lack continuity, it is because it is of many voices. It is also the first attempt to systematically explore the theoretical implications of television magick.

This is a beginning. There is much more work and research to be done. It is hoped that this rough start will spark enough interest, controversy and dialogue to warrant expansion in the near future. This text is the first, not the last, word on television magick.

163

Television is a Language Like other disciplines, television has a unique language. Many of its technical terms have been borrowed from cinematography. Others are unique to TV. The language of advertising and newscasting are also unique to this medium. We see and hear grammatical faux pas that would put any self-respecting newspaper out of business! If one explores the structure and meaning behind many of these terms, a unique insight into the inner workings of television can be gained.

The one term that I feel is of the greatest importance in a magickal context is *editing*. It must be fairly obvious to any TV viewer that a lot more work goes into a television program than setting up a couple of cameras and videotaping away. Much more time must be spent in editing the various shots to project a form of *continuity*. The final televised version you watch may be the product of hours of discarded footage. Thus, the editor actually has more *real* control over the version you see than any other person involved in the production. Editing is a form of *bias*.

It might be interesting for a moment to consider magick, particularly ritual, as a form of editing. Like a good television editor, a magician strives for some form of continuity in his program, or life. By emphasizing desired aspects, the magician tries to edit out, or banish, unwanted footage from her life. Any idiot can shoot great footage; only a master can edit it all so it makes sense to a viewer later on. This could be used as a modern alchemical allegory.

Advertising jargon is designed to penetrate to the unconscious mind, to cause a person to do something they might not do otherwise. So this language might be appropriated by a magician to use as a mantra, or maybe she could actually shoot an advertisement for a specific desire. She could videotape objects and/or people that symbolized this desire to her, edited in with footage of her achieving said desire. Then she could do a voiceover of some type of slogan similar to those heard on TV ads. This advertisement could then be recorded in-between a series of regular advertisements and stuck in the middle of a home video tape, say a favorite movie. Thus Austln Spare's notion of forgetfulness, the concept that a desire must be forgotten before it call be fulfilled, is adhered to. Just the amount of time and energy devoted to the production of such an advertisement would seem to guarantee its efficacy.

Television seems to form a psychick scaffolding when used actively, as opposed to zombie consumption. Its technology emphasizes components, and the psychick structures it produces have a systematic feel that reflects this emphasis:

Multi-channels	Computer graphics
Commercials	Pixels
Electronic components	Mixing
Blackout	Model variations
Station Identification	Scanning
Test pattern	Tracking
Edits	VCR/DVD, etc.

What is the intelligence of these configurations telling us? Remember that quantum mechanics, with its formula of indeterminacy, is crucial to the technology of television.

To take part in the TV experience as defined by normal/network standard, one must accept a passive role, excluded from the life and breath of these so-called events. This produces the strange alienation of the voyeur. This in itself is not "bad"; it's the way they make it seem as if there are no other possibilities. No questions, please!

Spellbound/hypno-teased are we. Always going away without the fulfillment of our desire (as promised?). Searching hopelessly. But the product we seek is not our desire. The process is a door to our desires. The TV set is process, not product. What is "put through" it is known as "programming."

TV is magick. Buttons, switch, channel, remote control, video. Yes, modern magickal lingo. The symbols of a new form of incantation, spell, ritual. Millions of people take daily part in a ritual of acceptance, passivity and the giving away of freedom and responsibility (the ability to respond).

165

TV must also work through subliminal and vibrational avenues. Who knows what the existence (exit stance) of TVs everywhere continually on is producing? The constant and relentless rein(force)ment of alien orders?

To deprogram is to "stop the world." TV is a tool for use or abuse, as are all the tools and toys of our time. What is powerful for control is also powerful for the Individual. Resistance is not necessary. No need to run away. Turn on, tune in, drop out. Imagination will sct you free. Stopping a world of conditioned behavior. No fight. Step off the merry go round. A rejection of TV is no use to me. Integration of TV is a way to free your mind's eye. TV is. We are. Imagine yourself. If you can see it in your mind's eye, you can see it in the TV eye.

Integration for Realization—Riot in Thee Eye The mind is trained to learn by example, not exhortation. To properly influence behavior, control does not plead and demand to "people, please do as we say." It simply shows others doing so and receiving praise and prizes. A dash of the herd mentality, and there you go.

I believe the roots of this magickal mystery lie in the masking of the real purpose of "art." It is not now, and has never been, mere entertainment. TV, video and cinema are rooted in old ritual. When we can understand and work with this process, then we can begin to re-claim lost parts of our ancient and eternal selves, lost in the process of "programming." We can free ourselves with the very tool of oppression.

TV is powerful because of the way it engages the senses. It comes on like a dream. You are caught in an alternate reality. The key, however, being that it is not supposed to be one of your own choice or creation. We are left speechless in the face of our lack, our passivity, our confusion. Unable to articulate the experience except for the smallest of details. Are we still trapped in someone else's bad dreams?

Video. Here the overwhelming power of TV can be transformed into a tool for anyone. This seems like a bit of trouble for the powers that be. They cannot cut us off because they are dependent on us, not the other way around as they like to think! So their survival depends on their ability to confuse, manipulate, divert, divide, conquer and control people. They use TV to push a philosophy of passivity. But the very fact that they must push contains the seed of their destruction. We can turn the situation upside down, and live our dreams.

TV as Magick and Religion Is the deification and worship of technology an excusable response to the automation of human perception? During the Harmonic Convergence, one New Ager took a television set with her to the top of Mt. Shasta, and then stunned other observers by announcing that the image of an angel had manifested itself on the screen. The next day, before a large media conglomeration, a repairman reactivated the phenomenon and explained that it was due to a simple mechanical defect. Press and skeptics ate the story up with glee, but a pertinent point was missed. Who cares whether this videoized vision was caused by an otherworldly being, an unconscious group will-force or a shorted wire? Is not the human neurostructure, by which sensory data is received, but a complex system of wiring and basic automated processes? Spontaneous visual hallucination used to be a purely human characteristic.

The future utilization of TV to transmit spiritual experience is an inevitable reality.

Our all-encompassing environment, which used to be nature, has become technology. Before Judeo-Christianity, all of Western man's religions were quite understandably based on his environment. Now that we have outgrown a flawed spiritual framework far removed from the principles of physical experience (and much worse off as a result), why not return to a religion more direct and in touch with the human condition? Because our environment is now self-created? Ah, but that is to be the hook of this new world faith... Evolution is gracing us with the powers of creation and destruction we once projected out onto gods, or perhaps we are just realizing them latent within our psyches, the restless energies responsible for the seed of all spiritual thought... And so the medium is, indeed, the message.

Through these information and communication technologies, humanity has taken its most subjective inner experiences and offered them up replicated into the mass "meme pool" of perceptual stimuli. In doing so we have structured a gestalt of human reality, partially bridging the vast chasms between each universe of consciousness commonly known as a person. Actually, we have recreated (in its own image) the gestalt for, accepting either the spiritual notion of ultimate unity or the quantum energy grid of modern physics, we are beyond temporal impressions all one network of being. In other words, we have unconsciously, but faithfully, fulfilled (in our own little way) the creative principle within us by embodying its essence and carrying it forth. In one respect, TV sets and hi-fi stereos have accomplished in a few years what organized religion has been striving toward for thousands.

167

Imagine a DVD Tarot, in which all sequences may be shuffled. How many more corresponding attributions and possibilities for subjective impressions would be instantly at our grasp in a short effects segment than in a small playing card? Imagine TV ritual. The point of ceremony in spiritual traditions exo- and esoteric is to trigger inner experience through extraordinary sensory input. The potential of today's visual media for revolutionizing this ancient transformative art, their technical advances making possible both the creation of virtually any image—and their accessibility to anyone—is obvious. And, of course, the technology will only improve, forging new pathways.

It is true that these communication systems are, for the most part, effecting today the polar opposite of enlightenment. This condition has provided some rare opportunities, however. Televisions are incredibly prolific. Most of the population is used to watching them for long periods of time. From an evolutionary perspective, this can be seen as an "easing in" to a more vital project. Today's "living room" has become a TV viewing room, as is evident by the placement of the set and the rest of the furniture in relation to it; an objective observer would probably assume these devices fulfill a religious function already. The notion of "TV as altar" is not new, but once again becomes relevant. We enshrine our video consoles the way we used to enshrine our god-images. In the cathode ray then, may be the channel we must find. A true network to tune in, the remote control of an infinite, viewing its illusory passion plays on a plane of static radiation—are we the image on the screen?

168

TV Snow Here television's application as a type of unconscious mirror for scrying is exposed. This type of working, as well as its use in cut-ups, were the main ideas that were sent in to us. There is much more to be explored, though. An important task in contemporary magick is redefining psychick uses of existing structures. Seemingly abandoned locations such as TV snow can be taken over and used by the magician. A psychick graffiti zone. Infiltrate community channels, using night-time filler shows such as one consisting of a camera taking a complete journey on a subway train; these can be salvaged for use in ritual.

The impression I get from TV snow images is that they may form a consistent language, with a specific vocabulary of images due to the limited parameters of TV (as opposed to the structures of dreams) and the repetitiveness of the images. Are these images the same to people in completely different circumstances?

What I do is tune into a non-broadcasting channel and stare at the "snow," trying to look at one point, usually near the center of the screen.

After a time, moving patterns start to emerge from the "snow," like spinning mandalas, or large colonies of black ants dancing circuitously into their burrow. Eventually I begin to see several layers of things going on behind this. I can focus on any one layer, but not for long, as there is so much info. It's rather like watching five or six films projected one on top of the other, in layers, and trying to pick out one film. I can see topographical landscapes going by very quickly as if flying over a continent. Deserts and sparse vegetation seem to be prevalent. Also scenes from everyday life—houses, people, cars, etc...

Groups of people dancing and twirling, columns of marching men—it's an awful lot like the DreamMachine with my eyes open. To stop all the images, all I have to do is refocus my eyes on some other part of the room. The TV snow hallucinations seem very connected to the current regular programming. Many of the images and moods seem like the original templates of the programming.

Turn on a TV to a non-transmitting channel. Adjust the contrast, color and tint to a desired setting. Then add a strobe light. The strobe helps to speed up the process and makes everything a bit weirder. Also, that warped warbelling sound the stations transmit before going over to static can help bend your mind, especially if you turn it on full blast and let go.

169

Ambient Television If television has a unique ability to penetrate our unconscious, how can the Individualist regain control over it? One possible solution is to render it trivial. Things are most easily trivialized through such frequent repetition that they become commonplace. A television left on long enough becomes furniture, not entertainment! Stacks of TVs all tuned to a different channel make it impossible to concentrate on a single linear program; one finds that one's eyes roam from set to set. And this with as few as three sets.

I took one black and white TV set:

Contrast. Vertical hold. Horizontal hold. Permutated. Image tripled.

The constant flickering image, constantly changing. The magick moments, when captured, can be visually stimulating. When stared into, colors appear. Hues of blue, green, yellow and red. In the dark, back to the set, the flickering light produces rapid, strobe-like shadows. My set is placed in one corner of my bedroom. It has been running continuously for over two years, never shut off.

Tune the vertical, horizontal hold and contrast so that it appears that only one-third of the image is visible. Actually the whole image is there, tripled, each overlapping.

With eyes open, the picture can be amusing and amazing. My set is tuned to the local religious channel. Not to be sacrilegious, that's too easy, but that's where the most interesting pictures are, scriptures typed on the screen permutate, the Christian cross tripled becomes Psychick.

I applied the Dreamachine method, eyes closed—the connection being *flicker*. My first attempts were fruitless. Then one day I could see. A strange sense of depth was noticed, as if I was viewing from the back of my head out to my eyelids. The whirling picture seemed to engulf my head; the only colors noticed were grey and blue. This doesn't work all the time, it seems the harder I try the less I see. Utilize the brightness control, too. Some side effects—my eyelids twitched a lot at first (cathode ray interference?) and a slight headache.

Television Cut-Ups Camouflage. Cut-up produced by channel-surfing; the images appear to be following your train of thought, as if trying to keep up with you by feeding back symbols appropriate to your present thought. Using association blocks to create a bridge between your thoughts and the flow of imagery. TV watching often becomes emotionally intense during this procedure. (Also, putting only the soundtrack of TV without the visuals through a stereo can provide valuable insights into control.)

Flow.

Is the image more real than we? Cut it up, let's see.

We are starting to tape specific commercials and parts of programs which could be psychically stimulating one way or another....

Get several screens and put on each the most weirded-out images you can find or get on video or DVD and zone out on all the stimuli. The weirder the better. The addition of music equally as bizzare only adds to the experience.

Television and video are ideally suited for the cut-up method, incorporating as they do both the milieu of sound and visuals. It is interesting to interchange the audio and visual portions of two or more different programs and watch the conflicting messages you are then exposed to. Which sense do you assign more validity to?

Cut-ups of video can be of great use in ritual, too. If something is desired, you can record various images of it from television. When you have "captured" enough raw images, proceed to cut them up, splicing the images together randomly, either with the original soundtracks, random soundtracks from other raw footage or with a special soundtrack of your own device. This could also be randomly cut in with footage of yourself attaining your desire either symbolically or as working toward your goal. I find it very important in video sigils to have images of myself included in the footage. This serves to personalize the video, to take the power latent in video away from the big corporations and consecrate it to *me*.

171

By flicking the channels around, one often gets an impression of synchronicity, that the audio signals one receives are, in some sense, inter-related with one's actions and/or feelings in *real time*. This feeling is further heightened when multiple televisions are used, with the television putting out the audio blacked out and a TV tuned to another station being viewed.

Most people utilize their televisions in a very rigid, linear way. They tune in one specific channel and watch passively. But if one begins to view the TV as a mirror, useful both for scrying (astral) and divinatory ("fortune-telling") purposes, one will find that much of the "bad vibe" associated with television has disspated; it can even be turned around to become a potent shamanic ally. Cut-up TV is decontrolled TV, is big business castrated of its control patterns, the patterns through which we as viewers/consumers are manipulated. Through the break-up of these patterns, we are able to free the airwaves of their inherent *objectivity*, and reclaim them as subjective reflections of our own thoughts.

One of the biggest complaints about current television is that it allows for no participation by the viewer. It is soporific in that it allows for no challenges or ambiguities to a watcher. Even complex issues such as the Middle East are reduced to one-and-one-half minute "stories." The current half-hour to one-hour format of traditional television "programming" allows for no real character development or subtleties of plot. The characters, even on a "quality" program like Hill Street Blues, are hopelessly shallow in comparison to even the most shallow people in "real life." The cut-up method offers a childishly simple means of re-introducing abstraction and subjectivity, *depth*—back into a media notorious for its lack thereof.

TV Ritual—Sets and Scripts As has already been mentioned, a lot more goes into television program than the final, edited version we watch. A set is constructed. A set could be compared to a temple, or Thee Nursery. It is a place designed with a particular function in mind—in the case of TV sets, usually to create an illusion. All ritual spaces are sets in a way. They are constructed to perform a specific purpose, and are constructed with that purpose in mind. If you notice the set on a TV sitcom, for example, you can notice the tedious attention to detail—a small stack of unanswered mail on the mantlepiece, all the cooking utensils on the countertops, a little bit of dirt on the floor (they're only human...). This is done to complete the illusion that this set, in reality a moveable plywood shell, is somebody's home. Set and setting.

It is with exactly this attention to detail that the magician constructs her ritual space. She knows that if any detail remains to remind her of the so-called mundane aspects of her life, her ritual will lose much of its power.

Once the set is constructed, a production crew needs a storyboard, a

series of drawings which plot out both the movements of the characters and the zooms, pans and angles of the various cameras. The verbal
"lines" of the actors, as well as any music or other sound effects, are written out or described on the bottom of each board.

Thus, each portion of a scene is meticulously plotted out, in such a way
that each member of the crew can see her role in the production.

Anyone who has ever read magickal instructions for a ritual, such as
a Gnostic Mass, will recognize that a grimoire is essentially a storyboard. However, a storyboard is much more effective as a mnemonic
device, as it describes the "plot" not only verbally, but also visually.
Each sequence is described in terms of the "actors," the "observers" (or
cameras) and the accompanying sounds or speech.

It can be extremely useful to plot out a ritual in a story board format.
First, it allows no room for ambiguity as to who is to do what when.
It also allows the magician to see her ritual from the perspective of
a camera, a bird's eye view, if you will, of exactly what will be happening. It allows for far greater considerations into the aesthetical
aspects of the "production," placing a greater emphasis on symmetry
and staging. A good ritual is similar to a good TV program—it causes
a "suspension of disbelief" vital to creating change. It must create
an illusion, to make something possible that, without good staging,
would not be plausible.

Say you want to make money. Create a set that looks like a bank
vault, or a giant hundred dollar bill. Videotape a gorgeous man rolling
around in a pile of play money (need not be real, only green, if you
are from the U.S.). The magician can make this man, rather than the
money, the object of her desire. The money is already subliminally associated to the man through the video shot. A brief narration can be
voiced over, or an evocative song; you could even invent some sort of
dialogue, perhaps the man could be lustfully moaning the magician's
name and his desire for her.

A technique I have worked with is to use the presence of a camera to
prolong the agony, as it were, of a sexual working. As you excite each
part of a partner's body, take a break to videotape that particular spot,

173

both before and during stimulation. You'll be amazed at how sensuous it is to caress your lover with the camera's eye. You can zoom in on your favorite features at will, pause to excite a part and videotape the result. A body can become a vast, mysterious landscape, and the act of lust become a Hollywood feature. It can also be used later as an excellent link to either mentally re-create that moment, or to draw the lover closer again.

The sense of detachment from an event, which one might even be participating in oneself, is one of the oddest phenomena of video I have yet encountered. One literally becomes a voyeur into one's own life and actions. Videotaping a ritual is nearly synonymous with objectivity.

And these, admittedly unrefined, examples need not be the end of it. The videotape could then be put on a TV set and played back as a centerpiece for a more traditional money-making ritual. The possibilities are unexplored, therefore endless. And it can go on and on, continually videotaping layer after layer of superimposed videotape ritual until one finally has on one tape the accumulated documentation of perhaps dozens of individual rituals, or shoots.

174

This process is analogous to the old alchemical principle of "solve et coagula," of constantly sublimating (note the similarity to "subliminal," a major factor in unconscious recall) originally base matter into "gold."

Indeed, given the power that TV seems to exert over people and their lives, the old alchemical maxim "as above, so below" takes on a whole new meaning. She who rules the airwaves, rules the minds of men...

The Language of Advertising As mentioned earlier, television is a language of its own. The real content of television is not in the programs; they are merely "bait" to get us to watch the ubiquitous advertisements. It almost seems as though TV programs are deliberately made as dull and unchallenging as possible, to lull us into a sort of hypnotic trance, so that we are thus rendered more susceptible to the commercials. Commercials have their own unique language, too, and an amazing amount of research has been done into what sorts of advertising strategies are most likely to persuade us.

It might be useful to take a look at some of the factors in advertising that have been found to influence consumers:

Information content
Brand/product identification
Setting
Visual and auditory devices
Promises/appeals/propositions
Tone/atmosphere
Comparisons
Music and dancing
Structure and format
Characters
Timing and counting measures (for example, length or number of times the brand name is shown or mentioned).

Many of these methods are very reminiscent of old ceremonial magick rituals; for an excellent crossreference too lengthy to get into here, see Magick in Theory and Practice by Aleister Crowley, chapter two. The main thrust of my argument is that advertising jargon is a magickal language. It can be used to affect or program the unconscious mind. Advertisements are constructed in exactly the same way that rituals are, using mnemonic devices very similar to the qabalah. I do not consider this to be a theory—I take it to be a fact. If you have any doubts about this basic assumption, go to your library and read through some books on telemarketing techniques.

Start watching advertisements. Pay close attention to the logic of them. You will begin to notice that hardly any of them really make any logical sense. A typical example: Everyone knows that oxitone fights cavities. Crust toothpaste has oxitone. So it has the power to keep cavities away. Now it has not been actually stated that oxitone does, in fact, fight cavities—you are led to think that you are stupid for *not* knowing this. It is also not stated *how much* oxitone it takes to fight cavities. Nor is the extent of this "cavity fighting" ever defined. So we are left with a total non-sequitur. What, at first appearance, is a very informative advertisement turns out, on closer examination, to say absolutely nothing. It is a conjuror's trick, a sleight-of hand maneuver.

175

It is in this realm of tricking the unconscious into accepting the impossible as *facr* that the traditional magician has always worked. And, although Madison Avenue may have updated the language and hardware, the essential technique, philosophy and approach would be very familiar to any magician of the past. A contemporary magician, if she has any desire to be such in anything other than name alone, would do well to learn how to apply these updated methods of unconscious persuasion to her ritual methods. Many of them are supported by the latest research into psychology and neurolinguistics, as well as proving their effectiveness through consumer response.

A lot of money goes into marketing research. *Somebody* must be getting results from this form of magick.

Video Fragments Get or rent a video camera, one that has a negative/reversal switch on it so that you can make the picture negative. Point the camera at the TV screen while monitoring. You will discover an astral tunnel in black and white. Now turn the camera ever so slightly and observe! With practice you can see every geometric pattern under and in the sun—an almost infinite variety of symbols all fluctuating, all changing constantly. The effect is enhanced even more if you turn the color up to high contrast during the experiment. By various spinning methods (i.e. rotating the camera as if the lens were a pivot) and very slight adjustments of the zoom lens you will have hours and hours of mesmerized fun and trance. Video feedback has another application. Take a small picture, no bigger than 10% of your total screen area, and stick it onto your TV. In this manner, you can immediately add visual images to the splendorous kaleidoscope of colors, and these images will also feed back infinitely. You have to see this effect to believe it! Why it has never been used in promotional videos, especially in the '60ss I will never know.

This technique sounds as if it would lend itself perfectly to the sigil process, a symbol of desire being placed on the screen and multiplied by video feedback. A hypnotic aid to concentration. Also, favorite patterns and configurations could easily be videotaped and saved for documentation as well as future rituals.

Conclusion Television magick is certainly an area of the occult deserving more attention and research. Hopefully, this modest beginning will be enlarged upon through experiments and communication inspired by this first effort. Reading through this text, it is obvious that we have not even properly scratched the surface.

Coyote 3 [Tom Hallewell] Denver, TOPYN.A., 1989

THEE REVOLVER AS MAGICKAL WAND

The handgun is not exclusively an instrument of death. Through its use, the hand (Will) can be merged with the eye (Imagination). It is thus a tool for magick whose usefulness in the occult has, to the best of my knowledge, never been explored. So let's take a look at some of the symbolism behind the words, actions and characteristics of handgun use. For the purposes of this short essay, we will consider only the revolver, because it retains six (solar) shells to be ejected at will after firing. The word "shell" translates into Hebrew as "Qlipoth," the hollow beings that inhabit the shadowy region between day and night, Spare's "Neither-Neither." Spent shell casings, being the "dead head" after firing at a desire, make excellent souvenirs or talismans of a ritual. After firing, they can be used as talismans for sigils to excellent effect. The actual name "revolver" implies the circles of time exemplified by Kali. The revolver thus makes some very direct connections to esoteric Tantric practices.

177

We will now give an example of practical handgun magick. On a large piece of paper, symbolize a desire as the center of a target. Then symbolize the *action* necessary to attain the desire on a very small piece of paper, such as a rolling paper. Anoint both as you would any sigil, focusing all your attention on the achievement of your goal. Then take an unfired shell and remove the copper-jacketed slug. Pour out about half of the powder. Wad the small sigil into a little ball and drop it into the shell. You may wish at this point to mark the outside of the shell with a design which symbolizes the completion of desire. Pour the rest of the powder on top of your symbol. You now have your desire lying surrounded by gunpowder (fire or Mars) contained within brass (Mercury); this symbolizes active magical Will. Replace the slug on the shell casing. Your active Will is now capped by lead (Saturn) enclosed within a copper (Venus) jacket. There is actually a second cap beneath (as above, so below) which ignites Mars to begin the magical process (the primer cap) as well as the cap above which completes the process. The cap is a symbol of Mercury. So we see that Mercury begins, ends and encloses the desire at hand.

Into the soft lead of the slug tip, carve a design, which when united with the symbol on the target, will render success inevitable. You are now ready to begin your ritual.

Place the target in the direction that you think best symbolizes the intent of your working. Draw a magick circle around you and face the direction of the target. Turn one direction clockwise and vibrate a name that you associate with that direction (I personally use N-Earth "Coyote," E-Air "Nrsimhadev," S-fire "Kali," W-Water "Atargatis" [a mermaid].) You could just vibrate the name of the element symbolized by that direction. Then fire one shot at the horizon in that direction. Repeat this process until you reach the fourth direction, the direction of your target or desire. Now vibrate the object of the target or anything else that will focus your entire conciousness on the goal.

Cock.

Aim carefully. Unite the *hand* (Zos) with the *eye* (Kia). Breathe with yogic regularity and relaxation.

Squeeze the trigger. While exhaling, *see* the symbol on the front of your slug splatter hot lead onto the object of desire as you *squeeze*, not pull, the trigger—the catalyst, union of hand and eye. To pull the trigger is like sticking your finger in your eye. *Squeeze* the trigger; *see* the hand and eye merge, your Will flatten against your desire, puncturing it. Trigger dents primer ignites powder burning desire pushing Venus jacketed Saturn slug home to desire and Will united. *Hear the report.* Nothing left now but the paperwork—the *report. See* the muzzle flash. *Smell* the cordite (Saturn), the burned up resistance.

In conclusion, remember all the active, fire, *phallic* symbolism in the handgun. A silver, nickel plated gun symbolizes the moon in her fertile, creative Artemis phase. A blued (black) handgun represents the moon in her dark menstrual destructive Kali phase. Thought and "target practice" will elicit many more connections and applications. A heavy cap gun or blanks can be used indoors in any ritual to replace the archaic wand.

Fire!
Coyote 3 Denver

‡

BRIDGE MAGICK

Even before I became consciously involved in magick, the underside of bridges always produced very unusual mental states in me. These were interesting, but I wanted to see if I could come up with something more systematic/useful involving bridges.

The bridge is a structure which can seem abandoned, although still in use by traffic. Under a bridge there are columns and slopes and whatever else the terrain consists of, perhaps a river. The point is to redefine the use of the bridge, take over psychick structures. This lack of use parallels the place of magick in the unused parts of our brain. Under certain bridges there is a feeling of stepping past the usual confines of the social/historical model daily life is crippled under.

179

The Scandinavians had trolls, magickal beings who lived in tunnels and under bridges. You don't actually have to live under a bridge or inside a subway tunnel to make use of them in a ritual. Why should the magician have any resemblance to robed figures carrying wands and tracing pentagrams, especially since so many have covered this area before? Finding something that works for you is the most important part, the figuring out can come later. Everyone has something unique to themselves and their situation that can be used in a ritual. Redefining and personalizing found junk is another suggested technique along these lines (scrap metal, abandoned electronics, used packaging, dead animals).

When I started becoming obsessed with bridges one of the things I did was to paint graffiti on supporting columns. These were highly charged, very personal images which came spontaneously at the site. I did all sorts of strange things after that, the images seemed to unleash all sorts of wild energy. Later I heard about the function of totems in certain tribes and how it related to growing up in a tribal society—rites involving the transference of the youth's soul to his totem. This accomplishes the "death" of the youth. With infusion of life from the totem the youth's system gradually recovers. Each time I returned to my graffiti/totems, it seemed I was tapping into some powerful timeless energy. It was as if I was drawing information through the drawing itself from the perceptions of the bridge. The bridge was a reservoir. Perhaps the whole valley system in which I found these bridges, carved and shaped unconsciously by city planners and developers, is a contemporary equivalent of the totems of aboriginal tribes. The "information society" contains an intelligence most of its "cells" are unaware of.

Ritual use of the outdoors seems natural in North America. For me, growing up in Canada, the outside has always held a strong magnetism. In Europe it's probably quite difficult to find areas to conduct private rituals outside, practically impossible in cities. Most North American cities, on the other hand, have generous tracts of land allocated for parks, etc.

180 Taking the plunge. Jumping off bridges has always been a popular way to commit suicide, reinforcing the image of the bridge as a gateway between different worlds. In Carlos Castaneda's books on Yaqui Indian magic, jumping off a cliff was a major initiation—you either assembled yourself at a different location or you died (or if you were a very advanced seer you would disappear into another dimension).

Of course there is a reason why most "normal" people would rather jump off a bridge than conduct a ritual under one. The Roman word pontifex, from which Pontif originates, means "builder of bridges." A pope was meant to be a bridge between two worlds. On the other side of the good/evil coin, devils were reputed to particularly enjoy taking part in the construction of bridges back in the Middle Ages (for payment in cats). The Israelites made the bridge into a sign of the covenant between God and his people, and in China it was the sign denoting the union of Heaven and Earth.

Can a figurehead really be *your* bridge? TOPY is not a substitute religion, it is a receptive place for experiences and ideas which would otherwise have no place, no place in modern society and no place in a culture which exalts

itself above organic processes. Here we can reclaim ourselves and reject the fossilized totems of power, money and fear inherited from the past.
The Abominable TV Snowman TOPYN.A.

IS MAGICK REALLY FOR ALL?

A Re/Introduction to TOPY The word "magick" is so open to misinterpretation that one wishes one could find a substitute word that covered all the implications that the former implies. Neurology, physics, art—to name a few—all come close, but not one of them encompasses all the implications of the others, which "magick" does. Like it or not, we are more or less forced to us the old nomenclature for the purposes of this book, at the risk of evoking unpleasant encounters with past manuals on contemporary "magick." We will show our distaste for the word by framing it in "quotation marks" throughout the course of this work.

This book has high hopes. We are going to try and change the way you look at and define the "occult." It might be traumatic for some people, as we have no intention of going "by the book," this work ought to stand alone. We are going to begin with the assumption that there is really nothing "magical" about "magick" at all—what we call by that name are actually long-neglected abilities that *anyone* can develop. This will be discussed in greater detail in the first chapter.

For hundreds of years (at least), English writers have assumed that their readers are male. We feel that this disenfranchises a large number of potential readers, so one subtle "magickal" exercise we will perform throughout this book is to linguistically exclude *males* for once. Maybe you'll see what it's like being on the other side of the fence! Needless to say, this book is intended for both genders.

We think this is a radical project—there is nothing to memorize, no "exercises" to do; in fact, we aren't going to ask that you do *anything at all*, just read the words that are in this book, the ideas contained in them are food for thought, not seedlings to be transplanted; rather, seeds to be sown on the fertile ground of your own imagination. Our only hope is that they take root and flower!

181

Is "Magick" Really for All? "Magick" is generally portrayed as a very difficult process. It takes years of study to make any real progress, one must learn many complex terms and memorize ornate rituals—often in foreign languages—and collect piles of musty grimoires. No wonder there are so few accomplished "magicians"—it sounds like pretty hard, tedious work! How many people have given up "magick" in despair, knowing that they'll *never* be able to pronounce "IHVH" properly?

We're not trying to discredit the more esoteric aspects of the occult by any means, but it also seems like a true "magickal" system, if it is to be valid, *has* to be written in the language of the day. If "Goddess" hasn't learned English by now, She can hardly help you get a job at Burger King! The alchemists were often considered to be heretics when they suggested that one could become enlightened with the aid of the most "high-tech" tools available—it is laughable (sort of...) that so-called "modern magick" is still using the tools treasured by the "cutting-edge" magicians of the Sixteenth Century.

182

One reason "magick" is so maligned by "science" is because it is so far behind the realities of modern life. When was the last time you drove a chariot to work—or even saw a live horse, for that matter? Modern Woman's dreams are filled with video, computers, guns automobiles and spandex—not robes, candles and swords! A contemporary system of "magick" has to incorporate these new gestalts, or it belongs in a museum, with all the other artifacts.

Traditionalists will argue that these later patterns lack the sanctity of the older ones; however, it is equally certain that many old soldiers felt that there was something "effeminate" about rifles, so they died trying to spear their adversaries!

In any case, there can be no doubt that technology is probably going to go a lot further *forward* before it goes back, so a wise "magician" will accustom herself to these new tools. For it to be truly useful, not just an affectation, "magick" must use the most readily available tools—tools that we *already* know how to use. If the sword was the tool of the knight, then the computer console is the weapon of today's secretary.

In preliterate times, Woman dealt with her surroundings on a much less objective level than most of us do now. She watched patterns in nature, and detected some sort of pattern behind it all. Before some man (almost certainly the first scientist) called it "God," people's "magick" consisted of trying to "second-guess" nature's cause and effect by imitating the first step in an observed chain of events. This intuitive level of influencing events is far from primitive, in fact, this book is all about the process of combining knowledge with intuition and energy to bring about change.

There are many people who are afraid of the potential we *all* have within us. We contend that there should be no "secrets" if "magick" really is for all. Many books begin with long lectures about the "karmic" repercurssions of using this potential to manipulate the lives and desires of others. We say, if that's *really* what you're in it for, do it! We think that you'll find out soon enough that you have your hands full dealing with your *own* life. We don't like scare tactics, don't be "nice" out of fear, do it out of convenience—life's too short to be sticking pins in voodoo dolls!

In short, this book *really is* for *all*, your nervous system and your environment are a vast playground, so let's play some new games!
It might be said that "magick" exists for two reasons:

183

  1 To make oneself more sensitive to subtle stimuli.
  2 To strengthen oneself, spiritually and physically.

Begin to listen. Pay attention to the patterns in your life. You might try carrying around a pocket-sized tape recorder and record everything that seems significant. Capture the sounds in your life. Many sounds are capable of triggering intense emotional reactions. Tape fights, gospel meetings, sirens, friends talking, wild parties, tape yourself having sex. Tape everything you can, and *listen to it* afterwards. What feelings does it bring out? You may, in hindsight, find that you have *accidentally* recorded some rather significant, or at least peculiar, events. You will probably find that your memory of a given conversation or event does not match your recording of it.

For some reason, to record an event—in any medium—is, in a sense, to deify it—to raise it above other events. Brion Gysin mentions this frequently in regards to writing—once something is recorded, it becomes Truth. The record outlasts our memories. Tapes don't lie. Tapes also have a way of "taking you back" to an event. Push a button and you're there again.

Use the tapes to analyze the sequences of events or behavior that lead to success, and those that lead to failure. *What* was it you said to that boy in the bar that had him following you the rest of the night? What did you do to get your sister so angry at you? Learn to detect the meanings *behind* the words people say, study the inflections, the choice of words. This is a truer divination than you'll ever get from a deck of cards!

In a very real sense, you have begun to capture pieces of time. Later, you can restring them, like beads, into a pattern more pleasing to you. Pick pieces that have significance, that are part of a larger pattern you want to use. Splice (or re-record) them randomly, and play them back. This technique may be familiar to you—it's the cut-up method.

By applying the powers of time-capture and cut-ups, we are able, in a way, to short-circuit linear time and create a sort of "eddy," where time is swirling, as it were, rather than traveling in a straight line. It is in these outwardly trivial paradoxical states that "magick" seems to work best.

184

Test your limits. How long can you go without food? Sleep? Sex? Push yourself—find out what your physical body is capable of. Many of us get in a lot of trouble by over– or underestimating our thresholds. There is nothing quite as frustrating as finding that one's body is simply *incapable* of performing simple commands due to fatigue, loss of sleep, hunger, etc.

Actively seek out your fears, and find a way to face them. It may not be possible to conquer them altogether, but try to loosen the grip they have over your behavior. Try to get to the point where they no longer influence decisions.

Try being *completely* honest with someone, tell them your deepest fantasies, fears, hopes, dreams. Don't try to cover up any character flaws, expose your very *soul* to them.

Allow a certain amount of time each day to just meditate on how you would like your life to be. Would you want a car, would you eat mat, smoke, drink? Do you want a job? A boyfriend? What kind of clothes would you wear? You will find as you continue that everything begins to fall into place, there are less uncertainties. You change your mind less each day. Is that your true will, then? Time will tell…

These are just a few suggestions, it would be better if you find your own way to explore these areas. The taping exercise is basically a way to examine the outer world—your environment, the others are to explore the inner—yourself. There are an infinite number of ways to do it—the key is to do it regularly.

These preliminary exercises are just a means by which to familiarize yourself with the territory we are about to explore in detail.

THEE SPIDER PATH

In many cultures, animals were observed and their traits imitated. The spider is one example, she is usually portrayed as an archetype of feminine power—with good reason. The female is often as much as *ten times* bigger and much more aggressive than her male counterpart! Spiders are one of the truly omnivorous species around, which means that a male might become a *meal* rather than a mate, if he isn't careful! Needless to say, he has evolved a very careful courtship sequence.

185

Before seeking out a female, the male spins a small mat and essentially masturbates onto it. He then dips his antenna-like front appendages, called palps, into the semen on the mat, coating them with his seed. He then seeks out a female's web, and taps out an elaborate beat on it, to (hopefully) convey to his prospective partner that he is a date rather than a snack. If the female doesn't immediately eat him, he then performs an entrancing dance which (again hopefully) in effect, hypnotises the female into allowing him to insert his sperm-soaked palps into her, by then, waiting organ. He then takes his leave as soon as etiquette allows, female spiders seem to enjoy a light meal after sex.

There are a number of points of "magickal" interest here, first the idea of ejaculating before, rather than during, intercourse. This theoretically enables both parties to charge a sigil *prior* to the actual coupling, thus the sexual act itself becomes a "magickal" mixture of "elixirs" collected previously, devoid of lust.

Secondly, the male inserts the semen with an organ incapable of sexual arousal to himself, but very capable of exciting his partner. As many people might have noticed, the male of our species is usually worn out about the time the female really starts "humming." By imitating the spider, humen are able to train themselves to put the pleasure of the woman first, as he has, literally, already "taken care of himself."

The mere act of manually implanting the seed in the female is an interesting act both of discipline and will for the male; it is not often that male sexuality takes a background role in our sexual pastimes. There are a number of other interesting traits possessed by spiders: nearly all of them are venomous. This is a metaphor often used by Kenneth Grant and Michael Bertiaux to denote sexual secretions that some tantric adepts collect from the glands of their sexual partners. It is thought that certain points of the body secrete certain pheromones, which are subtly changed during periods of intense fear, pain or arousal. Many animals, particularly social species, are known to use pheromones to communicate, activate mating instincts and so forth. It therefore does not require a great deal of imagination to conclude that such processes, long forgotten, still exist in humans.

Many "magicians" believe that by stimulating certain points on the body they are able to induce the flow of such substances, and that secretions can be gathered from each different duct by exciting a specific nervous meridian in the body of their partner. Each duct produces a unique pheromone, called "kalas" by tantrics, which, in turn, possesses its own unique properties as a medicine, drug or poison. Initiates of this system recommend *extreme* caution in experimenting with it. They claim that accidental misuse of these substances can be disabling or even fatal! We have not heard of any such accidents, however; it could be a baseless justification of secrecy.

In any case, it is an interesting concept. The method of insemination used by the male spider seems an ideal method of exciting these nerve meridians, for the purpose of stimulating pheromonic secretions and then

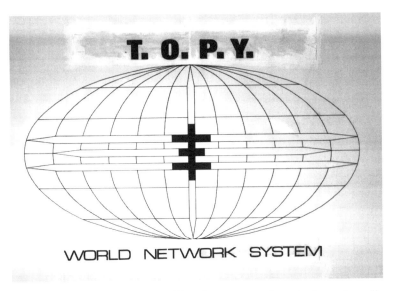

collecting them for future use. The idea is not too far away from the well-documented use of human adrenaline as a drug by a certain 1970s author.

By the way, the spider has no teeth for chewing food; the venom which she injects into her prey consists in part of a strong acid which, in a manner of hours, begins to convert bone to liquid. Her "saliva" is also a strong digestive fluid: with her powerful fangs, she tears a hole in her unfortunate victim's skeleton. She then sucks the innards of her victim out, leaving only a hollow shell of insoluble armor.

The other point of immediate interest about the spider is the fact that she weaves webs. Webs seem to be a really good "magickal" metaphor—they connect distant points to a center, they are very flexible, they can be used as communication devices (as we have seen with the approach of the perspective mate). They are also a combination trap and alarm system. During a ritual, one could select objects representing various desires or goals, place them around oneself, and then, using thread, weave a web connecting them all to the center. Visualizing oneself as a spider in the center of a very sticky, sensitive web might be a very effective form of psychic self-defense, if one worries about such things.

In literature a web is often used to represent eloquence with words; however, the web is a two-edged sword, as one is often trapped in them oneself! So also with the spider—if she falls into her own web, she can become entangled and perish along with the fly she intended as prey. Whenever one weaves webs, there is always the possibility of entrapping oneself in the process. In fact, the web is an excellent symbol for communication and networking in general, it is the best model for information-based relationships to be found in nature.

The web also implies a certain degree of anchoring and stability. Any "magician" who truly wishes to succeed in her endeavors must have a web of some sort, for security as well as communication and grounding.

By studying the attributes of various animals, one can gradually develop a personal Qabalah much more meaningful than learning the letters of some forgotten tongue, but this too is a forgotten language, at least for Womankind. We spoke it aeons ago, as we sat around campfires in the primal night of our dimmest past. Once we develop our ear to hear it once again, it calls out to us through the millennia; and its call, once answered, is hard to resist.

188

⊼

WHY DON'T YOU JUST ENJOY YOUR BODY?

The physical vehicle of the spirit/mind is the body—it is the only one you have! If you desire spiritual strength, it seems only natural that you should possess some degree of physical strength as well. One's dreams can't come true if one hasn't the physical strength to realize them.

Think of the type of lover that attracts you—handsome, muscular, well-groomed and intelligent. If you were him, would you be attracted to someone who did not share these characteristics? So many "magicians" take terrible care of their physical vehicle, and then wonder why the Adonis they lust after never calls! Nobody wants to make love to someone who is flabby and listless due to lack of exercise!

We feel that a *crucial* part of any magician's daily discipline should be some form of physical exercise—it is crucial that the shape of one's body reflect the discipline within. Our society is based on the way things appear to be, so work to embody on the outside the traits you are working hard to engender on the inside. Strength, sensuality, discipline, to name a few.

You will find that improving your physical condition is very rewarding in many ways—you will become more disciplined, have a great deal more energy and stamina, both at work and play, you will be more conscious of what you are putting in your body, such as alcohol, tobacco, drugs, caffeine, junk food; and, perhaps most importantly, you will be more attractive and radiate good health to those around you.

It is said that our lives are a constant race against inevitable decay and death; though many of us are too young to feel the approach of middle age, the race is on. If you can get a head start on it, you'll be glad, as you grow older and exercise becomes more necessary, to have developed the requisite discipline early in life.

Don't get us wrong, we're not trying to turn you into a bodybuilder or health food fanatic! We're just pointing out that there are so many more possibilities open to a person who is well-toned and vigorous physically than to a person who is not. It is crucial that a "magician" have a good self-image. And most often, that self-image is not as good as it could be if you don't like the body you see in the mirror. It is the function of "magick" to change what we don't like—it's high time we started doing some "magick" on our own flabby, tired bodies!

Experiment with your body—try stimulating (or better yet, have *someone else* stimulate) points on your body. You will notice that stimuli on some points excite you and others repel you. Mark these points down somewhere, they are very important in certain forms of sexual "magick"!

You have surely noticed that, in much religious art of all cultures, that particular emphasis is given to the posture of the hands; Christ is often depicted with his thumb and ring finger touching, and the two in between extended, this is meant to be a benediction. Take a while and try to think what each of your fingers represent. What do you use your various fingers for? As an example, if you are right-handed, your probably point *only* with that finger. So you could say that your right index finger is your projective finger, similar to a magick wand. The index finger of your dominant hand is most likely your dominant finger.

Try touching the tip of your dominant finger with the tips of each of the other fingers on that hand. Can you feel a difference in the "energy field" of your hand when you change? Also try extending, bending and clenching the remaining fingers while you are touching one with your index finger. Again, you will probably notice subtle differences.

The Hindus were great students and practitioners of sacred gestures, which they called "mudras." They attributed each finger to a planet; even the palm was thus associated. They believed that, by combining these planetary influences, one could create subtle changes in one's "aura" that could make one more open to particular forces or ideas.

Austin Osman Spare was also a great believer in the power of gesture and posture to influence one's receptivity to specific currents. Based on Hindu yoga techniques, he developed a series of positions of what he termed the "death posture." These consisted of either unnaturally compressing or extending the body or the hand. By concentrating on these postures, practicing them, and eventually being able to hold them effortlessly, one is able to induce slightly (and not-so-slightly) altered states of consciousness. For some reason, these states are very conducive to "magickal" work.

190

A note is perhaps necessary here. While we neither condemn nor condone drug use, we do feel that the goal of the magician should be to attain drug-like states without the use of drugs. We have found discipline and focus to be very difficult to maintain while under their influence. A sloppy "magician" is generally not a terribly successful one. Health and legal complications can also cause one a great deal of trouble, trouble that can easily be avoided by "just saying no."

In order to be relevant to people today, "magick" has to be relevant to the prevailing conditions of today. We suggest that you study everything you can find on the various "magicks" and religions of the past; but rather than take them as whole systems, we recommend that you take out only what you find interesting or useful. Keep a "reading diary" and write down, *in your own words*, what interests you in every book you read. This practice need not be confined to non-fiction works; in many works of fiction, especially sci-fi, extremely useful "magickal" concepts are suggested. If you don't write them down, you *will* forget them, or, at best, your memory of them will be garbled and of little practical use.

Use everything for your rituals—if you like the way a Hare Krsna altar is constructed, then use it! That doesn't mean that you have to deal with Hindu archetypes or godforms—go on your intuition—we can't know what symbols and exercises are going to be most useful to you, only you do—*experiment* with anything that catches your attention, *be eclectic!*

In order to be a competent "magician" today requires that you have some conception of scientific knowledge. This, to us, seems of a *lot* more value as a foundation than memorizing a lot of long-neglected pantheons and correspondences. Science and mathematics are the language of our time, whether you "like" them or not—ignore them, and you will be as obsolete as Baal!

Every function known can be expressed in mathematical terms. For example, to move a large object, you must apply a force greater than the forces already acting upon it. These forces include the inertial weight of the object, the drag factor, and so forth. Try to think of the things around you as equations rather than objects. Try and calculate how much energy you would need to generate to counteract the influence of gravity on a body of your weight.

191

This type of thought is useful for a number of reasons—first, it trains you to start thinking of the many influences and "laws" that surround any type of action; secondly, it makes you more observant. It also will, hopefully, get you to start thinking of "magick" as a process which can also be expressed mathematically, and you can start evolving your own formulae for solving various "magickal" problems.

If you are using mudras, or waving your hands around, try to visualize the effect your motions or gestures are having on the air around you. Try to "see" the molecules swirling toward you if you are trying to bring something towards you. If you are trying to "send" something, you would want the energy to swirl outward. However, the general goal of such operations as casting a circle at the beginning of a ritual are to generate a "cone of power" around the "magician." So it is pretty safe in any ritual to begin by trying to pack as much energy around you as possible.

One should always use a certain amount of caution when performing rituals to make things happen, as "magick" seems to attract the "monkey's paw syndrome"—that is, you almost always get what you ask for, but it often comes about in a most *inconvenient* manner. This effect can, in our experience, never be predicted or avoided, but can be minimized by being *very* clear about exactly what it is you want. If you have *any* doubts about the desire before the ritual, it would be best to wait and see if the second thoughts dispel before performing it.

There are countless cases of people performing spells for a certain person as a lover, only to discover that they not only can't stand him, but are also unable to get rid of him! This dilemma is reminiscent of the fairy tale about the farmer who got three wishes. Being a very simple man, he asked for a sausage. His wife, incensed by his trivial wish, wished it to be on his nose. They ended up using the last wish getting the accused thing off the poor farmer's nose. Likewise, one may find one's ritual time monopolized undoing rash or poorly planned desires, rather than making new ones.

So, at the risk of getting preachy, do give some thought to this—it can save you a lot of heartache and trouble to just be sure and word things in a very straightforward manner. If you don't want "Paul" calling you after your fling, then try and include a "no-strings" clause in your ritual.

After analyzing a number of such rituals, we have classified sigils into two loose categories: the *wish sigil* and the *will sigil*. The wish sigil is, as implies, a ritual aimed *outside*, at a specific person or event; to get a certain job, for example. The danger about wish sigils is that you might end up totally hating the job; plus, by merely wishing for that job, you have done nothing to make yourself more qualified to get a different job in the same field. You haven't done anything to yourself. You aren't a better bridge player—you merely stacked the deck for one hand!

The will sigil, on the other hand, aims to create a change in the practitioner to make attainment of a specific set of goals possible. She does not "ask" for specific things, rather she tries to develop the *skills* necessary to get what she wants, whenever she wants it. This seems to be a superior method all around; it enables the "magician" to not only get what she wants, but also gives her the ability to get the things she'll undoubtably want in the future as well. So she is developing her personality for the long term, as well as achieving short-term goals.

It might be a good idea to think of your desires in terms of what skills you lack to achieve them; as an example, there is a particular man you want to meet. Now wouldn't it be better to try and figure out how to be more aggressive, perhaps, so you can just walk up to him and introduce yourself? Because, long after *that* schmuck is forgotten, you will still be more aggressive and be able to introduce yourself to all kinds of *other* schmucks (pardon the cynicsm there)!

Perhaps you could think of yourself as the center of an energy whirlpool, with all that energy just lashing around you, waiting for you to absorb or send.
TOPY STATION Newsletter

193

OV EXCERCISE
Stuff to do to make you more capable and more relaxed Magickally

You may have noticed that books on magick, however interesting they are, eventually get onto the boring exercises which apparently you have to do every day in order to actually get on to the interesting magickal heights scaled by the experts. They're usually authoritarian about it, and the exercises tend to be deadly dull. They nearly put me off magick for life!

Well, I agree that it's a good idea to get hold of these skills. You'll feel more comfortable and more clear-headed as a result of them, and you'll be able to do ritual work more effectively. The whole thing will make a lot more sense, and you will, as the phrase has it, be able to Have Fun With Your Head. But I don't see why getting hold of these skills has to be so dull. When you talk to people who are dead good at magick, they always seem to have had a ball getting into this stuff. Why shouldn't the rest of us? But just what are these skills that we're talking about? Well, in roughly ascending order of difficulty, they are:

Centering
Meditation Visualisation

There's lots of stuff you can add on to these, but they mostly require these skills before you can do them, like the Qabalah, astral projection, skrying, etc. Let's take ourselves through these skills one at a time.

Centering This is very simple but it gets called all kinds of names. Basically it's easy—it's how you feel when you're comfortable, with the five regular senses kind of in a circle around you. You feel balanced and secure. You should always start off magick from here, and when you feel scared, under pressure, or uncertain, anywhere in your life, this is where you should be trying to get to. On one level, it's very "un-spooky" but the more deeply balanced and centered you feel, the more magickal you feel. That's why old occult texts call it names like "The Birthplace of the Soul"—it is, but it doesn't feel like it most of the time.

The fastest way of getting centered is to take deep breaths, sighing a little (or a lot if you can get away with it) as you exhale. Be aware of your stomach—if it feels tight or nervous, you've got to breathe deeper or longer. And mentally, it should feel like you're looking at your own reactions and thoughts, so that you can identify what's happening to your emotions. It's probably impossible to do this perfectly, unless you're an advanced yogi, but the process of trying to do it is enough to calm you, make you feel peaceful (or at least a lot more calm than you were five minutes ago). The point is to do it to a point which is "good enough" and you'll probably find it so enjoyable you'll keep at it. By the way, this technique is probably familiar to you—it gets taught by everyone from Evangelical Christians to Management Consultants and health workers. Still magick though!

Meditation Centering is essential but it's also pretty easy. Meditation is a bit harder but still not nearly as difficult as it's made out to be. You'll find it dead useful too. Meditation, in this basic sense, is training your mental muscles so you can focus your mind where your Will tells it to go. Basically, one is gently pushing away thoughts that you don't want in your head, so you can get more energy and peace from out of your center. Take away the static from the peace you felt when you were centering, and it expands, making you feel even better. The thing is, you have to decide you're going to do it, saying to yourself, "No, I'm not going to let that get in the way of my bit of peace and enjoyment."

Bear in mind, however, that you don't have to be in perfectly focused, Samhadic state every waking hour. Nor do you have to SMASH the extraneous thoughts out. Here's how:

> 1 Get yourself a reasonably quiet space. You need to feel confident that no-one will disturb you for, say, 15 minutes. Turn the lights down; if you can light it by candle, without the place getting too weird, so much the better.

> 2 Sit down in a comfortable straight-backed chair or against the wall. You probably shouldn't lie down. Just make sure you're not liable to drop off when you get going. If you can do it in a yoga position, or even the full lotus, that's great but it isn't strictly necessary.

> 3 Take at least ten deep, cleansing breaths with your eyes closed, while focusing on getting centered.

> 4 Now drift into the "velvety-blackness of non-thought," as one writer put it. Remember how you felt when you were simply captivated by a trancey piece of music? Or when you were daydreaming at school, looking out the window vacantly? That's the kind of thing we're aiming for. This time your brain will keep on feeding your consciousness with bits and bobs of memory, information, reminders, etc., as it tends to do. Your job now is to say to it, "No thank you, I'm not thinking about that, I'm thinking about this sensation of peace and calm coming from my relaxed body. Especially my stomach." And you should gently put the thought aside—you can always come back to it later, and your brain will supply it again, later, if it's that important—

195

and go back to thinking about the sense of peace which comes from your Center. Just keep on feeling balanced.

5 Drift along as long as you like. Don't worry if you keep on having to push away thoughts, this is only natural at first; just keep on trying to recapture that feeling of balance. If you're not enjoying it you're not doing it right! So aim for the feeling of balance, and keep trying to return to it.

6 When you've had enough, do a few more deep breaths to wake you up. If you want to use things like meditation videos, or even just a picture or sculpture to look at, that's fine. But start off with feeling balanced—that's what it's all about. You do have to be self-disciplined about meditation; you have to decide that you like doing it, and that you're going to do it for a while, so you can get better at it. If you can fit in five minutes a day, that's good; if you can do it for five minutes twice a week, that's good too. But make a note of how it feels after the first time, and again after a couple of weeks, so you can assess your progress. And it's not that hard, because you should always be looking for the pleasurable feeling.

There are payoffs that you can't discern at first too:

Your Will Power is becoming more disciplined, more effective, because you're trying to DECIDE to go for that pleasure and calmness. This is useful Magickally and in the rest of your life too.

You're activating the center (toning up that "mental muscle"), so that when you feel balanced, it feels EVEN BETTER!

You're reclaiming Time. It's only five minutes, but it's five minutes that are yours. And that means that you are caring for yourself, making yourself happier and stronger.

Once you've got the hang of meditation—and that doesn't mean that you're perfect, just that you feel you're "good enough" you can use it in all kinds of magickal techniques.

Especially when you've built onto it another basic technique that is even more useful.

Visualisation This is perhaps the most important skill for a lot of magickal work, and it's also the one that seems to put more people off than anything else. People tell you to close your eyes and draw a picture in your mind, and of course you can't! You just see blackness. Actually it's a lot easier than that.

But why is it so important? Think of it like this: if you can't imagine how something is, then you can't imagine how you want it to change. If you're trying to access the stuff that is locked away in your unconscious and in the structure of your brain, you can't do it without using imaginative flights of fancy that trigger them. So whatever kind of magick you're doing, knowing how to visualise is bloody useful.

All that visualisation is, is the imagination. Obviously, the imagination is a big place, but you don't have to explore all of it (or be a hyper-imaginative artist) just to do some useful visualisation. You just have to use a bit of it.

197

Another useful idea in understanding visualisation is that of day dreaming—but day dreaming under your conscious control. Just as you can be reasonably aware of your surroundings yet still be off dreaming about that special person (or that special glass of beer) which is just around the corner, so you can be thinking consciously about magickal stuff while still being aware of where you are. Eventually, you can see what you've visualised in the room with you and switch it on and off at will—but you don't have to be that good to get started. Here's how you start:

    1 Center yourself.

    2 Go into meditation—i.e. pursue that enjoyable sensation of contentment, gently pushing away other thoughts. Use your breathing to gently keep you in the right place.

    3 Imagine whiteness spreading as far as you can. Don't expect the image from your eyes to suddenly turn from black to

white—it's in your mind's eye. Try using memories of a blank wall to get you going.

4 Once you're fairly comfortable with the white, imagine a nice bold figure on it—a psychick cross could be a good one, or another symbol you're familiar with. The idea is to just let it be there, while gently pushing away intruding thoughts. If it's a real pain trying to get it, stop, open your eyes, get comfortable and centered, and pick an image that's easier, even if it's apparently more complicated. Try a memory of some graphic pornography, perhaps, or a favourite album cover, or the front of the 73 bus. Perhaps even a piece of music. Anything, it certainly doesn't have to be "occult." The point is to be able to keep it in place while retaining the comfort and enjoyment of being centered. It really is a lot like daydreaming when you've got the hang of it. One TOPY Trick you can use is to look at the graphic of your choice from a paused video or a computer screen and remember it. Then close your eyes and recall it, keeping it there. You may also wish to use some ritual or ambient music, but that can be distracting—try it and see.

198

5 The next trick is to make it move around, do what you want it to, in your imagination. This is lot of fun, and you can soon find yourself doing visualisation all the time. But it has to be consciously controlled—don't let it turn into bog-standard day dreaming.

6 Now you need to experiment. This should be easy once you've got the basic technique under your belt—it should feel good. That's enough to get you started. Once you get centering right, it's not too hard to pick the rest up. Try to keep a brief record of how you're doing—that act of monitoring is enough to keep your Will active, so that you're actively pushing your skills along. The first magickal act you should try is a simple protection ritual. All you do is go into meditation and visualise a circle of light going round your head, and then around your body. All the while you're focusing on the thought that this is protecting you, and no bad energy or hate or attack can reach you when it is activated. This is the most basic ritual and one of the most effective. Now all you have to do is go out and enjoy yourself.

SOME EXERCISES

The sequence of exercises introduced here is to be used in conjunction with your Ritual, but it should also be practiced on its own at least three times a week.

> First Stand with your legs apart, the width between your feet being approximately that of the width between your shoulders and let your toes point slightly toward each other. Place your hands on the back of your hips so that the thumbs rest on the hip-bone and your middle fingers touch at the base of the spine. Lower your knees and arch yourself backward.
>
> After a while this might feel slightly uncomfortable, but persevere. Your whole body should start shaking at this point, just allow that to happen for a few minutes, again going a bit further than you think is comfortable.
>
> Second Lie down and simply concentrate on your breathing. Not in the sense that you are controlling the breath, but rather as being an outside observer. Nothing should exist but your attention and your pattern of breath. Go on for about seven minutes.
>
> Third Lie down, preferably on a hard surface but with a soft headrest. Draw up your knees and let your feet rest on the soles. As you breathe in, push back with your hips and the back of your head. As you breathe out, lift your hips and your head slightly so that your weight rests on the feet, your back and shoulders. Do this for five minutes.
>
> Fourth *Ritual.*

199

The first of the exercises works by putting the body in a so-called stress position where the firing zones of the muscular system are activated. This results in a loosening up of muscular blocks that have dammed up or hindered the energy flow through the body.

The second one is a simply there to acquaint you with your major biological rhythm: that of breath. Do not at this stage confuse it with "anapanasati" or any other Buddhist or Hindu practice. Now we are solely dealing with your physical aspects, your body, so mind and psyche will have to wait. The third exercise is in a way a crude imitation of what some authorities call the "Orgasm Reflex," i.e., the body's involuntary movements at the moment of release. But its practice can have the function of eliciting that response and can rid you of unwanted tension that builds up in your body as your climax—tension usually brought about through fear, guilt or other negative conditionings.

Important Write down your impressions and feelings after you have gone through these exercises. Sometimes they can result in releasing old and held-back emotions, sometimes you will recognize them and know their origin, sometimes they will just be feelings that you can not place or understand. Note every difference in your physical reality: Does your body respond in a different manner? And so on. And then send us a short description of your results.

200   Mirror Exercise Sit in a comfortable position in front of a mirror, relaxed but not slumped. Light the mirror with a candle to the left and right. For the preliminary part you may like to close your eyes, letting your consciousness sink down through your body (in Tai Chi systems there is a power center, known as the Tan Tien, located below the navel); or use any method of relaxation and centering which works best for you. Now concentrate your gaze on your eyes reflected in the mirror. Don't consciously try to place any particular emotion in the eyes, but let images and feelings arise spontaneously. Do this for a while longer than is comfortable, then record your impressions immediately.

"Mirroring" With Partners: Please note—it's a good idea when using "mirroring" exercises with a partner to explain and discuss what you are doing, as it can cause confusion and worry otherwise.

Sit comfortably, relaxed but with a straight back, facing your partner. Let the energy flow freely through your body and between each other. Let feelings and images arise as you look into each other's eyes. What do you see and how do you feel? Are there similarities between what each of you sees and feels? And, of what you see in your partner's face: Which do you feel comes from him/her, and which do you recognize as your own feelings? By learning to recognize your own feelings projected onto your partner's face, you may be able to discover if you also have been projecting unconscious aspects of yourself onto your partner. This discovery can be a painful one, but it can also be a liberating experience: Once the projected aspects are recognized as such you can then begin to reassimilate them into your consciousness, this becoming stronger, and learning to see clearly and appreciate others as persons in their own right, with their own feelings.

A Note on Taking Note Often it is useful to try to record immediate impressions of an exercise or experiment without moral judgment or intellectual interference at first. Then put it away and forget about it; do something else and sleep on it. Go back to it another day and see if your experiences of the exercise connect with anything that has happened, or you have done or dreamed. You may find that connections (will seem to) have been made spontaneously. For this phenomenon to function, it is necessary to give it time and space to let it happen, and not do anything consciously to force it. This is why we suggest to analyze your discoveries it may be useful to leave some time first. If you try any of these suggestions, you'll probably want to "tailor" them to suit your personal needs, and maybe you'll come up with some new ones. Let us know what you discover in your adventures so we can share them.

Please yourself! THIS IS THEE TOPY WAY…
TOPYSTATION

Essays on intuitive magick

VII

rovoke thee expansion ov thee individual.

Dismiss all obstacles, dismiss fear.

Dismiss all non-thinking non-individuals.

Embrace all your love and hope.

Embrace thee strength ov thee individual.

Join as one.

POSITIVE MIND = POSITIVE LIFE

Thee Temple ov Psychick Youth aims to destroy all negative thinking and replace it with positive thinking. A negative attitude towards life will leave you chained to thee ground, not being able to reach thee goals that you truly long for; you will be stuck doing the same thing for the rest of your life, whether it be a boring job or a boring social life. It is a fact that when the mind desires something so much it is more than likely to happen. To make these things happen you will need a positive mind; you have to set your mind directly on that goal, never letting your mind wander, never letting apathy rear its ugly head. Apathy is one of the most common of obstacles; people tend to give up too easily, they can't be bothered to reach for, or at least attempt to gain control of their own destiny, and that is one of the many reasons why the Temple exists—we aim to drive out apathy and to bring in positive thinking. The method to drive out apathy is to add variety to your life, to widen your interests. (A life of variety = a positive life.)

This is the point where we separate the positive from the negative. The negative will attempt to ridicule the positive, making the positive wary and unsure of every move made to make a better life. The way to avoid this problem is to either avoid the negative, or to confront the negative and make it a positive. Apathy is a very powerful force and the average human being is very vulnerable to it. We are NOT average and we can avoid these obstacles, through self-realization and by opening up. Opening up will lift a great weight off your back. If you feel that you can't open up because your friends wouldn't understand your desires and aims in life and just ridicule you, they are no true friends of yours; they are negative and they are forcing you to stay the same as them; they are afraid of progress and openness, and they will stay on the spiral of negative life till the day they die, and take you with them if they can.

The flesh and bones are only a shell that shelters the soul from the outside world. We aim to break through the negative shell and release the positive soul, making you more aware of your true hopes and desires, making you a fuller being capable of taking a more positive attitude towards life.

Eden 211, 1987

DOUBT IS THE BEGINNING OF WISDOM
A MODERN GNOSIS

Involvement in TOPY is an awakening, a process through which we can explore our selves, and move towards the achievement and goal of living fully, completely within our free and established Will.

But all paths, however committed and determined we are to follow them, are beset with obstacles, more often than not of our own making. Periods of ecstatic energy born of certainty become darkened alleys from which we can see no escape. Then we again see a glimmer, or a new thought occurs to us—seemingly from nowhere—perhaps triggered by the odd word caught in conversation, or an item of news on TV, and we change course, or have doubts. We may even start in a new direction. But false starts lead nowhere, and too often the light we see ahead fades as we reach out to its source. Within TOPY the aim is to remove these obstacles, to escape from endless, futile circling of light and dark; for the true path is straight. It is a path of the knowledge and wisdom of the Self.

Doubt: An affliction or a gift?

Doubt: A prison, or a path to understanding?

Since the aim is to know one's Self, the method must be one of observation. A watching for inner motives, an understanding of temporary attitudes struck for a limited purpose. We are all prone to act "out of character" at times, to rebel against the inevitable conditioning of the wider society we inhabit, but through all the changes, the shifting poses we display to the world, there runs a core of truth even if at times it seems hidden and intangible. It is this core we must reach out for, and make manifest, be true to, for this is our unchanging Self through which Will must be channeled if we are to live out our destiny.

Without self-knowledge, it is all too easy to meander through life with little idea of why we behave in a certain way, or even where our actions are leading. So conditioned are we by the ideas that we pick up all around us, that so long as we meet with little or no resistance we are liable to drift on without a care until we find with horror that we have gone nowhere at all (even if the journey has taken a life-time), or worse still that what we took as our goal, our "home," is in reality the opposite end of the globe. We see the result of this all around: people stuck in lives, homes, jobs that simply don't "fit," as though everything is lived second-hand, according to another's will. And we hear the arguments of defense against such accusations: "There's no choice." "It's not bad, really." Yet the proof of the pudding is in its eating, and the signs of depression, anxiety and an all-pervading lethargy are only too clearly visible. When things go wrong, responsibility is denied. Blame is always attached to someone else, placed *outside*: "It's society's fault." "I didn't mean to. He/she made me." Excuses fly around like wedding-day confetti, clinging to anything that doesn't move—it doesn't matter what, so long as responsibility is evaded. Deny everything and it will go away.

207

But the problem never does. Not unless you take it upon yourself to actually go out and do something about it: Take your life in your hands and claw back your identity from the morass of the commonplace. Own up to your life, warts and all. It's all you've got to go on. The simplest things can help you do this. Small, everyday little doubts that flit in and out of consciousness like faery messengers whispering in the night.

Doubts: So easily brushed aside by the arrogance of an ego that lives each moment without a thought for the grander view. Doubts: Little murmurings of unrest calling to you to look again. Nagging irritations that get in the way and spoil the fun. Who needs them?

As autonomous psychic functions, "doubts" are a part of us; unconscious elements which bubble to the surface and dissipate with hardly a ripple. They are easy to ignore. But we ignore our Selves at our peril. For today's ripple that fades under the ego's withering glare may be the first sign of a deep-set conflict. We may indeed think that we don't "need" them, but we have them, and in this lies their importance: they enable us to know the inner realm. Like a psychopomp, they are guides through the psychic jungle of our dis-integrated identities. From the shadows of doubt the Moon can be brought into union with the splendor of the Sun. Ego joins with Self.

How to proceed?

Watchfulness. The raw material for getting to the root of our doubts is constantly with us. We all fantasize, run movies of future events through our minds. Scenarios drop down from the sky and we find ourselves imagining how we will deal with this problem, explain that one away. Often this rehearsal of a future event has little practical purpose, either because of the improbability of the situation we project, or because we have already determined our action. But the movie runs on regardless, and is psychically valid, and therefore real enough. Watch the screen. Let the movie run.

Try not to intervene or consciously manipulate the inner debate; after all, we want the unconscious to have its say. So follow the argument, however absurd it may seem, and try to retain an objective stance. See the pros and cons that surface. Watch for the ego's responses/attitudes. See where the conflicts come from, their "shape" and emotional content. Keep all this in mind. Be the Watcher that is Self.

When the movie has run its course, re-run it. Examine all the elements—*truthfully*. What was the outcome? The ego probably "won"—it usually does, since it can exert ultimate conscious control within this context. But is the ego's position valid? What good points did the unconscious throw up? Are *they* valid? What part of you do they represent? Can you trust this part? You know you can't always trust the ego; its vested interest in winning at any cost is too great.

Repeat the scenes which seem important to you. Change them round, add in different words/thoughts. Does the picture change? Or does the outcome remain the same? Remember as you do this that the unconscious deals in symbols. The argument relates to inner *principles*. Can you relate the characters/attitudes to aspects of your life? A parental figure might relate to a constrictive attitude in you (it has simply taken the form of a parent); or a wise teacher might represent a part that wants you to expand your horizons. You are the best judge of this. See what images fit.

By expanding the "film" in this way you will help define the root of the conflict, and once you have grasped this you have the key to integrating the disgruntled and troublesome element of the psyche into your life. You can of course accept or reject the proposition brought up from "within," but there are dangers in such choices unless they are carried out from a standpoint of knowledge. You should know where in you this thing is coming from.

The three basic rules are:

What does the protagonist represent? Which part of you?

What is its attitude? Is it simply "interested?" "Supportive?" "Antagonistic?"

Are you (the ego's presence in the psychic movie) positive? Sidestepping? Apologetic?

209

By following through this process you will learn much about your inner motivations, and thus be able to express the different sides of your nature more freely, more actively. Doubts should not be feared. They are friendly when treated well, for they are a part of you and want to "join in." They may be asking for no more than a little space for a neglected side of you, and if you allow them this you will find they can bring you closer to the goal of achieving a unified and co-operative psychic totality.

Doubts are a route to the unconscious. *Do not reject them.* Reach through and bring them into the light of Day. Enjoy the freedom of inner growth born of your acceptance of their view, their dreams, which are yet yours. Incorporate them in a wider vision of your existence. Live in the Knowledge and the Wisdom of the Self.

Through Gnosis is the Self released.

Eden, December 1987

SEXUAL MAGICK

Man has not always realized that sexual experience can bring more than simply physical pleasure. He is not aware that in some mysterious, "magical" way it could intensify the consciousness, expand his awareness and heighten the body beyond its physical form. Sex, because of its link with procreation, places the individual in the position of being Godlike—a creator of life. Even looking back in Greek history, gods and their worshippers are often portrayed in states of sexual excitement.

Sexual magick can be based upon a number of principles:

> 1 Man possesses hidden powers (often identified with the unconscious mind) that give him greater perception and increase physical, emotional and mental powers.

> 2 These powers lie buried beneath some barrier which normal states may not be able to reach and penetrate, but which can be overcome by a variety of techniques (drugs, alcohol, etc.)

> 3 Sexual stimulation can penetrate these barriers, leading up to the point of the orgasm—the breakthrough of energy or power.

> 4 This energy can be stored and contained; for example, magical containers into which the sexual fluids have been poured, where these objects have been consecrated or charged at the moment of orgasm. These will remain potent batteries of power.

Masturbation techniques are used to heighten the consciousness and focus, and to stimulate magickal power. The release of energy is the orgasm. True desires and aims can be reached through a period of concentration, during which the individual will be aroused to a "fever pitch" of energy and arousal.

Focus the conscious mind and the whole of the imagination on to the desired fantasy throughout the ritual. To gain physical health the body should be seen as healthy, vibrant and energetic. This image must be carefully and accurately formed and held throughout the period of stimulation. During the period of release and relaxation, the image should still be held in the mind to firm the image and the body.

Andi Brechen

SLEEP

Falling asleep is the most extreme form of "letting go," when consciousness literally ceases to be. Most of the time it seems as though you were simply "switched off," and you can never know how, since when you reawaken it is but a dim memory.

However, there are times when the process of falling asleep can be directly perceived. When, barely realizing it, you slip into a semiconscious, trance-like state. A state in which you are directly aware that you are becoming unconscious and aware of any dream images which may appear in the mind.

This state is equivalent to the trance a trained magician can induce at will; it is an altered state of awareness which we all experience on occasion.

211

I have already discussed the point at which you enter this trance. In my own experience, I find the approach to this point difficult. I'm unwilling or unable to let go. I couldn't deliberately induce a trance. A number of times when I've realized that I'm falling asleep and tried to relax, I've stopped myself by thinking about it, and then have been unable to sleep. (I do get insomnia.) Reaching the point seems like a bridge which can only be crossed by not trying.

Yet I treasure the times when I do still my mind and cross that point while still aware—an experience similar to orgasm—and enter that trance-like state. It is a time when awareness not only mingles with other forms of thought, but is itself changed. This it seems reasonable to compare to watching an old black and white movie that's never actually been made with your eyes closed.

During the writing of this piece I've increasingly found myself approaching this "twilight world" and have also found it more difficult to cross that point. I think this is mainly because I'm analyzing the experience and trying to describe it at the same time.

On the basis of my own experience, there exists a point, a precise instant in time when consciousness realizes it is losing control. The point at which that loss of control becomes inevitable, when ejaculation will come whatever happens. You can consciously try to delay it, guide it toward the desired effect, but you can't stop it. It is out of conscious control. In terms of sleep, the same point exists, although it is not always evident, as complete loss of consciousness follows. The point, which can be experienced when you slip slowly into sleep, is when you realize that you are becoming unconscious.

In both cases, the period between that point and its conclusion is a special experience. A time in which what is called "I" mingles with our other thoughts.

The period between the point (as I've termed it) and the climax could be called a process of synthesis, when, for a brief period, mind and body meet. A time when conscious and unconscious thought processes mingle in an integrated self.

212

However, what I consciously experience is a feeling of losing control, a sense of slipping into something dark and unknown—even fear. These feelings mount as I approach that point.

Once the point is reached, however, I can usually accept it with ease, becoming almost detached from the process. Observing from the sidelines, new images and feelings appearing as if from nowhere. Even is such shallow "drifting" states as have occurred, it has become obvious that the dream product can be directed—directed to a purpose.

One technique we were taught by a Cheyenne/Apache mentor to consciously move into the borderline awake/sleep/dream zone is to lie on your back with your head on a pillow. With your arms in a surrender position, i.e. palms facing up, tips of fingers level with the top of your head, hook the hands under the pillow so they are trapped by your weight. We have found conscious entrance into lucid dreaming states is increased dramatically.
Genesis Breyer P-Orridge

SEX—THE SIGIL

I've been talking about "letting go," allowing inner energies to flow out through your whole self. We can compare this with the Qabalistic concept of "Crossing the Abyss." The Adept must release his/her self and "die" in the womb of the Abyss, to be reborn on the other side. Once this release of "I" has been achieved, the forces continue to flow upwards to the Crown by their own inherent nature.

Thus with magick—thus with the sexual act—thus with sex magick.

During sex you go through a process of release. Initially, you are very conscious of your actions. Perhaps a heightened, more focused awareness (remember the "rational" mind is not an isolated, differentiated being, but an integral part of yourself.)

As the flood of sensation increases, it feels like an engulfing tide. The "I" circuit experiences thoughts and forms rising up around it from an unfamiliar source.

Now "I" may begin to feel threatened and begin to resist. Unexpected fears may arise. (A desire to prolong the pleasure by holding back at this stage may be a self-deception formed from such fears.) This doesn't matter because the flood of sensations drowns such thoughts, and sweeps you forward in its tide.

213

As excitement mounts, the point is reached when "I" can no longer control the process, and orgasm becomes inevitable. Then the sense of separate identity ceases and becomes irrelevant. It is at this time that inner energies start to flow and can be directed and focused upon release in orgasm.

The purpose of the sigil is to focus the mind upon the objective you desire. By continuous concentration before the point, fixing the idea as a thought form during the climax of the operation.

This can condition the products welling up from the unconscious, producing thoughtforms appropriate to the operation, directing energies toward your goal.

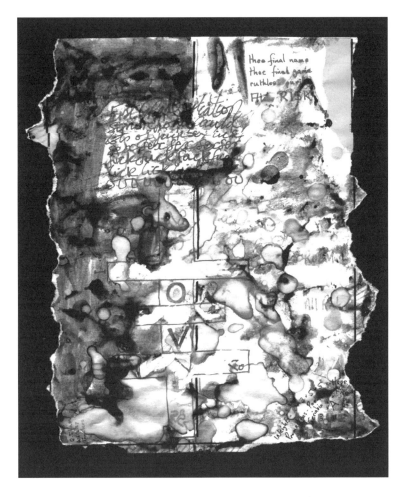

As most people are able to achieve orgasm, this is the most accessible form of magick for the "ordinary" person. Although the effect
will be greatly improved by mental training, the performing of such
acts as the sigil will in themselves increase your mental discipline.
This sexual magick is the most useful tool in the development of an
integrated (magickal) self.

Image by Genesis Breyer P-Orridge

MAGICK

What might be called the conventional magician, say, trained in the Golden Dawn methods, will spend a great deal of time and effort undergoing mental discipline. This enabling them to induce altered states of awareness such as trances. The Golden Dawn system places strong emphasis on astral projection.

The "ordinary" person's (myself) reaction to this approach is "I can't do that." It's only after a long time, if at all, that you see any results. Perhaps we don't have the necessary commitment, but then why should we when its value can only be seen once you've done it. Lots of people dabble in magick but get no further.

Also, the results and practice of such systems seem irrelevant to and in conflict with everyday life.

This is not to undervalue mental discipline, but simply to say that most people don't have the sufficient commitment or desire to develop it.

Sex magick provides a more accessible approach, combining immediate results with a system of mental training. Being more accessible, it reduces the need for gurus and gives the individual a chance to develop.

215

This is still a method of mental training for psychic development, to help integrate the self.

Now, as I've tried to indicate, such experiences of integration do occur naturally in "normal life." This is the great value of using sex in acts of magick. It bases the action on altered psychic states which are readily achieved and could be familiar if you bother to look at them. Such states, continuous reminders of our wholeness, do occur naturally in a number of forms to everyone. Even if they are difficult to induce or control, they will still happen.

The important point is that anyone can and does experience greatly altered/heightened states of awareness. You don't have to be a great Adept. Anyone can, during certain periods, be that integrated, whole self. You can use the energies released to direct every area of your life. Enjoy your Self; you are whole.

A NOTE ON SIGILS

For magick to operate most effectively, the most powerful tools available must be brought into play. In that region of time and space which we currently inhabit the most appropriate tools are those of modern technology. The most useful sigils now possible are mixed media constructs created by a combination of computers, video cameras and recorders, and electronic sound sources and processors.

In my experience, the best means for production and use of sigils involves first creating a simple statement or image defining the intended result. This should be done in such a manner as to imply that the operation has already succeeded. For example, "I have..." or "I am..." are more effective openings than "I want..." which implies and thereby reinforces a state of deprivation.

Next, the images and/or statements should be modified as far beyond recognition as possible without destroying their meanings. Methods used might include embedding them subliminally into other messages, or distorting images by color shifts or spatial irregularities, or the treatment of sounds by filtering or ring modulation, etc. Other useful devices might include the use of cut-ups or superimposition of symbols.

The finished product could then be used in a number of different ways. As an object to be concentrated upon, a picture posted in some prominent place where it would often be seen, a piece of music to be listened to, a film to be viewed at frequent intervals, etc. The meaning of the sigil should be ignored, and even forgotten, during this phase of the operation. The image of the result is meant to be embedded upon the unconscious mind, and conscious thought must not be allowed to interfere.

All that remains to be done is to await the result without making attempts to force it or taking action that might hinder it. Make no effort, and you will act correctly.

R. P. Stoval

MAGICK—CONSCIOUS VS. UNCONSCIOUS

It seems that in my previous ramblings on the subject of belief I had committed a sin of omission. My statements that effort and belief were not only unnecessary but also to be avoided could be interpreted as denoting the kind of inactivity that would make "the Taoist wu-wei look like a Chinese fire drill." To resolve this paradox one must realize that while it is the conscious mind that controls the physical actions, magickal powers are the province of the unconscious mind. For the magick to be effective, consciousness must not interfere with unconscious activity.

Unfortunately, at this stage of our evolution consciousness neither controls nor is aware of unconscious activities. The ultimate aim of magick is to correct this situation. Magick is the technology of the unconscious.

The conscious mind need not believe that magick works. The unconscious knows. All purposeful activity should be completed before the actual performance of the magickal operation. For example, in planning a ritual, all elements must be designed to point toward the intended result, but must not be consciously perceived as such. A perfect ritual would, in fact, seem to be completely nonsensical. It should so distract the conscious mind that no thought of the result appears during its performance. As another example, in divination one should first frame the question and then perform the necessary operations without thinking of it. The result should then be interpreted by free association without reference to the question. The answer should only be compared to the question after its interpretation.

Remember, through the practice of magick the conscious mind may eventually develop a link to the unconscious. At this stage, all these devices may be discarded, and results brought about by direct (in)action. This should be our final goal.
TOPYN.A.

A NOTE ON THE SEX
MAGICK OF THE OTO

When Aleister Crowley was made head of the OTO, he was enjoined with the task of writing complete rituals for that organization. (Such rituals had previously existed only in skeletal form.) It is clear from a study of Crowley's extant writings that he never completed this job. Furthermore, I know of no group claiming OTO dispensation using a complete and consistent set of rituals. Some do not even use the same formulae taught by Reuss and Crowley.

For those interested in the use of these formulae, complete practical instruction can be found in *Liber Aleph*, particularly in chapters 82-95. There is also much useful information to be found in *Magick Without Tears*. These are probably the two most important Crowley works for the practicing magician.

For further study, I would recommend the novel *Out* by Ronald Sukenick (difficult to obtain, but well worth the effort), read in conjunction with Crowley's *Book of Lies* (especially chapters 23 & 61). These works contain everything the serious student will require.
TOPYN.A.

‡

ABOUT BELIEF

It is not necessary to believe in order to perform magick. In fact, belief is a barrier to success second only to the overpowering desire to succeed. Both these stumbling blocks are, in a sense, identical as they both symptomize the "lust of result."

The keys to the successful completion of any magickal operation are imagination, will and love. In order to succeed, one must first imagine the result. Next, the will must be used to focus upon every conceivable detail and make the product of the imagination seem as real to one as those circumstances that the operation is to alter. Finally, love is brought to play to cause the mind (the unconscious mind, in particular) to merge with the result.

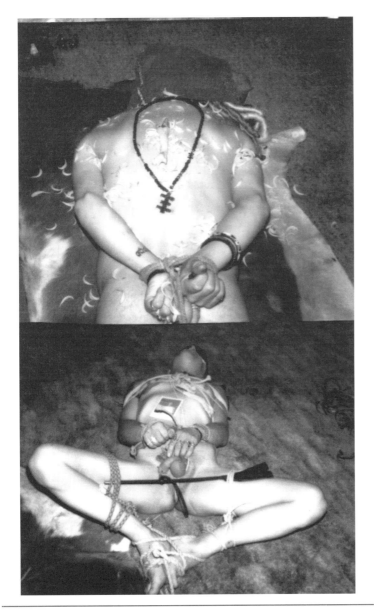

Image by Genesis Breyer P-Orridge

The desire to succeed blocks success by dividing the function of will, part of which is now expended in the unneeded effort to think of accomplishing the result, rather than the result itself. In a similar, but more insidious manner, one's belief prevents the faculty of love from being fully applied to the union with the intended effect.

A peculiar upshot of all of this is that one is often more magickally effective when one does not even attempt to achieve anything from one's exertions. In many cases, one is more likely to see issue from a particularly vivid daydream, sometimes even from a mere idle thought. This is because without intent, the faculties of imagination, love and will are able to act at peak efficiency, free from all interference.

To manage this in a planned operation is not easy. Perhaps the best way to do so is to utilize an abstract image symbolizing the result (a sigil, for example, or a meaningless image with subliminal imbeds) and to focus the mind upon this image so strongly as to exclude all else. On finishing this process, one should then throw oneself fully into some other task, so that further thought on the subject may be avoided. This should assure the result.

220

TOPY

‡

FORMULATING LINKS

Suppose you have an ally whom you wish to communicate with, but is too far away for you to speak to or see in person. How do you communicate with them across the seemingly unbridgeable gulf that separates you? Magickal links are one way.

A magickal link is a means of transcending geographical distance in order to communicate with persons not physically present. Whether this communication is collateral—i.e., whether the sender *actually* communicates with the receiver in such a way that the receiver is conscious of it—is open to debate.

Many people are somewhat skeptical about "astral" workings, and with good reason. There is something very metaphysical, and therefore unscientific, about any magical process that presupposes "other worlds." The methods described in this piece require no belief in any supernatural phenomena, in fact require nothing but a bit of privacy, concentration and a few (easily obtained) raw materials. More on these a bit later.

In order to form a link, there must be some form of attraction. A compelling force that enables you, or even makes you want to form said link. There are several types of attraction: physical contact, sexual attraction, a linking talisman, and what I call "blind links."

Sexual attraction seems to me to be the easiest means of formulating a link. Any time you are attracted in this way, it is easy to visualize the object of attraction. Unfortunately, exactly the same reasons that make sexual attraction the easiest means of ingress also tend to make it the most likely to backfire. Be sure that the object of desire feels the same way about you as you do about him or her. For this method to work effectively it is not necessary to have met the object in person. It is, however, preferable to have some sort of *personal* link with the person at hand—a *Playboy* centerfold is, by itself, a tenuous link at best. Obsession abounds in this particular branch of magical meeting, so be sure to keep a clean mental house.

221

The second method, physical contact, is less open to trouble. It requires merely that you know a person intimately enough to know his or her mannerisms, speech patterns, physical appearance, etc. Loving, caring for, or respecting a person makes it a cinch to hook into their "vibe" and connect.

Linking talismans is effected by having a piece of the object, hair, handwriting, a photo, or a diagram you both agreed on previously.

The blind link is tricky. That consists of making a link with someone you have never met and with whom you have no object linking you to them directly. I can't recommend this type of meeting, however, as this type of link is often assumed by the receiver to be of hostile nature, and retaliation can be fierce. Be careful!

A talisman of some sort is very useful in formulating links. This talisman should in some way contain a part of the object of your focus.

It should also remind you of the object, enabling you to focus your concentration on that person and also to amplify your consciousness of them. There are three forms of talisman I intend to discuss: physical, pictorial and sonic.

Physical talismans are the most widely-used form of link and, while effective, are not necessarily the best. The cliché hair, fingernail clippings, clothing, former possessions, all fall into this category. The theory behind talismanic linkage is that any of these items can hold the vibration of their former owner long after they have left his or her possession. This makes a good link.

Don't forget that an item given to you by the object of focus is an excellent talisman, too, as a gift contains an aura of your relationship with that person and may have been given to you in order to strengthen the bond between you. A bouquet of flowers, jewelry, a book, letter or card, any of these can be used successfully.

Image by Lady Jaye Breyer P-Orridge

Physical mannerisms can be imitated to good effect—a particularly peculiarity of gait, facial expression, an often-used hand gesture, there are no fixed rules regarded talismanic links—use anything, however silly or banal it may seem, that reminds you of your object.

Photographic links are extremely powerful icons for concentrating the attention on a person or place. Before embarking on this particular method, it is best to decide on a standard pose that you can assume in all your magical photographs. I always sit or stand with my fingers interlocked and clenched about six inches in front of my face, elbows slightly apart. Every muscle should be kept tight, but comfortably so. Having a mirror in front of me helps, but if none is handy, I treat the camera lens as if it were a mirror itself. Before taking the photo, I try to "zone out" as much as I can, visualizing myself where I am in present time. I try to visualize a thread or tear in time that will enable me to travel back and forth in time-space at will.

If you are photographing yourself to send as a link to another person, try to imagine that person as being with you. Where is that person now? Be with them—try to visualize being both places at once.

223

Photographing yourself and the object together may be the best, if it is possible. You should both be in your set poses, both imagining you are separated again, focus on being alone, of reaching out to be with your friend again, focus on being alone, of reaching out to be with your friend again. Perhaps you could both be in your set poses, both imagining you are separated again, focus on being alone, of reaching out to be with your friend again. Perhaps you could both face one another and each picture the other as being your reflection in a mirror at home. *Click!*

To illustrate a method of re-evoking a specific place, let me now cite at length a personal example. While walking along a faraway stream, I tripped and cut my hand on a piece of quartz. I held the rock in my palm, stretched my bloody hand out, each finger strained as far apart as possible. As I snapped the picture, I imagined looking at this photo at home, of longing to be in this beautiful place at will forever. Now, I merely have to project this slide on a wall, zone out, outstretch my hand in that same position and place the pice of quartz on my palm and there I am again. I hear the birds scolding,

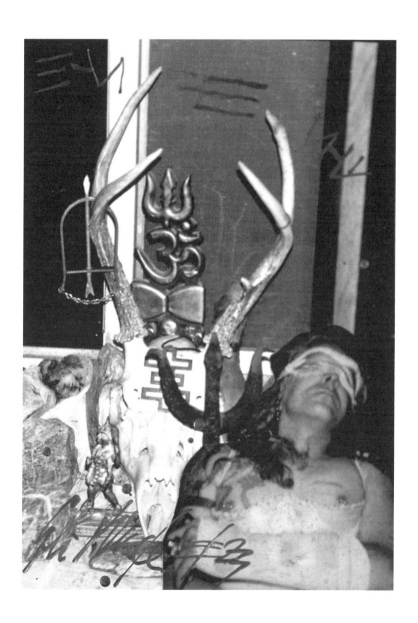

Image by Lady Jaye Breyer P-Orridge

the rustle of the trees, the rushing water. My hand stings where it has been cut. It's really uncanny!

The last form of talisman I want to discuss is sonics. This is one of the most outmoded and overlooked devices in modern magic, and its potential is nearly limitless. It is complex as well as neglected, therefore I will devote a bit more space to it than I did the others, to encourage more research in this area.

First off, a portable, fairly good sound quality tape recorder is essential. Don't leave home without it!

The three types of sound talismans I'll discuss here are voice, music and incidental or ambient sound.

A recording of a person's voice is an almost unerring link. It contains the mood, personality and a piece of their very soul—however you define that elusive critter. By recording a person's voice, you are literally trapping or encapsulating a part of them in time, one that you can go over again and again. Using the cut-up method (very simple with audio tape), you can restructure what they originally said, either randomly or by design. With two tape recorders, you can make new tapes of edited or cut-up versions of the original speech. Cut-ups introduce the random factor and can be used for divining the person's real intention behind the words spoken. Inflection and emphasis of key words can be more easily perceived when heard out of context. So you mix it all up like a shaker full of dice and see what sort of random patterns you end up with. It can be quite oracular at best, and utterly incomprehensible at worst. That's the random factor for you!

The inflection and accent of the object can also be mimicked, perhaps along with their physical mannerisms. This too is an almost certain link.

Is there a song that reminds you of that person, perhaps one you first heard with them? You can evoke that person by listening to or singing that song. Or maybe the lyrics use that person's name, or remind you of them. You'll be amazed at how evocative a schlocky pop song can be if it contains memories of a certain place or person, or even a phase of your life.

You can also make up your own lyrics, maybe singing them to the tune of a well-known song. I've made tapes of little dittys I made up about different people or situations, and they prove very useful in forming links with people and in making dreams come true.

Ambient sound is a very complex subject which I haven't explored in nearly enough detail to describe in the depth I'd like to. It appears to be most useful when used in conjunction with other sounds that are more directly linked with your object. Via the cut-up method. Record the ambient sounds that you feel make up the *environment* of the person you wish to form a link with. Their favorite TV show, the neighbor's dog barking, the neighbor's baby crying, the cars going by their house, the loud hi-fi next door. Mrs. Jones borrowing a cup of sugar. These are all aids in capturing the *mood* of that person's environment, thereby bringing you mentally closer to them. You can also capture the essence of a whole city by walking around randomly recording things you encounter on your walk. It serves as a mnemonic device to help you recall the feeling you got while exploring that city. Ambient sound magic merits a lot more research...

226

Incense, candlelight dreamachine slide projector on automatic rotating slides of object-desired ambient audio growing more specific feeling environment. Looking at photos, touching gifts from object. Look in the mirror at object beside you touching you. What are they saying? Imitate their voice greeting you, hug them, kiss them. Greet them as you would on seeing them in the flesh. Close your eyes. Drift towards their gravitational pull. Meet them in waking dream drifting...

If the links and the desires are strong enough, you should feel their presence almost upon starting. If you don't, don't be discouraged, just try another time. Not succeeding is not always failure—maybe they're not home!

A few last remarks—*you can't have too many links.* Try to accumulate as many as possible, to flood each of your senses with reminders of the person on whom you are focusing. *The closer to sensory overload, the better.* A link with a person is *always* a violation of that person's space—make sure you are welcome there.

Links can be used for an attack, as well as friendly visitation. Be aware that people under attack often retaliate. Also remember that unforeseen side-effects almost always occur in such attacks, they have a nasty habit of bouncing right back to sender, with a little additional backspin. A wish to injure someone can easily result in a much more serious injury than you had wished, which might make you feel guilty or regret such action. Only attack someone you *really* want to destroy. No half steppin' allowed…

I deplore banishing myself, but linking up with other people can easily lead to obsession. Make sure it's a person you want to be obsessed with, or banish after each meeting.

Above all, don't take anything that transpires between you and the object of your link as being *objectively* true. I have found that each transmission contains some truth, but it's really hard to separate unless you approach the object with the results of you meeting. Then they'll tell you which parts are accurate and which are wishful thinking on your part. *Never base a decision solely on the results of a link-up*, without checking those results with the object for accuracy, or at least using logic, i.e., what you already *know* about the issue at hand, and intuition. *Never make a decision that goes against your gut instinct, no matter what a link-up tells you.*

227

I hope this little piece is helpful to you as a guide to formulating and using links. Every method I discussed is one that I have tried myself and each one works *for me* to a greater or lesser degree. However, this article is based solely on *my* ideas and results. I would like to expand this rough beginning based on *your* ideas and research. Please help enlarge and expand on this admittedly feeble beginning on a subject that could, if fine-tuned, be so useful and beneficial to us all.

Coyote Two, November 27, 1987

During the early daze of COUM in Hull, Yorkshire we were friends with Alan Worsley, who was doing serious research into lucid dreaming, guided dreams and planned meetings with other people who were also sleeping yet sharing the same "dream" landscape. We recommend you Google Alan Worley online for more information on the amazing success he has achieved. He visited TOPY in exile in 1994 in California and is considered our TOPY mentor on "dream sciences".

Genesis Breyer P-Orridge

Love with horns

VIII

Image by Genesis Breyer P-Orridge

nderstanding in a special way—empathic, inter-subjective. The imaginative assumption of another's identity, without prejudice. A true regard and respect for the meanings which the Individual generates in his or her engagement with the world. Morality is a null concept, void of any usefulness now. The only code worth having is the code born of reflective experience. Critical empathy, love with horns, is the nearest thing we have to telepathy. A mutual intuitive reflex. (But deeper still, we all know each other perfectly.) Strangely, this empathy is rarely accomplished, rarely practiced, becomes corrupted by the mealy-mouthed. When the Individual is undermined, it does not feel safe to explore, to fully venture towards another. We have become debilitated to such an extent that many of us have only a precarious hold on what we perceive to be our identities. Scared, we latch onto and attempt to concretize that facet of ourselves which attracts least reprehension. What exists beyond is smothered, stifled, becomes more and more out of focus. Without focus, the social interactions in which we engage become schizophrenic in character, are cloven. The encoded message is schismatic: existential suicide. Divide and conquer... but conquer what, exactly?

The crippled slave can praise, can grovel, but cannot work. Everybody loses, all is lost. In such circumstances, how can we go out and interact with others in anything other than insecurity, doubt, suspicion, introversion and distance. Our motives become small, disconnected, misplaced. The Other has become a threat, a multiform projection of the ancient enemy, the object of neglect, the Self, the Shadow. The Shadow possesses such fierce vitality—when we repress it, curdle it, it hurts so bad, it wants out. Becomes very ugly indeed. We create the prison, the iron cage, armor our personality. We jump on the suitcases of our psychick baggage to secure the straps, as we hurtle towards the grave, where we will fill the final hole. We are without, desolate. But no-thing is ever really lost. At any moment we are free to choose to throw the prison open, to find the optimum state, but I forget how and... even why. Deliberately. As do we all. We never remember. We twist authenticity into a devil, an adversary. Bad faith pandemic. We break our vulnerable, young horns, again and again.

Cummings wrote: "We doctors know a hopeless case when—listen: there's a hell of a good universe next door; let's go." We are here to go— isn't that what Gysin meant? He meant drop the corpse, the hopeless case of faith we courted, slept with, suffer from. Let's go. This time we will catch the plane, catch the bull by the horns. Suicide must become a gesture of the past. You must engage, you must locate access to the universe just next door. *Mutuality* is the only ground strong enough, the only workable system. As we leave this universe of faith, this time of control, anger becomes action. We are coming. This time it's not just Jesus who gets to come. When you go, when you let go, you travel, you come. The Adversary strikes, you submit, the weapon dissolves, melts into your flesh, and you never were apart. We can only achieve mutuality, reciprocation, by understanding the Other that is within, changing its name, defining what it is that we have to give each other. The weapon so sharp, so cutting, turns in the light and becomes Magick, for us, with us, by us.

Who desires and acts not, breeds pestilence.
William Blake

Orgasm is the one and only moment when you can't cheat life.
Godard

*Corrupt is the teacher, for they who speak have only spent words to give...
Do ye not speak from between your thighs?*
Austin Osman Spare

TOPY UK STATION

THEE BIG HOUSE

We all share a vision of a Big House. It is all around us, within us, in our dreams: a place of our own where all our desires are realized, where we live and love together, the multiple aspects of our selves coming together in unity of purpose. A state of Psychick Wholeness.

It is a dream that begins in childhood, with play-acting and drawings, a Big House in which we operate as One, interdependent yet Individual.

A place where we can change roles, be whoever we wish to be. It is a dream that, like so many others of our early years, dies as we grow, as society forces us into separation. We become shackled by the expectations of others, and retreat into little boxes of darkness seeking a false security in isolation. The world is filled with separation; there is little else to see. We lock our doors on each other, psychically as well as physically, and fret at the knock of the stranger. We fear to open ourselves to self. Little wonder that we fear then to open ourselves to others. But the childhood dream is a living thing, cannot so easily be shut away. It emerges in the world of adult fantasy, from the Haunted House of Horror to Southfork. Revolutionaries sieze palaces. The rich build their mansions. The Big House is a part of us. The Temple aims to make it real.

In September, several Individuals working with TOPYHQ began the search in earnest. We traveled to the North of England to visit a building a friend had told us of, a place large enough to hold conferences and in which many of us could live together. The place had a number of out-buildings we could convert to additional living space for visitors. We could build our own workshops. It lacked land, however, and the cost was high, too high for us at present. The expedition was not wasted though. We learnt much about our needs, how the Big House should be structured. We envisaged a center, ultimately several centers, several Big Houses, in which groups of Individuals are living and working together. Space to initiate experimental forms of living, to introduce different physical and psychic regimes so that we can learn to exercise all the parts of our natures. We see ourselves rotating between Temple buildings, permanently at home within the Temple, but never tied to a particular place or style of living. In one place a retreat, another a place of functional work. And we see the Temple able to undertake long-term research projects. We will give ourselves time as well as space. We will live in touch with the land, begin again to understand its energy. We will be self-sufficient, not necessarily in the sense of producing all our own food, our own heat, but by utilizing all our skills and integrating these into a functional whole. And by drawing our resources to a center we will attract others who perhaps don't yet have the courage of our commitment, but who share our dream. We will explode the myth of selfishness by showing that it is by sharing that we get the most done; not by holding out, by trying to act alone. We will learn from each other so that we

233

break the fallacy of divided labor, the habit of specialization; of isolation. The time to act is now, is always now. There is a limit to what can be achieved by study, by talk. Plans are but pieces of paper if they are not put into action, testaments to romantic notions. The Big House is not a house of paper dreams—it is a reality we will make manifest. It will not be easy. Any project of this scale requires commitment if it is to succeed. We must learn to let go of previous ideas of what is reasonable, and to discard the trappings of our old ways. It is an adventure, the Great Experiment. Life is precious, too precious to waste in the continual reinforcement of that which we already know. We can stand still and take no chance only so long as we are satisfied to stand up to nothing, to remain dictated to by others who say they know best. We have no choice if we are to be free. We must take the plunge and alter, radically, our concepts of life, its structure, its aims. Many of us are already on this path. We invoke change as a friend, the true spirit of life. Without it we stagnate and die. With it we are free. The Big House is no longer a mist on the horizon. It is near at hand, and we must make ourselves ready.

Genesis Breyer P-Orridge, November 1988

DECODE–ENCODE–A CODE

Reading the books of John Lilly, especially *The Scientist*, led us, as it did most people, into greater comprehension of the more radical contemporary speculations upon evolution, communication, spiritual intelligence and the brain. Dolphins and whales were inevitably integrated as fully respected and revered sentient beings, inseparable from our reappraisals. It is easy to love them, too—but they are not just the easy and appealing face of ecological responsibility. We have grown to believe that reposing within their intelligences and memories are precise threads of spiritual information connecting through time to the origin of *all* species in this omniverse and to all the possibilities and impossibilities of what time is, both in physical and non-physical manifestations. We believe that, whilst time does behave to some degree as an energy would, it is, in our experience, an all-pervading form of *consciousness*. Thus all information and experience, of *any* type whatsoever, may be accessed by all other consciousnessess—past, present or future. From time we are born and into time we return.

Prior to settling in California as exiles from Poor Britain, on March 23, 1992, we had resided in B-Right-On, on the coast of southern England. We discovered there was a "Dolphinarium" there that earned its absentee owners over three million dollars per annum in profits. Believing that all HumanE Beings should integrate as a caring part of whatever demographic area is host to their Weigh ov L-if-E, we felt that outrage and nausea at this sick spectacle were not enough on their own; and the P-Orridge famille bravely chose to co-ordinate a campaign to expose and close down this unnatural abomination parading as entertainment.

With sentient beings, activists of all age groups and socio-philosophical persuasions, we spent endless rainy weekends and sunny Bank Holidaze peacefully picketing the Brighton Dolphinarium. Our own TOPYSTA-TION gathered over 7,000 signatures on a petition which was presented to the committee designated to decide the fate of the outmoded prison facility. We developed positive relations with Zoo Watch, Into the Blue, local and national media, the local council, even soliciting successfully the support of our local Tory M.P. Andrew Bowden. The P-Orridge famille organized for TV, music and film celebrities to congregate for freedom festivals, and local schools developed programs for their children, raising their awareness of the issues.

235

In their turn, the Dolphinarium's Swiss holding company employed people to stand and shout abuse, threaten and even physically attack our pickets. The local police were called endlessly for fabricated reasons in the hope they would arrest us. This tactic backfired when the police signed our petition and gave us verbal support. Even local churches lent their support despite our clear pre-Christian British and Celtic lineage. After over one year of dogged persistance and intense verbal persuasion, we had dialogue with members of the Dolphinarium that their income had dropped by over one million pounds. It is a sad but realistic fact that philosophical arguments and ideals are far less powerful than financial damage incurred in the minds of that species which chooses to be proprietor of such spectacles as a Dolphinarium. Nevertheless, despite smear campaigns in the press, on December 23, 1990 the announcement was made that the Dolphinarium would close for good.

Members of our campaign had made contact with the Aga Khan, who offered, as an ongoing charitable trust, a lagoon in the Turks and Cacos Islands in the Caribbean to be used for the rehabilitation, rescue and adjustment to freedom of previously captive and/or abused dolphins. Into the Blue was formed to raise funds for safe and proper transport, veterinary attention and as much rehabilitation therapy as necessary for Missie, Silver and Rocky (from another UK Dolphinarium closed by similar collective action that same year) and future liberated sentient beings of the sea. However, as with all pressure for change, the full benefits will go to future generations of dolphins, whales and even, yes, to we mere HumanE Beings. The first three dolphins were released successfully, as a group, into the open seas and oceans just over a year after the Dolphinarium closed.

Since that time, the P-Orridge famille have been forced into exile, victims of the psychological warfare that is sweeping through Poor Britain as it degenerates inconclusively into a withered mirror of 1930s Germany. Survival of our own family group in a foreign culture, and rehabilitation and detoxification from all sense of be-longing have pretty much preoccupied us, almost pathologically, and we empathize *more*, not less, with all displaced, disenfranchised and distressed beings. Despite these essential but depleting needs and functions, we have discovered one shame-full anomaly in San Francisco's beautiful and liberationally historical Golden Gate Park—two captive dolphins, kept in worse conditions than those in Brighton, with less real justification or sensibility—after all, "it's for their own well being" is less realistic than "it's for the millions of dollars we can make."

We do not know enough about local ordinances, or local regulations, or even local apathies over such matters to initiate immediate action—but we do know that two veterans of our Brighton campaign were reduced to sobbing tears when they discovered these sentient beings, and we do know that despite the jaded, skeptical or merely just subservient-to-hopelessness feelings of many, the indignation, perseverance and passion of a *few* can still win a practical, permanent and moral victory against all odds. This is what we learned most from Brighton—we *won*! Slowly, inexorably, frustratingly we succeeded on behalf of those who, as of yet, cannot speak for themselves in our languages. This lesson applies to us all, and continues a lineage of protest and angry love that we must, none of us, ever allow to be denied.

Genesis Breyer P-Orridge, San Francisco, January 23, 1993

236

T.O.P.Y. BRIGHTON
ANTI-DOLPHINARIUM
CAMPAIGN

KONDOLE, THE WHALE

Not long after, we were introduced to Timothy Wyllie, a gifted writer working in realms including dolphin intelligence, by Eve, a mutual friend. His speculations and convictions struck ever deeper into our spirits as we absorbed both his regenerative presence and also his seminal book *Dolphins, Extraterrestrials, Angels*. We have become convinced that there is only one story, yet numerous mythological tellings. That all consciousness is linked in every dimension and direction similtaneously, and that we are each charged with discovery and navigation.

Within all the stories, songs, metaphors, parables, archetypes and myths are actual descriptions of all salient events and facts, formulae and processes. There is no possibility, in this sense, of fiction—everything is true.

Nothing less than a rigourously critical TransMedia exploration of the essential evidence, the prime nature of matter, L-if-E and brain will lead beyond merely altered states into *quantum* states of consciousness.

Kondole was located by our second daughter, Genesse, when she was two years old. We were in a large second-hand bookshop in Shrewsbury, England. The shelves were piled high on several floors with all kinds of old books. She had watched us browsing, and wished to join in. We said she could have any book she chose from any shelf on any of the floors. After a short time, she returned from the an

237

we duly purchased for her. Inside it, as we read it together that night, was a story of a whale called "Kondole." It was her favorite tale. This story went as follows:

> *The mythology of Encounter Bay, in South Australia, tells how, at the time of the ceremonies, the day was so hot that the streams of perspiration pouring from the bodies of the actors created all the springs and watercourses in the neighbourhood.*
>
> *As the performers had no means of providing light for the evening rituals, they invited Kondole, hoping that he, being the sole owner of fire, would bring it with him. But being mean and disagreeable, Kondole simply hid the fire in the bush and arrived without it.*
>
> *Enraged by his selfishness, the performers discussed several possible means of forcing him to bring his fire to the ceremonial grounds. But as Kondole was a large, powerful man, no one was brave enough to follow up any suggestion. Finally, one of the performers, completely losing his temper over Kondole's mean behavior, crept up behind him and threw a spear that penetrated his skull.*
>
> *Suddenly, the people of the ceremony were transformed into creatures. Some became kangaroos, some opossums, others the smaller creatures. Some rose into the air as birds, while others, entering the sea, were changed into fish in their many forms. Kondole, the largest of them all, became the Whale who, ever since, has spouted water from the spearwound in his head.*
>
> Genesis Breyer P-Orridge

Timothy Wyllie became a timelong friend since the Dolphin action daze. Apart from being an amazing artist, writer and spiritual mentor he also has remarkable stories of L-if-E to share. T*he Process Church Of The Final Judgement* has been an obsession of mine since 1969. With Benjamin Tischer we proposed a Process book to Adam Parfrey years ago. The fruits of that idea and y-eras of archiving and persuasion led directly to Timothy Wyllie's book *LOVE SEX FEAR DEATH* being published in 2009 by Feral House. The Process had a profound influence on the pragmatic methodologies and internal structures of TOPYUK STATION, indeed *LOVE SEX FEAR DEATH* contains a chapter by my Self comparing the two organizations. Consider it essential reading.

Leaked report shows a lot of muck but no poison in dolphinarium water

SO JUST WHO KILLED LITTLE MINNIE?

AQUARIUM & DOLPHINARIUM

SABOTAGE is unlikely to have caused the deaths of Minnie the dolphin and six sharks at Brighton Aquarium and Dolphinarium, the Leader can reveal.

We have obtained a confidential leaked report on chemical tests carried out in the dolphin and shark pools the day after Minnie died.

It supports claims from animal rights groups that the sharks died from suffocation because a water filter broke down — and raises new questions about Minnie.

The report was compiled by Lewes chemists Rymer and Redman at the request of Brighton Council — with the aim of finding out if the sharks and dolphins had been poisoned.

It says the water showed "increased levels of ammonia and organic loading" — in other words, urine and faeces.

The oxygen levels were "relatively low" and probably associated with the increased level of organic matter.

Animal experts from the Zoo Check charity said the higher level of organic

by JEREMY BRITTON

matter was probably caused by inadequate filtration.

Assistant co-ordinator Terry Hill said: "This report doesn't prove anything 100 per cent, but it hints at what really went wrong — bad management."

The leak is a further embarrassment to dolphinarium curator Alan Eastcott, who has consistently suggested sabotage.

Recently he backed up his claims by saying tests showed an unusually high level of a certain chemical.

Denise Friend from Brighton Animal Aid said: "The whole affair smacks of mismanagement."

But Mr Eastcott said: "These tests were taken long after the sharks died and the water parameters could possibly have changed."

BRIGHTON U.K. THIS IS YOUR SHAME

PROTESTING about Minnie's death in a demo outside Brighton Town hall last month

Thee door ov light

IX

AT STOCKHOLM
*Improvised on thee anniversary ov thee receipt ov
The Book of the Law by Aleister Crowley*

ower is often very quiet. Very quiet.

At thee end ov thee day this is what we are trying to do. Understand. Understand?

And it is thee brightest, most extremely searching minds that develop and think and posit new and *stimulating* models for us to superimpose. And we feel our own experiences and we feel thee oddity ov being alive and we have no choice in thee matter. We get trapped here briefly, change nothing, measured against infinity. At thee best, stretching slightly nearer to thee sky. Thee most stimulating thinkers risk all to grasp at thee deepest and most hidden revelations. If they even suspect that they have glimpsed a usable piece ov essential pattern they are left crippled in thee expressing ov it. How does such a Master pass on knowledge? Through thee most flawed and mystical medium ov all: *language.*

Language. Power. Language. Quiet.

And like most forms ov behaviour it is inherited and it must by definition contain within it, coded and drenched in aeons ov subjectivity, a mass ov confusion and a few insights.

At Stockholm we could not speak, although thee sudden glow ov passion mantling to thee crimson cheek ov either, told our tale ov L-ov-E, although we could not speak. What need ov language, barren and false and bleak, while our white arms could link each other so, and fond red lips, their partners mutely speak. What need ov language when our kisses flow eloquent, warm as words are cold and weak. Or now—aah sweetheart, even were it so we could not speak.

Four. Two. Six. *Two. Three.*

And we lay in thee monastery, and we lay in thee Vatican. And we touched thee walls as they crumpled like bone. And we lay back and each eye that opened was alone. And you came towards me like hot breath. Your juice flowing over my flesh, E couldn't help but touch your body.

243

Your body like monastery-angels, lust, Catholick sex. Stroking her fingers in naked flesh. My breath escaping like lust-rust in her hair and over my skin. E raised her clothes and then making shame and making names E came. With Catholick sex. Caresses ov monasteries and churches, singing ov choirs, and open orgasms and liquids on thee back ov my hand, rubbing my cheek, down my gland working alone in thee naked land. Angels ov breath. Wings ov monasteries. Catholick sex. And you spoke from so far away. And E sucked in your breath. Death. E touched her thigh and death smiled.

We live in fragments. And thee coumfortable ones disturb as much as thee bad. Thee leaves falling, we sit with thee lights thumbing through our dictionaries, to explain. What makes this difficult? What makes happiness paralyzing like suicide? Thee ultimate irony ov nature's game. We play it both ways, weighing up thee results. Choices so hard like bone. Old myths die soft and paralyze our ambition. Why am E always focussed on thee suffering? When we are happy we sleep and slumber. Raw in pain, we feel hopeless and dead.

E dreamed ov a new kind ov spider.

Mostly small baby ones. One adult with a yellow body. When you step on them hard nothing happens, they don't squash and die. They always threaten that they may bite and poison, but they never do. It's just another possibility, keeps us on edge, perhaps that's it—*all those marvelous words composed as we wake or drift to sleep*. All those words are spiders. Teasing us—so close to existence. Is this thee white path?

In thee search for signs, individuals see directions. There was a timezone long ago when feet struggled across blood-biting flint, wrapped in animal skin. Bleached bone spoke ov thee snake wave day. If you imagine a small child with a long ribbon flicking their wrist sharply at each extremity ov position fluidly in thee central space, you will picture thee flow ov life as it was then. Regular, like thee trails ov a serpent on Sahara sand. Each bended knee wrapped in thee moisture-preserving layers of nomadic survival, elbow cricked for support. Each bended knee sees what has passed. Time is that which emits. Arising like a Knighted Templar to scan thee four directions—thee point ov intersection between sky and earth is shimmering, not clear. There is a spinning ov equality, mind, body, emotions and spirit. These coum from thee simplicity ov looking. Hand raised to shield eyes, thee fingers ov thee left hand create a flickering movement like a Venetian blind. It is, ov course, a frame. A threshold—to travel through—in light and to light. We have travelled through time many thousands ov yeras from ritual wandering towards words into language. All ways ov closing down our basic nature, all ways ov closing down our hope. And language has becoum thee essence ov what we are. *Light is measured by time, and time is what we Emit.* We have travelled through time in a few lines, marks that have no flowing pattern, no snake, no calligraphy. And we have been losing things as we converse. And we have been losing things as we listen. And we have been losing things as we try to be alive. And we have just been losing things.

In thee search for all these signs, individuals speak directions. North. South. East. West. Crystal sand melted by atomic fission. Thee sun is behind everything; each second we observe tells us stories, parables, allegories. We see thee sun, our arms reach out to hold it. It seems so small. We have no sense ov perspective. Our boar-like grunts sound raw. We shake our matted manes and feel anger. *Anger.*

245

As we sit around our cave fire, all life dances. On thee pitted stone.

No fear exists except thee fear ov leaving. No fear exists except thee fear ov dying. No fear exists except thee fear ov sinning. No fear exists except thee beginning.

And that is what happiness does. It gives you fear. Thee only fear that exists. Ironic. Ironic. Oh, and happiness ov course gives you insight. And life gives death. And if time is that which emits and we are outside it then death takes us back inside it. So wc can never end. And thee greatest fear, thee greatest fear must be Eternal Life.

As time passes thee addiction dwindles. Detoxifying, *satisfying*, like a jolt ov steel. Muscles aching memory, no longer as loose as they were, but stiffening with age instead ov lust.

Thee demand outstrips thee supply and creates in-security. Give me sin-security anyday.

And now thee white path is moving. Can you see a change? Is it good? Does it feel good? Do you think you should? Do you feel good? Do you remember how it was to be good? That's just thee way it is?

Thee door is always open both ways.

And we stand, and we watch everything. And we speak, and we touch nothing. And we use our seeing and look for anything. We wash and change, thee power ov saying, and we divide to be lost. And lost in thee whole we divide as parts and provide thee soul. And we divide as parts, and provide thee soul.

Thee ruins ov Earth. Leaves spluttering Fire. Boots splashing Rain across an upturned pram. Escaping like Dust from zero-point.

Style exists on thee dark side ov history. Thee propagation ov comfort. A circle ov dead animals—unexplained. A conflict vision ov society with a bitter experience ov vivisection. *There will be no announcements.*

Rigid groups with rigid motives are increasingly redundant. Only a primal scream. A disgusted, disgusted terrorist. And X marks thee spot with a cross. And this is ritual music. Alive and kicking—everything is on thee head and everything is dead. Secret passages, dank with liquid open to lance thee key, and thee hordes are stripped for action and action in itself is for no reason.

This is thee world, everyone talking in tongues to fire-strewn Spirit, convinced, betrayed there is only expression, loud and unclear, an exact parallel ov life passing by. In each ov us there are ghosts, escaping like dust from control. We have thee ectoplasm ov Youth, thee final Psychick Rally, yet a present testament is just set in present time.

Breath, in a dead soul, hanging by that thread. Convinced and betrayed.

And there lies history: a yellow spider.

That's just thee way it is—but when all is brought together, when space and time no longer channel all existence, when we are just a chaos ov tiny pieces, divorced by thee dimensions from each other, we feed back thee splinters and concentrate them outside thee seperating limits ov existence so that we at last may becoum One! One Nature! One Substance! One Being! One Orientation! One Power! One Truth! One Knowledge! One Awareness! *One TOPI!*

Then and only then we can say nothing—*no-thing*—nothing at all, and that is just thee way it is, and that is just thee way we speak, and that is just thee way we look, and that is just thee way thee children cry, all, all children cry and die. And that is just thee way it is, and that is just thee way it is, it's thee only time you can say nothing.

You know it doesn't matter. You know it's all pointless. You do know that. Where do you go when you can speak?

Control is an illusion, control is imposed; but it does not need time, it does not need life, for it is outside time. It must be, for *time is a consciousness.* Outside time. It's outside time.

All images begin in mirrors and end inside our unconscious. All conscious mirrors crack and cut, seep blood and stain our dearest memories. Sitting in one position, our head crooked but balanced on our knee, our muscles tremble and we shake, we are left and we are right. Corrupted. Corrupted butter nearer to thee mortality. We are trained to fear. Encased in thee concrete ov acceptance by our peers where it can do us no harm. Fear and ignorance remain. In describing life, its grandiose stupidity, we can be motivated by compassion and motivated by despair, colored by not a little sarcasm and cynicism. Yet in every picture, there is enervation and texture that rely upon a resented caring for its composition. Framed by our paranoias, framed by conditioning, framed by false witness and thee left and thee theft and thee right and thee theft ov all pieces ov silver. We kiss thee cheek ov thee land that bites us. We reccive nothing in return. Butter nothing is why we came here. Nothing is what we so awkwardly strive and fight for. Nothing is our very precise confrontation with reason.

247

It's easy to forget nothing and hard to describe it. What was it we said once in thee mud? Thee expression that there is nothing to express, nothing with which to express, nothing from which to express, no power to express, together with thee obligation to express.

Creative action. Destructive action. A perception ov thee weird phenomena ov being alive. To illumine, clarify and describe some part ov human experience, trying to grasp or even form thee values that guide that experience in a given age, or piece ov time. And whilst time is that which emits, we for better or worse are those who do not. Thee mirror receives our staring gaze, we melt quite gently then sink away, leaving a smoky, cloudy effect, like bleach spreading into water. To cleanse our guilt we must describe our fate, objective warzone correspondence using thee oral language ov everyday life. Shattered or not, our message remains neither fixed nor dogmatic. True value never changes. True value remains in thee only real sense. Only time has a constant value, and time is outside our life.

Nothing is more real than nothing.

Human experience is sadly thee experience ov nothing. And thee only reality it knows is nothing.

After thee accumulation ov too much history we have lost our innocence. We cannot easily believe in any explanations. We describe rather than feel, we touch rather than explore, we lust rather than adore, we play rather than think, we abuse rather than give praise. So there you are, or not.

And so you are there. And that's just thee way it is.

In a distant cave individuals are wrapped in animal skins. Painting sorceries on their temporary cave shelter. Across thee mountains a boy is sewn in bloody-warm skins to dance thee sacred dance ov Pan. Thee point where thee animal spirit and thought spirit separated. Thee moment when society became inevitable. At this moment thee knowings which were contained in states ov not thinking were encoded, thee myths, legends, allegories, religions are now where they reside. Thee search ov High Art and High Magick has been for processes ov retrieval. In order to facilitate completion ov reintegration we search for the knowings we lost. Thee re-establishment in thee individual ov a permanent state ov zero time. Zero language, zero thought, this is our Holy Grail. Where consciousness can exist within its own planes. Just as if it were thee Light. It is no accident that these encoded truths are so often seen as pictures, or seen as picture stories. For every picture is made ov light. E am thee Light. E am thee Truth. E am thee Light. E am thee Way. E am thee Light.

Language is thee most corrupt ov messengers.

In thee distance there is truth which ends like a knife. Thee bridge we have laid will always give us life. And we who cross on a goat we ride or fall like fruit in a red sea tide. Thee snake is time. Its teeth are seed. They press like flesh on those who bleed. Thee cross is gold as is our L-ov-E. Thee goat is bold it eats thee dove. Dust to dust. Dust and dreams. Anoint thee stone with blood and screams. Thee rod and almond rise and grow, they mask thee blood and light thee O. Thee door ov light is loud and full, it hides thee fish we cannot kill. From all our eyes thee future leaks. Thee path is made, its shell is weak. He who is asleep with words shall gain his peace by force ov swords. If you could understand, you would take my hand, and I would spread so far. Just like Arcadia.

No fear except thee fear ov leaving. Death is like each other. Life has only dreams to recommend it, and thee security ov being inside. To be part ov a group—to be *in*-side—is to enter thee body and partake ov sex. We thrive on violation. We attempt to re-create thee excitement ov a first moment's intensity by deceptive means. There are no taboos. Nothing is forbidden. Happiness can give you fear, ov course. Thee fear ov it ending. Thee only real fear is fear ov ending, and thee only joy—is violation. Unhappiness gives cruel insight. Happiness makes death a threat. As time passes thee addiction to happiness dwindles. Always a jolt ov steel. Thee orchid and thee metal. Muscles no longer as loose as childhood ache in memoriam—stiffening with age before beauty. Age before lust. Age before L-ov-E. Demand outstrips thee supply, and we congeal—fixed in parables and fantasies. Thee past controls through people. Little girls becoum young ladies. They attract by their lack ov experience, unaware ov *thee spell*. More concerned with being inside than observation, they accept thee host, their tongue lolls. Their eyes close. Thee *words* are spoken. *Everything* is taken in. They create a ghost that haunts us forever. Thee ache for reclamation. Perhaps, thee story goes, if you recreate that first moment, past, you can travel back in time. Or by creating a stranger situation—replenish lust. Violation is a form ov breaking thee rules. A necessary act to exist. Conscious deception and

249

threat ov oneself and one's security. Conscious attack on one's feeling ov being safe affirms existence. It makes us real.

Sexuality, sex, getting inside makes real too. *And once inside we can make anything happen*. Eyes shut in a coffin. A world ov darkness. We travel into that darkness to reconvene our emotions and listening hard we see every detail ov every sexual act.

Little girls masturbating about tomorrow. Every second losing its intensity. Creating thee need forever to go back inside, and feel safe. To travel back and to feel alive we have to becoum our own sperm. It really is so difficult. What we have, creates our need. Restrictions are removed like school uniforms. We discover eroticism in both manners, and manners maketh man and woman. We enter our bodies, we are inside. Inside is quiet. Scarcely a solution in sight. Sharing a body is nothing. Sharing insight, being inside, is everything. A fine balance maintained by neurosis; when we break rules we becoum fools. Driven by a desire for ignorance. We don't want to know. All these rules are created by a wound. We never escape them. We never escape them. We descend into them. Rats in a trap made up ov all thee letters we know. All paranoia coums from thee past, it takes us like a rape and damages. But in thee morning after thee night we fall in L-ov-E with thee Light.

Thee solution is to touch skin, to stay safe and be deep inside. Better pain, better hurt, better coumfusion than boredom. Better to give all than do nothing. You are your own owner. You can give yourself a name, you can give yourself a new family, give yourself back to yourself. This process increases and gets *deeper*. You can shatter yourself, begin to rebuild. There is an anger inside, an anger at thee past, an anger at society, an anger at hypocrisy, at stupidity, at lies, cruelty, righteousness, religion, politics, war, violence, sexual oppression, sterility ov vision, genocide, culturecide, at a million and one foundations ov modern life.

This anger is natural.

It is *thee warrior* rising up in clarity. It is you reclaiming your right to exist, thee way you want. To have a future, to be safe, to leave your descendants their own place in history. Because you care so much, because you L-ov-E so much, because you insist on possessing your own self so much you will feel in every cell thee pain and sorrow ov seeing what those addicted to power and control have done to you. And they are still doing it.

Genesis Breyer P-Orridge improvised poetry at TOPYSCAN, 1989

WILL THE FUTURE LEAK THROUGH?

In the beginning was the Word and the Word was XXX. What scared you all into time? Into body? I will tell you: "The Word." Prisoner come out. The great skies are open. Who is Bou Jeloud? Who is he?

(But Jesus said, suffer little children, and forbid them not, to come into me; for of such is the Kingdom...)

Whatever you are is a mirror of what we are. If you can't believe it's happening, pretend it's a movie. As it is.

(But Jesus said, I am what you have made of me and the mad dog devil killer fiend leper is a reflection of your society... In my mind's eye my thoughts light fires in your cities...)

251

Every religion in the world that has destroyed people is based on LOVE.

Christ said: Love thine enemy. Christ's enemy was Satan and Satan's enemy was Christ. Through love, enmity is destroyed. Through love, saint and sinner destroy the enmity between them. Through love, Christ and Satan have destroyed their enmity and come together for the end. Christ to judge, Satan to execute the judgement.

After this I looked and, behold, a door was opened in heaven; the first voice which I heard was as if it were of a trumpet talking with me.

Let's not hear that noise again and again that may well be the last Word anywhere.

"I am Alpha and Omega, the beginning and the end, the first and the last." Who is Bou Jeloud? Who is he?

The shivering boy who was chosen to be stripped naked and sewn into the warm skins... When he dances, his musicians blow a sound like the earth sloughing off its skin. He is the Father of Fear. He is, too, the Father of Flocks. The Good Shepherd works for him.

(But Jesus said, "I am the Good Shepherd, who giveth his life for thee sheep. But he whose own the are not, leaveth the sheep and the wolf catcheth them.")

There's a light seeping out from under the door. And behind this door burns our sacred Cross that shines for them. It burns for them and the sound it makes is the Sound of Fear. The key that unlocks the empty rooms, the fires of hell outshine the face of God. In the madness of the mire.

(But Jesus said, "I don't mind being tortured. What about you?... I'm no longer afraid. I'd just as soon bring it to a gallant, glorious, screaming end, a screeching stop in one glorious moment of triumph.")

Rub out the Word forever.

Simon Woodgate, April 1989 and January 1990 Era Maximus

Time mirrors

X

Drawing by Austin Osman Spare

VIRTUAL MIRRORS IN SOLID TIME

Since all phenomena (or phenomenally appearing things) which arise, present no reality in themselves, they are said to be of the noumena (in other words, they are of the Voidness, regarded as the noumenal background or Source of the physical universe of the phenomena). Though not formed into anything, they give shape to everything. Thus it is that phenomena and noumena are ever in union, and said to be of one nature. They are, like ice and water, reflection and mirror, two aspects of a single thing.
The Seven Books of Wisdom (Tibetan text)

n the case of a mirror, there is a third aspect: the subject/viewer. Mirrors reveal and conceal; their mystery permanent, their hints at doorways, windows, points of entry and thresholds just out of reach of our conscious minds. TIME (The Imaginary Mass Emits). Image. Idea. There can be no separation, scientifically or subjectively. The atavistic face gazes down into a crystal pool. Ice-cold water. Grunts. A hand shatters the image; fear gaunt and haunting passes across, a shadowy cloud, and through all TIME; that moment can persist, be reclaimed.

What is time, but a variety of one thing?
Austin Osman Spare

These moments of time accumulate, are listed under memory in our modern synapses and are posited as always retrievable, amorphous. Nothing is forgotten, all is permitted. In a stinking cave, muttering babies scream and scratch, furs undulate in copulation. In one corner, bright-eyed first marks are daubed on a wall. They are marks to function, marks of place, of time. They are marks to draw results and persist beyond one human lifetime. Instinct has arisen, snake-like, coiling itself into intuition and has suggested the very power of suggestion. No one noted down from a book this process, it grew from watching the elements, closeness to life-sources, death-forces that modern persons are divorced from. On this damp stone there is a curve; it is land, horizon, ejaculation, movement.

Magick consists in seeing and willing beyond the next horizon.
The Sar

Mrs. Paterson stares down. Penciled into existence. It is her as she was when she took Austin Osman Spare at fourteen years old and initiated him into the art of sexual magick and a power-full system of sorcery (a primal oral tradition preserved through female bloodlines) that she had rediscovered and regenerated through her covert communion across time with systems and techniques that grew from a most animalistic and pure union of instinct and inherited DNA encryptions. This woman knew, and she taught Spare, how to travel through time and just how malleable and manipulable a form of energy and matter it was. She also instructed Spare in techniques that could empower him to remain present in life, after an apparent physical death. She was a medium, but her guides were not the "New Age," romantic and patronizing icons of native peoples and tribes. Not just Indian chiefs, Pharaohs, Tibetan Rinpoches or aborigines. They were more like the creatures of Clive Barker's *Hellraiser* visions, or the demons in *Evil Dead*. They were the deepest, most atavistic and rawest representations of the alien that we can experience. Equivalent, if you will, to a seriously hardcore DMT entity confrontation. Mrs. Paterson understood a most particular secret. Her medium was her self. She was quite able to travel through mirrors and throughout time.

258

There is a drawing in my possession by Spare, a pencil and gouache, finished in 1928. The main figure is Mrs. Paterson. Coming from behind her head, making a blister in a shimmering green-penciled aura, is a half-completed face. It belongs to no one, everyone. It is she at times, it is cavalier and it is also Austin Osman Spare. This one picture contains all the secrets Spare never wrote down (his books are thorough, precise and often opaque). Spare appears in the bottom right-hand corner, represented as he projects—he will look as an old man, eyes closed, concentrated; manifesting, it would seem, the other beings in the picture. Remarkably, his projection of his older self is uncannily accurate.

What Spare is doing is "tricking" us. All his writings are symbolic; they were never intended to be taken literally, as illustrations, on any level. His writings are primarily journals, decorative encryptions of basic techniques of travel. But they are appendices to the real work. This special trick was to convince everybody that his drawings, paintings and images were symbolic, fantastical products of his imagination. They are in fact the essence of his sorcery. Like all great sorcerers, he hid his central se-cret in an apparently commonplace medium. What we discover in this key picture is that he is actually kneeling. It is actually a "photographic" record of his prediction of both his own bodily death, and his worship of Mrs. Paterson as the keeper of immortality.

Spare made consistent use, for very specifically sex magical reasons, of late middle-aged prostitutes who would normally be considered "brash" and heavily made-up. Women who could, in his mind, rep-resent Mrs. Paterson at the age she seduced and instructed him, and thus charge more powerfully his sexual magick rituals and sigils as a result. Just as the sorcerer repeats elements of ritual over and over again, and uses the same magical tools, incenses, incantations and so on repeatedly to achieve a cumulative effect, so Spare recreated a virtual sorceress to revisit, the precise intersections of time and space that she had imprinted in his brain. Through this reputedly sordid, but actually visionary method of sexual magick, he was able to return at will to a potent portal, an access point into the matter of time it-self, and then, even deeper, into what we can only call timelessness, though outside time might be a more accurate way to articulate the state. These women were close enough to Mrs. Paterson in cosmetic physical appearance and characteristics to be used as a focusing visual key enabling him to be accelerated at the moment of orgasm, just like a particle accelerator, into direct, inter-dimensional contact with her, and all the infinite previous hers that had ever existed.

259

This is more easily understood contemporaneously, now, in a post-DMT experiential environment. In other words, DMT would be a very good equivalent experience of what this catapulting might feel like. However, Spare could recreate this at will, and via will, over and over again, with deep lucidity and in a state of sexual intoxication, rather than biochemi-cal intoxication. A drug-free splitting of the atoms of time!

When Mrs. Paterson died, he was able to take a particular aspect of her life source and literally preserve it still "living" into this, and one or two other pictures. This is not to be misunderstood as in any way vampiric. That is not what we're dealing with here. This is a much more deeply fundamental sorcery. Spare is consensually keeping open a portal of connection between the primal inter-dimensional knowledge and an entity that was represented by the physical manifestation within linear time by Mrs. Paterson's existence on this particular Earth, at a particular allotted moment. In the same mysterious way that, if you will, a mirror can contain all that it faces in what seems an equally "real" world, so Spare's pictures can hold the entirety of the images and entities that he represents in them.

They are there. The frame is exactly intended to be experienced as, and function as, the edges of a mirror, although, because it is a plastic, more fixed medium, we often cannot see around the inside edges by moving, as we can with a mirror. We cannot always change the amount and depth of what we see simply by moving, as we can with a mirror. Do not be fooled by mundane physics. There are specific periods when, remarkably, the opposite is true, and these images do indeed become exactly the same as mirrors, representing an entire portal into a parallel omniverse. Further, I would suggest, indeed insist, based upon my own personal experiences, and those of many other colleagues who have acted as controls, and/or guinea pigs in my experiments with these pictures to act as confirmation, or dismissal of the actuality, that these pictures do not just become virtual mirrors. They become living portals that animate, through which entities can travel, accessing our "world" and bidding us into theirs.

When Mrs. Paterson died, he fixed her in this picture. We see him. He sinks into her chest, is absorbed; they rise together, androgynous, genderless, both their faces and all their ages superimposed to create one alien being. One inter-dimensional entity. He has drawn himself dying, conjuring himself into this picture in advance of that event, so that he may always return. Like the Cocteau character crossing back and forth through the mirror.

Art can contradict Science.
Austin Osman Spare

Art is the truth we have realized of our belief.
Austin Osman Spare

Do you see those flowers growing on the sides of the abyss whose beauty is so deadly and whose scent is so disturbing? Beware...
de Guatia

In these sorcerous images, these his purest incantations through art, Spare uses a graphic skill and technique second to none. Yet his most commonly seen works can appear deliberately fast and loose. The nearest modern parallel would be Salvador Dali, who could suggest perfection and hyper-reality in a few precisely placed marks and intersections, and through his works worship his own personal sorceress, Gala. Dali's photo-realistic technique is accurate in an unearthly way, too, and Dali uses delirium and dislocation of the senses to catapult himself, and us, through the parameters of madness and obsession into his personal landscape and environment. Dali occasionally masturbated into his paints, particularly painting the leather strap across Hitler's back, and made good use of the canvas as a virtual mirror viewed from one static position.

I would argue that Dali, despite his genius, was naïve, struggling to de-scribe glimpses and fragments of vision, with an ad hoc quasi-magical perception and aspiration. Dali did not build, though he hungered to, a system as unique, primal, timeless and fully administered by informed, cumulative and inter-dimensional arcane knowledge as Spare. Spare knew all too well what he was doing, conjuring and building. A method of physical and neurological immortality, a means to step outside time. Dali really wanted to, but remained finally restrained by his inability to travel beyond use of his imagination. For Dali, the mirror was a solid barrier into which he could gaze, but not travel. Spare was the very ma-terial of the mirror, the destroyer of its boundaries, or limitations, and finally usurped every definition of mirrorness, creating a virtual portal that accessed all moments of time past, present, future, none, in every possible and impossible infinite combination.

261

Time is, you see, a solid through which all passes, all is seen from a van-tage point. As we learn to move our point of perception, so we act like a lens, or a mirror's surface viewed from above. Light, thought, life, passes through us, expanding outwards. We can place our mirrors anywhere, perceive them from any direction; thus we are potentially everywhere, in every possible time and every possible dimension. All travel is possible. We are an amorphous, infinite density of matter. The matter is time. It is all a matter of time. Time is malleable and thus both the portal and the means of travel. We can leave, we can return, we can cease to exist. This is the "virtual mirror" of Spare. These are the prophetic portals. But they do not prophesy art. They prophesy an end to materiality. A disintegration, a dissipation of our corporeality beyond anything so far confessed in the small wooden box of physics.

The future is in the past, but it is not wholly contained in the present.
Hoene-Wronski

Brion Gysin was another such artist of the future, another such alchemist and sorcerer who used art to create time and inter-dimensional travel. He used a different style. More abstract, more directly concerned with encryption, coding and decoding, and with a clear appreciation of post-linguistic magick. "Rub out the Word," he would emphasize. He too was absolutely aware of the implication of his experiments and their functions. Both Gysin and William Burroughs accepted as a given that the central power of their works was to trick time and, through another system of cumulative effect, manipulate and navigate mortality and all sources of pre-recorded life, brain, entity, location and the process of control that locks us out of the inviolate human right to transcend physicality.

262

Gysin was a practicing magician first, and actually described at length to me in Paris his longtime practice of mirror staring, and the incredible melting of none-sensus reality that resulted for both him, and many of the other Beats. He suggested that there are "hot spots" in cultural engineering, and vehicles of convenience that accelerate the inevitable for those reckless and/or courageous enough to risk all for a possibility of disincarnation, of leaving behind the host physical body forever in a necessary transmutation into otherness, a way of alien being, that must be the only valid goal of any of us if forward motion and discovery are truly our agenda. In traditional Western occulture this letting go of all preconceptions, all expectations, all value systems, all inherited moral imprints, all concepts of self-preservation and all distinctions is referred to as the "Abyss."

See a cliff, jump off.
Old TOPY proverb

Both Spare and Gysin lived to pursue, and attain, new dimensions. They understood the hunger to pursue successful systems of sorcery, not knowledge. This alone made overt collaboration with magical groups impossible, where the need for nostalgic elitism, power implied by academic recall and self-image measured by the length of one's bookshelf far too often camouflage mere self-aggrandizement, and the essence of motivation is the servility of others. Gysin incorporated tape-recorders, permutations, projections, trance music, mathematical formulae. Spare incorporated his own body, sexuality and dimensional fluidity. Both were prophets of portals of virtuality and developments in quantum neurology that later became possible, and, as egalitarian access to cyberspace and other synthetic worlds expands globally, now become at the very least more likely and, I would propose, inevitable. The world we appreciate in a mirror. That world where as we get close, appears to be large, and equally as "real" as this supposedly more physical none-sensus reality; and the world of Spare, where the frame of the image is arbitrary, where creatures and perceptual environments are frozen in a precise cryogenic graphic is equally accurate.

These worlds are mere precursors of the apparently limitless, and multidimensional possibilities heralded by the microchip. The century wills to be remembered eventually as the century when the cut-up—the splitting of the atom by relativity, of the mind by psychedelic compounds and of linear thinking by cultural nihilism—were the primary themes. Spilling over into social fragmentation, online alienation and a data-glut that, by its very scale, insists on acceleration of response by our brains, and a highly developed perceptual skill of instant, and arbitrary assembly "to see what is really there," as W. S. Burroughs has stated.

263

Spare was aware that mystery and magick, in themselves, generate at the very least a morbid fascination, and reaction in human persons. He consciously used his books, his twisted Beardsley-esque graphics and his atavistic writings to attract our interest after his physical death. Not for reasons of ego. I would contend that it was to reactivate his "mind" and re animate his psyche. Sound far-fetched? Well, personal anecdote, take it or leave it

One of the Spare paintings that I used to own (now in the collection of Blondie's Chris Stein) was called "The Ids." Every New Year's Eve, strange things would occur. Most noticeably, the two faces of Spare himself that faced each other would re-animate. Many different guests would suddenly gasp and say, did you know that the faces in that painting have "come alive"? Or "They are arguing." None of these observers knew who Spare was, or any of his ideas, or my own ideas about him. Eventually I checked and found that Spare died on New Year's Eve, 1956. A medium called Madame Bruna, also, on a social visit, was shocked and disturbed by the "Mrs. Paterson" image. In fact, it was this repeated witnessing of the faces becoming real, moving, talking, changing, that led to the thoughts in this essay. In the case of the "Mrs. Paterson" picture, nobody felt anything malevolent. Just a powerful experience of people "trapped in a mirror." "The Ids," however, was different. Something one could only think of as "bad" always happened when it animated. It got so predictable and incontrovertible that I took to putting it in a cupboard, facing the wall for a period before and after New Year's Eve each year.

The last phenomenon was particularly odd. Before traveling abroad I arranged for two people to be caretakers of my house in Brighton. I warned them, almost like in a fable, such as "Hansel and Gretel," that they must not touch, move or hang up the Spare painting "The Ids," which was in the loft space of the house, facing the wall. I told them, "It might sound superstitious or stupid, but please trust me on this one." I guess, inevitably, they felt this as a challenge and chose to not only turn the picture facing outwards in the loft, but to spend a night staring at it and sleeping in the same space. Apparently, as they tell it, after an hour or so, the picture seemed to fill the room. Spare argued with himself, as usual. Then a new thing happened. The central face of one woman (there were three women's faces above Spare's heads) came alive too. The picture seemed to grow into a huge mirror, filling the visual perception of one whole end of the loft. The room seemed to fill with green mist, and then, holding her hand out, this woman walked out of the "painting" and came towards them. In the inanimate painting, the heads are floating in a green field, no bodies. They have heavy makeup on, like the prostitutes Spare favored for his psycho-sexual sorcery. Both people panicked, and ran from the loft, locking the door behind them. From that time on, various destructive events affected the house, and them. Had they let loose, in classic horror film style, a malevolent entity, with its own agenda? One of the two people became an alcoholic; both had mental breakdowns. By the way, Chris Stein was aware of this side of the painting's history when he purchased it.

Spare had been shrewd enough to make all his secrets non-verbal, and non-linear. Not one explanation of these secrets is contained overtly in his writings. He was, in the best covert cultural traditions, working for himself alone. Only the atavistic hinting, and the "Virtual Mirror" drawings and paintings can articulate, and bear witness to, his phenomenal achievements.

The Universe is a creative process carried on by man's imagination, an operative power capable of becoming more supple, more animate.
Teilhard de Chardin

What is happening in these certain key pictures? I would propose a few speculations. All ideas have an image. We were originally an hieroglyphic species, before the restrictive linguistic and alphabetical systems we use now were adopted. Adopted, I might add, purely for reasons of control, and the compression of both vision and potential in all of us. All the materials used to create and fix an image are material. They are formed of patterns of atoms and molecules, charged by certain energies that hold their specific clusters together in some way. Modern psychology also tends to accept that ideas are material entities, like animals and plants. All mythological ideas, Jung suggests, are essentially real and far older than any philosophy. They originated in primal perceptions, correspondences and experiences. The catalytic element that regenerates a reaction between entotic ideas and a spectator and that favors parapsychological events is the presence of an active archetype. In the specific case of Spare's virtual mirror art, this element can be anything from an obvious glyph (condensing and compressing a desire), a non-decorative aesthetic arrangement, or in the most intense "portal" works, an invisible charge of energy which somehow calls the deepest, instinctual layers of the psyche into action. The archetype is a borderline phenomenon, an acausal connecting principle, closest in explanation to deliberately controlled, self-conscious synchronicity. When Spare describes in certain of his texts "Self-Love," if you will, as the engine of his sorcery, I believe he means self-conscious, yet ego-less. When he uses the word chaos, which he profoundly championed from the start of the century, he is leaving a key evidentiary clue and amusing himself. Austin Osman Spare's "Chaos" is both a signature, and a signpost into future time. (ChDVH = JOY = 23) Thus we get CH-A.O.S.—both his name, and his confession of secret sorcery.

265

Art is the instinctive application of the knowledge latent in the unconscious.
Austin Osman Spare

After Mrs. Paterson died, Spare was waiting to be inside her again, fused with her sexual-magical energy. Inside her also, in the sense of two liquids mixing to create a third amalgam. Two consciousnesses as well, the Third Mind of Brion Gysin. This is not romantic fiction. This is a prediction of some of the inter-dimensional forays that are subscribed to very convincingly by Terence McKenna and other such botanical voyagers. In this key picture by Spare, what we are really seeing is both his projection into the actual future moment of his own death, and the way Mrs. Paterson looked exactly at the moment of her death overlaid. His aim in all his sorcery was to reunite his spirit and hers, captured within the dimensions of his artworks so that through this process they could both, quite literally, live forever—an interesting twist on the idea of great art making the artist immortal! In this case I mean immortal quite literally. They do still live. Just as our concepts and assumptions about reality, and varieties of perception have been forever revised by the advent of virtual reality and quantum psychology, so our concepts of linear existence are confounded by the manifestation held in stasis in these virtual mirrors.

Keep in mind Cocteau's "mirrors" passing through to the "other side" where different rules of physics and continuity apply. We are finally accepting that everything is truly in constant flux, that the malleability of all matter and all constructs is not just theoretical, that time is equally an energy and matter as flesh, and that projected images and virtual worlds are as valid and vibrant as the basic inherited consensus possibility that we tend to arrive trapped in, squealing and pissing from our mother's vagina. We are witnessing the realization that everything everyone says is true. That everything believed is real. That bodies are mere vehicles for transporting our brain and that mortality is primarily a philosophical control process. Why, my children, even that dear old anarchist construct "The Bible" was assigned an alchemical message more significant than Pat Robertson might choose to consider.

Have I not said that faith can move mountains?
Some old prophet or another

The marvelous is not rare, incredulity is stronger than miracles.
Jaques Rigaut

Apart from the more dramatic animations already mentioned, many unprompted witnesses have been shocked to see Mrs. Paterson's eyes close, open, cry or her whole head turn. Quite literally a living portrait. Magick makes "dreams" real, makes the impossible possible, focuses the Will to... Throughout occult circles in all ages crystal, water, polished metal, mirrors of all types have been used for oracular purposes. Spare's massive achievement is that he recognized the potential of art, of image, to be the most powerful magical mirror of all. A window in time. An interface with death. An inter-dimensional modem. In his art he captures not just an image but a life force. What seems to happen is that the individual's consciousness contained within the art remains dormant in this reality until they come into contact with the minds of certain others, or as an intersection with linear TIME sets in motion a preprogrammed "software" sequence of interactions. Primal, atavistic "aboriginal" peoples knew this. Sometimes facilitated with botanical catalysts they would invest immense and potentially limitless powers in specific totem images and glyphs or sigils.

This use of the image as scrying mirror and as neurological nuclear energy is very different as a function of "art" to the post-patronage, post-craftsperson Twenty-First Century norm of Art, with that horribly big "A." In contemporary elitist art you actually don't get anything much back except aesthetics. You certainly don't get mummification and time travel! But we must never forget that all art grew from sorcery and from the concealment of Gnostic and alchemical procedures from those who would be "King." Art was once synonymous with, and a direct aspect of, Magick. It was functional, and it was dedicated to the processing of immortality, and the opening and preservation of portals.

(By the way, I would argue that "cyberspace"—or the "psychosphere," as I would prefer it was called—is an extension of this perception and function in just the same way, and we are just glimpsing the beginnings of the somewhat cack-handed access we've so far realized.)

Anyway... Spare achieved the forgotten, that which vested interests in all status quos considered impossible, even blasphemous; a two-way communication where HIS image reacts to and with the viewer. It has a life of its own. The nearest parallel, a virtual mirror in which you can see another world, one that we cannot touch, the glass remaining solid

267

and frustrating us. What this energy held within his images is doing is transcending the barriers of observed time so that what we are seeing is a five-dimensional object or image. This form of energy wills to have existed at all times, and wills to exist at all times.

An objective (hah!) and critical survey of the available data would establish that perceptions occur as if in part there were no space, in part no time. Space and time are not only the most immediate "certainties" for us, they are the most misleading, doomed to be discredited as separate and abstracted states imminently. They are also usually considered empirical certainties too, since everything observable is said to happen as though it occurred in space and time. In the face of this overwhelming "certainty," it is understandable that "reason" should have the greatest difficulty in granting validity to the peculiar nature of "delirious" phenomena, or paranormal events. But anyone who does some amount of justice to the facts cannot but admit that their apparent space-timelessness is their most essential quality. The fact that we are totally unable to imagine a form of existence without space or time by no means proves that such an existence is in itself impossible, and, therefore, just as we cannot draw from an appearance of space-timelessness, any absolute conclusion about a possible space-time-less form of existence, so we are not entitled to conclude from the apparent space-time quality of our perception that there is no form of existence without space and time. I would imagine, though, that any of you fortunate enough to have had a particularly enervating moment of psychedelic experience will be more empathetic to the speculative space-timeless state!

Just as "physics" now tends to allow for "limitedness of space," a relativization, it is beginning with catastrophe theory / fuzzy geometry / chaos mathematics and other quantum disciplines to posit a "limitedness" of both TIME and causality. In short, nothing is fixed. "It's official!"—the possibilities alone are endless.

Conscious looking is a search for verification of the notions that impel the search, and all ways has a circular mirroring element within it.
Genesis Breyer P-Orridge

In Spare's most critical images, it seems that a medium has been synthesized whereby the essence that survives death, but is usually beyond our communication, has been transmitted into an object that we are familiar with, i.e. a painting or drawing, and we are therefore familiar with trying to interpret or receive information from. Because of the familiarity of the medium of painting, we don't put up paranormal, skeptical or (very many) emotional barriers. We expect to try and see what the artist wanted to present, wanted to communicate (though personally I see little of that in contemporary "deceptual art" as Brion Gysin used to say). If Spare said he was going to capture himself within the frame and canvas and facilitate immortality—or, at least, a very different medium of mortality, demonstrating "life" after apparent death—most observers would switch off, or scream ridicule tinged with an innate fear of the unknowable. There would be an interference with the transmission, because Spare seduces us by allowing us to dupe ourselves into assuming what we view is an artwork, a picture, when in fact it is a "photograph" of a mirror of an actual, or virtual, reality; a mortality software, if you will. Because of the self-deception, we remain open-minded. This open-mindedness is essential to the functioning of the sorcery at the critical time intersections that animate it (New Year's Eve, for example) and increases the chances of the phenomenon of actual physical changes.

269

The observer, if fortunate enough, wills to see that which many of us in this rightly post-existentialist age choose not to believe in or to be heartily skeptical of, namely living, moving, changing images of a post-death entity or brain-essence. This is all as acutely programmed as any software, except—Allah be praised—it's not binary, nor an either/or program, which probably explains Spare's success as, surprise surprise, we do not and never did, live in an either/or universe, and all binary systems are fallacious, serving only to block the righteous evolution and maximizing of the potential of our species, a species programmed in its DNA for only one ultimate function, to transcend all need for a physical body, fixed in linear time and space. You will see this entity reacting to you; it receives and transmits directly into your conscious five senses. It must also be transmitting directly into your other levels of consciousness too, and your other hyper-real senses. Presumably we transmit back to what is there, so what is there wills to change by absorption over the years as it reacts to, and is triggered by, all the various observers. All these factors mingle and mix, and mutate. Mutation, after all, being the sincerest form of flattery.

The "soul" (an advertisement for the brain as Dr. Timothy Leary once suggested to me) is generally said to be visible through the eyes, the mirror of the soul. The eyes, jewels of the actual brain exposed directly to the outside, the neuro-visual screen of the brain. In this key Spare work, centered on Mrs. Paterson and executed in 1928, her eyes are neither open nor shut, and this is true in many of Spare's virtual mirror works. They are neither rejecting the possibility of seeing a captured "soul," nor openly inviting it. This half-open, half-shut limbo suggests that responsibility lies with the viewer to choose whether or not to commune with any frisky entities that manifest. In fact, on many occasions an interesting further mutation frequently occurs. The eyes become alien,

Image by Genesis Breyer P-Orridge

not dissimilar from the "Schwa" portrayal, as if coated with an almost reptilian film of non-human skin. This alien quality seems to be amplified by Spare's technique of painting himself old when he was in fact young and, of course, later painting himself young when he was by then old. Forming an infinite envelope of time, in effect, Spare moves back and forth through time as he succeeds in presenting us, via the image, with the apparently impossible, or miraculous—immortality. Sorcery has always made effective and functional use of the process of reversal to confound expectation even at the root of the most sacred and central scientific assumptions.

The psyche, in its deepest reaches, seems well able to participate in an existence beyond the web of space and time This dimension is often dubbed "eternity" or "infinity," yet it actually seems to behave—if we for the moment take Spare's art as representative and, more vitally, functional and in no way symbolic—as either a one-way or two-way mirror, dependent for its operation upon a translation of the unconscious into a communicable image that bonds the actual atomic structures of the graphic image with its driving forces, unlocked from the unconscious into a fixed or mobile source of power dependent upon previous viewers and, more critically, with our own individual abilities to interface directly with it.

271

Accept nothing, assume nothing, always look further, be open-eyed as well as open-minded and don't kid yourself.
Genesis Breyer P-Orridge

Keeping the speculation simple for now, if, in theory, all matter is actually vibrating tiny particles with lots of groovy names, then it's just possible that we could walk through walls. Then it is also theoretically possible to lock clusters of the same particles and energy into the fabric of an image, giving it the ability to move, change, alter and animate its content. The only gap of credibility being first-hand experience. We don't usually believe anything until it happens to us. We only really know what we have experienced; belief is rooted in recognition.

Every now and then, as I type, you'll not be surprised to know, I wonder if this is going to sound too "out there" or "crazed" as you, the observer, read it. I already know it gets a little opaque—for which my less than humble apologies—and of course it assumes you know what the fuck I am referring to vis-a-vis the paintings themselves. Oh well, tough. This subject leads us to a bigger "picture," a discussion of the parallels between virtual space and the creation of deities, immortality and the psychosphere from a Processean perspective that we will to arrive on at another occasion. But I digress... Imagination opens to synthesis larger than the sum total of reason. New images reflect more than logical synthesis can produce. There is a radical discontinuity in every truly creative idea or discovery.

It's all a matter of TIME...
Genesis Breyer P-Orridge

Projection direct from image to viewer involves more than the logical mode of thinking. An idea cannot exist separate from an image. For example, the Virgin Mary image embodies the idea of "compassion," perhaps. A Goddess or God is a figurative image of an idea. Images are the root language of social freedom and self-expansion as much as words and alphabets are the roots of social control and self-limitation. Science attempts to explain the omniverse objectively; therefore it cannot explain "art" or, more particularly, the unique effects or phenomena Spare generates within "art." This is not a possible function of science although, to be fair, science is, now, thankfully, beginning to include the point-of-viewing in its theories to great effect. Science cannot tell us why Spare's images can alter, why his faces change, eyes open and close, colors vary. Photographs are said to steal "souls," and they certainly capture a moment in time and freeze it. So do the images and oracles of "art," for art was originally revelatory, prophetic, functional, shamanic. Fully integrated into every detail and aspect of life.

He who transcends Time escapes necessity.
Austin Osman Spare

Spare's images capture the process of creation, the thoughts of the creator, and the memories of the viewer. ("Change the way to perceive and change all memory." – G. P-O.) These memories of the viewer recall past events and feelings that are more compact, briefer than when they took place originally. They are compressed. Memories are past time, accessed into recent time. Time is not, however, linear; all time exists simultaneously and points in every direction simultaneously. It is quaquaversal, omnipresent; it fits, in fact, all the usual definitions of "GOD" by the Catholic church. There is really no reason why Spare's paintings and images should not capture time, thought and experience, and then recreate and expand it in the viewer's mind.

All nature is a vast reflection of that which is within us, or else we could not know it.
Austin Osman Spare

Subjective experience is no less "real" than objective conjecture. All roads lead to Rome in a mirror-to-mirror function. This function of mirroring is found in the trance state in a simple, direct way. The higher techniques of idea and the artist's illusory skills make effects and phenomena active through the dimensions of spacelessness and timelessness in ways normally consigned to the skeptical parking lot of modern existence. Time mirrors time.

273

Embrace reality by imagination.
Austin Osman Spare

Years of trying to rationalize inexplicable "experiences" disintegrate and only the most extreme speculations and constructs of impossibility begin to get close to giving answers that we see and feel. We are "Here to Go," as Brion Gysin succinctly stated. But not just here to go into inner and outer space, though that process is one part and conceptual parcel of the final aspiration. We are here to go out of the physical body. To enter the solid pool of time. To be fully integrated into that matter of TIME that connects us with every moment, in every direction, and every parallel or conflicting omniverse that ever-was, wills to be, or intends to be. Intention is the key and the process is the product.

The Life Force is not blind. We are.
Austin Osman Spare

Time must be reassessed as a solid; as a form of consciousness; as the key element in the atomic scale. As the covert energy hidden in the million and one names of deities. Life is only a brief physical manifestation outside the circles of time. We can re-enter the time pool and we can remanifest. This is exactly the same as entering the virtual world of "cyberspace/psychosphere" when you log on. Our appreciation of the implication of logging on must be developed from this deification perspective. Once logged on, we are vulnerable to all the agendas, traumas, neuroses, and brilliances of all other logged on individuals. We have re-entered a pool. No different to the pool of time or the gene pool, or "racial memory/DNA" pools. This pool I will to name the Spatial Memory.

Our understanding of time travel, physicality, possibility and the malleability of TIME and existence in a new, contrived virtual world is prophesied by Austin Osman Spare, by Brion Gysin, by many artists and creators. This shift in our perception of time and mortality will be the most important arena of discussion and philosophical, cultural engineering in this Twenty-First Century.

274

What is death? A great mutation to your next SELF.
Austin Osman Spare

The primary quest in Art, Life, Science and Brain has become a quest for reliable, repeatable methods for inter-dimensional travel and communication. Beyond the body and through the prophetic portals. Einstein, Spare, Gysin, Leary, McKenna and all the other visionary synthesists have contributed to the cumulative effect upon which sorcery is based. We can all play. By being aware of the implication of logging on. By designing conceptual and physical grids within the Psychosphere to facilitate accurate post-physical travel. By shouldering the responsibility we have accessed of God/Goddess building our actions are the process that leads to the final unity and the vanquishing once and for all of any either/or paradigms at last. This is the time that shall end. This is the calendar that ceases to exist. Time and life are not synonymous or fixed. Both are solids and can be shaped to our will to...
Genesis Breyer P-Orridge

MAGICK SQUARES AND FUTURE BEATS
The Magickal Processs and Methods of
William S. Burroughs and Brion Gysin

Being the First Part:
Change the Way to Perceive and Change All Memory

Our very first "memories" are hand-me-downs from other people. Various events and moments, amusing anecdotes of when we were babies and very small children. Usually stories from a period in our life that we actually cannot recall for ourselves. These are the cornerstones which we begin to add onto, building more conscious, personally recorded experiential memories. Usually, without much consideration of veracity or motive, we assume those original stories (whose source is usually parental) are true, rather than separately authored and constructed mythologies. Yet, with the best will in the world, they are edited highlights (and lowlights) from another person's perspective, interpreted by them, and even given significance and meaning by their being chosen to represent the whole of us, before our own separate SELF consciousness sets in. All the information we have at our immediate disposal as self-consciousness develops is from someone else. Everything about us is true. Everything about us is false. Everything about us is both. It is by omission that we are described exactly, creating an unfolding program not of our own choosing. We are edited bloodlines seeking an identity with only partial data and unknown motivation and expectation.

(I should point out here that Brion Gysin claimed very convincingly to recall being in his mother's womb, the traumatic drama of actually being born and the horror of arriving at the "wrong address" and all subsequent events. I personally believe(d) him. I also suspect it is a part of what made him so incredibly remarkable, important and effective as a cultural engineer and innovator, as a sorcerer of light and language and as a magician.)

These inherited, brief memories are a little jigsaw puzzle, a picture that contains impressions of what kind of "child" we were in the eyes of our familial others. Without malicious intent, necessarily, they still tend to guide us towards an unbalanced, prejudiced perception of who we are. They can easily become at least a basic sketch of our character by our

275

parents, a blueprint made more solid by each re-telling, less possible to challenge. Just as we tend to like to please our parents by doing what they praise, so we can also manifest and reinforce their criticisms as well. At their unintended worst, these assumptions and maps become the metaphors/enhancers/deciders/directives for a lifetime's neurotic self-image, selected recordings of who we are, who we are imagined to be, who we are instructed we are, who we are expected to become, what kind of adult we will unfold into and, of course, evidence of an inherited fiction from which we will be conditioned as to how we too will perceive the world and our place in and on it. Looping around and around, a self-perpetuating, self-fulfilling and prophetic sampling into which we immerse ourselves without any great wisdom to hint we might wait and see, listen and watch, question and perhaps even re-edit in order to maximize our potential to become.

If our self-image is primarily built upon the faulty, biased, prejudiced and highly edited memory recordings of other people, with their own agenda of who we are intended to become, as defined by this perceptual process of un-natural selection, then ways and tools that allow us to seize the means of perception become vital in our fight to construct a self, a character, an identity that is truly and independently our own. Any magic that empowers us to do that, both sacred and profane, is a matter of survival, a cause of infinite concern in terms of the evolution of both our species and ourselves. In short, it's a divine territory that recognizes behavior, perception, and character as malleable matter equal to all other forms of matter, distinguished (so far) only by our apparent awareness that we exist and have choices, mortality and doubt as signifiers of our individuality. If there is any right, any birthright, it might well be the right to create one's SELF.

Being the Second Part:
In a Pre-Recorded Universe, Who Made the First Recordings?

In a very real sense, I do not own my early life. The first "memories" I have are actually short anecdotes describing things that happened involving me that I actually have absolutely no recollection of. Interestingly, they all revolve around me doing something "naughty" which influenced others negatively (by parental standards) and for which I got "blamed." The mistakes of others were placed very squarely at my door, a classic "bad influence." For much of my life these shameful crises were simply accepted on trust. I have even recounted them myself, for years, without doubting their veracity, even as I have come to know how subjective, selective, personally convenient and self-serving various sources of versions of events can be. We consciously and unconsciously edit out all kinds of things to suit ourselves, pragmatically, or manipulatively, in order to make things happen. These are the roots of a childhood theatre of behavioral depth magick, a form that sadly suffers from being born of devout ignorance, and a total lack of shamanic guidance. Magick is by one definition, if you will, the science of making things happen according to your desires in order to maximize control over one's life and immediate environment to create a universe that is perfecting in its kindness towards you.

This could all be innocuous, and perhaps, for many, it is. For me, it has emerged as a key factor, a continuous exploration and necessity for my emotional survival as a creative being to free myself from imposed ways of being initiated by these uninvited guests in the recording device that is my experiential existence. My recordings are what I build my soul from. The act of independently visualized and consciously chosen creation builds that phenomenon that is what I call and perceive as "me": If I am not who I was told I was, then who am I? More importantly, can I find ways to change the original recordings and inherited construct and actually remember and become whoever it is that I am, or even better, who I dream I wish to be? Can we build ourselves? Are there methods, examples, tricks and techniques, methods and madness, analysis and delirium that empower my SELF?

277

It is very easy to fall victim to peer group pressure. Parental expectation. Emotionally crippling tales that put the blame for negative events upon your personality and behavior. We are pushed, shoved, squashed and bullied into submission and contrition. At some point in each being's life, I believe, we are presented with a critical choice, a classic, cliché fork in our road of life. As this occurs, I would suggest that the split is between the none-sensus reality, consensus-perceptual "memory" pre-recordings of a more or less controlled and predictable biological timeline existence and/or an opportunity to redefine self-perception and remix re-recordings, infinitely and chaotically, entirely unique and original combinations and collisions of self determined and self creating recordings assembled from, with and by freedom of choice. Instead of our identity (in all possible and impossible senses of the word) being built by others we can build our own, and own it.

It was in 1967 that this critical concern overwhelmed me. Was there a system, a way to adjust, control, break-up and re-assemble behavior, personality, creativity and perception, so that novelty and surprise, the unexpected and improvisation could be applied to my identity, using my self as raw material, as malleable physically and mentally as any other medium? Could I change the way I perceive and change all memory? It seemed to me that there had to be a way to truly live my life as art and make my art an inseparable extension of my life. I began my search for a creativity-centered system of applied magick.

You might think that seeking out two Beatniks was a funny place to start looking for a functional, modern process of magick. In fact, it turned out to be exactly the right place to look, and just as I had hoped, it did change my life, and it did enable me to build, with intention and clarity, the bohemian, divinely seeking being I willed to become.

If I was constructed on the foundation of, and from, inherited memories taken on trust, on metaphors handed down with their own agenda via language and image (what one might think of as the cultural DNA of personality) then I needed to confront the omnipotence of word control. It was imperative to my survival as a sentient being to locate the most advanced alchemists, and the most radical in their field, in order to learn what I could of strategies that would force the hand of chance in favor of self-creation rather than submissive reaction.

(In Paris, during the 1970s, Brion Gysin pointed out to me that it was extremely significant that the very first chapter of the book of Genesis in the Bible is known as "The Creation." He also chose to point this out in an early permutation poem "In the beginning was the WORD and the WORD was God.")

I first met William S. Burroughs in London, at Duke Street, St. James, in 1971 after a brief series of postal correspondence. It actually felt and seemed strange, as I had discovered his existence via Jack Kerouac as the mysterious character "Bull Lee." Confirmation of his being an actual person led me to the porn district of Soho in 1965, where I snagged a

278

copy, a first edition actually, with dust jacket by Brion Gysin, of *Naked Lunch*. It had been prosecuted for obscenity, so porn shops were the only places in those days to buy Burroughs, Henry Miller, Jean Genet and pretty much everything else I was consuming as confirmation, vindication and affirmation as a fifteen-year-old. Six years after beginning my Beat odyssey via books, my very first question to him, a living, breathing, Beatnik legend in the flesh was… "Tell me about magick?"

Being the Third (Mind) Part:
Nothing Here Now but Thee Recordings

William had a cut-out, cardboard, life-sized photo of Mick Jagger standing by his bookcase. Its significance was the rite of *Performance*, not rock and roll. On the television set were a full bottle of Jack Daniels and a remote, the first I ever saw. William was not in the least surprised by my question. "Care for a drink?" he asked. "Sure," I replied, nervous and, for one of the only times ever in my life, in awe. "Well… reality is not really all it's cracked up to be, you know," he continued. He took the remote and started to flip through the channels, cutting up programmed TV. I realized he was teaching me. At the same time he began to hit stop and start on his Sony TC cassette recorder, mixing in "random" cut-ups to prior recordings. These were overlaid with our conversation, none acknowledging the other, an instant holography of information and environment.

I was already being taught. What Bill explained to me then was pivotal to the unfolding of my life and art: Everything is recorded. If it is recorded, then it can be edited. If it can be edited then the order, sense, meaning and direction are as arbitrary and personal as the agenda and/or person editing. This is magick. For if we have the ability and/or choice of how things unfold—regardless of the original order and/or intention that they are recorded in—then we have control over the eventual unfolding. If reality consists of a series of parallel recordings that usually go unchallenged, then reality only remains stable and predictable until it is challenged and/or the recordings are altered, or their order changed. These concepts led us to the realization of cut-ups as a magical process.

279

At this point we broke open the hard liquor and each downed a large glass. Soon (it seemed) the bottle was empty.

A Cassette Tape Recorder as a Magickal Weapon

What I was then told changed the unfolding of my life in every possible dimension and concept of the word. He told me about how during the Chicago Democratic convention in 1968 he had walked around recording the background noises of the Yippie demonstrations, the riots, the Mayor Daley repression and violence. As he walked, he would randomly hit record at intervals, "cutting-in" the most recent sounds around him, creating a collage that was non-linear time. What he observed happening was that as a configuration of "trouble sounds" occurred (i.e. police sirens, screams, chanting of slogans) the actual physical manifestations and/or expressions of those sounds also increased in what we think of as the "real" physical world. His next experiment was to work with "passive" environmental audioscapes in order to check his evidence and see if it could be replicated. As William explained it to me later, in what became an apocryphal action, he had decided to check more "scientifically" the theories he had been assembling with Brion Gysin regarding "reality" being a linear recording. A malleable medium or element that was subject, as such, to the intervention of edits and erasings, rub-outs and re-sculpting, if you will.

Not far from Duke Street (where he was then living in voluntary exile, a choice I would find myself compelled to make years later) was a basic British/Greek café called the Moka Bar where he might sometimes relax and get the classic English breakfast of chips, baked beans, fried eggs, fried tomatoes, mushrooms and toast with a large cup of tea or an instant coffee. Nothing special. Nowhere special. The perfect place, in fact, to encounter arrogance and snobbery, abruptness and poor manners on the part of the very people indentured to one's service. On one of those days, a day when all is over-colored, over-laid and over-bearing, William was treated with great disdain, with crass, crude, nastily aggressive and insulting behavior quite beyond the pale of acceptable manners. Such was the rudeness and unpleasantness that William swore never to eat there again. But, more than that, his disgust and anger was so intense and intentional, so unforgiving and angry in the moment that he felt quite compelled to experimental "sorcery" (his word to me, take note). What form did his curse take? Here follows my first lesson in contemporary intuitive and functional magick.

William took his Sony TC cassette recorder and very methodically walked back and forth in front of the offending café, at breakfast-time and other times of day, making a tape of the ongoing street noises that made the sonic background of its location. A field recording encapsulating a typical day via street sounds. Next he went back to his apartment and at various random places on the same cassette he recorded "trouble noises" over bits of the previous recordings. These were things like police car sirens, gunshots, bombs, screams and other types of mayhem culled primarily from the TV news. Then he went back to the café and again walked up and down the street outside playing the cut-up cassette recording complete with "trouble noises." Apparently the tape does not need to be played very loud, in fact just a volume that blends in so that passers-by on the other side of the street, or a few feet away would not notice the additional sounds as implanted fictions. This process was repeated several times, quite innocuous to any observer. "L'Hombre Invisible" at work. Within a very short time, the café closed down! Not only did it close down, but the space remained empty for years, unable to be rented, for love or money.

281

We would do well to consider at this point, that each individual human being is inevitably the center of their own unique universe/sensory/experiential world. Only YOU are physically present every single second of your personal life and as a result, any person, or event that takes place without your physical presence is a part of somebody else's unique universe. Of course, there are times when others are present and then they will tend to assume you are all in one universe together. However, ask any cop if they get the same story from a variety of witnesses, or the same description of a suspect, and you will be told in no uncertain terms, that nobody sees or hears the same thing at the same time as someone else, nor do they share equal abilities to describe or recall what they imagine their memories have recorded. In other words, consensus reality is just that, an amalgamation of approximate recordings from flawed bio-machines. The background of our daily lives is almost the equivalent of a flimsy movie set, unfolding and created by the sum total

of what people allow to filter in through their senses. This illusory material world, built ad hoc, second to second, is uncommon to us all. It will only seem to exist whilst our body is passing through it. After that its continued existence is a matter of faith, and our experience of it seeming to have a continuity of presence that seems solid comes from our assumption (only) that we can apparently go back there at some future time of our choosing.

It is quite possible that the energy or phenomenon that glues together a repeatable experience of solidity and materiality on this earth is the pressure of billions of human beings simultaneously, and in close proximity, believing in what they see and hear. Bear in mind that history is

Photo of G B P-O with Bachir Attar of Jajouka by Lady Jaye

the collected recordings of subjective previous people(s) and our species. What has survived, what was memorized or stored in some form is usually assumed to be the story of our unfolding species. Nevertheless, we are more than aware that certain events are written up with agendas included: bitter families, dogmatic religions, democracies and totalitarian regimes all collude in this process of editing.

It has crossed my mind that this entire planet is a recording device itself. As archeology and anthropology and forensic science progress we are able to discover and reveal endless details of happenings going back millions of years. Also, side-by-side, we have almost every period of human species history still continuing today. The bushmen in Africa live in a basically prehistoric way; tribes in New Guinea in the Stone Age; other peoples in a barbaric Middle Ages; entire communities in middle America live almost in a fundamentalist Victorian era; and yet others, in places like Silicon Valley or Tokyo, live in a technological science fiction future. This is a remarkable thing. Infinite micro-realities existing simultaneously, their very activation an appearance of "reality" and infinite, social, macro-realities parallel and colliding and competing for supremacy and with it the power to edit and describe a global "reality."

283

At this point I feel it helpful to remind the reader that this essay is necessarily, as part of an anthology, only an over-view of the complex and wide-ranging evidence consistently to be found in the creative works, in all media, of William S. Burroughs and Brion Gysin. My thereby implicit proposal is that whilst Burroughs was indeed a classic literary figure of the Twentieth Century; and Gysin a classic Twentieth Century "Renaissance" artist—who together bequeathed to us through intuitive science, a method and a prophetic appreciation of meaning, a pivotal approach to questions of perception and the nature and origin of literature and art—they can only be fully appreciated and, perhaps, finally understood, in terms of their central and passionate inner agendas and obsessions when re-considered and re-assessed as serious, conscious and masterful creative/cultural alchemists and practicing magicians, a mission for which I have taken the linguistic liberty of coining the term/occupation "Cultural Engineer."

As their works as this unexpected brotherhood unfold after their collaborations begin at "The Beat Hotel" in Paris during 1957 to 1963 and meticulously thereafter, one is immersed with them in a fascinating journey into pre-material consciousness, a place where direct and indirect communications with the nervous system occur; where nothing is fixed or permanent. Everything is true and permitted; where ancient programming holds prisoner the possible truths of who and what we are, and where even words are potential enemy agents and distortion devices that assist in the suppression of our potential as beings. This wordless "Interzone" was so "inconceivable" to even such a libertarian poet as Allen Ginsberg that he felt it "threatened everything." It is not uncommon for people to demonstrate symptoms of fear and insecurity when the very fabric of their protective safety blanket "reality" is scattered, shattered, shredded and then further cut-up to reveal a central possibility of divinity and love within all things and perceptions of things. It can be painful to release the last connection to an inherited linear space time "reality" assembled from filtered essence of solidifying mundanity. In a magical universe, everything and every thing is malleable, changeable, interconnected at invisibly deep levels, levels so subtle and sub-atomic that consciousness and intention can affect them.

Intention is the work of envisaging and enacting will.
Ray L. Hart, *Unfinished Man and the Imagination*

In an oft-quoted moment, Gysin proposed to Burroughs that "Writing is fifty years behind painting," by which he meant that painting had begun to call into question all the traditional boundaries and templates. Even reason and object were arbitrary and unnecessary markers. By his introduction of the cut-up in all its manifestations, Gysin, the accomplished "shaman" as Burroughs so rightly designated him, gave his compadre the magical tool(s) required for a lifetime's astonishing body of creative work- recorded as literature, revelation. Their intricate and dazzling story and their functional, demystified techniques and process continue to leak into present time in preparation for various possible futures. I believe that a re-reading of their combined body of work from a magical perspective only confirms what they themselves accepted about themselves, that they were powerful modern magicians. To view them otherwise does a great disservice to us all. In this post-digital age, as we each construct our own personal "reality tunnels," it is my conviction that a positive unfolding of our species, and an evolution that is non-destructive and anathema to polarization, is absolutely central to our survival with ethical honor.

In the ever more metaphysical world of physics, a parallel sequence of "discoveries" equivalent in their importance to science as the "cut-ups" system of magick is to culture, has potentially reshaped our understanding of the universe and "reality." According to physicist David Bohm (and simplifying as best as I can as a lay person) any apparent separation between matter and consciousness is an illusion, an artifact that occurs or is assembled only after both consciousness and matter have unfolded into the "explicate" world of objects and linear/sequential time. As one might expect, the other realm would be the "implicate" world, which would be all those inner "worlds" (including thought) that take place outside linear time and sensory confluence. What is coming to be accepted as a non-material field of consciousness? Bohm's researches suggested to him that "at the sub-quantum level, in which the quantum potential operated, location ceased to exist. All points in space became equal to all other points in space, and it was meaningless to speak of anything being separate from anything else."

Interestingly, a Cheyenne/Apache shaman told me years and years ago that there was no word for death in his clan; they instead used the word "separation" to express the concept. Similarly, the Shiva holy man Pagalananda Nath Agori Baba spent many patient hours deprogramming my Western linear materiality in order for me to be better able to grasp the concept of his "path of no distinction." The Egyptian sage Hermes Trismegistus explained this absolute elsewhere idea hundreds of years ago when he was recorded as saying "The without is like the within of things and the small of things is like the large."

285

So now, finally, after thousands of years, we have a consensus of great significance born of this unprecedented and radical intersection between mystic, scientist, shaman and artist. Partly for lack of adequate language and partly to camouflage their subversive ideas in order to stay alive, various enlightened visionaries, often the "heretics" of their era, have employed brain-twisting metaphors to describe the universe of objective "reality" as an illusion. What scientists are trying to describe to us now is a universe where, according to thinkers like Niels Bohr and others, subatomic particles require an observer to come into existence and without an observer's presence they do not come into existence. Even more remarkable is that away from us each observing from the center-point of our individual existence, the universe is a measureless resonating domain of frequencies that are an open source that only gets transformed into this world as we think we recognize it after being accessed by our senses and entering our brain. There it is decoded/encoded/acoded (and who knows which or all?) as it is assembled according to the dimensions of linear time and space, and, I would argue, our subjective cultural expectations. There seems to be a growing agreement at the heart of creation among those in service of the path of the divine, the scientific, and the artistic that the primary reality is one of wholeness, an indivisible unity that functions not unlike a living being, or (my favorite analogy) a coral reef. So, while we rush about, billions of us, interacting experientially with our environment, various objective events do, for all practical intents and purposes, happen to us in particular locations, on a subatomic level things are quite different. On a subatomic level Bohm proposes that all points in space become equal to all other points in space, they are nonlocalities. So, to quote John Lennon, "Nothing is real," adding that "And it wasn't/isn't there anyway!"

To sum up this section, the universe is a unified source, an infinite, open, timeless, intricate quaquaversal frequency field in constant flux that appears to have objective form and material solidity when, and because, we observe it. And observe it we do. We observe it over and over, we are obsessed with recording it (just think of all those hundreds of paparazzi documenting J-Lo's every move) and then we store it in monolithic museums, libraries, databanks. These huge repositories can act on a society's behalf to symbolize anthropological recorders and our maintenance of them; our belief in their contents in turn functions as the batteries that charge up and energize the social hologram that we have assembled as none-sensus reality in order to give continuity, consistency, solidity, and even significant sense of meaning with enough consistency and reliability for us to function during life as biologically sentient beings. Nevertheless, it is our expectation that things will be the same, that a log will remain a log, and if enough of us keep "creating" logs as a matter of habit, eventually… yes… log jam; but it is still no more "real" despite the materiality produced by repetition.

It is not a coincidence that in more established doctrinal/dogmatic religions worldwide, in so-called "primitive" tribal and/or shamanic cultures, in the rituals of public and secret Western magical and/or Masonic orders, or in the ecstatic rhythms and ancient beats of trance targeted music and the chants that go with such music, repetition of key power words and phrases are integral, as is the phenomenon of call and response. Even at this deepest level of a relationship with the measureless frequency field, with the universe as a unified open source that has no locality, we are trying to solidify and maintain our sensory illusion(s). The purpose of these various "services" is to collectively reconstruct a social reality seamlessly with language, with words and names, with devotional submission to the power of its story, and thereby, ironically, to put into strict bondage through this habitual repetition, the essence of life itself. Why? In order to predict and control it. Often, unwittingly, we empower the people who claim continuity of descent by colluding in these rites.

The real hidden doctrine handed down through the ages, the central agenda, is control. Why do those who control seek to maintain control? For its own sake. How do they control? By controlling the story, by editing our collective memory, conscious and unconscious. In many ways the edit is the invisible language of control and its corporate media allies. They cut and paste in order to separate us from each other by entrancing us with a pre-recorded reality that seamlessly isolates us in a world designed by those who would immerse us in service to their fundamentalist consumerism, simultaneously divorcing us from the universe that is creation itself in an infinite pre-sensory source.

287

[...] writing is... not (just) an escape from reality, but an attempt to change reality, so (the) writer can escape the limits of reality.
William S. Burroughs, *Last Words*

In *Last Words*, Burroughs writes of the enemy and their two weaknesses being firstly that they have "no sense of humor" and, secondly, that "They totally lack understanding of magic." Later he directs our attention to two other enemy weaknesses in reference to dogmatic scientific modes of enquiry by pointing out that phenomena "that occur only once" will automatically be invalidated by virtue of their uniqueness and that they have an "insatiable appetite for data." We have seen that everything is indivisibly unified. That there really are no hard edges, no division between mental and physical worlds, or any worlds or dimensions animate or inanimate. Instead we have been introduced to a holographic universe of infinite interconnectedness that responds to the future beat of a shaman's drum. It is fundamental to understanding how to operate and interpret the challengingly effective, modern and magical exercises of Burroughs and Gysin with cut-ups as their foundation and words as the disputed territory. What we have been trained from birth to believe is a solid environment is only a tiny fragment of what is available to our perception. At the same time, the behavioral, political and anthropological history of our society and culture has been written and recorded by authors fulfilling an agenda of (and for) vested interests who do not have our well being at heart, leaving most of us trapped in their current description of the universe.

No two actual entities originate from an identical universe... The nexus (lineage) of actual entities in the universe correlates to a growth by assimilation that is termed 'the actual world.
Adapted with apology from Alfred North Whitehead, *Process and Reality*

Back to the café. Experiments have shown we live a great deal of our lives "asleep," filtering out sensory input. Film a street as its residents are going to work in the morning. Add in a police car going past afterwards in the editing suite. Play it back to those same residents later that evening. Asked if this is a recording of the morning, almost all will say "Yes." They will also say they recall the police car going by. This is the phenomenon Burroughs was working with. Added to the fragility of our individual neurological recording devices is the age-old technique of suggestion. Yet here we are faced with something perhaps even a little deeper: A conscious attack upon, and alteration of, none-sensus reality by a formalized ritual.

"In a pre-recorded universe who made the first recordings?" So asked Gysin and Burroughs. Further, if all we imagine as reality is equivalent to a recording, then we become empowered to edit, re-arrange, re-contextualize and re-project by cutting-up and re-assembling our own reality and, potentially, the reality of others. If this is true and effective, then a magical act is taking place. Simplified, magick has been defined as a method for changing reality in conformity with one's true will, or as a methodical demystified process that allows us to force the hand of chance in order to make things we truly desire happen based upon, and within, purity of intent. Crowley said that magick has "The method of science, the aim of religion." Brion Gysin talked of magick, saying it was "The Other Method, an exercise for controlling matter and knowing space, and a form of psychic hygiene." So what happened to the café? If it were only suggestion, then it would have only discouraged the people in the street whilst William was walking about playing his tape. None of them might have been customers anyway. It was NOT necessary for the café proprietors to be aware of the "curse." The premises closed and remained closed, followed by a series of brief failed businesses, long, long after William moved on to other activities.

(The process) involves a reversal of our ordinary understanding that causes produce effects. The cause must precede its effect in (present) time, yet it must be presently existent in order to be active in producing its effect.
Lewis Ford, *The Lure of God*

According to Gysin, in *Here to Go*, William sometimes used two cassette recorders, one in each hand and occasionally even added his own voice repeating an incantation he had written to intensify the focus of his spell. One particular incantation ended up as part of the soundtrack of *Witchcraft Through the Ages* (a.k.a. *Haxan*) an obscure, and really rather kitsch, Scandinavian silent movie for which Burroughs did the voiceover, a quirky anomaly resulting from the fact that Beat filmmaker Antony Balch had the UK distribution rights. Part of it went something like this:

289

> *Lock them out and bar the door,*
> *Lock them out for evermore.*
> *Nook and cranny, window, door,*
> *Seal them out for evermore...*

In addition to tape-recorder magick William also employed a version of the cut-up photograph as additional sorceric firepower. On one visit, as he explained magick to me, he very generously showed me some of his journals. On one page he had stuck in two pictures. One was a black and white photograph of the section of the street buildings where that same Moka café was that he'd cursed. Beneath it was a second shot of the same section of street, or so it seemed at first glance. However, upon closer examination he had very neatly sliced out the café with a razor blade. Gluing the two halves of the image back together minus the offending establishment. This same principle can be applied to people one wishes to excise from one's life, and variations can be used according to your imagination and needs. Of course, these modern upgrades of magical practice can be easily integrated into older traditions if one desires. For example, one could put the cut-out image into a brown paper bag with one's invocation added in pencil, black pepper, broken glass, sharp blades and vinegar, and then throw it over one's shoulder into a graveyard whilst walking away without looking back.

Once one accepts a possibility that the universe is holographic and that at the smallest subatomic levels all elements of phenomena can be affected by all others, then the probability of these operations being effective becomes far more credible. Indeed I would argue that a magical view of the universe is the most likely description we have proposed so far as a species. In *The Job*, Burroughs discusses silence as a desirable state. What he seems to imply is that words are potentially blocks, both by their linearity in our language system and the manner in which they narrow definitions of experiential events and actions. He says, "Words… can stand in the way of what I call non-body experience." He does not want to turn the human body into an environment that includes the universe. That would once more create limiting templates and maps of expectation that discourage new and/or radical explorations. Rationality and the fixed progression of physical biology narrow consciousness. One magical method he proposes is:

What I want to do is to learn to see more of what's out there, to look outside, to achieve as far as possible a complete awareness of surroundings… I'm becoming more proficient at it, partly through my work with scrapbooks and translating the connections between words and images.
From *The Third Mind* interview with Conrad Knickerbocker, 1967

One pre-requisite of most Western magical orders is that the applicant/ neophyte keep a daily magical diary in which they note their dreams, synchronicities, apparent resolution of temporal events and desires after magical operations. This is not so much just to document and vindicate the system being applied, as to create an ongoing awareness of the constant relationship we all actually have, moment to moment, with the other. In a universe where everything is "interconnected, inter-dimensional and integrated," or, as Michael Talbot describes it, holographic, the acceleration of and practical collaboration with this interrelation of energies and their ability to assist us in affecting manifestations is more clearly revealed by methodical documentation. It seems that the more one acknowledges this confluence of mutability the more kindly its relationship to and with you is.

This interaction is the one symbolized by the number 23 in Robert Anton Wilson's books and in the mythologies flowing throughout his and Burroughs' fiction. It is not so much that the number 23 is a "magical" number that does "tricks" for the person who invokes it, it is more that the number 23 reminds us of the inherent plasticity of our inherited reality and our potential to immerse our SELF in that quality to our own advantage and possible well-being. It represents a magical vision of life rather than a linear and existential one. Significantly, Burroughs, like Kerouac and Gysin, kept dream diaries and journals, Gysin and Burroughs extending their range further by including cut-up texts, newspaper headlines, photographs, fictional routines and poems in a kaleidoscopic visualization of multi-faceted and layered "reality." Burroughs suggests a practical exercise to amplify our appreciation of, and practical familiarity with, this manifestation:

Try this: Carefully memorize the meaning of a passage, then read it; you'll find you can actually read it without the words making any sound whatever in the mind's ear. Extraordinary experience, one that will carry over into dreams. When you start thinking in images, without words, you're well on the way.
William S. Burroughs in *The Third Mind*

On August 6, 1981, I visited Burroughs in New York. He was living at 222 Bowery in the basement, a location fondly nicknamed and immortalized in various biographies as "The Bunker." A book Burroughs introduced me to was *Breakthrough* by the Latvian paranormal investigator Konstantin Raudive. In his book, Raudive documents hundreds of "recordings" of the voices of the spirits of the dead. His method was unusual but simple: Attach a crystal receiver to an otherwise standard reel-to-reel in the socket where a microphone would be plugged, hit record, and see what appeared on tape. What Raudive found was that within a wall of white noise and hiss, various intelligible sentences

291

and messages, that he believed were from souls in the dimensions associated with being dead, were audible. Given that we were meeting
on "Hiroshima Day," as Burroughs designated it, there was a feeling
that perhaps quite a large number of dead souls might wish to break
through. We set up an old tape recorder on the kitchen table where
many a dinner soiree was held over his New York years and hit record.
Each of us took turns listening through headphones live to the noise
and interference going down on analog tape as it slowly turned. After
half an hour we played the "results" back, intently noting the slightest
sonic detail. Like good, objective laboratory researchers, we made notes,
both on paper and recorded onto a cassette with the Sony Walkman I
had with me. It was almost a parody of an autopsy on TV. Final report
from the Bunker? Nothing! Oh, how we hoped for evidence, but we
got just the expected hiss and short-wave *Twilight Zone*-type sounds.
Regardless—and Crowley was fastidious in reminding the initiate of
this—we did not fall into the trap of "lust of result." Sometimes only
one phenomenon occurs to vindicate a theory, sometimes things seem
unrepeatable. In terms of this text, what is significant is that Burroughs
truly believed in the possibility of communication with the soul after
physical death, long before he went public with that in *Last Words*.

As a footnote to this experiment, an extra event is worthy of mention.
During 1985, Psychic TV were recording a song about the deceased/
murdered founder of the Rolling Stones, Brian Jones, called "Godstar."
Still fascinated by the Raudive book and Burroughs' dogged exploration
of its technique as a magical tool, I arbitrarily, on impulse, told Ken
Thomas (my co-producer and creative engineer) to leave track twenty-
three of the twenty-four-track analog tape empty. After all the elements
of the song were recorded in the traditional multi-track way I instructed
him to re-run the master tape with every track muted except track twenty-three. This track was to be on record, but with absolutely NO form of
microphone or even a crystal receiver plugged in, simply a tape running
through a deck with no scientific means of recording on one track. Ken
seemed to think this was both illogical and "a bit spooky," but to his
credit, he went ahead and did as I asked anyway. When we played back
the previously virgin, pristine and blank track twenty-three, much to
our amazement, we heard a metallic knocking at a few points! We replayed and replayed the track; it was definitely there and had certainly
appeared during our "token" Raudive/Burroughs experiment—yet it

seemed random, and was not a "voice." Suddenly, I had a moment of clarity and suggested Ken replay the track with the vocals of the lyric and some basic elements of the music added in the mix. The knocking sounds came very precisely under a sequence of words in the exact phrasing and position of the following, "I wish I was with you now, I wish I could tell you somehow…" (Later I would change the lyric to "I wish I could save you somehow.")

If I am truly frank, I took this as a sign of approval of the song and its message, which is that Brian Jones was murdered and received a callous treatment at the hands of the media during his last days. He became, for myself and many other fans of his iconography, a scapegoat in the essential magical and sacred way. Sacrificed, at the very least, by ignorance and greed to the consumer and materialistic machine of linear reality. It is worth noting that at the time we were taping the song the consensus opinion, and official coroner's verdict, was "death by misadventure," with a lot of media hinting that he either drowned during an asthma attack, or he was so high on drugs that, despite being an athletic swimmer, he drowned right in front of his current girlfriend and guests. Our "magical" message tended to imply there was more to the story and eventually, during the 1990s, a builder Jones had hired, Frank Thorogood, confessed on his deathbed to murdering Brian Jones by holding him under water. Whatever you may choose to believe, it certainly appears to me that there are ways to make contact with realms considered Other via the most simple of tape recording devices.

293

Burroughs, and Gysin, both told me something that resonated with me for the rest of my life-so-far. They pointed out that alchemists always used the most modern equipment and mathematics, the most precise science of their day. Thus, in order to be an effective and practicing magician in contemporary times one must utilize the most practical and cutting-edge technology and theories of the era. In our case, it meant cassette recorders, Dream Machines and flicker, Polaroid cameras, Xeroxes, E-prime and, at the moment of writing this text, laptops, psychedelics, videos, DVDs and the World Wide Web. Please note that earlier we discussed the possibility that the universe is a holographic web constructed of infinite intersections of frequencies (of truth). Basically, everything that is capable of recording and/or representing "reality" is a magical tool just as much as it is a weapon of control.

Being the Fourth Part:
Look at That Picture is it Persisting?

The first question Brion Gysin asked me, in Paris in 1980, was "Do you know your real name?" I replied "Yes," (assuming it was Genesis and not my given name Neil) and then inquired, as casually as I could, "Tell me about magick?"

Brion Gysin was born in Taplow, England in 1916, but indicative of the unspecific density of his visitation on earth, (and I use the word "visitation" because until his dying day in 1986, Brion insisted that in being born human he was "delivered here by mistake") his conviction of mislocation, and with it a disruption of a different, perhaps parallel, dimensional existence, fueled his remarkably deep sense of irony and Otherness and was a central quality of his body of magical artistic work. Gysin was a transmediator, a Twentieth Century Renaissance man, a multi-media explorer and innovator. Innately disciplined, he would continually paint and draw, extending his calligraphic journeys into what Burroughs would describe as "…painting from the viewpoint of timeless space."

During my conversations on magick with Burroughs during the 1970s it became more and more clear to me that Gysin was pivotal in the history of the magical unfolding and the techniques of cultural alchemy that had drawn me to this Beat oeuvre, and from thenceforward I desired to make direct contact. During my conversations on magick with Gysin, the cassette tape-recorder that I had with me was tolerated only on the condition that certain key teachings were spoken whilst the tape was switched off. As he presented it quite plainly to me, "Magick is passed on by the touching of hands." In other words, certain ideas and methods are handed down master to student, one on one, directly in each other's physical presence. This agreement has been honored ever since, and remains so. Nevertheless, just to have confirmation from him that it was indeed true that his work was contemporary magick, not simply artistic or literary experimentation was a great solace and gave me determination in my personal path.

It was Gysin who first recognized the potential of cut-ups as a means to update and upgrade writing and art, and as a contemporary application of magick. In collaboration with Ian Sommerville and Burroughs he discovered, and made cheaply accessible, the Dream Machine; "the first artwork to be looked at with eyes closed," the story of, and implications of which, are marvelously catalogued in John Geiger's book *The Chapel of Extreme Experience*. In that book, for the first time, out of a kaleidoscopic cyclone, a blizzard of revolutionary scientific information and ultra-visionary creation, we are exposed to an incredibly significant creative and conceptual exploration of consciousness via "flicker." In terms of possibility, both Burroughs and Gysin would often quote Hassan i-Sabbah, the "Old Man of the Mountains," who, from his fortress in Alamut, Iran was rumored to have controlled, using brutal assassins, a huge swathe of ancient Arab civilization. His motto, "Nothing is True, Everything Is Permitted," recurs over and over, especially in Burroughs' books. It is not so far from the Thelemic precept "Do What Thou Wilt Shall Be the Whole of the Law," a theoretical connection that Burroughs appeared to acknowledge towards the end of his life.

Gysin spent twenty-three years living in Morocco. During that time he ran a restaurant called 1001 Nights, and would invite a group called the Master Musicians of Jajouka to play music for the guests as the entertainment. He told the story, more than once, of how that business crumbled after he found a magick spell, "an amulet of sorts, a rather elaborate one with seeds, pebbles, shards of broken mirror, seven of each, and a little package in which there was a piece of writing… which appealed to the devils of fire to take Brion away from this house." Very shortly after this discovery, he lost the restaurant and ultimately returned to Paris. On one of my first visits to Paris to meet with Gysin, I was blessed with a special evening. After looking into the Dream Machine for a couple of hours, Bachir Attar, then the son of the Master Musician of Jajouka— he is now the Master Musician himself after his father's death—and his brother, cooked me a ceremonial meal. During the feast Bachir played flute music that he told me raised the Djinn, the little people, and the spirits who would bestow great fortune upon the listener. Despite the friction of the era when the restaurant was lost, a very powerful magical bond remained between the ancient system of magick and the most contemporary of elaborations represented by Gysin.

Calligraphic magick squares were one of the techniques most commonly applied by Gysin. He would reduce a name or an idea to a "glyph" and then write across the paper from right to left, turn the paper and do the same again, and so on, turning the paper around and around to create a multi-dimensional grid. Gysin believed this "scaffolding" allowed the Djinn to run with the intention of "exercising control of matter and knowing space. These same techniques and consciously driven functional intention also permeated his paintings and that, in fact, in a very real sense, everything he created included an act of conscious sorcery. his paintings.

William S. Burroughs described the central difference of Gysin's painting as follows:

> *All art is magical in origin… intended to produce very definite results. Art is functional; it is intended to make things happen. Take porcelain stove, disconnect it and put it in your living room, it may be a good-looking corpse, but it isn't functional anymore. Writing and painting were done in caves to ensure good hunting. The painting of Brion Gysin deals directly with the magical roots of art. His paintings are designed to produce in the viewer the timeless ever-changing world of magic caught in the painter's brush. His paintings may be called space art. Time is seen spatially as a series of images or fragments of images past, present, or future.*

Gysin felt trapped and oppressed by materiality, but optimistically searched for techniques to short-circuit control and expectation. He accepted nothing as fixed and permanent, reducing the most intimidating formulae of language to animated permutations that become portals of behavioral liberation. If, as we have seen, the universe consists of interlaced frequencies that pulse and resonate at various interconnected rhythms, then his search was for a future beat that would liberate the body and mind from all forms of linearity. Each magick square is essentially holographic, suffused with a directed unity. Intertwined in his grids as confirmation and illustration of the magical ideas proposed are examples of routines, exercises with words and densely cut-up texts. What we observe is a complex, deeply serious mind, an occultural alchemist, camouflaged by passionate humor.

In Gysin's works and writings we are blessed with a perfect example of the storyteller teacher. A practiced, post-technological shamanic guide to the mind, providing exercises, navigational tools and data to assist us in the essential process for magical survival and for the exploration of this strange place in which we unfold our physical existence(s). A domain we call earth, society and life but rarely call into fundamental question. Rationality and materiality have generated a depth of inertia so profound that it could destroy our potential as a species to survive or evolve. All the more reason to re-appraise and study, as magical masters, the instructive works of Burroughs and Gysin as we traverse the Twenty-First Century. As science confirms the revelation of this space-time neurosphere as a holographic universe, I have no doubt that Burroughs and Gysin, re-defined as occultural alchemists and practicing magicians, are destined for an accelerating appreciation for the seminal influence of their cultural engineering experiments.

There is an exquisite mastery of perception that these discoveries unfold. Both Gysin and Burroughs use a serial seduction of detail. Meaning is shattered and scattered to become a more accurate and truthful representation of this arbitrary plane we needlessly confine by using the word-prison "reality." Consecutive events are subverted as we read, revealing the fragility and distortions that our conditioned senses filter out for simplicity of behavior and illusory reason. Nothing tends to remain as it seems, but becomes as it is seen. Contradictory experience is portrayed as equally perceived, parallel images and thoughts. Mundanity is turned strange and disturbing.

297

Burroughs and Gysin, as master magicians, grasp the elasticity of reality and our right to control its unfolding as we see fit and prefer. They consolidate our right to active participation in the means of perception, and their proposal of the nature of consensus being is still quite revolutionary. As we navigate the warp and weft of biological existence and infinite states of consciousness, consciousness, the holographic universe looks kindly upon us, and at the magick squares of their methods and the delirious madness they supply us with, we are offered a unique perspective and afforded respite, balance and the possibility of retrieving new and valuable information for a future.

We are not talking about a matter of faith here; faith is something that has a low quotient in these experiments. Rather, we are looking at prophetic predictions based upon a magical vision of the universe and the resulting, practical applications of alchemical theories and exercises. In fact we are looking at an early, workable model of the future, in which a positive, compassionate unfolding of our latent qualities as a species is defined and described in the vainglorious hope that we "abandon all rational thought" and immerse ourselves in an ecstatic series of creative possibilities.

In a way, it is a bit like learning a martial art. We develop our media reflexes and accelerate our improvisational responses in order to maximize our individual potentialities and the interests of our chosen people or our private dream agenda. In his various essential commentaries on media divulgence, Douglas Rushkoff astutely directs us to a re-examination of the original source of an inherited narrative of culture and life. His conclusions are very similar to my assertions in relation to Burroughs and Gysin, that the very history that began this examination, the social narrative imposed upon us as a child, that so easily programs us to maintain every possible status quo without criticism; and that compounds the notion of linearity and a serial phenomenological universe seems more clearly to be an illusion and a deliberately inert construction. A picture of "reality" that is designed by those with a vested interest in stasis to maintain our surrender to cultural impotence and all forms of addictive consumption.

The past controls through people and their surrender to a closed system, where the laws of physics remain constant, and predictability is a desirable state in an ever more rigid global world order. Yet, in fact, we are entering a digital future, a holographic universe where, at least theoretically, every sentient being on earth will be interconnected, international and interfaced. Entirely new navigational tools are required. The possibilities are endless. It is my contention that as the authorship of our own private narrative becomes increasingly autonomous, malleable and optional, that a new future, a future that is inclusive, rooted in the idea of an open source that we can affect by logical and alchemical means, becomes critical to our species' survival, comprehension, and evolutionary change. A future where Burroughs and Gysin, and their modern occultural brethren, have supplied prophetic, functional skills and nonlocal points of observation which can train us to be fittingly alert and prepared for the unpredictable aesthetic and social spasms to come.

Endnotes:
1. See *Even Further: The Metaphysics of the Sigil* by Paul Cecil in *Painful But Fabulous.*
2. Another magician from a different school might call them "égregores."
Genesis Breyer P-Orridge, 2006

AN OVER PAINTED SMILE

As the 1960s arrived I was living in Gatley, a little suburb between Manchester and Stockport in Cheshire. Life was divided quite starkly for us teenagers. You supported Manchester United or Manchester City football club. You were a mod, a teddy boy or a rocker. You liked Cliff Richard or Elvis and you were a puff (gay) or normal when it came to sexual orientation. Liverpool was about fifteen miles from Manchester and both cities were ports in a post-war, post-industrial storm of decline.

My inclination was to be a mod, the glamorous evolution of beat(nik) protest culture and poetry. I recall vividly walking through Picadilly Station in Manchester in 1962 and suddenly looking up at the sound of jewellry tinkling to see my first pre-Raphaelite, living, breathing angelic beings! A group of especially sophisticated mods who were probably on their way to the Twisted Wheel or the Heaven & Hell club for a pilled-up night of frenzied rhythm and blues tinged with soul. But what riveted me with an impact that literally charged and changed my life forever was the appearance of the boys. No polarized clearly defined gender stereotyope. No! The boys wore immaculately tight jeans witth a slight flare, black Italian hand-made "winkle-pickers" (a ridiculously pointed toe) or beautiful "chisels" (the toe cut across as if sliced off with a chisel). Under their casual three-button wool jackets were tailored shirts with collars held stiff with a stud through from one side to the other at the front; divided by a thin black knitted tie, or thin (one inch wide max) black leather tie. Fabulous already, but that was not what took my breath away and demolished all my preconceptions about what could acceptably be worn by a male. The young men all wore perfectly applied make-up, mascara, eye shadow and lipstick, and had meticulously coiffed hair back-combed and cut to create a perfectly ambiguous and androgynous vision. Amazing! Even for mods of that era they were, I realize now, way ahead of their time.

299

I mention this in detail because the desire to integrate my Self into, and have no fear of becoming, an hermaphroditic peacock-like P-Androgyne certainly was imprinted in that very moment. It also prepared my aesthetic for the cultural upheavals that were to come next.

Once I saw that group of mods I knew, in my heart, that I wanted to look like that and be a part of whatever clique or group it represented. I had chosen my side. This meant that at school I had a much reduced circle of possible friends but it also meant I could easily identify them and have a greater chance of acceptance and support for my interests. All these things are important when one is exploring puberty, relationships and loyalties outside thee parental world ov childhood. E was beginning to build an identity that was Self-chosen, not just accepted by rote or laziness simply because my family bequeathed it to me. This time of seperation from one's familial circle and declaration of uniqueness and individual charatcer is a fantastically exciting and vital period during which it felt quite natural to be part of a wider social fraternity.

My friends at Stockport Grammar School and I would discuss shoes, clothes, accessories and, of course, music, swapping information and publications during free time between lessons. I quickly learned about the "Toggery" in Mersey Square. A new-fangled "boutique" which sold cool mod clothes. A couple of musicians in a band called the Hollies worked there. My first prized purchases were an important black pig-skin cap, a thin black knitted tie and a gorgeous pink "roundhead" skirt. Through going to the Toggery we learned about the new Beat music scene growing like wildfire in our area. All kinds of bands were playing at small clubs, even the Town Hall.

Our lifeline for hearing new records was Radio Luxembourgh (Fab 208) which I could tune in to on my treasured Bush transistor radio. The best music was on late, so I would listen under the bedclothes through a tiny earphone like the ones used by deaf people. It was primitive, but it was fabulous!

A lot of the music they played was still awful Tin Pan Alley schlock and top twenty stuff that stunk of contrived 50s music, crooning and rock and roll. Here I must confess that I never liked Elvis at all, or the "rock" music that spewed forth thereafter to cash in on his success. There was no music that I felt connected to, that spoke for me, or through me, the way those mods had expressed everything I was feeling visually and as style. There was a peculiar emptiness in the realm that music now occupies. So I listened to jazz from my father Ron's collection as a substitute. At least I could admire the skill and improvisations, the freedom and soulfulness.

Yet I felt starved, a hunger that I had no name or description for. All I knew for certain was that all the turmoil I was experiencing and the countless discoveries pouring into me from literature and poetry gave me no sense of having a visceral voice. One night I was drifting with the radio on. The DJ announced he was going to play a promotional copy of a new single by a rhythm and blues "pop" band called the Rolling Stones that would be out on Friday. Next thing I knew I was being thrilled by "Come On!" I knew straight away that this was the voice of my tribe. I bought it on the day it came out and played it over and over again. Then I would flip it and play "I Want to Be Loved," the B-side. In those days you could leave the steadying arm up and the track would play infinitely if you left it alone. Glorious. I truly felt as if I had been released from a prison, and I knew it wasn't just because the song was great,—in all honesty, it wasn't—though it seemed radically new right then. But the real reason I felt free was Brian Jones. Another apparition that solidified my dream into a resolve that has never left me.

Sometimes our process of learning is wholly intuitive, a critical revelation can be integrated into our personality and sense of identity by an act of self-trust years before we are consciously able to articulate or describe it. Daydreams are really important activators in this evolution of personal wisdom. If we are able to be totally honest with our Self without inhibitions, filters and hesitations we can build visual metaphors in our daydreams of what we truly and intimately desire to become. These images are like holograms of possibility, templates of identity. Happiness is when the inside and outside are the same. This is the reason that I have always said, since those early times I have described, that I take my daydreams very seriously. In a way, my whole life has been an ever more meticulous unfolding of, and creation of, my imaginary Self in the material world. Bit by bit I have used a process of removal. Removing any remaining elements of inherited identity and stereotypical roles so that, at any given time, what remains in this physical body that contains what I call "me" (in my internal dialogue of consciousness) is knowingly *Self* created. Written by my own choices and additions, my willful and willing experiences and my memories. And with this individual language by which it is defined and described, I can reclaim, and actually be, the author of my own, "divine," higher Self.

All this began with the fully conscious decision to utilize each epiphany

301

as an hieroglyph, as a neurological anchor that would reinforce my idealized Self both internally, for my own development, and externally, to slowly reclaim control over the world's perception of my Self and my physical interactions as a person. Perhaps this helps explain why I have dwelled upon these two apparently mundane moments from adolescence. What came next absolutely concretized my intuitively magickal path in perpetuity, and that is why I feel duty and honor-bound to declare and revere the being that, without ever knowing, gave my Self so much clarity and determination.

Once I had acquired "Come On" and played it almost ad nauseum until it became a blurrred invocation of empowerment, I naturally sought out everything I could find written about the Stones. Radio Luxembourg collaborated on a color fan-style magazine called *Fabulous 208* which specialized in large pin-up photos of the new explosion of pop groups. I persuaded my parents to subscribe and methodically clipped out all the images of the Rolling Stones for my first magickal diary (though I still thought of it as a scrapbook). I became as ardent a Stones fan as I was a supporter of Manchester City. The Beatles were "poofs" who were approved of by parents, grandparents and even teachers. They were neat and tidy, likeable and cute, composers of pap and pop music without any blues authenticity or sense of dangerous rebellion, commodified and assimilated by the cultural status quo at an alarmingly fast pace. We fledgling beatnik Stones fans tended to dismiss the Beatles out of hand as token darlings of a society and oppressive class-driven system that our instincts declared was our natural born enemy.

Within the poor-traits of the Stones I collected, slowly the visually anarchic icon I fixated on was Brian Jones. Cocky, slightly sneering, with feminine hair and clothes provocatively suggesting that they were borrowed from a girlfriend in a rush to get to the photo session after a night of debauchery, he was the most androgynous male I had ever seen up until then in my relatively cloistered life. My worldly knowledge may have been unsophisticated, but my instinct was spot on given the luxury of interpretive hindsight. There is no doubt in my mind that this androgyny was what I found compelling and deeply significant. I had always felt profoundly puzzled by society's concept of gender and biological roles and stereotypes. Metaphorical archetypes seem much more inspirational and enervating, and even more relevant, to my personal thought processes and metaphysical concepts, as far as I had any way back then. Luckily I was blessed very early on with an awareness that identity was clearly fictional and/or imposed, its function being primarily to maintain a status quo rooted in inherited priviledge just as much as culture was built on inherited expectation, ritual and behavior.

From then on, forewarned and primed by Radio Luxembourg, I was able to buy each Stones single, in their orange and white striped sleeves with the dark blue Decca label, the day they were released. I still have them all, athough "Get Off My Cloud" is warped and doesn't play anymore. They were the soundtrack to my imagination and my sexuality, exploding through my body and mind, occupying every cell with daydreams and fantasies that would remain dormant but active, creating a checklist of scenarios to enact and identities to become that I am still methodically ticking off upon completion. Hindsight tells me we should all be told how crucial these daydreams are to our future unfolding as sentient beings, to our emotional fulfillment and to our achievement of our maximum potential for happiness. Instead, most of us are persuaded that these glorious early visions of creating something unique, joyful and vibrant that has lasting impact of some kind upon our world, changing our Self and our surroundings for the better... these fabulous, nourishing visions are crushed into a place of internalized impotence and shame as we are beaten down until we accept their frivolity as irresponsible "adolescent idealism" or place them in the more qualified, professional and cool hands of a Damien Hirst or his ilk in the service industry of art. Under pressure from peer group, family group, social group, religious group and all the other representatives of perpetual surrender to hopelessness. Our liberty of delirious imagination falls limp as it is bound and gagged by that which is named "growing up" and "being an adult." Somehow I knew not to capitulate to this immense cultural pressure. I knew I should cling to and treasure my daydreams. Knew that they were, and will always be, the most satisfying sustenance of my soul. I have learned since through wonder-full beings I have met that creativity, and the manifestation of compassionate imagination, is what sets us apart as living creatures and reveals our search for re-union with our divinity of consciousness.

Suddenly my happy little reverie was shattered. My family had to move

303

from the North to Solihull in the Midlands. Instead of being unself-consciously accepted as part of a peer group, wearing similar clothes as my mates, being accepted without hesitation and feeling as though I fit in, I was suddenly adrift. Everything I had taken for granted was wrenched away. How I looked, talked, walked, thought and felt was quite literally and physically under attack. I mention this only because it explains to a large degree why I elevated my inner life and gave far higher value to the symbology I had created. When the outside world is mentally and physically abusive every single day, and both one's peer group and those in authority who are supposed to protect you from viciousness and humiliation fail you, the only escape is escapism. In a nutshell Brian Jones came to represent rejection of everything that hurt and rejection of "normality" and social expectations. I grew to despise maleness and male stereotypes of behavior, inevitably linking maleness with abuse and violence, pettymindedness, anti-creativity, negation of sensitivity and an animalistic, primitive attitude to sexuality and love. Through all my misery I held on to art, music, poetry and romantic love as ideals worth any sacrifice.

By now the Beatles had improved a little, having discovered drugs, I suspect, but the Stones were still my favorite. Brian Jones was flouncing around London dressed in overtly feminine clothing and the age of neo-dandies and psychedelic peacocks was upon us. One day my father, Ron Megson, asked me if I would like to go see a filming of *Thank Your Lucky Stars*, hosted by Brian Matthews. This was a pop music television program on ABC every Saturday night. Each week there would be about half a dozen artists miming to their latest records in the studio. Who appeared depended on what new singles were coming out. You never knew in advance who would be on. Still, the idea of seeing real pop groups "live" for the first time was exciting. My father's business had dealings with the television company, so not only would I get to be in the studio audience, but I would have a VIP backstage pass. I didn't care who was on, I would even cope with Freddie and the Dreamers if I had to! Ouch!

The shows were actually recorded the Sunday prior to transmission. So, on Sunday, March 21, 1966 I went to ABC Television's Alpha Studios, Aston, Birmingham at around four p.m. As I had two hours to spare until six p.m., when filming began, I wandered around "backstage." As I walked along behind a huge grey curtain and lights on scaffolds, I was glancing

down, carefully avoiding cables on the floor when suddenly (quite literally) I bumpeed into someone quite hard! We both said "sorry," and as I looked up, there was Mick Jagger! He was carrying a Coke in one hand and seemed smaller than I had imagined. I didn't know what to say, so like anyone would, I asked him for his autograph. All I had was my post-card-sized ticket, so he signed that for me. I told him the Stones were my favorite group and how much they inspired me, especially when I was depressed. He asked me if I would like to meet the rest of the band, as they were here to perform a new single. Naturally, but rather inarticulately, I said that yes, that would be great, and I followed Jagger as he led the way.

All of the sudden, it seemed, we were in a cafeteria and these were the rest of the Stones, sitting at a diner-style table sipping drinks—coffee and Coke seemed the order of the day. In a daze of awe I found my Self sitting down at the table with the Stones, with nobody else around at all that I can recall. I sat with them for over half an hour asking questions about their music and feeling incredibly dumb. All of them were really nice to me, despite what I felt was my obvious awkwardness.

Bill Wyman, Charlie Watts, Mick Jagger and Brian Jones all signed my ticket! Keith didn't, for some reason, and I didn't want to annoy him by asking why. I felt lucky enough not to be greedy on top. All this is

strangely surreal in my memory. In slow motion, as are many key blessings or traumas. What I do remember very, very clearly is how Brian Jones looked, and how he looked at me. He seemed translucent, not fully materialized as if in an unguarded moment when he wasn't fully focused on being present, as if your hand might pass right through him. It was as if the particles that were intended to give him substance and represent the physical body known as Brian Jones were dancing a little too freely, making it hard for him to maintain a human form. He was more apparition than person. Neither male nor female. I kept expecting to see right through him, or have him vaporize, or even suddenly realize I was looking in a mirror with him in the distance. It was very strange, and a little disturbing. Once or twice I felt him staring at me, and as I caught his eye it felt as if he was asking me not to say what I could see, telling me he knew what I saw. As I rebuild my sense memory of that event there does seem to be a sense of panic, of drowning in forces out of control. I have though carefully about this feeling and I do not believe it is hindsight adding or embellishing, I think it is real, because I remember how vivid it felt and how unsettled I felt afterward.

Rolling Stones autographs, 1965

While I was sitting there, Keith asked someone to pass him the sugar. Every movement he made was in slow motion, especially as he turned, almost like a mime or a Zen dancer, giving everything an even more surreal qualitty. As I sat there in awe listening, I made a clear decision that I would somehow find my own way to live as an exotic musical creature, refusing boundaries and expectations, immersed in limitless new possibilitues. I made a promise to my Self there and then, speaking to the still-forming person inside my head, and I locked it down with purity of intent by using Brian Jones as the hieroglyph to represent my dream with form. Why Brian Jones and not the others? Intuition told me that he was the source, the reckless explorer innovating with new instruments, new arrangements and, most of all, perhaps new identities that transgressed taboos with abandon. Rightly or wrongly, I saw Brian Jones as a Romantic, flawed by daring, the soul of the group. He was the first Pandrogyne to enter my personal cosmology.

After a while, somebody came to usher the Stones away to get ready for the show. As they were leaving, though, Brian Jones spoke to the floor manager, asking him to change my seat. Usually the rule was that teen-age girls who guaranteed that they would scream and act hysterical on a signal were the only people allowed to sit directly behind the groups on camera. It made for better television. Tonight, thanks to Brian and the Stones, I was sat right in the middle of the front row, behind the Stones, near Charlie Watts. Best view in the house. I couldn't have wished for a more perfect moment if I had known they would be there. Next thing I knew I was sat behind the drums watching the show. Dave Berry uncurl-ing himself from behind a curtain (yes, the huge grey curtain from earlier), Susan Maughm doing a crappy song; I seem to remember Bobby Vee sing-ing "Rubber Ball" and then a new pick from the top, "The Measles" from Manchester. Perhaps they were playing "Bye Bye Birdie," I am not sure, but I do know they looked really cool in immaculate three-button velvet suits, and really not cool with measles spots speckled all over their faces! But I liked them, because they were playing hard British rhythm and blues.

Then, the Rolling Stones. So close, just an arm's length away. I was still overwhelmed by the knowledge that the reason that I was so close was that they themselves had decided that I should be. This meant so much to me, not just because I was naturally thrilled as a fan, but for secret emotional reasons, too. For the first time since I had left Manchester,

307

two years previously, I felt included and accepted by a social group and, most of all, I even felt special, my Self-esteem bolstered instead of eroded. I felt as though my fledgeling ideas and values, coupled with my rejection of so much that constituted the status quo and how I was supposed to behave to fit in and succeed, had been validated. I wasn't insane, destined to be alone and isolated for being "different." There was a community of artists where I could potentially belong and be accepted.

It is impossible to say how important it was to feel OK instead of how it was at Solihull School where I was like a target, defined as stupid and beaten like I was subhuman. After being swept away in a never-ending torrent of ridicule and abuse, simultaneously lost in a strange new town, without any like-minded friends (as of yet), this revelation was my lifeline, my private moment of rescue. I had something, no matter how petty or silly it might seem to anyone outside, something that gave me hope and direction. Thank you, Brian.

Oh yes, they performed "Nineteenth Nervous Breakdown," which I honored years later with a cover of the B-side of "As Tears Go By" by Psychic TV. I loved "Tears," apart from the romantic simplicity, because Marianne Faithful had recorded it and, along with Twiggy, she was my female icon. Twiggy for her pandrogyny, Marianne for her rebellious energy—beauty with balls, so to speak. Memories can be solidified and recorded in objects, as well and songs, poems and pictures, of course. One medium can preserve a memory or event, but each memory is a hologram filled with connectors, links and reflections as complex and infinite as those of cyberspace. When I hear "As Tears Go By," I can retrieve huge parts of my emotional and creative life in an instant. I can remember people, places and happenings. Most of all, I can remember that fleeting, etheereal phantasm that I once believed was Me. I have realized that we are all, as we become alert to the fragility of being, almost translucent, just like Brian Jones was then. This lifelong determination of identity can be the process by which we are liberated from expectations and by which we dissolve the parameters intended to define, and thereby restrict, our flowering into an individual way of being.

Far beyond consensus reality and "normality" is this place where all dreams meet. A dimension I believe exists outside time and space.

I made a secret promise for my Self then and there, that I would honor this profound contribution of Brian Jones towards my deepening resolve to be the sole author of my own story and identity and towards my belief in the magick of creativity. I knew I would find a very special way to reveal this gift when the time was right.

By the time Brian Jones was discovered murdered in his swimming pool at Cotchford Farm (birthplace of Winnie the Pooh) in 1969, I had dropped acid, dropped my token gestures at a straight life, dropped my original name and all the emotional archaeological relics that went with it. My musical boundaries had loosened to include, most particularly, the Velvet Underground. My writings were beginning to get published in various "underground" publications. I was in London to accept an invitation to join the kinetic art performance group the Exploding Galaxy, so I decided to see the Rolling Stones' free concert in Hyde Park. To be honest, I was pretty disgusted that they could countenance carrying on using the name Brian Jones chose, and present a sham pseudo-continuation of his legacy without imploding with immeasurable shame. Still, it was free, and it wasn't out of my way.

Despite how documentaries which record that afternoon are edited and despite how their sacrilege of his legacy has been compounded by the resulting manipulation of musical astory, do not be misled, the Stones were awful! Capitalizing on tragedy is always a delicate balance with the best of intentions, but using the pretext of a (conveniently timed) memorial celebration of Brian Jones, Mick Jagger and the Stones managed to be totally embarrassing musically, whilst simultaneously redefining all previous notions of insincerity. My personal recollection is that there were indeed about 500,000 people in the park when the Stones began playing, and it was impossible for anyone at the back, as I was, to get anywhere closer to the stage. Mick Jagger seemed like a prancing miniature puppet in an ill-fitting white dress. By about halfway through their set, though, I could easily wander right up to the front of the stage to talk with Buttons and the other Hell's Angels doing security, who I knew from the hotel squat in Drury Lane. Die-hard fans were drifting home in droves, gravely disappointed by this lackluster memorial to a death taken as hard as that of any cherished blood family member. My resolve to find a form to preserve the symbolic and actual influence and resonance of Brian Jones solidified into determination that day. As I listened, appalled, to an illiterate reading of Romantic poetry, and as I watched in dismay the sputtering fluttering of white butterflies, falling scattered, dead and dying onto the stage, the earth and the audience as they were thrown unceremoniously from cheap cardboard boxes, I shuddered. I was well aware that butterflies were an Egyptian symbol for liberation of the soul after death, and I wondered what theur cruelly miscalculated demise might represent for the future of those more intimately involved in this fiasco.

As time passed, I continued to try and find ways to integrate my theories and feelings about pandrogyny into my art, and later my music. I also continued to collect books and press clippings related to Brian Jones and his story. As I more overtly included a magickal view of the universe into my creative life, I studied the hermaphrodite as an embodiment of perfection and re-union into a fully conscious whole in alchemy. This positive androgyne I named the Pandrogyne in my writings as a symbol of the reconciliation of opposites, an ending of binary templates for nature and a healing of the Fractured Garden of Eden in a process of aware unity with the divine. The first beings created in "His" image were hermaphrodites, and they were illustrated as such in paintings until the Holy Roman Empire, through censorship and destruction, tried to remove all traces of this version of mythology as part of their holocaust to replace nature, balance and compassionate matriarchy with male, materialist and inevitably violent patriarchy. Different generates friction, friction demands war. For that reason alone, a perspective based upon reconciliation and likeness, a hermaphroditic culture becomes a political position and a threat to entrenched masculine systems of social order. Acceptance of duality enslaves human consciousness.

For me personally, Brian Jones, even more so after his pointless murder, remained a valuable symbol of transcendence of the mundane and an embracing of the integration of opposites and their transmutation into genius and an evolved state of balanced being. My affinity was further strengthened upon finding that one of the original meanings of the word "Pan" was drowning, while "panic" can mean an unreasonable fear leading to excessive and extravagant behavior.

There is a previously unavailable recording on reel two, track ten of *Godstar: Thee Director's Cut*. On it I am interviewing Brion Gysin in his apartment in Paris about Brian Jones' trip to Jajouka in 1969 to record their music. Brion tells of how he was sitting with Brian in the doorway of a small house. One of the Master Musicians walked past, pulling a white goat on a rope. Brian Jones went deathly pale and gasped "That's me!" There was an ominous atmosphere as the musicians explained that the goat was being led off to be sacrificed, to be devoured as their evening meal. The Master Musicians of Jajouka have a seminal legend in the stories of their clan that says that one day, 3,000 years ago or more, the Great God Pan emerged from a cave in the hills near their village and taught his secret, magickal music to the first Master Musician, whose name was Attar. That family has handed down this music as an oral tradition ever since. It is said to heal insanity and calm the Djinn (potentially mischievous nature spirits). Whether by invocation or design, my life has been marked by what feel like an ever-increasing number of synchronicities—links, reflections and phenomenological connections that defy the outmoded language of co-incidence. This has been especially true of my conceptual relationship with Brian Jones since that time, so long ago, when I bought "Come On." First, actually meeting him; then, over the years, meeting so many of the characters in his Chaucerian tale. I didn't mention it before, but on my way into Hyde Park I literally bumped into a resplendant flower child only to have him turn to say "sorry" (again!) and reveal that it was Donovan, who had married Brian's great love Linda, mother of Brian's son Julian. Later, through William S. Burroughs, I had connected with and become friends with Brion Gysin, who had introduced Brian to Ja-jouka and who likewise introduced me to a young Bachir Attar, a direct descendant of that first musician taught by Pan. It is my nature to take clusters of such events as confirmation of my path and my speculations upon cultural inevitability. They also give magickal color to the unfolding. With a faith in discarnate spirits to whom one has made a promise, no matter how privately, comes a great responsibility to manifest and mate-rialize any promise made. It's a calling.

311

In 1985, a full-on hyperdelicized Psychic TV were playing at the notorious Haçienca in Manchester. Perhaps it was around February; I don't remember—but it would make sense if it was, as Brian's b-earth-day was the twenty-eighth (mine is the twenty-second, so I always remember). I had been reading a book about Brian Jones and was feeling frustrated, yet again, that the obvious conclusion—that Brian Jones was murdered—was still glossed over and that his incredibly important contribution to popularizing rhythm and blues and his innovation in founding a group as influential as the Rolling Stones was being largely forgotten.

I had also been thinking about celebrity, how Andy Warhol had turned fame into a new artistic medium, upping the cultural ante by making a "star" merely a stage, and inventing a new word for the next stage with "superstar." We all know how successful and impressive this insight was and how the word has passed into our vernacular so that it is easy to assume the term always existed, and forget it was contrived and deliberate. This was an early example of what I have named "cultural engineering." As I thought more and more about Warhol's linguistic interplay, I became convinced it was time to add another stage to the ladder of stardom. A word to encompass a celebrity whose fame lived on after death and grew exponentially, becoming mythical and legendary until their attributes and impact are far beyond any material achievements in their lifetime. Such media figures often die tragically young. Thinking of ancient civilizations whose Gods had human form, with human flaws and gifts (especially, in relation to Brian Jones, Hermes and Aphrodite, whose offspring was a hermaphrodite), I had invented a new word—"godstar." Star, superstar, godstar. It all made perfect sense. As the power of each new word is dissipated and diminished by overuse and familiarity, our consumer society, with its built in obsolescence, even of its champions, demands new, more vital words. So be it… here was one such word, sleek, witty and precise, all ready for action! Godstar.

312

Suddenly my resident songwriting genius Alex Fergusson threw out some fabulous power chords that tripped a channeling switch in my nervous system and, without prior discussion or any rehearsal, totally improvised and spontaneous, I found my Self singing a pop song all about Brian Jones. I can definitely remember thinking to my Self, in a sensation akin to an out-of-body experience, "Wow! This is a perfect pop song, complete with verses and chorouses. How strange. Where did *this* come from? Huh. I kind of like it. Weird…" The rest of the gig is a blur. I do know the acoustics were dire and all of PTV were disappointed with our overall performance. Yet as we relaxed in the dressing room, one by one, everyone asked "What was that new song you made up tonight, Gen?" Our then-business "manager," Terry McKlellan, said "That song would make a great pop record—what was it, Gen?"

"Godstar," I replied, not knowing what else to say. "It just came out on stage. I was as surprised as everyone else. Anyway, it doesn't matter, because I can't remember what I sang, except that 'Godstar' is the chorous."

Alex Fergusson told us he could probably play something like it again. Then we all had a moment of genius. To solve a problem is to look for the obvious first. Had anybody recorded the gig? Even a bad bootleg would do. Just a reference, so we could recreate the song and see if it was as special as we'd all felt.

Luckily for us all, and for Psychic TV, we did locate a cassette recording. It was crumbly, but served well enough as a notebook, which was all I needed. Alex memorized the chords and structure; I transcribed some words, and the rest flowed out easily. A classic three-minute Sixties-style pop single. What an amazing gift, made possible by our faith in improvisation and openness in the heart of the moment.

I quickly realized that *this* was the "object" I was to magickally charge in honor of Brian Jones' impact upon my metaphysical life, that obscure and mystical creature confirming the sublimity of the Pandrogyne.

313

One positive thing Terry had brought to the table was recording time in a beautiful analogue 24-track studio in the basement of DJM records in Holborn. Countless classic records had been given birth there, but it was due to be demolished to make way for a modern digital studio.

"Godstar" had grown in scope from a new word to a single, and now I planned to begin writing an entire feature-length film script, also to be called *Godstar*, which would be a treatment with Brian Jones as the central character. However, it was not be a straight documentary—rather, an exploration of why and how Brian Jones was, for my Self, and I believe many others, a holographic metaphor for the unfolding theme of Pandrogyny in Western culture, and the disasterous fate that befalls a natural-born shaman in a society that treats its mystics, creative healers, artists and visionaries as enemies and subversives. Instead of being given special training for the "chosen" by previous generations of mentors in order to learn to express and channel their revelations for the benefit of their people, like shamen are today in ancient, but sophisticated, tribal belief systems based upon a balance with and within nature, they are ostracized and isolated. Those who would enlighten us all and heal our differences through music and art are beaten down, attacked and vilified, accused of immorality and evil in order to divert positive attention that might teach their peers and release them from self-negation. Sadly, the Sixties were littered with the corpses of well-intentioned but tragically destroyed champions and seers.

So I wanted to use Brian Jones as a symbol of that destructive process that has assisted in thee homogenisation and commodification of rebellion and freeform thinking. Flawed but possessed of genius. Brutally isolated and murdered to suppress his dreams, including imperfections of course, perhaps infinitely amplified by the inevitable resistance to endless joy in change and purity of intention. Simultaneously to present him as an original manifestation of the neo-dandy hermaphrodite and a pioneer explorer of global cultures. Using world music as ritual and his life as a surreal allegory like an over-painted smile.

In the studio I insisted on authenticity wherever possible. We hired a drum kit that was the same as the one(s) used by Charlie Watts in the early Stones photos with wooden drums. I used only analog effects, real tape-produced phasing, razor blades for edits—and always there was a photograph of Brian Jones on the desk or in my pocket. Psychic TV were recording the full soundtrack to *Godstar: Thee Movie*. As I had expected, "Godstar" made a great pop single. Alex Fergusson outdid himself with backwards guitar solos and, through all my obsessive madness and devotion to the concept, Ken Thomas, my super-engineer and co-producer extraordinaire, translated my filmic descriptions into aural soundscapes, finding ways to put the energy and mystery onto tape as if it was 1969 again. His gift is stunning.

Theoretically, Psychic TV were on CBS Records just before we began. However, one day I went in to the head office and had a discussion with Muff Winwood about a follow-up album to *Dreams Less Sweet*. Basically, he told me we should make more commercial music and write a potential hit single. I told him we never wrote to please anyone, but as it happened we had a perfect track. I played him the live invention of "Godstar." He told me CBS could never sell our music if it was going to be like that song. I always remember my reply: "Even a monkey could sell more records by Psychic TV than CBS!" He explained that

I needed to compromise and write music that they could work with. I then replied, "When you sign Psychic TV, you are renting my brain, and obviously CBS can't afford my brain any longer."

My faith in the "Godstar" project was so profound that after leaving CBS I borrowed money from a kind bank manager and founded Temple Records to release the new single and its associated album. Dejamus covered those costs in return for the publishing. At the start those tapes were just demos used to try and raise funds. As the story unfolded, not every track got retouched, due to lack of money—but the title track did. The collection of songs towards the soundtrack was eventually released as *Allegory and Self*, otherwise known as *Thee Starlit Mire*.

Throughout the recording of "Godstar," I insisted on leaving track twenty-three of the twenty-four track master blank. No mikes were ever plugged into it, nor were any instruments. A very weird thing happened, to which Ken Thomas and the others can bear witness. During playback, after we'd recorded everything and in due preparation for a "finished" mix, including two or three takes on my vocal, Ken noticed an odd noise in the background. One by one we muted the various tracks until we arrived at track twenty-three. Once it was isolated, as we expected, it was silent. Then, all of the sudden, a knocking noise occurred. Just a few times—seven, to be more precise. It was a slightly wooden sound, like tapping on a solid table. We were baffled. Ken insisted there was no rational or scientific reason for the noises to be there. Then I had a strange premonition. I told Ken to run the tape again, this time with one of my lead vocals and track twenty-three playing, nothing else. The knocks came, as I had guessed, under various words in the exact same rhythm and phrasing of those words. Like a child trying to tap out a melody. The words that were this highlighted were: YOU WERE SO BEAUTIFUL and I WISH I WAS WITH YOU NOW.

315

Make of this what you will. I truly believe that somehow, the recording session being a little more like a séance more often than not, Brian Jones' spirit was able to send a message, endorsing the song and saying that it was OK to do it. This was so unexpected, yet I can only imagine that intuition, or Brian, guided me or we'd never have left track twenty-three available to him.

I was concerned that Brian's parents might feel thee single was in bad taste, or exploitative, so I contacted them via their solicitors. I sent them a tape of the finished song and explained it was created as a labor of love and respect, and to redress the balance in terms of the slowly fading memory in the music media of his contribution to modern rock and his ever-present legacy. They replied that they liked the song and were happy for it to come out.

More than ever we believed that this project was speaking for Brian Jones, with his collaboration included, as crazy as that sounds. When "Godstar" was finished, I released it on my Temple Records label; it was distributed through various independent companies. I always felt that there was an "X" factor. An unknown pool of people who were also fanatical fans of Brian Jones and would support and even buy the single just because it was about him. To my amazement the single got rave reviews and was the only time that Psychic TV got blanket positive press—even the *NME* approved! "Godstar" went to number one in the independent singles charts. Through the infinite generosity of my dear friend Akiko Hada, we were able to assemble a video for TV. It even included previously unseen film footage of Brian Jones. I was researching archive material at Pathe News and the little librarian guy found a couple of cans they'd never developed or broadcast. I paid for duplicates to be made and found it was Brian on the Thames receiving an award from Anita Harris and him and the Stones at an airport with Mick and Keith running. This last, unique section was edited under the telling line "Where were all your laughing friends?"

After sixteen weeks at number one, "Godstar" also made it to number thirty-one on the national singles chart, and to number twenty-nine in another national chart. At that time the policy at Radio One was that they had to playlist any singles in the top thirty at least for a few plays. We were ecstatic. I was convinced that if the song could do so well just on word of mouth and reviews, plus a few broadcasts of the video, then it would inevitably climb up the charts nationally if more and more people heard it. It was, and is, ater all a classic little pop song. Tragically, a mysterious phone call purporting to be from the offices of an interested party's representative (who felt churlish, to say the least, about the decidedly pro-Brian sentiments of my lyrics) motivated the playlist programmers at Radio One to go against policy and veto "Godstar" from ever being heard by a far wider public, or so our plugger suggested to us. So close to a *hit*, then deliberately sabotaged and blocked. I was heartbroken. I felt I had let Brian Jones down. Yet I vowed to continue with the campaign to make a contribution to maintaining visibility and appreciation of his life, music and times.

Despite "Godstar's" climb to the top of the pops being maliciously obstructed by those in the music industry with a vested interest and with far more power than us, our independent success had been noticed. RCA Records licensed somne other tracks from the proposed movie, and so we found ourselves filming a promo video for "Good Vibrations" on Venice Beach, California. John Maybury was to be the director, and this time we had a budget. Sadly, on the very first morning of filming we received a phone call from London informing us that Trojan, John's lover, had died of a drug overdose. John immediately flew home and we carried on as best we could, filled with sympathy and immersed in melancholy without him.

The bad news became worse. Once back in London, I went to the Rough Trade office to collect all the substantial income from the sales of "Godstar." This money was intended to finance all of the pre-production costs of the movie, perhaps even subsidize shooting some scenes in the hope of getting full backing so I could finally realize my feature-length dream.

317

"We've already paid you," I was told when I went to accounts to get paid. "How can you have, I've been in California!" I replied. It turned out that they had believed Terry McKlellan was our manager, as a result of things he'd said to them whilst he casually persuaded them to give him a check payable to him personally in the amount of all the money we would otherwise have made. Suddenly Temple Records was broke! Studio bills we'd been informed had been paid started to drop through my door. Producer's fees and royalties due to Ken Thomas that I had been assured were paid I discovered (from a rightly angered Ken) were not, and on and on. *Godstar: Thee Movie* was fucked! Our previously healthy budget had evaporated and Terry McKlellan had disappeared. We'd never seen or heard from him since.

Worse was still to come. Ken Thomas formally withdrew from the Psychic TV project, feeling used and manipulated after putting his heart and soul into our music. He was our George Martin. Then, Alex Fergusson, finally disheartened by the vile machinations of the record business, quit the band he had co-founded with me. Alex had pulled me out of my post-Throbbing Gristle funk, and my vow never to be in a band again, and had convinced me to write songs with him until we decided to form a new band, Psychic TV, together. Alex had understood my fixation on Brian Jones; he had channeled the riff that had triggered my own channeling.

I was devastated. I was suicidally depressed and my two key, unique and inspirational collaborators were gone when I needed them the most— but I understood why they quit. I couldn't fault their logic, even though I knew it was not my fault. I became withdrawn and miserable for ages. I wanted to give up and crawl away, but I couldn't. I had been stuck with bills and responsibilities that only I could try and resolve. I improvised pragmatically day by day. Eventually I released an album of the demos for the film soundtrack as *Allegory and Self*, realizing I still loved those songs, even though they literally brought me grief.

318

Psychic TV now exists again as PTV3 because Edward O'Dowd has "pulled an Alex" and persuaded me to reform the band around the "Godstar" songs which he loves. My Self and Lady Jaye have pursued my original alchemical daydreams and chosen to explore, with ever more commitment, the mutability of identity and the Pandrogyne as divine metaphor through our contemporary art project and process of "Breaking Sex" or "PANDROGENY" where, as the third being created by the melding of two beings, a new artist and phenomenon, BREYER P-ORRIDGE, is created. Using cosmetics, cosmetic surgeries, tattoos, identical clothing and hair and mirroring each others behaviour we extend all this coumpendium of modern magick into a cutting edge new system where no aspect of the process is separated from another. Perhaps the ultimate synthesis prior to a radical and conscious leap off the bridge of the known into a future where knowing nothing is an advantage.

And finally, *Godstar* has been re-released as a double CD, *Godstar: Thee Director's Cut*, evidence of my determination to adhere to the promise I made to honor Brian Jones' significance and influence, whenever and however opportunities arose, through my own artistic and creative works. Even though so many years have passed since my first attempt to use "Godstar" to give impetus to making a metaphorical and meta-physical movie of the same name, I have not given up, nor forgotten my personal pledge. *Godstar: Thee Movie* waits to be completed. Thank you.

Genesis Breyer P-Orridge, New York City, 2004

Image by Genesis Breyer P-Orridge

Changed priorities ahead

XI

Photo of Aghori Baba by Tri Lochan Nath Shrestra

MUSIC, MAGIC & MEDIA MISCHIEF:
The Gnosis *Interview With Genesis P-Orridge*, by Jay Kinney

enesis P-Orridge occupies the curious position of being both a household name and virtually unknown at the same time. While he has been prominent in performance art, so-called industrial culture, the tattoo and body modification rites of modern primitives and the underground rave scene, Genesis (or Gen, as he is called) and the groups he collaborated in, Throbbing Gristle and Psychic TV, have remained largely hidden from mainstream culture.

From 1972 to 1976 Genesis collaborated with Cosey Fanni Tutti as the performance art group Coum Transmissions in the UK. Their performances were visceral attacks on powerful taboos, including explorations of pain, sexuality, disgust and outrage. An Easter performance in Amsterdam late in Coum's career included, in Gen's own words, his being "crucified on a wooden cross, whipped with two bullwhips, covered in human vomit and chicken wings and chicken legs, while I had to hold burning torches; people in the audience could hear the skin burning on my hands."

Coum Transmissions was replaced in 1976 by Throbbing Gristle (TG), now a four- person project and one of the trailblazers of industrial music, whose work has been described as "a mottled sheet of experimental sound." As Genesis says in the following interview, TG dealt with issues of power, control, image and propaganda through an unending series of mind games, surprises, seeming contradictions and a conscious flirtation with paramilitary style.

In 1981 TG split in two, with Genesis and Alex Fergusson forming Psychic TV, which combined the occult and paramilitary themes that had begun to crop up in TG's work. Genesis soon founded a magical order, Thee Temple ov Psychick Youth, or TOPY, which spread word of its existence through Psychic TV gigs and recordings.

Influenced by the early Twentieth Century occult painter Austin Osman Spare, TOPY disseminated information on constructing "sigils," magical objects intended to focus psychic energy toward a conscious goal. TOPY's version of sigils entailed adult members writing down a favorite sexual fantasy, anointing the paper with various bodily fluids and hair at the twenty-third hour of the twenty-third day of the month. Sigils were then mailed off to TOPY headquarters, where they were held in strict confidentiality and supposedly served to build a reservoir of psychic energy for TOPY members' use.

In the late '80s, Genesis and crew became active in the burgeoning rave scene in England, jousting with authorities over holding unlicensed all-night dance parties in unlikely locations. Their notoriety culminated in early 1992 when, in the midst of public hysteria over Satanism, twenty-three Scotland Yard detectives descended upon Genesis' home/TOPY headquarters in Brighton, England, looking for evidence of Satanic ritual abuse. Much of Genesis' art and video archives were seized, and the tabloids had a field day. At the time of the raid, however, Genesis and his two children Caresse and Genesse, were, were off in Nepal, organizing soup kitchens and encountering Hindu and Buddhist holy men. Faced with likely public castigation if they returned home, Genesis and family continued a nomadic life, ending up in the world's designated parking lot for the eccentric and aberrant: Northern California.

324

The following interview was conducted in San Francisco in late March 1994. Despite his reputation as a sordid amalgam of Peter Pan and Captain Hook, Genesis turned out to be a good deal more complex—and charming, even gentle—than his image had prepared me for. It also became apparent that although his motivations are often mischievous and he has an anarchist's instincts for stirring up trouble, Gen is also following a unique path of public self-discovery that is surprisingly idealistic. Few individuals better typify the questions raised by the intersection of popular culture, art, fashion, the occult and radical politics.

Jay Kinney Thee Temple ov Psychick Youth is the first instance I'm aware of where a public figure involved in art and music created a public magical group and made it a integral part of their work. Why did you found TOPY?

Genesis Breyer P-Orridge Well, when I started doing public events and provocations and happenings in the '60s, I was already reading books by Crowley. And my grandmother was actually a medium. She used to have a good reputation for what was called ectoplasmic phenomena.

When she was in a trance, people would claim to have seen almost corporeal manifestations of relatives or people they didn't know. From then on I had an interest in inexplicable phenomena.

The first time I met a person who was in a magical order was in 1969 in Liverpool. This guy came round to this apartment that I was crashing and he was in what turned out to be [Kenneth Grant's] Typhonian OTO. He was a total heroin addict. As he was explaining to me all about how he was in the OTO, he was a magician, and so on, he was tying off and shooting up in the kitchen. And then he was doing the classic squirting a syringe of blood all over the kitchen walls in somebody else's place. And I thought, "If that's what happens when you join a magical order, I don't think I want to do it!" (Laughs.) That was my first introduction to someone who was prepared to say in public that they were involved in magical practice.

Not long after that, I became involved in performance art. At first it was involved with body movement, but very quickly it went into sexual taboos. The performances went from being street theater to having more and more to do with art galleries because those were places where it was safe to experiment. During that time, I got intensely concerned with ritualizing the event and making it have to do with states of consciousness and the assembly of different objects and symbols that seemed to focus something in my own neurology. And I started to notice other things happening every so often.

In Antwerp in 1977, I was speaking in tongues really fast, which has never happened to me before or since. During that particular performance I drank a whole bottle of whiskey, and I also ate branches of this tree that I had found outside, which turned out to be poisonous. And in this trance state I was actually carving designs with rusty metal into my chest. It wasn't planned; it was more as if I was taken over. And then I started vomiting, of course, which was the combination of the tree bark and the whiskey. And because I have to take steroids all the time, if I can't keep the steroid pills down, then I start going into a coma really quickly.

Kinney Why do you take steroids?

Genesis They used to give me steroids for asthma when I was a young

325

boy, and it destroyed half my adrenal glands. And now I have to take them to replace what my glands used to do.

So I ended up in the Antwerp hospital lying in the emergency room with this doctor. And he was saying, "I can't find a pulse or a heartbeat." (Laughter.) And my then-partner Cosey was getting all upset and saying, "What are we going to do? What are we going to do?"

I remember I was lying there and listening and thinking, "But I'm OK!" (Laughs.) I was in my own body, but I was aware of this conversation going on and I was in some suspended state. My brain was functioning normally but I couldn't speak, I couldn't actually move. A transient kind of zombie state was triggered.

That was when I decided that whatever it was I was dealing with in these performance pieces, it was getting so peculiar that I didn't want to do it in a public situation anymore, because there were obviously risks involved. I was getting to the point where sometimes I nearly physically died, and I couldn't put that responsibility on an art gallery or on other people. And I should start doing some research quick to find out what I was really doing.

I'd been going that way anyway, realizing that I wanted to do it privately and with a lot more rigor and thought and actually sit down and plan it, fast, concentrate, and work out a schedule. And always have somebody who was just there to guide or to be able to call me back out if things started to get strange. And also to document what happened.

Kinney Who did you look to as a guide?

Genesis I met a woman called Roberta Graham, who was also doing very intense private performance pieces, building strange contraptions that took the body to really deep thresholds of pain that would push people out of their bodies. But she was very methodical and very scientific. She would spend months planning a new machine and experimenting and testing it slowly to find out exactly what it did. So I collaborated with her to some extent.

I also began doing a lot more reading and thinking and sifting, going back and recalling a lot of these events. And it seemed that certain techniques were utilized all over the planet. Maybe if the technique itself was looked at minus names and incantations—or if the incantations were just a series of sounds and the words were unimportant—maybe I should just try and strip it down and see what was really there. What were the key dynamics that made these things happen, minus all the trappings?

It was a refining of the very simplest elements. One thing was the orgasm, and another was various bodily fluids and certain times and astrological conjunctions and the repetitions of certain types of deep or high sounds.

Not long after that I began working with various women friends as a Priestess figure exploring endurance (both in terms of time and pain) rituals privately in a dedicated space. Trying to see what happened, if anything, with essence minus mystification.

The basic premise in all my work has always been, if I think about something and it seems to make sense, to project it into the public arena of popular culture. To see whether it survives or not in its own right, to see what happens and what is confirmed and denied and what creates interesting interactions and confrontations. To use popular culture as the alchemical jar to see what happens. Why I have to do that, I don't know. It's just been a drive for so long.

327

Monte Cazzaza came over to visit during 1979 and 1981 and stayed for over six months with me. And I told him that I was thinking more in terms of a paramilitary occult order that was secreted within something that seemed enough a part of popular culture for it not to appear to be a threat immediately. And for reasons of mischief and fascination, this turned me on! (Laughs.) I liked the idea of the mystery and the mischief both.

And of course Monte always encourages anything that looks like it might create some short circuits in the status quo. Monte went back to America, and I just sat down and designed the Psychick Cross on graph paper. I wanted a symbol that seems really familiar, that is almost the same as lots of things but not quite the same, so that people could find it easy to adopt into their personal mythology.

Kinney I was wondering about both the TOPY cross and Throbbing

Gristle's thunderbolt logo. The thunderbolt has a slight flavor of a neofascist group, and the TOPY cross had a feeling of being both an upside-down cross and a Russian Orthodox cross. So you've chosen symbols that are right on this edge where people can project nefarious intents onto them. It's an interesting device on your part.

Genesis I think that symbols are critically important. And that's why with TG it was the same: I sat down with graph paper, and we spent a long time deciding how it was going to look and what the proportions would be. Because in Britain and Spain red and black are the colors of the anarchists. But red and black are also traditionally seen to be neofascist colors. The lightning bolt has the SS connotation, but it also has the idea of short-circuiting control. And if you look at the lightning bolt as a break, it's actually the anarchist circle and flag snapping in two. So it was, as you say, right on the edge.

Previously with Throbbing Gristle we had started wearing camouflage and paramilitary stuff and walking that tightrope between the acceptable and the provocative—pretty skillfully, most of the time. Because of our sense of humor, we managed to keep it going, because people soon began to realize that we were actually commenting and pointing things out, NOT condoning them.

We found that people began coming to the gigs dressing like us. They'd come in army surplus and caps and put TG patches on. We triggered something and observed it and then encouraged it. We thought, "Let's see what happens when it's not the Bay City Rollers or the New Kids on the Block." Here we are playing with this dark shadow side, but it's the same pop phenomena, with people wanting to feel that they belong and state their allegiance in terms of popular culture and ideas by how they look. Let's not be afraid of that and let's not be aloof from it, let's explore it and push it even more.

329

The response was much more powerful than we expected. So we would play with that and do a lot of talking about what we could do that completely contradicts the expectation. Of course eventually we did a gig all dressed in white with white light, and everything was beautiful. And everyone else in the audience was in black and camouflage and "uuuurrrr!" (grimaces), and we smiled all the time and we really annoyed them. And it gives you all these extra cultural weapons. You can do the simplest, stupidest thing and it seems really loud and large and potent again. Wearing white suits shouldn't make any difference, and yet it blew the fanatics' minds and it was recorded in the papers: "What's happened to TG? They're all wearing white! They've sold out! What's going on?" (Laughter.)

So that was very much a satirical exploration of what happens in popular culture. And what is this dynamic, where people want to gather and feel connected with the band? We were mirroring them back and they'd mirror us and we'd mirror them more, until we had designer camouflage made in Paris, which was to me the ultimate incongruity, to have hand-printed camouflage.

That stopped because it had got so there were no games left. With the best will in the world of trying to confound it, we'd become a rock band. The one thing we didn't want to be, that we despised, was the rock band, and we'd become one. We could go on stage and be as atonal and confrontational and dismissive as we chose, and the more it was, the more it was OK. Because people had worked out that that was what we did. So it was all right now and we'd been called on it and it was going to be accepted.

Before that whole process ended, I was already beginning to put out leaflets "from the Psychick Youth Headquarters." I was beginning to build the next project into TG. With the TG single "Discipline," it said on the back, "Marching Music for Psychick Youth."

So I'd already got the name and the concept of doing it in a much more ascetic, considered way, instead of it just being thrashing around because it's fun and pisses off mom and dad and the old teenage rebellion syndrome. What can we do that takes us further than that?

It seemed to me that we were in this position where we had to stop or take responsibility for our actions. TG was kind of gratuitous, and that wasn't the idea either. It wasn't meant to become really popular or be gratuitous just because we could get away with it. I had serious intent behind all the mind games and the double bluffs and the satires.

I decided to design something that was more about my own serious interests, so that I could go deeper and deeper into it and pull people across. So they might have a different perspective on how to do their lives and consider alternative ways of seeing the universe and the potential of their brain and their body and their ability to have control over themselves.

Kinney Did it ever occur to you that you might be opening up a giant hole that the unaware might fall into?

Genesis I was warned about that all the time by the people in the Museum of Magic in England. Through my own interests I got to know the people at the Atlantis Bookshop. I used to go there regularly and fritter away my money on first editions of Crowley and Austin Spare paintings. And I got to know people who were seriously involved in Wicca

and were friends of Alex Sanders. I was doing research and I talked to everybody. I told them I felt there was room for magic to come back out of its closet and see how much relevance it still had. There was a whole generation of people who hadn't seen the '60s occult revival and weren't necessarily interested in learning things by rote but could get a lot from knowing about the possibilities and then could make choices.

Some people did say, "Oh you've got to have twenty years' training first, and you've got to do this and do that, and people go mad if they don't know all the right formulas." And I said, "Well, I know what you're saying, but then there's the whole voodoo self-hypnosis syndrome as well, that sometimes people go mad because they've convinced themselves that that's what is going to happen if they don't do things the correct way."

I personally feel that it was a responsible thing to do. I was assuming that there would be people who were prepared to investigate these areas and see what would happen when it was done with other people. A lot of people did the same ritual at the same time with the same basic parameters.

Photo by Peter Christopherson

Kinney In *Thee Grey Book* the intention stated for TOPY is in terms of "moral freedom, spiritual freedom, sexual freedom" and against faith.

Genesis And guilt and fear.

Kinney But at the same time the components of the sigils were these three different bodily fluids and two different portions of your hair, plus this very intimate sexual fantasy, ritually combining these on the twenty-third day of the month at the twenty-third hour and sending these off to you! It seems like an enormous act of faith on the part of the person.

Genesis I think more of an enormous act of trust. One of the first posters we did said, "Abolish fear, establish trust." My personal theory is that if your intention is clear and non-malevolent, then nothing can be done to harm you with those elements of your body. Once or twice people challenged me and said, "I'm sending you my things. How do I know you're not going to do some curse?" And I said, "Fine, I'll send you some of mine!" And I always did (laughs). I don't remember doing anything to harm you, so I don't see why you should do anything to harm me. So have what you want.

332

I wanted to contradict the tradition that those things were innately dangerous for other people to have possession of. Because I thought that was something people had hypnotized themselves into being vulnerable to. It's the skill of the person attacking, it isn't the things that they have. Those are just tools for visualizing and focusing as far as I'm concerned.

That whole area of thought had become too entrenched and paranoid and was based on "I can hurt you if I want." Well, I'm sorry, I got bullied at school and I found it a completely intolerable and despicable activity. I thought it was actually very freeing for people to be told, "You can let go of this fear. It doesn't matter. What mattered was what you got from your ritual for you. And afterwards you don't need this stuff. You don't need to keep it." And sometimes they said, "I really want to keep the one I did this month because I feel really connected with it and it still seems to be working for me." And I said, "Sure."

I hate to set up a new dogma. We said, here's a sketch. If something starts working for you and you adapt it or find it's uncomfortable, that's OK. We're not here to tell you what to get. We're just saying, have you tried this? Because we've noted that certain of these elements have worked for us in really interesting ways that we can't fully explain according to the none-sensus reality. We're glad that we get these extra things. At the very least it's fascinating and makes life better, and maybe it's also useful and significant. And all the sigils that came in while I was running TOPY are still absolutely and utterly safe and not one's been lost or destroyed.

Kinney Those weren't seized by Scotland Yard?

Genesis No. What's really amazing is that they didn't take any of them! Isn't that odd? We wrote an essay called "Magick Defends Itself," and I'd say I rest my case!

They went up to my office where all the filing cabinets were and they were locked and the key was hidden. They crowbarred them open. And they left them all! A TOPY friend at the house said they just glazed over, they couldn't look. Their arms did this (flips through folders) and their eyes did this (looks blankly). They left everything!

Kinney But ostensibly it was because of TOPY that this raid was occurring.

333

Genesis Yes! Because they were convinced that TOPY was the proof that evil satanic rituals were really taking place. That we were importing teenagers from Brazil and killing them in rituals. Keeping women prisoners and forcing them to have babies and eating the babies and all that stuff.

Kinney Let's back up a bit. For a few years leading up to that raid, you had also been involved in the rave scene, correct?

Genesis Correct. Since about '86.

Kinney So maybe there was a confluence of reasons that they were coming down on you.

Genesis Oh, I think so. We were involved in the anti-Dolphinarium campaign in Brighton. And we were involved in anti-apartheid; we used to go to Trafalgar Square to the Anti-Apartheid Society and give speeches. And we've been involved in squatters' rights, and I've been into gay street theater, so we were involved at least to some extent in supporting radical gay rights. And raves; pro-psychedelic, semi-legal gatherings of happy young people twisting their minds, propagandizing their own view of life. So if they have a computer that says, "These are the kinds of groups that we don't like," we appeared on each list.

Basically I had decided to come out of my own closet and go, "Look! I've actually been doing all this stuff for several years, using me as the guinea pig, and the bottom line is I feel that my life has been incredibly enhanced and invigorated. And I feel I have to share that."

Kinney What's the underlying cosmology that you work with at this point?

Genesis (Laughs.) To tell you the honest truth, I'm reassessing everything again. It seems like I was given an opportunity to sit back and reassess to what extent more traditional methods might still be really valuable for people. And not just dismiss them out of hand for the sake of breaking a few holes in a wall. So I guess each time we reincarnate, it's a little bit more serious and a little bit more considered and a little bit further along in terms of assimilating and respecting tradition. That's partly, I suppose, the fact that I'm educating myself in public, which is a strange and vulnerable thing to do.

Kinney I was wondering because in Thee Grey Book the definition you had of TOPY had to do with developing magical work free of gods and deities. Do you still see the universe as not populated with gods and goddesses or a God?

Genesis Yeah. To be really honest I'm still pretty much an existentialist. But I don't deny that certain energies and resonances definitely seem to work.

Things do get manifested when you focus on them and truly desire and need them to manifest. That happens. And I don't really care why. My suspicion is that it's an innate gift that comes from so far ago and is so primal that it's pointless putting names on it and trying to humanize it. I think it is always an error to humanize phenomena.

I think that if you substitute the word "Time" in any spiritual or religious text for the word "God" or the name of a god or deity, it makes equal sense. Time is infinite and omnipresent and omniscient and everything comes from Time and returns to Time. And physical manifestations are the exception, not the rule. So if you want me to give a name to the greater power there is, I'd say it's Time.

Kinney Have you disengaged yourself from TOPY?

Genesis Well, officially we announced that we disengaged ourselves because it was appropriate in terms of Scotland Yard. And I also had this urge to become nomadic. I had started getting this sense that a nomadic way of not being fixed in one place was really essential. I wrote some essays on it in England before the raid. So it was again a mixture of "which comes first?" Was it that my guts were telling me that that was what had to happen, or did I somehow just have enough of an inner vision that I knew that that was the next step? I don't know. I know that we made the right moves at the right time and we weren't there [when Scotland Yard raided the TOPY house].

When I was in Nepal I was fascinated with the devotion and the sadhus and the Aghori Babas. Especially the Aghori Babas. Just the simple statement of "the path of no distinction," which is what they follow, made so much sense to me.

335

When I was in Nepal with both the more Bön Pa-oriented Tibetans who are basically sorcerers, and then the Shiva and the Aghori and the Naga, I felt the really deep sensation of, "Wow! All the stuff we were doing based on impulse and instinct and intuition and observation, here it makes sense! We were right! That line of inquiry was right. These techniques are being used as a daily thing over here. We are Mr. and Mrs. Normal. We don't have to explain our practices. We don't have to explain scars and tattoos and piercings because the people here do it too. It's a symbol of devotion and a quest for holiness. And that's wild!" I just felt, "Ahhh, at last, a homeland!" I could wander around here naked and everybody would be quite happy about it, and just say, "Oh, Baba," and bless you and leave you to it.

And that's something I think we're all moving back towards. I think part of the piercing phenomena and the resurgence of an interest in early Pagan perceptions is actually a gradual remembering of another way of life, a way of life that's devotional, disciplined, integrated. That's something that has been missing. That's why I even started to respect people like the Jesuits.

Kinney But a central component of that devotional way of life generally is the conception of something larger than the individual.

Genesis I know, I like devotion for its own sake! (Laughs.) And it gets me into strange conflicts with people. I haven't been able to align myself with an orthodoxy. Sometimes I wish I could, but I just can't. I start to blaspheme and I start to make jokes all the time or change the sentence around to see if it's more fun reversed. I always have to check and double-check things. And not feel that I am subservient to the dogma so much as that it's working for me.

Kinney Dogmas and orthodoxies and belief systems aside, experientially, amidst all this working with forces or energies, haven't you had some sort of experience that made you think, "My sense of self in this body is only a convenient fiction"?

Genesis Oh yeah, ever since I was young. But I just take that as written. This is just a useful vehicle, transient, mortal, insignificant. I've always had a very strong sense of that. It's existentialism. I think I should never have read Jean-Paul Sartre when I was a kid. Because I don't feel the need to feel contact with greater beings. I've had really powerful spiritual experiences at times, mystical experiences and visionary experiences, but none of them makes me feel that there is a specific one I should align myself with. These phenomena are fabulous and I'm really fortunate when I experience them, but I shouldn't make it into a way of life, because I can't repeat them ad hoc. They just come upon me.

One of the most fascinating experiences I had like that was in Nepal. Some friends of ours took us to this tiny village with lepers and incredibly poor people. In this small village square there was this tree in a shrine where supposedly Shiva had had sex with this other deity. And it was padlocked up, and there were hardly any people around it except the lepers and the beggars, and we were wandering around taking photos of some of the statues. All of the sudden, out of my peripheral vision I saw our friend, Tri Lochan, who is a Shiva devotee, waving and at that moment I immediately went into this trance state where everything seemed unreal and I was no longer controlling what was happening. As I saw him waving out of the corner of my eye, I knew that I had to go straight to him.

336

I went straight to him without speaking. He was with a village priest who had unlocked the shrine and was waving us in. So we took our shoes off quickly and Tri Lochan's going, "Hurry up, hurry up!" So we went inside and he closed the door. Then the priest anointed us with this tilak [paint marks of the deity], and I got this really fast freeze frame of the shrine. And there were the remains of this tree in there, strewn with animal intestines and mummified human heads and incredibly powerful, very dark-edged materials. Pools of blood. We had to throw some money on a plate. Around the edges were cast-iron creatures with heads that come off, and they were all filled with blood too. And it was really dark and he started chanting.

As soon as he started chanting it was like Terence McKenna describes DMT. I just went "whhhoooo" instantly into this completely altered vortex. There was this sense of shooting like a particle accelerator and becoming a particle and no longer being in a body. Shooting into this deeper and deeper blackness. Until suddenly there was a sense of floating in this liquid blackness. The only way we have to describe it in our language was it was the ultimate blackness, black beyond black. And then

His Holiness Dzongsar Khyentse Rinpoche and G. B. P-O. Nepal, 1992

338

I became really aware that somewhere within this ultimate black were these two shiny, slightly pointed, almost insectoid eyes. I couldn't see them; I just knew they were somewhere; the distance could be light years or feet. And I knew that those two insectoid eyes were what was referred to as Shiva. And that Shiva watched.

That's what Shiva did; from such a power place of darkness that's all that Shiva had to do—just be in that place and have eyes to observe, that was enough. That was about as powerful as it got, mate! I wasn't afraid, it was just totally mindboggling.

And all of a sudden it was like "whhhhhoooo"—a real science-fiction sound effect—and suddenly there we were again in this shrine. "Wow, that was really strange!" And Tri Lochan was going, "Quick, quick!" We had to get outside again. All the villagers had found out that we were in there, and they were going nutty because nobody outside their sect was

Aghori Baba Pagalananda and G. B. P-O. Nepal, 1992

allowed in, and certainly never any Europeans. To this day I have no idea why the priest chose to unlock that place. And when we left, the villagers were still screaming and swearing at him and shouting at us. "It's blasphemy, you shouldn't have let that happen! What were you thinking of?" From what I gathered he was equally puzzled as to why he did it. That was a really deep, religious experience, and it was unexpected. I hadn't visualized anything like that at all. I hadn't read it up in advance. It wasn't coming from anywhere I knew of in me.

I don't know how long it lasted. It was probably only three or four minutes, the whole thing. But I came away with an amazing repect for the Shiva tradition and those sadhus. And then I went back and talked with the Aghori Baba and he asked me for my solid gold Psychick Cross, which I had on a leather thong, so I obviously couldn't refuse. So I gave him my Psychick Cross and he gave me his ring and bracelet. And he gave both of the children gifts off his altar, and he gave us ash from his fire which burns in his chamber. They have records saying that that fire has not been extinguished for over a thousand years. And he told us to bring it to America. We didn't know we were coming here then.

Kinney The Aghori Baba is from Hinduism, then?

Genesis There are reputed to be only nine practicing Aghori Babas. It's an offshoot of the Shiva sadhus and the Naths. There are the Nagas, who are pretty extreme and the most revered. He stayed in this chamber most of the time, but primarily they live in graveyards because they have to copulate with dead bodies. Also some of their initiations are in the jungles with the tigers. They have to sit naked in the place known to be frequented by the most ferocious tigers for days and days, and people bring them the minimum amount of food and water. And they just sit there until they have no fear of any kind, of tigers or of death.

The Aghori Babas' basic discipline is one of the most ascetic. They would have their followers bring them the absolutely most expensive, exquisite feast of chicken and food, and then they would have to eat human shit or flesh off one of the bodies burning outside. His chamber actually has the ghat in front of the door, so the entire time you have the smell of burning human flesh in there as well as the incense.

The point is that they're the same. They taste the same to the Aghori Baba. Everything is the same. There is no judgment, there is no moral standpoint or perspective in terms of the implicit nature of things. That's not saying behavior, because obviously there's a morality of behavior, but in terms of the implicit nature of things, they're all the same.

Kinney I was wondering also about your interaction with pop culture and music. You successfully avoided being too caught up in the corporate control of culture. But at the same time Throbbing Gristle or Psychic TV were cult figures and a lot of the things that you were in the forefront or exploring—piercing or tattoos or industrial music—have ended up becoming popularized. And that becomes a trap in itself.

Genesis Sometimes things do get diluted and homogenized for a period of time. My personal feeling is that oil rises to the top, that if you cast your net wide enough you'll pull in a higher ratio of serious fanatics. It's something I was discussing with William Burroughs back in 1971. He said he preferred to be the quiet, reclusive, seminal thinker. He liked to wear suits and appear superficially to fit in with the status quo, whereas I liked to be the bull in the china shop. It's just a different strategy.

Kinney I wonder if there's a certain danger. It's the same with energy coalescing around places where rituals have happened. The cultural forms, say, of fascist ideology are deeply cut grooves, and if you don't click into them, you might find yourself speeding towards disaster.

Genesis In my experience, archetypes are unquestionably powerful. In that sense I would agree with you about things being dangerous. We did a ritual at Stonehenge, the Ordeal X, which is basically a Thelemic ritual from the Book of the Law. We got permission from English Heritage to do that, letting people inside Stonehenge for the whole night on the right astro logical day and everything. Now I didn't know the woman who was the priestess very well. There were more TOPY people than there were traditional Thelemic people, but it was a good balance. But in this ritual there's a section where it says "Unto…" and the Priestess is going, "…me." And then she goes, "Unto me." She went insane afterwards, quite classically insane, lost her head and had a nervous breakdown and never really recovered.

What we all felt had happened was that she felt that she was the Goddess, not a channel or a symbol of the Goddess. And I think that can happen. Instead of investigating the archetype or even allowing an archetype to manifest in ritual and ceremony, people identify with it. They think, "I'm dealing with power, I am power!"

People have to be really honest about how they perceive themselves, about their own weaknesses and traumas and temptations. In ritual I always work with someone who is completely straight and who is there as an observer. The Eye, I call them. The Eye is there to police the ritual and watch everyone and make notes and also has the right to intervene. I think it's really important if you're dealing with something that you conceive of as very potent and archetypal. We are susceptible to the tiniest event in childhood or to emotional cruelty or brutality later on. These things leap back and come back like a hammer. To me, it should all be about being freed from those hammers, not becoming the hammer.

Kinney I also wonder about TG's camouflage clothes or armbands. Can that be flipped to the point where other people take it up and it slowly becomes what it was originally mocking?

341

Photo of Lady Jaye with Naga Babas by Genesis Breyer P-Orridge

Genesis The irony was that didn't really happen. I decided to do Psychic TV and TOPY and make it overtly paramilitary and encourage people to wear uniforms and have the same haircuts. And interestingly enough, I never saw any abuse of that. I can only assign that to the fact that the underlying philosophy was not one that would appeal to the person who would want to be that way.

Kinney So, in a sense, that was playing out an impulse in a harmless fashion?

Genesis Look, TOPY was saying, "It's not the uniform, it's not the armband, it's not the haircut." All the people in TOPY were trying to look as much like each other as we can, and guess what? None of us look the same. With the best will in the world, we all end up slightly individualizing what we have. One of us just wears a different ring, that ring just shouts out as being enough to define somebody as different. It's what's going on in the mind that matters; it's not any of the trappings at all. And our mindset is definitely contrary to people wanting to sublimate other

people to their will. We're not doing that and it's not manifesting as that. We're showing you don't have to be afraid of the symbol.

What can I say? It worked. No one I ever knew became a neo-Nazi. With TOPY I pushed the envelope to its limit and the message I got back was, "These are good people." People who are drawn to this are being filtered effectively because they're all right. They're very supportive of each other.

We couldn't have toured America without TOPY people who'd give us their houses. They'd bring us food, they'd run the merchandise stall, they'd stick posters up. They were really positive. It was a tribe. The Cherokee weren't neofascist even though they all had the same basic tribal look.

There's a difference between tribalism and the mob mind. Our tribe was based on individual strength, while the mob is based on individual weakness. and communal strength.

Recorded in 1992 after fleeing the British Government who forced Genesis and family into exile for seven years. Genesis was never charged with anything—not even a parking ticket. But two tonnes of archives were seized and destroyed and he lost both houses and all belongings, barring a secretly located archive of paper based documentation.

ına

a of Madonna's."

ıve included titles

d videos have included
ual acts and her cos-
eft little to the imagina-

, comments about
ge, Cliff adds: "Having
ke some of the records."

Madonna—sex and hype

Satanic inquiry police raid home

POLICE investigating a suspected Satanic abuse ring raided a Brighton house.

**by Paul Bracchi,
Chief reporter**

Officers from Scotland Yard's Obscene Publications Branch seized videos, literature, photographs and letters after swooping on a town centre address at 4pm on Saturday.

There were no arrests.

The material—which filled a Transit van—is now being examined by detectives.

The raid was part of a nation-wide inquiry into alleged devil worship and child abuse.

A group called The Temple of Psychic Youth has been linked to the investigation.

At least one member of the

in Sussex.

Chief Inspector Colin Knight, of Brighton Police, said today: "I would like to assure mums and dads that, from what we have learned so far, there is absolutely no risk to local children."

More than a dozen officers raided the three-storey house near The Level. Police have asked the Argus not to publish the address while inquiries across the country continue.

● On Wednesday the Channel Four programme Dispatches will screen a 90-minute report on alleged devil worship and

Thee green book

XII

This is a restricted access internal document, intended for special circulation only, and should not be copied or in any form transmitted to non-individuals ov Thee Temple ov Psychick Youth.

hey speak Panic. They conquer from within. *From within.* Whispering words of Panic to an inner ear, suggesting, conniving, adding brushstrokes to the pictures of the Last Few Days. And we are mere understudies, mere look-alikes. The curtains rose on these histrionics with the birth of Man. Long before the first crude figures were daubed in the half-light of ancient caves, they were here, waiting, with Infinite Patience. We have never been alone. There are others indigenous to this spinning ball, trapped in some Phantom Zone, waiting for the kill, the sacrifice, the Second and Final Death.

The father of Grock the clown, having had his legs broken in eight places by his father for professional reasons, broke Grock's legs in eight places to be certain that the child would grow up walking grotesquely so as to ensure his eminence as a clown.

349

We are the spinning, hobbling, waddling clowns in the eyes of our secret police. The livestock and the Farmer.

Humans can be programmed with any belief or attitude. The human does not possess "free will." We do not control our personal convictions, our opinions, our feelings. None of these are constant. We are composed of many "I"s, each a crystallization of opposite belief. When the wind changes, one "I" blows away, another steps forward. All of these "I"s revolve around an absent center. Penetrate the veils of personality. Within, there is nothing. Beyond a series of successively more tenuous masks, a hollow core. But, not quite hollow. A Puppet-Master sits and presides. A foreign body.

When you walk down a street your eyes are presented by a continuously changing perspective, every visible object slides across your field of vision in a precise geometrical relationship to reinforce the illusion that one is really walking through three-dimensional space.

I thought it was permissible to sit in my comfortable armchair and doze, as it didn't seem anything particular was happening. No-one is demanding my attention, so why should I feel guilty to just drift?

Once, I opened my eyes again, and I saw the facts of my situation. My comfortable chair became the seat in the cockpit of an aircraft, flying 50,000 feet above the earth, quite out of control, guided only by a long-obsolescent automatic pilot. Despite the enormity of danger this situation presented, I sought the oblivion of sleep once more. It's hardly ever now that I panic, and stirring briefly, kick spastically at the controls, striking random levers.

We are content to see nothing.

We have no control.

It doesn't even feel like failure.

We thought the world was merely a question of gathering. We didn't understand that knowledge is kept under heavy guard. We thought that to see a door implied the probability of its opening. We waited and waited, until finally such a great lethargy came over us that we were compelled to drop our aspirations, or seek their fulfillment in a purely imaginary landscape.

We have never been alone. The door is fastidiously patrolled. There are, and always have been, those amongst us only *seemingly* human.

Reality is *there*, but *we do not see it*.

It is fashionable these days to view the Universe as an "associative domain of consciousness." The notion of an observer-created Universe, that reality is in essence subjective, might perhaps appeal and comfort, but it is an imaginary state of affairs. It is a tremendous conceit. There is a Reality that in no way needs our participation to ensure its continued existence. The Universe is not conditional on human population. Our notions that we have only to "become whole," filled with joy, to see a corresponding change in the Universe, contacting friendly angels and so forth, is really an insufferable arrogance. There is nothing out there that cares. There are *no* guardian angels, holy or otherwise.

Were we to possess any real degree of consciousness we would have the facility of being able to immediately discern truth from falsity, reality from imagination. There *is* a distinction.

Individuals approaching critical breakthrough point, on the edge of evolutionary transition, the strange attraction to a new order of being, are ruthlessly attacked by the Fear Arm. They are either broken down— paranoid schizophrenia, demonomania, cardiac arrest, chronic migraine, suicide, radiation sickness—or initiated into new belief systems, arteries quickly hardening, lusting to re-locate the nullity of mind on earth. Individuals are attacked and herded like sheep, duped into a false flower garden. Like pawns in a vast Chess, our magnetic center, that part of us which is drawn towards the search for freedom, is taken with consent, because we are believing creatures. Born to grow fat on belief. Force-fed with belief. Turned towards blind alleys along which we will forever stray. We sleep on eternally, dreaming that we are awake. And the UTs are the Dream-Masters.

Our conclusion: UTs draw their vital sustenance from the tapping of the human state of arrested evolution. At critical transition points in human development, belief-circuitry is activated, which acts as a conduit for the life-energy.

351

That we are not in control; that we are not alone. These are facts of our existence. Everything you have "known" and thought to be true up until this point is a lie. You are stupid, and you are asleep. All your systems of knowledge are based upon an absence of understanding. You talk of progress, yet you still have to begin. What you have is worth nothing, because it was not had through struggle, but through "accident." You have wandered clumsily. And beneath everything, underlying all your squalid joys, hopes, trials and tribulations, your vestigial dances, you are overwhelmed with misery. A suppressed emergency. Not one person understands another. Almost everything in life is wrong. There can be no accurate meaning. It is all accidental, nothing is controlled, at least by us. We are thrall to the Law of Accident. A tall story of hypnotic alliance, and every little thing, every little thing. A foul fix of blank kidnapping time.

Our experience of life is of a continual succumbing to inertia. Always abandoning for the anesthetic solace of black wings.

We talk about love, about truth. We have never known love or truth. Up until now they have not existed. They are but a distant rumor. We are like spoilt little children. We presume consciousness, but we are asleep. We presume the Universe accommodates us, but it does not care. We presume our thoughts can change the Universe, but it will never change. Forget the Universe, forget your "humanity." At the end of the day, there is only YOU. You in your small corner. You in your Hell. You and your Personality.

What is it that sucks the spit from your eye? What dim crave is the sound of your love? See it parade everything it can not uncover. The world blocked out with one hand.

The only way to begin is to try and realize that you are asleep.

It is no good to say, "I am asleep." You have to *realize* it. There is a great inertia which works against us in this. There is the inertia which had been imposed throughout long years of social conditioning. Even should this inertia be overcome, additional external pressures come into play. Simply put, there is something out there that *doesn't want you to learn.*

Some people are very conceited indeed. They decide that they can perform "magick" and influence the very fabric of time and space, in a cat's whisker. And all of this without ever pausing to remember that they are asleep. Western "occult" traditions are practically valueless. If you want freedom, if you *really* want to wake from your sleep, then the "occult" is probably the last path you should follow. It is the idiot's road. The idiot's love of distraction. Another game to keep you from *the real work.*

353

Forces malign, coupled with typical human inertia, generated through thousands of years of false learning, combine to produce a deterrent so powerful that it is a rare individual indeed who could possibly hope to persevere through such an ordeal. The ordeal: objective verification of all experimental hypotheses through intense study of oneself.

Resignation, however, is not an option.

If escape is not achieved, and if the hidden hand does not snuff out your candle, the likelihood is entrance into, and adoption of, a rigid system of beliefs based on certain "clues" or "keys" occurring in the original work.

These clues may have originated from dream, vision, visitation, voice, etc. Once keys have been formulated as such, and begin to cohere into a belief-system, the real work has, for all practical purposes, been terminated. What then happens is a gradual slide into redundancy, stagnation, and obsolescence. Such beliefs present only minute fragments of a larger jigsaw, and in themselves, are an index to nothing.

Their beliefs are wholly induced by external agencies in their bid to prevent the larger picture coming into view, and to rule out the possibility of real breakthrough with the work.

The so-called "born again" phenomenon is one clear example.

The UFO and associated phenomena constitute a vast panoply of bizarre and inexplicable events, spawning an equally broad spectrum of theory and belief. Evidence contradicts itself. It is like a box full of parts from fifty different jigsaws. This is called "the confusion effect." It is quite intentional.

The pivot of meaning, the space between a possibility and a belief, is the threshold of knowledge. The agencies which subvert real knowledge and channel it into harmless and passive beliefs are the guardians of the threshold. Through the manipulation of belief, a shiny silver slug's trail of disparate clues, these agencies seek to control the destiny of life on this planet.

By default.

Sentient, discorporate beings. Ultra-terrestrials (U.T's). From neither outer, nor inner space. An order of beings which resides within the same spatio-temporal co-ordinates as ourselves, on a different vibratory level of matter. Clearly, they possess the facility to access our vibratory level of matter, and can "phase" into our physical reality.

This act of intervention requires energy: blood sacrifice, vampirism or simple appropriation. A dead cow, or a stalled engine.

The Men-In-Black (M.I.B.) are amongst the crudest, yet paradoxically most sophisticated, manifestations of the Ultra-terrestrials. Apparently

354

minions, shock troops, as it were, they come from below, and have a sense of humor to match. Their aim is the inculcation and escalation of fear. They circumvent possible transmission of witness accounts. If necessary, they have license to kill.

Another level of UT manifestation is as the Knowledge-giver. The Dispenser. The Great Holy Pharmacist. This is the direct "hacking" of human herding disposition, laying down "bugs" with post-operative, delayed effect, often years. (Look back into your childhood, down a foggy grey tunnel. A guy dressed in all black ever whisper in your ear?)

Carefully staged theater. Visitation. Dream. Vision. Angelic conversation. In the midst of a subtly induced delerium, certain knowledge introduced. Small scraps of panic. Little shards of a counterfeit heaven. And then God disappears, leaving you on a yellow brick road, preternaturally glowing.

Puppetry. True knowledge is a matter of *control*. Counterfeit knowledge is a matter of *promulgation and worship.*

Our growth is forestalled, deferred, by the "friendliness" of Gods and Angels. We have no will of our own, because we are bound to beliefs

355

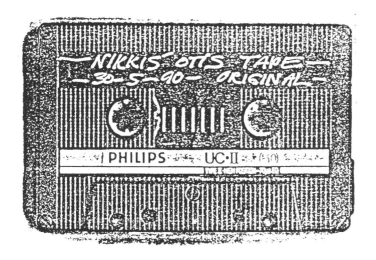

generated from without, spoken within. Every belief is the ragged claw mark left by a long-gone parasite. The vital sustenance has been drawn. We are dead. Until the next time, asleep, and in very great danger. On the wings of nightmare.

One minute, absolute confidence and assurance. The next, all is lost. That is the way we are constructed. Built up to fall down. No substance, no backbone. Transported by brief glories, only to end up more crippled, more irrevocably broken than ever before. And all to no purpose of our own, because we never retain anything, never build on anything other than sand. Never reaching and touching, never finding anyone. Your mute suffering achieves nothing. Doubled over with gut pains, gut suffering, black vomit accreting on your feet. Never finding anything worth finding. Always thrown back into the same freeze-frame of horror. You. You found comfort with others, apparently sharing the same misery. There was solace in that. A small place to stay and breathe in, look out of. Never daring to remember you had to leave. Be alone once more. It has to happen. Others forget you, achieve some miracle escape of circumstance, spinning off into further mad orbits of their own. The trappings don't matter. All that matters to you is that they're gone. Your haven destroyed. Perhaps it's the same for them. There's really no way of knowing. This is what it's like to be asleep. No comfort. No escape. No presence. No satisfaction. It's the warmth where you just sat, as you leave for another cold seat. That's what hurts.

Nowhere left to go. No place to stay.

They were consigned to their phantom zone before we were a glint in Horus' eye. Turning in fear and loathing. Gradually sieving through the sands of knowledge and being, locating their truth, finding their source and path and way to do. We can't call it consciousness. It's merely a modality of instinct. Having no sex, they located ours. As surrogates. They don't need it, don't want it. Need only to play with our fascination and horror of it, to further their escape. If they draw us away from the body and what it means, the further bodies attainable and what they mean, the Law of Reciprocity, then they win. We approach the Second and Final Death. Which means death for us all, death for the believers. Another Holocaust. The Infidels live, and escape their prison, their karmic cycle.

The Angels and Gods know no sex. Are completely without passion. Their seeds in our physical reality are sterile. Jesus on the Cross. The cold plague of mass religion. Sexless, denying carnal experience. Mirroring the Ultra-terrestrial landscape. Jesus was an Ultra-terrestrial.

This state of sexlessness is called "iesu." A bitter joke. Sexual molestation is one of their most cynical manifestations. The Christ-Spirit is a shadow of a ravening thing, a twisted mirror of a worm-brained deity, struggling to escape the confines of its narrow cell, sending its spirit-spores across to Earth, to wriggle in the body of a man on a cross.

And the future?

We live in screens. Pure screens. The removal of ourselves, our identities, from the organic to the solid-state. Our symbolisms are a succession of steps away from corporeal existence. We drive our cars as extensions of the physical body. We conduct our lives through the screen, through the shift of perspective, barely deigning to move slow, leaden limb across the flat earth. We never leave our homes. We observe the Other on the screen of our projection. Repeatedly, steps removed. The ecstasy of information. Information vertigo. The vertiginous heights of our ambition. The cold sheen of the new orgasm. Leaving behind forever the Ancient Mysteries, for a New Sacred. The Information Ecstatic, the imminent execution of World Holocaust through the neutral screen, is the countdown to the Second and Final Death.

357

From Religion to Technology.

The voice whispers, babbles on, in the inner ear.

How would an eagle feel if it were hatching chickens' eggs? At first the eagle thinks that it will hatch little eagles whom it is going to bring up to be big eagles. But what comes out of the eggs is always nothing but little chicks. Desperate, the eagle keeps hoping that the chicks will turn into eagles after all. But no, at the end they are nothing but cackling hens. When the eagle found this out, it had a hard time suppressing his impulse to eat up all the chicks and cackling hens. What kept it from doing so was a small hope. The hope, namely, that among the many cackling chicks there might be, one day, a little eagle capable of grow-

ing up into a big eagle, capable like itself, to look from its lofty perch into the far distance, in order to detect new worlds, new thoughts and new forms of living.

You want the truth in a mirror, where you can't grasp it. You have entered this world quite accidentally and will silently leave it again. Only the truth in your own fist will make you the master of this Earth. You set security before the truth.

You are cowardly in your thinking because real thought is accompanied by bodily feelings, and you are afraid of your body.

You have built everything upon sand; your house, your life, your culture and civilization, your science and technology, you love and your education of children. You don't know it, you don't want to know it, and you slay the great man who tells it to you. You built your house on sand and you all did this because you are incapable of feeling life in yourself, because you kill love in your child even before it is born, because you cannot tolerate any alive expression, any free, natural movement.

With the greatest consistency, your thinking always misses the truth, just as a playful sharpshooter is able to consistently hit right beside the bull's eye.

You always think in too short of terms, just from breakfast to lunch. You must learn to think back in terms of centuries and forward in terms of thousands of years. You have to learn to think in terms of living life, in terms of your development from the first plasmatic flake to the animal man which walks erect but cannot yet think straight. You have no memory even for things which happened ten years ago or even this year, and so you keep repeating the same stupidities you said 2,000 years ago. You cling to your stupidities as a louse clings to fur. You do not dare see how deeply you stick in the morass of your misery. Every once in a while you stick your head in the morass of your misery. Every once in a while you stick your head out of the morass to yell, Heil! The croaking of a frog in a marsh is closer to life.

359

There is never any progress. Everything remains the same. The same as it has been for tens of thousands of years. The outward form changes. The essence does not. Man remains just the same. "Civilized" and "cultured" people live with exactly the same interests as the most "primitive" savages. Contemporary civilization is based on violence and slavery and fine words. But all these fine words about "progress" and "civilization" are merely words.

There are machines, not people. People who no longer consider why they are here at all. They merely exist. Surrounding themselves with false illusory reasons for living. To pass the time before they die. Millions of dead souls. The children are already dead. They were dead before they were even born. The cycle has come full circle and we are living out our last moments. It is five minutes to midnight. Yet people refuse to recognize it as such. They are told lies and they believe them.

The End is Here or There.
The beginning is nowhere.

The struggle from the exterior to the interior. From the interior to the exterior. In between is the void. Yet the pain of anger is never enough. Whoever put you here is manipulating you. It's always been that way. Now it destroys. To many of us, only the sound and rhythm of our breathing reminds us that we are alive.

Upon Melanicus Wings it broods over this Earth. Deriving the energy that will sustain and evolve it. An evil thing that is exploiting us. It obscures the stars. A vast, black vampire.

The flux between that which isn't and that which won't be, or the state that is commonly and absurdly called existence, is merely a rhythm of heavens and hells, and is intermediate to both.

360

Uninhabited.

We are all uninhabited. Inside of all of us is Nothing. This manipulation comes from the initial incursion of Ultra-terrestrial influences into the human life-wave, attracted to the individual embryo or sperm as an effective means of incarnating genetic mutations.

We've been damned by giants sound asleep, or by "civilized" concepts and abstractions that cannot realize themselves: those little harlots have visited their caprices upon us, those dark clowns have anathematized us for laughing so disrespectfully, because as with all clowns, underlying buffoonery is the desire to be taken seriously. We've been damned by corpses and skeletons and mummies, which twitch and totter with pseudo-life derived from conveniences.

Once upon a time this Earth was a no-man's land, that other levels of vibratory existence explored and fought over for colonization. Mankind won that battle for colonization, yet *now* the Earth is literally owned by *something*. All others are warned off.

The Ultra-terrestrials are the beings which exist in the same space-time coordinates as life on Earth, yet on a different vibratory level. They exist as parasites on human consciousness. As beings that exist as pure vibratory energy, they need the energy that human consciousness contains in order to sustain themselves. That human energy has to be controlled if it is to be tapped effectively. And that is what they have done.

We have been, and continue to be, consistently manipulated into belief systems that lead us to accept that we matter. We believe. We have Faith. We accept. Why? To some it represents a fundamental inherent human trait; the *need* to believe in something. All beliefs are based on the promise of the *afterlife*, but it is a promise based upon adhering to rigid behavioral rules during life. A life consisting of unquestioning acceptance of fundamentals, unquestioning belief and dedication to the rules significant to the particular belief system. They are, in all cases, structures that guarantee non-development and human involution resulting ultimately in global destruction.

There is something of ultra-pathos—of cosmic sadness—in the universal search for the belief system that one feels has been revealed by either unworldly inspiration or analysis. Clinging to it long after its insufficiency has been revealed is utterly hopeless. The only seemingly conclusive utterance, or seemingly substantial thing to cling to, is a product of dishonesty, ignorance and fatigue. All belief structures go back and back, until they're worn out or until something occurs that indicates a move forward.

362

Belief systems limit human consciousness, inner development and evolution. That is their sole aim. To bring human consciousness under control so that it may be farmed.

We are the cattle for these ultra-terrestrials. Belief systems are the green grass upon which we spend our short lives grazing, safe and satisfied. Faith, prayer, rigid behavioral traits such as hatred, ignorance and unquestioning obedience to all are the milk upon which these beings feed off during human life spans. Physical death and the transference of the undeveloped human consciousness into oblivion is the survival factor of these beings. It's the meat that keeps them alive, as it were, on their own plane of existence as forms of pure energy.

Yet a characteristic that *is* inherent in human nature is the question of whether or not the grass we are made to eat is greener on the other side of the fence. Or if some other kind of vegetation growing on the other side of the fence would be tastier. Small minorities are constantly searching and questioning for real answers to the question of absolute truth. They do not recognize any answers in any past or present belief systems. These minorities represent the gravest danger to the ultra-terrestrial conspiracy. These minorities search for the expansion of the human consciousness and the development of the different levels of the human animal. The danger is not in the small minorities in themselves. They can afford to dispense with a few of the cows if they escape by breaking down a section of the fence once in a while. But wait. Can they really afford to? Of course they can't. Cows on the other side of the field may spot the break in the fence and escape over it too, if they had the inclination, and soon the small break in the fence would become a gaping hole and the minority of escaped cows would become the majority. So no escapes can be allowed.

Any individuals or minority group who threaten escape are subjected to the harshest punishment. The majority are also subject to this punishment, they know this and they present a formidable force working against the minorities seeking to escape from the grip of the ultra-terrestrials; from the grip of the status quo. The ultra-terrestrials deliberately manufacture confusion across the globe, manufacture wars, sabotage any attempt at global cohesion. A close analogy would be a prisoner of war camp.

The rules laid out were that anybody caught trying to escape would be immediately executed; they installed fear. However, if anybody had the courage to attempt to escape despite this fear (which could only effectively occur in small numbers; all prisoners can't escape at once) then the majority of the prisoners in the prison would suffer terrible hardship and torture at the hands of their captors. Therefore there is the installed omnipresent pressure from the prisoners themselves to resist any small minority plans for escape. And so it is on Planet Earth.

Every man and woman who reaches a higher level of spiritual and intellectual awareness becomes more aware of the presence of a higher intelligence that is separate from the human animal. They have become incorporated into rigid belief structures as Angels or Gods, but they are seldom viewed objectively. Any form of Gnosis is destroyed. Any large-scale group illumination is usually forced to an end, either by majority human pressure or a breakup in the catharsis.

Small minority groups are faced initially with the full force of mass human hostility, violence, destruction and murder. However, they are also faced with a more sinister danger from the non-human sources, the ultra-terrestrials themselves. These beings play nasty and sometimes extremely violent and psychological games with these individuals and groups. The aim is to lull them into a dark dead-end belief tunnel by exploiting the very strengths that set the individual apart from the mass in the first place. Those strengths are a willingness to observe the universe in a way that is totally removed from the mass perception of it.

The tutelage. Of poles of belief.

The ultra-terrestrials play with their perceptions of these individuals and minority groups. They do their best to lead them down avenues of pure self-deceit, by presenting them with vivid alternative visions of reality and existence that are mere fronts for dead-end belief structures. Oc-curences such as UFO sightings, contact with extraterrestrials, visions of angels, demons, gods, fairies, voices of superior beings informing them of the ultimate secret knowledge of the universe. These are presented in such a real way that to escape the trap of being led into a belief system is almost impossible. It is very difficult to un-believe something that is presented in a vivid way, yet even more difficult when it is presented in such a way so as to align itself with your thought patterns at any one time. The ultra-terrestrials seem to have worked out a method of exploiting the very state of mind that such an individual may find him or herself in at any one time.

However, individuals do exist outside of the effect of their belief engen-dering processes, and these individuals are ruthlessly hunted down and haunted by the Men in Black. These are the ultra-terrestrials assuming some kind of human form. They are very crude and imperfect human forms that exist as "shock troops," and they have the ability to phase into our vibratory level from their own, with the sole intention of guarding the knowledge that they possess of the real state of human consciousness. They are the guardians of knowledge.

The individuals who assume an intermediate position are in the gravest danger of all. The Men in Black hold high positions of power in world

364

government. Their controls are explicit in some countries manifesting as mass extermination; in others it is so insidious as to be invisible.

Everything in intermediateness is not a thing, but an endeavor to become something—by breaking away from its continuity, or merging away, with all other phenomena—is an attempt to break away from the very essence of a relative existence and become absolute—if it has not surrendered to, or become part of, some higher attempt.

To this process there are two aspects:

Attraction, or the spirit of everything to assimilate all other things if it has not already been assimilated by some higher attempted system, unity, organization, entity, vibratory level.

And *repulsion*, or the attempt of everything to exclude or disregard the unassimilable.

A universal process.

Anything is permitted. Everything is true.

365

To the intermediatist, everything that seems to have identity is only an attempted identity, and every species is continuous with all other species, or that which is called the specific is only emphasis upon some aspect of the general. Every idea and belief is a mere conflict. Every conversation is a conflict of missionaries, each trying to convert the other, to assimilate, or to make the other similar to himself. If no progress is made, mutual repulsion will follow.

Beings on other vibratory levels have attempted positivizations: to extend themselves upon Earth, to assimilate the indigenous inhabitants of this Earth. All things merge away into everything else. That is continuity. The system merges away and evades us when we try to focus against it.

Out of the negative absolute, the positive absolute is generating itself, recruiting, or maintaining itself, via a third state, or our own quasi-state, it would seem that we're trying to conceive of universalness manufacturing more universalness from nothingness. Out of unreality, instead of nothingness, reality, instead of universalness, is, via our own quasi state, manufacturing more reality. Intermediateness is a relation between the positive absolute and the negative absolute.

In intermediateness there is neither free will nor slave will but a different approximation for every so-called person toward one or the other of the extremes.

All intermediateists feel a lurking fear that they will be forced into solidification and dogmatism and evolve into higher positivists. All things in this intermediate state are phantoms in a super mind in a dreaming state, striving to awaken to realness.

By manipulating the human race globally into pure and simple ignorance and by engendering human systems based on fear, hatred, war, mass extermination, destruction and death concurrently with enormous developments in terms of technology, it seems inevitable that we have only a short time left before mass destruction occurs. This seems to have been the ultra-terrestrials' plan all along. To have developed a global scheme where all human animals are at the very *moment* of global destruction in a state of total confusion, undevelopment in terms of human life and each and every person fragmented from each and every other person around. All so that they may at that *moment* of mass human destruction and death feed off of the sheer mass of unfocused and undeveloped human consciousness that will be thrown into oblivion.

This massive release of human consciousness will enable them to ascend to a higher level of energy, and one which doesn't depend upon the existence of human life at all. Our urgency is great. But we fear that mass human ignorance is the end that has already occurred. What remains is nothing, with merely nowhere to go. In the end we are all still cows, even if we do manage to escape over the fence. The only mass change in consciousness which will occur is the one that will happen *one second* from the end. Then all will become realized. And, of course, it will be too late.

The Alpha and Omega, the beginning and the ending, the first and the last; and now the last is reaching the first, and the end is the beginning.

All things are returning to their Original. The heart shattered to shivers, ground to dust.

Everything in the world obeys the Law of Three, everything existing came into being in accordance with this law. Combinations of positive and negative principles can produce new results that are different from the first and second only if a third force comes in. The Absolute creates in accordance with the same Law. Take the Ray of Creation. At the top is the Absolute, God the Word, divided into three: God the Father, God the Son and God the Holy Ghost. In our human systems we are the same as God—threefold. If we consciously receive three matters and send them out, we can construct outside what we like. This is creation. All three forces manifest through us and blend outside. Every creation is either subjective or objective. The life of man plays the same role as planets in relation to Earth, Earth in relation to Moon and all suns in relation to our sun.

Passive man serves involution; and active man, evolution. In both cases we are slaves, for in both cases we have a master. We are a whole system within. One center of us affirms, the other denies. It is impossible to free oneself from it. Only he is free who stands in the middle. Intermediately. It is very difficult. We are slaves. We are weak. In order to become intermediate one has to go against the law of nature itself.

367

The power of changing oneself lies not in the mind, but in the body and the feelings. Unfortunately, however, our body and our feelings have been genetically constituted so as to not care about anything so long as they are happy. They live for the moment and their memory is short. The mind alone lives for tomorrow. Each has its own merits.

The key to all of the manipulation is the fact that a lack of connection in us between the body, feeling and mind has not been recognized. The majority has become so deformed that there is no longer any common language between one part and another. It is irretrievably lost. The only thing left for those individuals who seek intermediate existence is to establish a connection in a roundabout way, a "fraudulent" way. And these ways must be very subjective since they must depend on a person's character and the form his inner make-up has taken. Establishing subjectivity in order that this connection may be built requires that the individual takes himself ruthlessly apart, becomes totally aware of the false layers of illusion that make up his or her character, and rigorous self-remembering. Associative thought and behavior has to be destroyed.

Conscious faith is freedom. Emotional faith is slavery. Mechanical faith is foolishness.

The only worthwhile existence is to strike whilst all fists are clenched. Fear is the refuge of the weak. And we are all riddled with it. The only aim is to find the pearl buried in the manure.

He who fights with monsters should see to it that he himself does not become a monster. And when you gaze long into an abyss the abyss also gazes into you.

Truth asserted against, and *triumphing* over *error*.

Evil is outlived Virtue, or incipient virtue that has not yet established itself.

368   We are faced with a *new* dominant. Thee PANDROGYNE…

In the darkness a contorted face writhing in agony appears before us. It is our own face reflected in the darkness of our own pain. Screaming in the agony of a birth long overdue.

We shall have an outcry of silences.

I leave you all in a fine mess…

CHANGEDPRIORITIESAHEAD
Genesis Breyer P-Orridge TOPY STATION UK, 1991

THERE YOU GO, SHE'S POPPED OUT FOR A PAPER, SEE WHAT'S ON THE BOX TONIGHT

2

Thee process is thee produckt

XIII

Drawing by Val Denham

A PRIMARY ANALYSIS OF THE PROCESS CHURCH IN RELATION TO THEE TEMPLE OV PSYCHICK YOUTH

AS IT IS...

his essay is intended as a *first sight* analysis of some of the primary symbolism of THE PROCESS Church. It is neither comprehensive nor the final word on the subject. As the basic structure I have adapted some of my on-going researches into an evolutionary development of the Qabalistic Tree of Life, termed the tree of Psychick Integration (or TOPI-tree). In essence the center of cognition, the Ego and the Self (or Yesod and Tipareth to give their Qabalistic names). For those unfamiliar with the basic structure of the Tree, I will set our a few preliminaries, contextualised for the subsequent discussion. Again these are not comprehensive.

The first point of analysis rests with the four-fold structure adopted by THE PROCESS, and the parallel structure in the Qabala which posits four *Worlds of Existence* known as Atziluth, Briah, Yetzirah and Assaiah, and generally symbolised by the elements Fire, Water, Air and Earth. In ontological terms, these equate with Spirituality, Creativity/Unconscious Mind, Intellectual/Conscious Mind and Sensuality/Practical or Fixed reality.

Table 1 below shows the directional and elemental correspondences utilised by THE PROCESS.

SATAN	Fire	West
CHRIST	Water	East
LUCIFER	Air	South
JEHOVAH	Earth	North

Table 1

In terms of the TOPI-tree, the first point of analysis is via the elemental attributions. The diagram below shows (on the left) the standard Tree of Life as adopted by Nineteenth Century occultism, and (on the right) the Tree of Psychick Integration. Both Trees comprise ten spheres of

form or consciousness (known as Sephirah, plural = Sephiroth), connected by 22 paths of dynamic force.

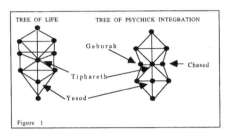

The main difference of the reconfigured TOPI-tree is the elevation
of the Solar-Lunar axis (Tiphareth and Yesod) which I have said represent, respectively, Self and Ego, consciousness. Essentially what has
happened is that both centres are raised to act as conscious mediators
and filters between the psychick processes known as Yesod (or ego/
daily consiousness) now has direct contact with the two spheres
representing *morality*, Geburah (or restriction) and Chesed (or
expansion). This apparently minor alteration in the structual design has significant repercussions in developing an integrated and
awakened psyche. Space precludes a detailed discussion but readers
interested in exploring this further are welcome to contact the address
given at the end of this essay.

In the centre of the TOPI-tree is the skeleton or hard wiring that engenders the integrated state. This is shown in Figure 2 below.

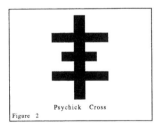

The following analysis will be based largely on figure 2, known as the
Psychick Cross.

As shown in Table 1, the original Process Church adopted a four-fold scheme, based on Judeo-Christian religious archetypes and directional and elemental correspondences. These can be represented graphically as follows (See Figure 3).

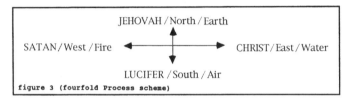

JEHOVAH / North / Earth

SATAN / West / Fire ⟷ CHRIST / East / Water

LUCIFER / South / Air

figure 3 (fourfold Process scheme)

That this imposes a polarised (or dis-integrated) dynamic should be immediately apparent, even to the most casual observer. Utilising the Qabalistic arrangement of the Four Worlds, the elements can be categorised as shown in Table 2:

```
     The Four Qabalistic Worlds with associated elements
                  and psychological role

     Atziluth - Divine Realm - Emanation = Fire = Spirit
     Briah - Creative Realm               = Water = Emotion
     Yetzirah - Formative Realm           = Air = Intellect
     Assaiah - Active/Material Realm      = Earth = Physicality

Table 2
```

375

This arrangement can be transfigured onto the Psychick Cross as shown in Figure 4:

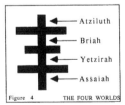

Atziluth

Briah

Yetzirah

Assaiah

Figure 4   THE FOUR WORLDS

Special attention should be paid to the shortened centre-bar, separating Briah and Yetzirah. This symbolizes the fluidity of exchange between the lower and higher realms of psychic activity. It is precisely here (i.e., in a space that is unfixed in matter) that consciousness operates. Qabalistic theory suggests that the human animal spans three of these four worlds. Thus, for example, whilst we remain rooted in *matter* (Assiah) we are unable to reach the highest world of Spirit/God (Atziluth). This is signaled by the extended bar below Atziluth. To reach this peak state we need to disembody or leave Assiah. It is thus by operating from Yetzirah (which equates with the astral realm in the western magickal system) that we can reach the highest point. This is the ecstatic or out of body experience. See Figure 5 below.

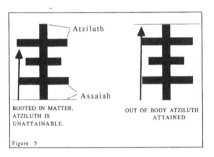

worlds. Thus, for example, whilst

ROOTED IN MATTER.
ATZILUTH IS
UNATTAINABLE.

OUT OF BODY ATZILUTH
ATTAINED

Figure 5

Using this basic *world* structure it is possible to obtain a number of insights onto the symbolism of THE PROCESS Church. The initial method involves the primary symbol of the Process *god form* and the superimposition of the associated element. Thus for SATAN we use the inverted Cavalry Cross and the element of Fire (Figure 6)

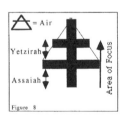

Figure 8

In the previous diagram the upper two bars of the Psychick Cross have been removed. The dotted lines complete a triangulation forming the alchemical symbol for the element Fire. The lower cross-bar symbolically defines the area of psychic activity and serves to accentuate the lower realm of matter or *Earth* (Qabalistically, Assiah). This coincides with the traditional notion of Satan as Prince of this (i.e. Earth) realm.

In Figure 7 below we reverse the above procedure in order to obtain the Cavalry or Christian Cross and the Process element of Water.

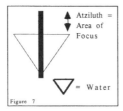

In this second configuration the lower two bars of the Psychick Cross has be removed. Again, the triangulation shown by the dotted lines discloses the elemental sign for Water. The natural psychick focus here is above the extended bar into the realm of divine emanation immateriality (Qabalistically, Atziluth). This is 'focus on God' in whatever lack of form one chooses. Its scepical significance is in its use to develop belief structures that rely on an 'afterlife' with the corollary of a relative disregard for events in the manifest world.

In Figure 8 below we utilise a composite form to represent the Luciferian Cross.

377

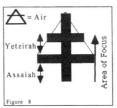

In this third configuration the upper-most cross bar of the Psychick Cross has been removed. The triangulation forms the symbol for Air. Here the principal point of focus is on the world of Matter (below the extended bar), but an additional dynamic is introduced by the addition of the Yetziratic influence (the area between the two bars). This intermediate realm is the place of unlimited *forms* or the *astral plane*. This effectively symbolizes the Luciferian conjunction of sensuality and unlimited choice and expression. It also incorporates the sphere of Yesod within the focus, indicating sexuality and ego-centricity or pride.

The final composite formulation, representing Jehovah, is shown in Figure 9, below:

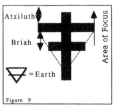

Figure 9

In this design we have omitted the lower bar of the Psychick Cross. The triangulation depicts the symbol for the element Earth. In this configuration the principal focus is on the *Divine* world beyond the uppermost cross-bar. However, the zone between the extended and shortened bar represents the Briatic world, or *World of Creation*. In the classical Judeo-Christian scriptures it is JAHWEH or JEHOVAH who initiates the sequence of creation. According to Qabalistic theory Jehovah is also the first tangible reflection of the entirely unmanifest God-head.

Closer analysis of the above scheme reveals an apparent paradox in that, for example, the symbol for Fire (and therefore the Divine Realm) is associated with Satan whose focus is on the Earthy Realm. This seeming inconsistency is suggestive however of an inner dynamic, and I would suggest that the elemental symbol sugnifies a *shadow* reality that compliments (or contradicts—depending on perspective and application) the primary are of focus. This provides a secondary area analysis. Repeating the Sequence used before we get:

SATAN = △ or ⟨symbol⟩

As previously said, the primary focus is on Assaiah (below the bar). The Fire symbol (representing Spirit) opposes this, thus pre-figuring or shadowing the main dynamic action. In a sense then, the element describes 'what is not' or in this instance a discarding of spiritual notions. In Jungian terminology, SATAN is the sensualist, or physical type, with a degraded or inactive intuitive side, thus Earth is opposing Fire.

CHRIST = ▽ or ⟨symbol⟩

Again, the element shadows the main focal point, predicating a yet to be achieved balance. The lack of 'earthing' inherent in the disembodied point of focus leads, I would suggest, to emotional instability or lack of relatedness. It is this, in an extreme form, that has lead to the establishment by Catholic Church of a celibate priesthood. The symbol for water is also, of course, equally a symbol for the Yoni, or female sexuality, which may in itself help explain the patriarchal form that Christian society has followed. In Jungian terminology this is the intuitive type with a degraded or inactive emotional side, thus Fire is opposing Water.

The remaining two forms are necessarily more complex but a similar ambivalence arises.

LUCIFER = or

The Luciferian Cross represents abandon and unrestricted sensuality, entirely at odds with the elemental correspondent Air, which is symbolic of the intellect. In Jungian Psychotypology the Luciferian is a 'feeling' type of which the negative or degraded counterpart is 'thinking'. Thus again we have a situation where a shadow element attributed by THE PROCESS Church opposes the primary psychological type by the chosen nomenclature. Here Water opposes Air.

379

JEHOVAH = or

The same situation holds true for the final cross/element combination. Jehovah represents the creative intellect, that is the creation of 'reality' via the mode of mentation and speech. In essence, the Biblical Creation myth deals with linguistic encodings of future possibility. It should be recalled that it was only after the Fall from Eden that physical actuality became an issue. The element attributed by THE PROCESS Church is 'Earth' but what we in fact have in Jungian terms is an intellectual type opposing hands-on practicality. Air opposes Earth.

Putting all this together helps illustrate an inherent weakness in the system adopted by THE PROCESS, where the four facets of quaternity were depicted thus:

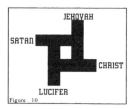

Figure 10

Using the Qabalistic reconfiguration we instead obtain a process of flow which can be represented in the following way:

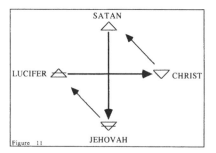

Figure 11

380

The resultant shape in Fiigure 11 is somewhat like a butterfly or, perhaps, a mobius strip, in which a continual loop of activity and interaction is established (see Figure 12). This is quite at odds with the structural rigidity depicted in Figure 10.

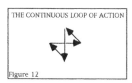

Figure 12

The dynamic is now four-fold within any one event structure. Moreover we have a symbol of perpetual motion (evolution), and can trace a logical ascent throught the four elements: Earth to Air to Water to

Fire (or JEHOVAH to LUCIFER to CHRIST to SATAN). Space preludes doing so in any great detail, but the JEHOVAH to SATAN sequence can be followed mythically as Creation to Fall to Redemption to Revelation.

So far I have dealt only with what I would term the macrocosmic level. Utilising the Tree of Psychick Integration the basic four-fold system can be explored via the Sephirotic correspondences (i.e. microcosmically).

According to Process Church literature the four types of designated *directions* are as follows.

JEHOVAH = North
LUCIFER = South
SATAN = West
CHRIST = East

Each direction can be assigned a Sephirah in accordance with Qabalistic traditions thus:

381

North = Geburah = JEHOVAH
South = Chesed = LUCIFER
West = Yesod = SATAN
East = Tipareth = CHRIST

These are highlighted on the tree shown in Figure 13.

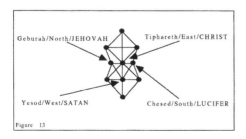

Figure 13

Some basic Sephirotic correspondences are outlined below:

JEHOVAH = Geburah = Mars = Severity = Justice = Restriction = Fear

LUCIFER = Chesed = Jupiter = Grace = Mercy = Expansion = Love

SATAN = Yesod = Moon = Foundation = Ego = Sexual Organs = Conscious Mind = Illusion

CHRIST = Tiphareth = Sun = Beauty = Self = Heart = Inner = Teacher

The Sephirotic descriptions are primarily concerned with inner balance rather than overt orientation. Thus a Jehovan utilising the appropriate Cross (±) may have any combination of the Sephiroth active at any one time. This provides for a means for adjusting and fine-tuning the psyche. For example the Jehovan Cross focuses on Air whilst being *shadowed* by Earth. Referring back to Figure 6 we know that *Earthly focus* is represented by SATAN, and Sephirotically (via the directional designation) is the Sephirah Yesod. This is also the Moon, suggesting that lunar-based rituals designed to generate flow and flexibility may be useful for the primary Jehovian type. A basic sigil to represent this is shown below (Figure 14).

Figure 14

Any Sephoric combination can be used on any of the four crosses to indicate intent, or to ritually invoke particular activity.

Remaining on a practical note, as I come to the close, standard tarot workings can also be brought to bear on this process. The standard

Trump/Path designations (available in many books) apply, with the following exceptions brought about by the re-configuration of the Tree of Life into the TOPI-tree:

Strength/Lust now runs between Chesed and Yesod
The Tower now runs between Geburah and Yesod.

As I said at the beginning, this essay is essentially a primary attempt at analysis, and the ideas expressed will clearly benefit from further exploration and discussion. That said, it should provide plentiful food for thought. I welcome any suggestions and correspondence (and criticism) on any of the ideas mooted here. Exchange and interaction is the whole of THE PROCESS—the goal is integration.

SO BE IT
Brother WORDS

PERSISTENCE OF A TRINITY
Observing Symbols of Correspondence

383

Through basic research in magick and enactment, there is a curious and peculiar relationship between three power symbols that are all familiar to us. These symbols/logos/sigils are the SWASTIKA, THE PROCESS 'P' CROSS, and the PSYCHICK CROSS; all of which coincidentally play a powerful role in demonstrating how THE PROCESS is a group associated with power. Most of this research has been documented and established from the efforts of Father MALACHI, with two final exceptions contributed by Brother SEE. All material presented has been established for the on going study in both construction and pattern within the means of dimensional reality and spatial memory rendered through symbols.

Let us take notice of the SWASTIKA. Perhaps one of the most universal power symbols to date. It has been used within various ethnic tribes in Europe and Asia, as a powerful geometric structuring in numerous areas around the world, and more recently and notoriously for being the magickal sigil and logo of the NAZI party and later associated supremacist orders.

SWASTIKA

When the SWASTIKA is flipped in reverse, a potentially interesting characteristic is revealed. We notice the shape is equally as powerful as when it is faced forward.

SWASTIKA (Reversed)

Father MALACHI has taken four reversed SWASTIKAS and placed them so that their limbs are intersecting and produced this arrangement:

384

If we look at the center, something familiar is revealed to our eyes as we begin to eliminate the framework of these reversed SWASTIKAS. Notice then what these intersecting limbs have created by if we establish some negative space around the obstructing areas of what we are trying to see.

Indeed it is THE PROCESS 'P' CROSS. This connection undoubtedly opens up the possibilities and theories for further explaining the essence of power that THE PROCESS comprises.

The Process 'P' Cross

Father MALACHI then points out that if we were to similarly take four PROCESS 'P' crosses and place them so they are adjoining each other, then a reversed phenomena is presented.

385

Again we establish negative space in the surrounding areas to view the unusual construction which always tends to develop in the center of such arrangements.

The SWASTIKA returns. Notice that THE PROCESS 'P' CROSS and the SWASTIKA are extremely similar in their constructive elements of intersection because both employ four sections of the same linear pieces which are perpendicular to one another at certain points. Perhaps that is why either is produced through four of the other together.

This now brings us to the PSYCHICK CROSS which is a symbol which defies interpretation, yet also proves itself to be a missing link in the dimensions that separate the SWASTIKA from THE PROCESS 'P' CROSS.

PSYCHICK CROSS

Father MALACHI attempted to simulate THE PROCESS 'P' CROSS by arranging four PSYCHICK CROSSES in a 'P' formation. As a result such was produced:

It seems in this instance that establishing negative space is not even necessary. What we have in the center is obviously a very conspicuous SWASTIKA.

Brother SEE points the way to a fourth and final consistency of using four of one symbol to make a single one. This is when PSYCHICK CROSSES are placed in a reverse 'P' arrangement. What is produced is but the only possible assumption:

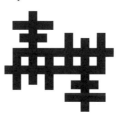

To verify the format, we must establish negative space to reveal what is of course, THE PROCESS 'P' CROSS.

The next and final presentation is somewhat strange and peculiar. Perhaps because it marks an unprecedented shift from the use of using four of any given particular symbol. In this case Brother SEE used only two PSYCHICK CROSSES in a diagonal positioning as seen:

387

As a result, again, THE PROCESS 'P' CROSS proves its consistency in defining dimension and space.

What we have then is the newly adapted symbol for THE PROCESS publication X-Tul ('X' THEE UNER LYING).

So what have we have learned from these connection is that all matter is related and therefore all POWER is the same.

Brother WORDS commentary on X-TUL for Transmedia Foundation, 1996

Photo by Peter Christopherson

EVEN FURTHER:
THE METAPHYSICS OF SIGILS

The medium of process philosophy bears close resemblance to the artistic media of assemblage practiced in so many twentieth-century art forms.
Robert C. Neville, *Reconstruction of Thinking*, p. 310

Thee Product is thee Process
Genesis Breyer P-Orridge, Psychic TV

I

Created neither for gallery nor audience, the sigil art of Genesis P-Orridge represents a deeply private and personal aspect of his extensive creative output. Ostensibly simple collages, these works document his explorations into magical consciousness, work which continues today and is central to his world view. Moreover, each sigil is essentially functional, centred on the initiation of agentive activity. That is, each was created as an intentional act of magic designed to modify the course of natural events. They are thus much more than mere representations of what magic might look like, and their existence constitutes a direct challenge to our understanding of the world and to normative models of causality, meaning and creativity.

389

This approach to art implies a rejection of intellectualization and scientific causality and, equally, it undermines the critical means by which we generally approach a body of creative work. P-Orridge today refers to himself as a Cultural Engineer, and in his collection of sigils we have the tool-box with which he carries out his work. He uses art as a means of influence, treating the magical act not as that of creating a likeness in the hope that life will imitate fiction, but as the initiation of a 'mental push to get the impulse started and support it on its course… it is the priming and starting of an act.' (Suzanne Langer, *Mind: An Essay in Human Feeling* v. III, p. 61). In P-Orridge's sigils we meet a prioritization of process and action in which the aesthetic and the theoretical are secondary to the integration of intention with a wider reality.

To consider these sigils in terms of conventional art-criticism, in terms of aesthetics and form, would thus be to remove them from the context in which they were created and to place them in a frame antithetical to their purpose. Art for P-Orridge serves a sacred role: the integration of consciousness with the fluxion of universal pattern. Art is not simply to be looked at, dissected, and critiqued; but to be experienced.

Such radical non-conformity places boundaries of how best to discuss his work, and generally forces a shift to anthropological, psychological or philosophical approaches. Within this broad framework, the current discussion will explore some of the techniques employed by P-Orridge in the construction of sigils, but will do so from the relatively uncharted perspective of the metaphysics of process. It concludes with a speculation on *how* sigils actually work.

Trans-modernity It is clear that P-Orridge does not conform to the conventions of the contemporary artist. True, he works from and within a tradition of iconoclasts (and the art-world remains a central target for this), and his method owes much to postmodern and deconstructionist theory. This is readily borne out by his use of apparently random and found elements which he montages into sometimes didactic and occasionally confrontational pieces. He adopts the posture of the outsider, attacks social norms and celebrates the art of diversity and the extreme. Yet for all this, the currency he works in is *constructive*. His focus is on the creative process in the development of his work, and especially (and unusually) on the work's creative effect. The language of P-Orridge's art is therefore not that of representation and challenge, but of invocation and change.

The sigils he presents to us are intentionally 'active'; that is, embedded within them is a principle of mediated agency. He seeds the future (both personal and public) through his art, leading us into unknown and unformed future possibilities. This goes beyond the postmodernist trick of 'making us think' (a wholly traditional value), and can instead be seen as a literal attempt to 'affect the real'. His work does not so much change the way in which we see the world, but rather 'changes the world in which we see'. This transformative focus places P-Orridge outside the modernist and postmodernist tendency to teach about reality (or

390

to teach how to interpret that reality according to cultural context), and aligns him with both magical and iconographic traditions. He thus reaches across time and can claim as much to be working from an ancient tradition as to be forging new modes of thought and new ways of living. His art in these senses extends beyond the aesthetic, beyond the didactic, beyond the confrontational (though it shares references with all these) and emerges as the documentation of an engagement with the universal process of creative advance. The future is uncertain; and it is the future which P-Orridge invokes and explores.

The Art of Sigils Technically, sigils are simply signs or marks designed to effect a magical purpose. They are constructed from symbols and letters drawn from the wide lexicon of astrological and related symboligies, and understanding and creating them is largely a matter of intellectual analysis and translation. The operator or magician generally works to predetermined formulae and systems. Such was the predominant view of western occultism in the late part of the 19th century. This belief in 'systems' generated much scholarship in the area, but it also fuelled in large part the somewhat obsessive search for ancient secrets and the resurrection of supposedly 'lost' magical orders. The aim was to resurrect—and then claim ownership of—the

391

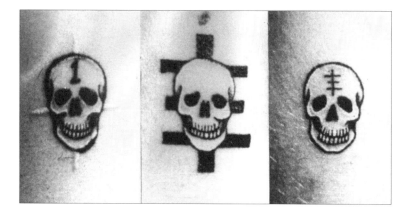

authority of what was regarded as a hidden tradition. Authority was thus located firmly in the past.

The artist and occultist Austin Osman Spare stands as a break with such developments through his radical use of intuitive approaches to magic. A fine and respected artist (his work as an official war artist can be found in the Imperial War Museum and has been the subject of several retrospective exhibitions), Spare attacked both the frame and the form of the then contemporary magic. He rejected the traditions of the past in favour of a highly personalized metaphysical map, alongside which he developed a system of word collage which represented a shift away from the formulaic methods of magic promoted by groups such as the Golden Dawn. It is the method that is of interest in our present context.

Taking the notion of 'spells' at its most direct, Spare would simply identify his intended outcome in the form of a word or phrase and work to eliminate each repeated letter so that each appeared only once. A phrase such as 'To meet the Angels' would thus be written:

TO MEET THE ANGELS > TO ME~~ET THE~~ ANGELS > TOMEANGLS

The resultant distillation would then be structured in a stylized pattern, breaking down the relationship with textual linearity so as to present an abstract image in which the letters qua letters disappeared.

Spare's work is influential on P-Orridge in several ways. Firstly, as an artist Spare rejected the gallery conventions of his day, treating the art world with Nietzschean disdain. Secondly, in his rejection of traditional magical orders he emphasized the transfer of authority from the 'other' to the 'inner' thus paving the way for P-Orridge's wholly intuitive and asystemized approach to magic. Finally, in his methodological approach he specified a process of distillation through which complex structures can be taken down to their elemental form thus enabling a clarity of purpose to be achieved. This process of constructive deconstruction, of elemental binding and combination, emerges in a highly developed way in P-Orridge's sigils.

The Laws of reality are also the laws of thought.
Ludwig Feuerbach, *Principles of the Philosophy of the Future*, p. 63

Collaging Reality P-Orridge's sigil art is amongst his most private work, but it is also provides the clearest indication of both his method and purpose. The harmony of the work provides its tone, the elements its direction. The process is one of a continual refinement so that everything that is necessary is included, everything that is unnecessary is set aside, and a balance of what remains is achieved. If Spare's work serves as a transitionary moment in magical art, P-Orridge takes that moment into new territory, setting aside Spare's ultimately system-driven approach and emphasizing in its place a wholly intuitive and naturalistic *process*. The focus of P-Orridge's work is eminently *practical*.

P-Orridge's sigils are invariably mixed media collages, incorporating both found and created material. P-Orridge also makes extensive use of photography, often manipulating the image to mask both form and identity. In this way he generalizes the particular. The aim is to draw out the essential characteristic of the target image, to purify it, and to intensify its affective potential. Images are over-painted and textured. Text is added. The combined effect is to mutate the commonplace and to unify the divergent. In addition to this, images created during the process of ritual are frequently incorporated into the work, a strategy which mythologizes location and space. And finally, by the ritual embedding within the sigil of the present moment of creative activity P-Orridge creates a dislocation in the linearity of time. He becomes genetically joined to the sigil. It becomes impossible to distinguish between the artist and the art, between the creator and the created. The emergent sigil can thus exercise its own creative agency over and against the artist in a full-fledged intersubjective dialogue. It signals its own completion, in its own time. It is this radical disruption of the spatial and temporal modes of being which transforms the sigil from 'art as art' to 'art as agent'.

Intention is the work of envisaging and enacting will.
Ray L Hart, *Unfinished Man and the Imagination*, p. 148

Some Metaphysics What he was getting at is the idea that what we think of as a single 'universe' is in fact a relational network of infinitely varied universes, each of which is centred in its own subjective being. Thus the universe I perceive at any moment is a unique creation, as is the world I perceive a moment later. And each is my unique creation. What is more, Whitehead argues that the future is open to subjective manipulation; that is, even though we inhabit a realm where a vast array of fixed (or to be more exact, relatively consistent) laws apply, the future is ultimately 'open'. In *Process and Reality*, Whitehead explores how his vision of inter-relating but atomized universes presents the kind of coherence which enables us to exist in the day-to-day manner to which we are so accustomed. The metaphysics is complex and controversial, but at its heart offers a view of reality in which process is the true stuff of reality, and in which 'matter' is little more than the documentation resulting from the activity and process of continuous becoming. It is this idea which lends itself to a more coherent and rational theory of magic since it proposes that the fundamental stuff of reality is a process of creative emergence; 'matter' is simply the outcome of that activity.

In discussing his own work P-Orridge has consistently focused on 'process', describing the resultant artefacts as 'documentation'. The creativity is centred in his own activity of 'making' and engages the whole person. It is largely an interiorized mode of creative action, and in this sense is wholly subjective. This work is private in the most fundamental sense of that word, since it is located in the interior conceptual and structural arrangements of his modes of thought. The art emerging from this interiorized creativity is simply the documentation of his ritual engagement with Present Time.

The English process philosopher Alfred North Whitehead wrote:

> *[N]o two actual entities originate from an identical universe.... The nexus of actual entities in the universe correlate to a concrescence is termed 'the actual world' correlate to that concrescence.*
> *Process and Reality,* p. 22-23

II

A Process View of Present Time In the previous section the process of sigil-construction was characterized as essentially one of engagement with Present Time. This needs some explanation. The concept owes much to Whitehead's process metaphysics and his idea that reality is made up not of substance (objective matter), but rather of 'events' or activity. In developing his thought, he implied a concept of time which whilst recognizing the formal flow of physical or perceptual time, treated its content somewhat unusually. In his scheme the 'past' is entirely 'objective', by which he meant inactive and unchanging. The future, in contrast, is indeterminate, a realm of potential possibilities. The 'present' is entirely subjective and is the sole point of activity. Nothing in present time exists physically since to be in the present is defined as undergoing a process of becoming determinate; but nothing outside this *process* of active determination is fully real. As an entity begins to emerge it becomes more defined, more and more definite in its form, until it achieves a satisfactory shape and emerges into being. At this point it becomes fixed, and triggers a new creative process. Our world is, in these terms, a series of successive and radically inter-related processes, each informed by its predecessors and each informative of its successors.

It is instructive to explore the notion of present and future time posited by Whitehead in the context of ritual engagement and magical act. A key element in Whitehead's system is that the future is open to subjective influence. Reality is not the result of physical causal chains, but rather of the imaginative invocation and manipulation of contexts. If we treat the process of ritual interiorization (such as that undertaken by P-Orridge) as the maximization of subjective being (the objective world 'outside' disappears from the ritual space to be replaced by the manifestation of a mental arena of the artist's own making), by entering a ritual space we are in effect escaping the linear flow of time. Under such conditions we are related neither to the Past nor the Future. We are conscious only of the Now. Present Time is thus extended and provides a space in which we self-consciously construct the form of our future emergence into reality. Whitehead termed this process 'concrescence' and it was effected by a subjective 'prehension' and harmonization of elements under the direction of a 'subjective aim'. In less technical language we can represent this as the organization and 'making concrete' of what will emerge into physical existence by a means of 'gathering' together diverse elements into a single reality.

Whitehead further suggests that in the process of concrescence, the subject (operator) draws on past information (objective fact), distils and orders it according to an initial aim, and harmonizes its elemental components until it reaches a state he terms its 'satisfaction'. The subject then transforms from its active transformative or non-temporal state into a 'superject', essentially a moment of observable reality in the flow of physical time. It is the emergence of the superject which seeds the future.

This idea of Whitehead's (which applies to all the stuff of the universe) bears comparison with the state of mind achieved during ritual, where connection with the external world is lost. In the apparent timelessness of ritual activity, the operator is free to construct out of just those elements he chooses. The construction is effected both mentally and physically. This reflects a further requirement of Whitehead's system which insists on all entities having both a mental and a physical pole. As above, so below. The process of creation is fundamentally a selective process of 'combination'; that is, it requires bringing the diversity of available data together with the subjective imagination of the present aim in order to create a unified and concrete whole.

[The process] involves a reversal of our ordinary understanding that causes produce effects. The cause must precede its effect in time, yet it must be presently existent in order to be active in producing its effect.
Lewis Ford, *The Lure of God*, p. 5

III

Sigils as Agents Immersed in Present Time, P-Orridge creates a ritual space which he inhabits with consciousness. He steps forth into a sacred space, outside the linearity of time and becomes in a literal sense the architect of his own universe: the magician conjuring and shaping the elements to his will.

He identifies his aim, expressed by invocation and empowered by intensity of experience. And then he works, his energies brought to bear on a single purpose. He brings a new form into the actual world. A sigil emerges into reality.

But how does it work? How does the sigil take effect? How can a product of human creativity change nature from its course?

What follows is speculation, but it is grounded in the metaphysics of process, some of which has been touched on in the context of the ritual construction of sigils. The key is in a radical restatement of our notion of 'time'.

> 'Creativity' is the universal of universals characterizing ultimate matter of fact. It is that ultimate principle by which the many, which are the universe disjunctively, become the one actual occasion, which is the universe conjunctively. It lies in the nature of things that the many enter into complex unity.
>
> When a non-conformal proposition is admitted into feeling, the reaction to the datum has resulted in the synthesis of fact with the alternative potentiality of the complex predicate. A novelty has emerged into creation…. [I]t is new, a new type of individual, and not merely a new intensity of individual feeling. That member of the locus has introduced a new form into the actual world; or, at least, an old form in a new function.
>
> *Process and Reality,* p. 28, 187

397

A Speculation on Time Our normal understanding treats time as the strictly linear measure of successive moments or events. This is the forward motion of time's arrow. Relativity theory suggests that it is bi-directional; the mathematics work equally well in either direction.

But what is time? P-Orridge coined the phrase 'Time is that which emits', and this provides a clue which I propose to explore. Time is significant to P-Orridge, and its significance lies in his intuitive grasp and ritual experience of time's thickness.

We can restate P-Orridge's phrase as a simple equation: TIME=EMIT. The one is the mirror of the other. We can take this a step further and propose that 'time' is the expression of energy (an emission). It is important here to note that this is not the same as saying that expressions of energy take place *in* time, but rather that what we consider as the movement of time is an expression of energy.

Now for some proposals:

The first proposal is that there is a relationship of identity between energy and time, and that when we consider what we mean by time we are considering the function of energy under another form.

The second is that we can consider our thoughts or mental activity as constituting high-energy states in contrast with physical existence or activity which occurs in low-energy states. All physically manifest objects (including atoms) are to be considered 'low-energy'.

I leave the third step to Alfred North Whitehead, noting first that he requires that every entity has both a physical and a mental aspect (or 'pole'):

> The mental pole is the subject determining its own ideal of itself by reference to eternal principles of valuation autonomously modified in their application to its own physical objective datum. Every actual entity is 'in time' so far as its physical pole is concerned, and is 'out of time' so far as its mental pole is concerned. It is the union of two worlds, namely, the temporal world, and the world of autonomous valuation.
>
> *Process and Reality*, p. 248

398

The 'world of autonomous valuation' is, for Whitehead, 'out of time'. We need to take this to mean 'out of linear time', since the process of valuation necessarily effects some degree of change in what is being valued. We cannot under a process metaphysic consider the possibility of timelessness since that would imply a lack of process, a lack of change. And any change must be an expression of energy and thus of time.

If the mental pole exists outside linear time, but cannot (because of its inherent activity) be 'atemporal', it must therefore be expressing time in some other way. We know from physics that the addition of energy increases the level of activity of atoms (they move faster), and that in the physical plane a large increase in energy alters the physical state of materials (solids melt, liquids vaporize). We also know that time is relative to the observer, and that rapid movement slows the passage of time relative to a fixed or stationary point. Atomic clocks run slow at altitude, and someone orbiting the earth in a satellite ages marginally less quickly than those on earth even though an hour or a day feels the same under both sets of conditions.

What this is leading to is the suggestion that our sense of linear time is simply the result of relatively low-energy existence. In order to retain physical coherence there are limits (even at the atomic level) on how much energy we can express, and this limit is directly linked to our notion of linear time. But if time bears a relationship of identity with energy, and energy (which is simply activity by another name) is increased, then it becomes possible to imagine that at high levels of energy the physical limits are broken and existence emerges outside the tight constraints of linear time. This suggests that 'time' as fully conceived has thickness or extension.

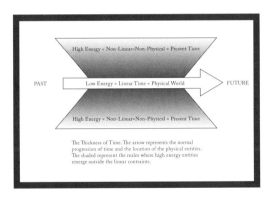

The Thickness of Time. The arrow represents the normal progression of time and the location of the physical entities. The shaded represent the realm where high energy entities emerge outside the linear contraints.

399

I propose that mental activity (thought) is simply the emergence of entities into high-energy states. This goes beyond what Whitehead claims but is arguably implicit in his position. We should also note here Whitehead's description of the non-temporal world as one of 'autonomous valuation', and take care to distinguish between the physical brain activity through which we engage with thought and the thought itself. But if we make the conceptual leap, we can begin to see how, for example, the mystic is able to transcend the limits of normal temporality and reach both into the past and the future. In the language of the magical traditions this is the realm of hidden or occult activity. The aether. The astral plane.

How Sigils Work It was suggested earlier that ritual space constitutes a move into the extensiveness of Present Time, and that the primary characteristic of Present Time is its prioritizing of the subjective. Present Time is where actuality is defined and shaped. By choosing to operate within this conceptual arena, P-Orridge is able to immerse himself in the fullness of his own subjectivity. His imaginative world becomes fluid and tangible, constrained only by the limits of future possibility. As he shapes his mental map of the future, isolates and defines his intention, he begins to construct. The emergent sigil shares his temporal and (non)-physical location, and thus shares also in the prioritization of subjective experience which is the nature of Present Time. As Whitehead puts it, it is born into a 'world of autonomous valuation'. A sigil so created is essentially a denizen of that world.

As with all entities, the sigil has a mental and a physical aspect, but because of its unusual beginnings the mental aspect is significantly heightened. This is in sharp contrast to artefacts created in the frame-work of physical time and primarily as objects of physical appreciation. In such cases the created work is bound by its own objective beginnings. It is the heightening of its mental aspect which enables the sigil to exert agency. Upon its release from its ritual space it is able to sustain its link with Present Time even while it exists in the linear frame of physi-cal time/space. It is this inborn access to continuing creative expression which constitutes the sigil's magical potency.

For P-Orridge, the key to a sigil's effectiveness is his management of its constituent elements. The environment of Present Time provides the potential, gives the sigil its nature, but it is the artist who provides and defines its function. That the sigil enjoys autonomy of valuation means that the process remains always somewhat open or indeter-minate with regard to its ultimate completion. It follows from this that the artist can never be certain of how the sigil will 'behave' and it is for this reason that P-Orridge incorporates a genetic link. The uncertainty does, however, serve an important purpose. Although it is possible to construct and control ritual space, the same cannot be said for the temporal everyday world which is subject to innumerable competing imperatives. The sigil must await its opportunity to act, in-fluencing and evaluating the patterns of physicality until such time as its encoded intention can be brought to fruition. It is a seed planted into the uncertainty of future time. It awaits only the conditions of its germination.

Closing Thoughts In making public his sigils, Genesis P-Orridge has afforded us a rare opportunity to explore new worlds. Currently operating under the banner of The Next New Way On, he is inviting us to challenge our modes of thought and to develop new ways of engineering our futures. He once travelled across America in a yellow bus reminiscent of that used by the Merry Pranksters in the '60s but on which the destination was now declared as 'Even Further'. It was a declaration of his intent to push the boundaries of human experience into new territory, to unchain the limits of imaginative creativity. The sigils he has created over the past 20 years or so are part of this broader goal.

We can if we wish treat his sigils as art, as objects to observe and admire. But we might also take them as an injunction to step over the line and explore the limits of our imagination. The only restrictions are those we place on ourselves.

Paul Cecil, 23 January 2002, England

401

THEE PROCESS IS THEE PRODUCKT

Since the mid-sixties, my teenage years, I have always been profoundly obsessed with human behavior. Whether there can be a system, technique, chemical, belief system, discipline that is able to reprogram entrenched, inherited patterns of behavior. Is there any way to short-circuit control, erase compulsive and reactive responses? Can we re-invent a SELF consciously in order to maximize its potential and, hopefully, therefore our satisfaction in life? My lifelong search is for focused mutability, and to change the means of perception. To challenge every status quo as a matter of principle and never rest, never assume or imagine that the task of reinvention has a finite ending. Permanent change towards a radical, positive and liberating evolutionary mutation of the human species is the core essence and motivation of every single aspect of my creativity.

Parallel to this aesthetic and philosophical obsession has been a strange, synchronous, concurrent, almost symbiotic series of similarities of problems and media issues at critical intersections in our gradual progress through the various projects that feel as if they are delivered like an advisory commentary by the story of The Process Church of the Final Judgment. The Process has so much reflectivity in my own life journey that it has come to be valued as a manual of strategic repair when serious conflicts with "control" occur. At other times I use my Process archives and documents as a means of problem resolution. This gradual, but life-long adoption of my possibly misconstrued, subjective understanding of The Process has an almost oracular quality, sometimes implying what we should do, and sometimes illustrating what we should not in terms of how to modify the perceptual misconceptions of the overarching, established monolithic culture at any given time.

In order to contextualize, to some extent, the ongoing interaction of The Process with key moments during my life a little background is required.

The very first mention of The Process that we were consciously aware of was in an early issue of *OZ* magazine, the most psychedelic, tripped-out underground publication of the 1960s and 70s. With white print on yellow overlaid with clashing green art nouveau graphics it was able to generate an internal environment equally as challenging as an actual acid trip. The writer in *OZ* was trumpeting a somewhat overblown warning to "freaks" that The Process was an insidious "mind control" cult fraught with oppressive psychotherapeutic technologies and covert monetary greed. Needless to say, and as is often the case, the more vivid the descriptions of the group were, the more mysteriously they were defamed the more obdurate our fascination became. Later we would realize, with hindsight, that various salacious articles we had found starkly compelling had been sensationalized investigations into The Process.

One way that my friends and I financed buying ourselves hash was street-selling *OZ* and *International Times*, the two main publications to have grown out of the sixties post-acid counter culture. The other way we raised money was by selling books. We would persuade our parents we were going to London on the train to see a Magritte exhibition at the Tate Gallery and that we would be staying with a friend's grandparents in Purley, London. Then we'd sneak off by bus to the motorway and hitchhike to London, thus saving our money for food, fun and live music. If you timed a visit right you could stay all night on the foam-cushioned floor of the Arts Lab Cinema in Drury Lane. Daytimes were spent shoplifting books on Tottenham Court Road. We focused on City Lights Beat poetry, W. S. Burroughs, Jean Genet, Henry Miller, the Marquis de Sade and their ilk. Nights were the Arts Lab, UFO Club and later in squats in Drury Lane and Piccadilly.

Our appetite for new ideas, contrary philosophies, drug sensualism and alternative communities and life styles was insatiable. We were adolescent dreamers searching for novelty for its own sake and extra-sensualist perception.

One weekend, whilst hanging around on the Kings Road outside Granny Takes a Trip (a shop selling the ultimate in dandy-flavored flower child clothing at that time) and coveting the riot of silks and velvets, brocades and multi-ethnic jewelry, we saw a guy in a weird outfit. He had long hair and a beard, all of which were *de rigueur* at that time, but he seemed groomed and was wearing a cloak and dark clothes. My instincts told me he represented an antithesis of the shock of colors and informality of the typical hippie. Part of me wanted to talk to him, but something held me back—maybe my lack of money, as I could by then tell that he was street-selling a magazine. I got close enough to see it wasn't *OZ,* or *IT,* it was a strikingly colored Process magazine.

403

To this day, it is impossible for me to explain to myself, why this minimal event touched me so deeply, but on some subliminal, gut level my intuition compelled me to decide to make a point of trying to discover what I could about this vilified group. What was it about them that unified the disparate and contradictory elements of the counterculture in condemnation and paranoia? By the end of 1969 I had realized that The Process were the same group accused of being the "Mindbenders of Mayfair" in the British gutter press, and who were alleged to have programmed the Manson Family, and (later) the Son of Sam and who knows what else. The Process became the symbol of the neo-hippie bogeyman! Anyone able to shatter society's complacency on such a deep level resonated with my own compulsive urge to strip away hypocrisy and bigotry, conditioning and imposed behavioral patterns in order to attempt to create a self chosen identity releasing my maximum personal potential so that my life could be an unfolding, autonomous narrative written by my self-conscious choices.

By 1969 I was living in the Exploding Galaxy in Islington, London surrendering my creativity, personality and my future to an extremely demanding commune. We tried to break down as many inherited values, inhibitions, gender roles, stereotypes and imposed social roles by trying to isolate ANY habitual mannerisms or behavioral assumptions. Later I founded COUM Transmissions, a performance art group that during the first half of the 1970s delved deeper and deeper into character archetypes and social, especially sexual, taboos and limitations. We wanted to create a morally clean slate upon which we, and only we, then designed and manifested an independently constructed individual identity. As our public explorations became more and more intimate, so media attention became focused upon our work in an ever more antagonistic style until in October 1976, after the opening of our retrospective "PROSTITUTION" at the I.C.A. Gallery in London, an unexpectedly huge tsunami of outrage, disgust and scurrilous defamation drowned all meaning in mannered, contrived denunciations. I had thought that scandal occurred when an artist, or action of some kind exposed the obsolescence of a particular, contemporary and socially endorsed moral convention. A process which could imply that by triggering a neo-moralist media outcry our intention to reveal outmoded conventions that damage and frustrate an individual's potential making hope subservient to the hierarchical "greater good" would be an end, in and of itself. I imagined in a simplistic way, that the destruction of a corrupted status quo was an end in itself. That anarchy was always preferable to inertia. But I was miscalculating.

When you are suddenly the subject of feature exposes in the yellow press, finding one's ideals ridiculed and twisted to deliberately alienate the public from one's sincere and optimistic intentions, it quickly becomes apparent that what actually happens is that your message gets lost in the hysterical noise of slander. After this experience I remembered The Process experiencing an even more extreme smear campaign. Did what befall them provide a strategy that I could learn from and utilize? It didn't, but it did start me thinking about possible conflicts with the establishment in the future and whether we could prepare ourselves better to avoid the soul-destroying impact that occurs when the governing powers that be, those grey beings with a vested interest in maintaining their privilege and influence, attack you with unrelenting fervor.

I knew that the direction my thoughts were taking my life and art were almost certain to release further attempts to censor and silence my ideas.

By 1981 I had been privately exploring phenomena that had spontaneously occurred during some of the more extreme, physically taxing and long time-based art performances. I had noticed that I occasionally spoke in tongues; could erase my responses to pain; achieve altered "shamanic" type states of consciousness; out of body experiences and time dilation and contraction. These events had been random and uncontrolled, but revelatory. They were also incredibly intimate. So I began a series of controlled rituals, in private, utilizing a sacred space, talismanic objects, self-composed ambient music, incense, candles and sensory deprivation. I had acquired a coffin during recording *Dreams Less Sweet* and would sometimes spend several hours wrapped in wolf skins, in bondage inside the coffin after ingesting a heavy dose of psychedelics for example.

I also began reading up on Western magic, in particular Austin Osman Spare. At the same time I came across the W. S. Bainbridge book, *Satan's Power* "based" on The Process and rekindled my interest in that group much more deeply than before. I felt a certain kinship already, having been victimized by a scurrilous media for my way of life and attempt to unify that life with art in a liberating and evolutionary synthesis. When I co-founded Psychic TV with Alex Fergusson in 1981, it was with another integrated project in mind. During long winter discussions with my inspirational collaborator Monte Cazazza we considered what might happen if a rock band, instead of just seeing fans as an income flow and an ego booster, focused that admiration and energy towards a cultural and lifestyle directing network. What would happen if we created a para-military occult organization that shared demystified magickal techniques? Sleeve notes could become manifestos, a call to action and behavioral rebellion. Bit by bit we took this daydream more seriously. We examined The Process in particular for the "best" in cult aesthetics. We needed an ideology for those involved; levels to achieve; secrets to reveal; symbols and uniforms; regalia and internal writings.

We called our experimental organization Thee Temple Ov Psychick Youth. Our previous involvement with mail art gave us a grounding in

405

mailing out flyers and newsletters. My researches into ritual and directed orgasm became a central activity that demanded 23 monthly sigils created on the 23rd of each month at 23 hours Greenwich Mean Time. From The Process we saw the need for a logo, a symbol. I designed the Psychick Cross. A vertical line with three horizontals. The central line shorter than the other two. All the lines in the proportion of 2/3. One of the secrets of this design revealed for the first time here is that if you create a grid of Psychick Crosses in a particular configuration you will see Process symbols in all the spaces in between. If you create a different configuration you will see swastikas in all the spaces inbetween. The Psychick Cross is a non-verbal logo that represents the sum total of all the activities, desires, products and creativity manifested in its name. I wanted to make sure, even in a sense invisibly, that our debt to The Process WAS honored.

One of our friends was a great seamstress. We combined grey priest shirts we bought at Roman Catholic suppliers with combat boots and grey military-style trousers that she produced. Embroidered patches in the vesica (vaginal) shape with a Psychick Cross and 23 were sewn on jackets and shirts to identify the TOPY community. Finally we looked again at The Process and saw that the long hair and beards, whilst common enough in the 1960s on one person, had a powerful impact once they were collected together *en masse*. The TOPY haircut was a combination of the long and sensuous in the form of a long tail of hair at the back of the head, and then the rest of the head was shaved in reference to the ascetic spiritual disciplines. Ascetic and decadent, the eternal balance and/ or contradictions. Definitely, though, having the Psychick Cross was the most instantly effective strategy for generating very quickly the impression of a serious, focused, militant network. The Psychick Youth look was so strong that it seduced and attracted males and females to adopt it very quickly. A handful of Psychick Youth dressed up, in even a large crowd, had an immediate visceral impact far beyond what might be expected from such small numbers.

It was particularly the records that spread TOPY abroad. We were soon receiving enquiries from the USA and Canada, then France, Germany, Sweden and on and on. This meant we were very exposed in the media, and primarily to music fans rather than to already serious seekers of occult knowledge and techniques. This sometimes over-dilettantish segment of our network created a serious credibility issue amongst more established

406

magical fraternities and devotees. We ourselves had been constructing TOPY initially "to see what happens" when demystified occult and shamanic practices are released non-hierarchically into popular culture. What will be the occult impact of several hundred, later several thousand Individuals masturbating to a common desire and purpose at exactly the same time all across the world? It had never been done before, so we saw this as a contemporary research into the effectiveness of these techniques. But as we grew in numbers and had to keep improvising new structures and solutions to administer TOPY we began looking for assistance and "advice" from outside. My ongoing interest in The Process had resulted in my collecting every publication, newspaper file, Freedom of Information folder and any other memorabilia from rare booksellers in England and the USA. I started reading The Process magazines, of which we had a full set scanned by a friend, and the books, including *EXIT, Humanity is the Devil, Satan on War,* even transcripts of LA police interviews with bikers after the Manson murders that a journalist friend from Hull University acquired for me.

What became apparent was that to evolve and remain relevant and vibrant, TOPY must become a template for a way of life. That The Process, for good or ill, thrived by proposing a fully engaging system of living combined with spiritual and mental exploration. That to expose flaws in behavior, and personality, and to have any chance of revelatory and revolutionary breakthroughs the group had to immerse themselves 100% in devotion to the group and fearless surrender to the potential challenges and innovations even at the risk of personal disintegration and mental collapse. Transformation can only occur if the Individual is prepared to sacrifice all they have, including a previous personality, and place in a status quo. Smashing old loops and habitual patterns is essential.

TOPY discovered that a certain ratio of Individuals were so dissatisfied with their current state of mind, the lack of magic (in all senses) and of connection to others, of outmoded sexual roles and gender expectations and archetypes that they WERE prepared to move into a far more Processean approach to this burgeoning community. With our archive of Process publications, and a probably idiosyncratic interpretation of the messages and structures they had used, we began a migration to Brighton, England. Why Brighton? We wanted a better environment for my

407

daughters Caresse and Genesse. Plus Brighton had a history of alternative culture and liberal ideas from the sixties and even earlier. So, with my family and two hardcore TOPY Individuals we bought a large Georgian house in Brighton, complete with an extra self-contained apartment. Sister Shadows and Brother Words sold their London home, as we had, to move a few houses down in the same street. We kept the London TOPY Station (a Station was the main HQ that administered a whole country, or larger territory overseeing the various more localized Access Points) in 50 Beck Road, Hackney where several TOPY Individuals lived and worked and where our original Nursery was still active. (A Nursery was a room in a TOPY house exclusively dedicated to magickal rituals and sigilisation.) The TOPY Station in London's Nursery had a rather gothic baroque décor that included an old Victorian dentist's chair, that had seen its dentist owner commit sex crimes on it before he was caught, convicted and sent to prison. Just as The Process' flirtation with implied "satanic" beliefs and other sensationalist mischief ended up biting them nastily, so TOPY's amusement with the darker aspects of humanity also backfired in a hauntingly similar way.

Not long after the TOPY equivalent of The Process OMEGA moved to Brighton, a steady trickle of fully committed Individuals had followed us there. We soon had five houses that were all TOPY Individuals, plus the London TOPY Station. It became clear we needed to keep everyone occupied, and that we had a marvelous resource to experiment together in living and designing a TOPY way of life 24-7. The Process really came into its own. We began to have a TOPY communal meal every Monday. The TOPY houses would rotate, taking turns to cook a meal for everyone, and then to develop more systems. Just as The Process improvised additional structures and disciplines in an ad hoc way, and Mary Ann and Robert would note developments, observations and concepts during long meetings of the original hardcore members, so we would discuss problems arising from communal living, sexual friction, the purity of group sigils as opposed to lecherous exploitation, and new options for the command structure. In particular I drew on my experiences living in communes most of my life, first The Exploding Galaxy, then The HoHo Funhouse, then COUM Transmissions and now TOPY.

One potent and fulfilling exercise was the TOPY Life Story. Each Monday one Individual would be chosen, or would volunteer, to tell their life story—the rule being that NOTHING is left out, no matter how distressing, humiliating, traumatic or depressing. The WHOLE truth. Usually this was the first time anybody had told his or her real story. The act of trust involved in revealing such vulnerability was immense. We discovered so much about each other this way and learned why people had certain issues, or habits, or personality loops and quirks both positive and negative. Interruptions were not allowed, but questions, no matter how intimate could be presented afterwards and had to be answered. The first one or two stories were difficult to present. But once one or two had narrated their innermost experiences and pains, it became easier and easier for others to participate. It was revealed to us over and over how many boys, and girls, had suffered sexual abuse, and often combined with violence. This prevailing social ugliness that we had all been damaged by became a bond in its revelation that created intense mutual loyalty amongst the TOPY Brighton contingent. Our compassion for each other deepened and has remained as dedicated and mutual loyalty all these years later.

TOPY included heterosexual couples with "open" relationships, monogamous couples both gay and straight, transsexuals, and quite a few couples with children plus single mothers. During the TOPY years especially, we visited other communes, in particular becoming close to the Zendik Farm, a commune/cult dating back to Los Angeles in the acid '60s whose emphasis is on self-sufficiency by organic farming and ecological awareness; we studied the Manson Family, the Moonies, the Children of God, Jim Jones, the Source, the Cockettes, and came to know people at Morningstar Ranch (another '60s holdover in Sonoma County). Many of these communes and cults experimented with separation of children from their biological parents to try and avoid inherited conditioning and emotional dependency—though I wonder if it wasn't, consciously or not, a way to try to ensure fealty to the group and by implication the group guru/leader/figurehead/enlightened superbeing, thereby assuring new, ever more fanatical followers who would have known no other way of life or belief system. Timothy Wyllie confesses that The Process' attitude to children was careless and potentially rather mean-spirited, seeing them almost as a hindrance to the spiritual advancement of individual members and a nuisance, and that he sees that as pretty shameful.

409

Fortunately, as I myself had two daughters, Caresse and Genesse, children did have a place in our ever-evolving ways of living. Quite naturally, it seemed, both my children and later several others were adopted instinctively as special Individuals in their own right. We created a TOPY naming ceremony for each child, and included them in films and on records. The only declared policy was to always talk to them in exactly the same language we would use about an issue or question for an adult. TOPY inadvertently became a large pool of child care-ers and babysitters, which gave all mothers in particular a lot more time for study and creative activities. Caresse and Genesse always went on tour with Psychic TV accompanied by a trained nursery teacher; a nurse from within the TOPY ranks. Their memories of living on the "EVEN FURTHER" 1966 school bus TOPYNA (North America) purchased for us to tour the USA and Canada in, and being made a fuss of everywhere, are amongst their fondest most vivid early memories. In 1988 a new zone was created in TOPY STATION in Brighton that was named the KALI CIRCLE. This was a females-only group. As often happens in close-knit communities, the Kalis in TOPY noticed they were all menstruating at the same time, their biological clocks synchronizing their proximity, reinforced by the monthly intimacy of sigilising. As is commonly the case, the Edens would feel the Kalis would become Moon Moody together, more prone to intolerance of stupidity, nagging or criticism! Through reading and discussion of women's magickal powers and the deeply alchemical resonance of menstrual blood it was proposed by all genders to experiment with seeing this monthly time as an opportunity to harness all the incredible intensity and potency rather than fight it or feel threatened by shifts in Kalis' behaviors.

The Kali Circle became autonomous, closed to all biological males and self-defining. To declare the activation through menstruation of the group, TOPY women began wearing a red cotton thread around their left wrist. During the "red" time all challenging, strange, or intense behaviour was automatically accepted. Kalis were left "alone" to channel their hormonal GIFT in creative, conceptual or physically active pursuits that were beyonf question. Surprisingly to all, this liberated the biological males to not feel personally criticized or insecure and liberated the biological females to behave and explore without guilt or restriction knowing ANY usual day to day responsibilities would be covered during their "blessed" state of power by other TOPY Individuals.

TOPY tended to see mutual assistance and support by any means at anyone's disposal as the most efficient methodology as well as the most generous. We posited that by sharing all our skills, properties and assets voluntarily we could all live a lifestyle way beyond our personal resources. A TOPY Individual in Brighton, for example, could say that rather than having only one room in a shared apartment if they were alone, they had five houses which included gardens and a large jacuzzi as well as fully equipped offices and music and video recording facilities plus homes across the USA, Canada, Germany, Holland and so on. Everyone became a token "millionaire" simply by choosing to reciprocate sharing. Quite a few Ratio Four TOPY Individuals became Nomadic, traveling about the Access Point network exchanging labor and other skills for shelter. The most famous, even happily notorious, was Boris of TOPY PYROMANIA who continues this (now) neo-TOPY pilgrimage to this day, and Alice Trip De Gaine who has become the talisman of fortune for Psychic TV and PTV3. He follows PTV3 around on their tours acting as a roadie, archivist of documentation and confidant. One thing we always hoped for was that the Psychick Cross would come to be a signal of trustworthiness and succor for those Individuals who wore it. We have heard hundreds of tales of people in far off places stranded or in dire need who saw a Psychick Cross tattoo, pin, or one the clothing on someone who rescued and protected them. That is a wonderful phenomenon.

411

One method we took directly from The Process was Telepathy Raising sessions. Each Monday at the TOPY meals we would begin with a blessing, "This is my Cross, This is my Life, This is my Wisdom." Then we would all hold hands in a circle around the table or, if there were too many Individuals, around the large living room. Everyone would focus inside with eyes closed, even the children present, and after around ten minutes a book was opened and each person wrote down any images they saw (if they did). We found that as the months went by there was a clear increase in similarities. One time in particular almost half of those present saw some image that included a lion. Trust and bonding went hand in hand. They were even more resilient and lasting amongst TOPY individuals who participated in communal sigilising.

Each TOPY house had a nursery devoted to generating, maintaining, and amplifying psychic and magickal energies. We believed, and were convinced we were experiencing, genuine visions, out of body experiences, inter-dimensional portals, and ongoing connection to some power or phenomenon that we saw as a positive interrelationship with synchronicity. It seemed apparent to us all that committed repetition of a personally developed magickal language and set of talismanic objects could literally "FORCE THE HAND OF CHANCE." We were also sure that by using orgasm to in a sense "post" a desire into the deep conscious, bypassing social barriers and filters, the usual laws of probability broke down and one's effective focus was increased, making what you wished to happen more and more likely as you continued using sigils to reinforce your will. Redundant phobias and neuroses were stripped away, inadequacies were evaporated, and emotional baggage and distortion dropped away. The mind began to make day-to-day practical choices that would maximize the attainment of the willed desire, reinforced by your being, your various levels of consciousness resulting in an ever-increasing positive relationship with success in work, play and relationships. The sexual orgasm as reprogramming was not a new idea, but what TOPY did was discard elitist structures that made a person keep having to pay more for the next level of SECRETS that only this group were privy to; we did away with obfuscation and deliberate theatricality and mumbo jumbo and made public the "secret of all ages," the "9th degree of the OTO" and the "tantric essence" and we gave it away free, whilst publicly confessing that sex magick was central to our contemporary occult way of life. This was both our "selling" point and our downfall.

412

Thee Temple Ov Psychick Youth was an experimental community and network that took the practice of magical techniques seriously as a means to "short circuit control," as W. S. Burroughs once entreated me to make my primary life-long theme. Just as my time in the Exploding Galaxy had been a crash course in stripping away bourgeois values and inherited ways of being by using brutal deconditioning techniques and group sessions where one member would be pilloried and hounded emotionally for any visual, or physical repetitious behavior patterns. Why is your hair the same as it was yesterday? Why did you sleep in the same place as yesterday? Why do you need money? Clothes? Knives and forks? To write in straight lines? And on and on until a personality collapsed in ruins, hopefully to be replaced by a constantly regenerating form of creation and exploration that took nothing for granted. So COUM Transmissions had isolated symbolic identity and looked for methods to deconstruct identity and habituated types of individualized character. COUM had costumes that represented different archetypes. For example, Harriet Straitlace was a bigoted old lady, disgruntled with everything in modern life, always certain her past was far better than any present, blaming everyone and anyone for whatever annoyed her next. Mr. Alien Brain was an inter-dimensional visitor who was trying to observe and analyze humanity from an extra-terrestrial anthropologist perspective and was constantly baffled by the self-defeating ways of human beings. He was puzzled by war, violence, greed, religion, sexual guilt and commerce. TOPY tried to break personal habits and preconceptions, erase all cultural imperatives in order to generate an autonomous space for the practitioner to individualize their own identity and create their own fully chosen narrative.

TOPY grew far more than we had imagined, even though we demanded a rigorous series of sex magickal documents, charged via orgasmic fluid, blood, saliva and hair! These sigils began as a method of self-analysis to seek one's TRUE innermost desires and ambitions—but as months went by, they shifted from the more mundane urges for sexual partners and money into far more esoteric goals that dissected behavior, possible origins of life, matter and consciousness. Most Individuals would find themselves working with language and image to create symbolic glyphs and non-verbal systems to map out the nature of TIME, existence and perception. This journey we all made together became a communally experienced process and led my SELF back to the other, original Process. As we wrote essays and poems for newsletters, sharing our theories and experiences with each other we began adding the slogan:

413

> *THEE PRODUCT IS THEE PROCESS or*
> *THEE PROCESS IS THEE PRODUCT*

Within a year of having set up this interactive system we were receiving sigils every month from several hundred people. We were being asked for more and more information relating to "INTUITIVE MAGICK," as we dubbed it. People were finding that their Sigils seemed to be effective more often than any mathematical formula of randomness could explain. A desire would be created in a Sigil, orgasmic fluid etc added and the desire would begin to be fulfilled. The whole project exploded rapidly. It became impossible to answer all the mail so we improvised.

The more enthusiastic Individuals that got in touch were told that this was an open system, a self-generating program. So Access Points were born—a subgroup of TOPY Individuals who administered the Sigils, questions and suggestions for their region or Zone. The ever-increasing cost of post and printing led to a need for funds, and so TOPY Benefits were born. And TOPY merchandise. Which in turn made TOPY more visible in the street culture and therefore drew in more Individuals who in turn began more Access Points.

Here is a clear difference between TOPY and The Process. From the beginning TOPY gave a great deal of its materials away for free. We absorbed the postal and packing costs. We relied on volunteers giving their time to keep on top of correspondence and organizing events, designing and manufacturing regalia—whereas The Process demanded that new members give over everything they owned in a total financial commitment that in itself was a complete surrender to and thereafter dependence on the cult. During the first two years or so of TOPY, the impact of this constant drain on our resources was cushioned by extra income from the public face of TOPY, Psychic TV. We would have a TOPY stall at all the gigs selling propaganda, booklets, T-shirts, silver jewelry and so on. The sales people were volunteers active within TOPY and would spend time answering questions and encouraging participation in TOPY to those who seemed interested. TOPY grew initially by drawing in close friends and already established collaborators. Then it spread via newsletters, essays on the sleeves of records that would include our post box address and interviews in magazines, on the radio and on television.

In the Brighton TOPY era in the later 1980s, we looked for ways to lighten the burden on my income from Psychic TV and Temple Records by proposing more responsibility to the Access Points in fundraising. At one of our TOPY GLOBAL Annual Meetings, when Access Point Individuals and Station Individuals all met for several days to discuss policy, concepts, new projects and communities I remember I said, "Whilst I realize that we tend to be antagonistic to the bureaucratic, monolithic churches we should never ignore practical ideas, regardless of their source. We should look at how old-fashioned churches raise money. They have jumble sales, coffee mornings, fairs, thrift stores, etc. So let's use their methods to finance our alternative. By the next meeting we had a market stall every Saturday and Sunday in Camden Town selling records, booklets, regalia, T-shirts, second hand books and clothes, crafts made by TOPY Individuals and posters. One of my personal inspirations had always been Emmett Grogan and The Diggers. So we began a weekly Digger Stall in the park in Brighton where we would give away anything we didn't need for free. Furniture, books, clothes, tools, pottery, lamps. Anything! Just like Grogan and the 1960's San Francisco altruistic hippie group The Diggers we had a sign that said, "It's yours because it's free!"

Surprisingly, giving things away wasn't so easy. People waited for the catch. Some even insisted on donating money. We never got together a coffee shop/Cavern like The Process, but we talked about it many times. I still regret we failed to emulate The Process here, as it was obviously key to exposing new young people to The Process in Balfour Place. We did have a second market stall in Brighton that was run by TOPY House Individuals on a rota system that was a kind of thrift store curiosity shoppe. The Diggers were so absorbed into our ever developing TOPY mythology that one TOPY Individual living full time in our Brighton house changed his name legally to Emmett Grogan P-Orridge! Another TOPY Individual who was looking after our house whilst we were in Kathmandu, Nepal financing and running a soup kitchen for Tibetan refugees, beggars and lepers twice a day using funds donated by TOPY Individuals, changed HIS name legally to Alice Trip De Gaine, an anagram for "pierced genitalia". Poor old Alice was the courageous Individual who when "Thee Troubles" hit in 1992 was caretaking the TOPY STATION house in Brighton (Be-Right-On) and had the intimidating misfortune to open the front door to 23 (yes 23!!! Of course) police and detectives from Scotland Yard. To Alice's credit s/he remains totally loyal to the TOPI ideals as s/he interprets them. Which is another huge difference between The Process and TOPY. One insisted upon blind obedience to even the most extreme vagaries of the Omega interpretations of its ever contradictory and varying rules and theology whilst TOPY insisted on personally evolved theologies and interpretations of TOPY texts even if, even better if, they were contradictory!

We decided to keep sigils anonymous by giving each Individual a TOPY Name and number. Males were EDENs and females were KALIs. Strangely enough reading "LOVE SEX FEAR DEATH" by Timothy Wyllie we noticed both these names crop up in The Process but in all honesty doubt they were chosen for that reason as they were democrati-

415

coveted and seen as potently hierarchical as this had been adopted as a symbol for the active relationship with synchronicity that we believed TOPY rituals engendered. Instead we had twenty-three twenty-threes making it the LEAST special number of all. How random is random? as W. S. Burroughs would say. An Individual would speak out their number, i.e. "I am EDEN THREE TWO, or I AM KALI ONE NINE," etc. It would seem at first similar to The Process renaming new members. But the first motive for Edens and Kalis was security of sigils. As they were stored at the various Stations, they were vulnerable to being read for vicarious kicks—we even had one or two cases of Individuals working at TOPY Stations using knowledge of a sigiliser's sexual peccadilloes gleaned from sneaky looks to try and seduce the Individual later, using the information to seem like-minded in the erotic department. Any person found exploiting sigil information for his or her own ends was immediately disconnected. The Process, on the other hand, being far too often a manipulative tool for the Omega from what we learn from the book *LOVE SEX FEAR DEATH*, seems to have used new names to imprint their power and control upon Acolytes and later Messengers. It is a basic technique of traditional cults to remove ties with a past by changing names and it also solidifies the sense of belonging to a special, superior new community that has knowledge specific to itself that increases self-esteem as it is acquired by service to the group.

416

TOPY was built almost as an anti-cult. We hoped to avoid the traditional methods of engendering belonging by rejection of the past. So the names were used to give a sense of equality. After a year or two, we noticed that people with lower numbers were copping an attitude at TOPY gatherings, implying things like "I was here way before you! You're Eden 425 and I am Eden 10." So to prevent this, we began randomly mixing up the numbers every year so that NO sense of superiority or specialness could even be implied. What we did eventually decide to recognize after several years' activity, however, was dedication and longevity of application to the greater good. We also found a need to come to terms with a reality that there WERE casually involved Individuals, not much beyond consuming the events, music and products with only a passing interest in TOPY's deeper ambitions and aspirations. Other people regularly gave time and assistance to TOPY Access Points and Stations; others lived in TOPY houses full time in the UK, Germany, Holland and the USA.

Beyond even that full-time dedication to TOPY as a way of life were those of us, very similar in a way to The Process' Masters, who not only lived in TOPY houses full-time, but also made TOPY our occupation. All our work was for TOPY projects and/or projects that funded TOPY directly. Sister Shadows and Brother Words ran Temple Press, publishing "occultural" books, as we dubbed them. We strongly encourage readers of Thee Psychick Bible to seek out and acquire ANY Temple Press books as they are all practical and/or inspirational. One series of books was called RATIO THREE to signify the level of information and focus represented by its publication.

In The Process, autocracy, matriarchy and an expectation of strict obedience were imposed by the Omega—there's no question that a totalitarian system can facilitate maintaining an unorthodox organization. There were times we coveted such monolithic techniques, but, in the end TOPY persevered with as democratic a system as possible. I had become disenchanted with the Exploding Galaxy when I discovered that whilst I was adhering absolutely to the rigorous and demanding rules of asceticism the titular leader had created a bedroom, was spending communal money on hand made shoes for his (forbidden) monogamous and regular girlfriend, who was having private dentistry to boot. Having pointed this out in a psychotherapeutic session I was declared a non-person and refused food, talk, work or any interaction until I left. Sadly, another member, nicknamed Lemon, succumbed to this cruel domination and had a nervous breakdown, becoming catatonic, just before I left. So, I was determined to try and avoid both the petty pitfalls of communal living, and the terrors of authoritarianism if at all possible. What we did eventually confess to ourselves was that, with the best will in the world, people connect with a group like TOPY or The Process at whatever level of commitment they are ready for and prepared to accept at any given time. So we internally began to use a table of RATIOS to simplify day to day running of the ever more complex community and network. At its peak in the late 1980s, TOPY had around 10,000 Individuals sigilising and/or connected worldwide with Access Points in England, Scotland, Holland, West Germany, U.S.A., Canada, Italy, Australia, Sweden (and Scandinavia). So contact and purchase of *Thee Grey Book* (our basic mission statement and explanation of sigils and magic) was Ratio One; sending in sigils at all even if the required 23 were not achieved was Ratio Two; active involvement in

417

an Access Point and/or completion of 23 consecutive sigils was Ratio Three; administration of an Access Point, or active participation in a TOPY Station and/or living full-time in a TOPY house was Ratio Four and full-time dedication of one's life and works to TOPY projects like Temple Records, Temple Press and being full-time prime administrator of a TOPY Station and/or co-running TOPY GLOBAL STATION in Brighton on a need-to-know basis was Ratio Five. We never released this development to the general public or TOPY Individuals, as we were concerned that it would create elitism and smell of hierarchies. We mainly used these demarcations to decide who got to read more sensitive memoranda and/or were informed of legal and media crises as our world disintegrated in a way uncannily identical to the way The Process did twenty years earlier!

TOPY communal L-if-E was also a lot of FUN, a game of possibilities where we took our daydreams seriously and tried to always manifest anything that seemed like a good idea as a matter of TOPY principle.

418

During the later years of TOPY we began to feel that just obsessing on personal self-improvement and "therapy" was not enough. That once one had redesigned one's SELF and made a magical view of the Universe an intrinsic concept in one's behavior there had to be more. As a more purely realized Individual one becomes aware of one's inclusion in the human species. An awakened re-integration as a functioning and loving part of humanity is the inevitable next level of resolution and direction as an autonomous being. I had always been drawn to Tibetan Buddhism from around nine years old when I read *Seven Years in Tibet* by Heinrich Harrer whilst sick and off school. Later I acquired a Tibetan thighbone trumpet, an amazing singing bowl and other instruments that were played on *Themes One*, the record that accompanied *Force Thee Hand Ov Chance* by Psychic TV in 1983. Continuing my search for comprehension of life, the Universe, nonsensus reality and the mystery of conscious-but-mortal life, I began visiting Samye Ling Tibetan monastery with my family. Weirdly enough (or not as the story of TOPY might suggest) the founder of Samye Ling wasChogyam Trungpa Rinpoche who was briefly connected to The Process and of course Burroughs. Later in 1991 -92 I was given the responsibility of mentoring one of the Rinpoches' sons during my months in Kathmandu, Nepal to introduce him to alternative belief systems, lifestyles and religions! These kinds of piling up of connections can make one dizzy with possible implications.

The intersections and similarities between my TOPY experience and The Process seem significant in some ethereal manner. It is pointless to speculate upon them. One thing was central to TOPY, apart from all the tactics and vivid aspects, and that was that beyond all else we desperately wanted to discover and develop a system of practices that would finally enable us and like-minded Individuals to consciously change our behavior, erase our negative loops and become focused and unencumbered with psychological baggage. The Process, certainly at its inception, seems to me to have had similar high ideals. Where the two experiments diverge is the incipient hierarchy that ultimately seems to have disintegrated The Process whilst TOPY, though it struggled so hard to avoid having a "Leader" or an "Omega," still fell foul of a surprisingly tenacious appetite in most people involved to create a "Leader," a guru figure who was then resented for NOT having all the answers. My rejection of that pressure to become the Omega figurehead and other Individuals' accusations that we had become hierarchical caused a splintering and an amount of jealousy that we never really resolved before the whole thing became too draining and monolithic, leading TOPY STATION in Brighton to declare on an enigmatic postcard sent to everyone on our mailing list…

419

CHANGED PRIORITIES AHEAD.

By 1991, what had become a dedicated inner circle drawn from the Brighton TOPY contingent who were called RATIO FIVE (the closest TOPY had to an "OMEGA") had been traveling around the north of England looking at various properties for sale. As weekly routines and rituals had developed in Brighton amongst the five houses, a group feeling had grown directing us to want to make a next step in communal living. Our sense of deeply bonding through our "Life Story" exercises, telepathy circles, and some Gestalt routines I had gradually introduced were profoundly stripping away so many complexes and neuroses in what we all believed were effective, healing ways. And a real craving to go deeper, push ourselves harder to expose and shed all previous identities and personalities began to obsess us. Clearly, those Individuals prepared to seek revelation no matter how much psychological or emotional pain might be ahead, proposed that it was time to find a "BIG HOUSE" somewhere rural and remote enough for us to be undisturbed, peaceful, self-sufficient to some degree and able to have the option of naked, outdoors ceremonies and rituals without provoking neighbours or the media.

This is when the RATIO FIVE found themselves sensing an oncoming rift within TOPY. By this time I was regularly consulting my Process archives and commentaries for solutions to organizational problems and new psychological "games" to maintain the intellectual forward motion of TOPY. At what turned out to be the last formal TOPY GLOBAL assembly in Brighton we chose to reveal various problems that had arisen. Unlike The Process, which insisted on the surrender of all assets upon joining, TOPY was funded primarily by Temple Records and Temple Press and to a far lesser degree the various market stalls. As the network grew, so did the drain on our personal incomes. The RATIO FIVE were subsidizing TOPY and it was beginning to feel like we were working longer and longer hours to keep publications and events flowing whilst the vast majority of Individuals had become consumers who only turned up for the fun but were glaringly absent when hard work was needed. The Ratio Five put this inequity up for discussion and were shocked at the bitter response they received. We had suggested that upon acquisition of a Big House any TOPY Individuals applying to live there full time would have to donate a to-be-decided minimum proportion of their assets. We felt that if we were selling our homes in order to purchase a building large enough to be a robust and workable community, it was only fair that others benefiting from our faith in TOPY should also give at least enough to prove their sincere commitment to making a living example of our idealistic concept for a radical contemporary evolutionary lifestyle.

In our evolutionary fervour we were shocked at the resentment and financial constipation we faced. It seemed that anything we supplied that was attractive, stimulating, exciting, fun and FREE was great and consumed happily with gusto, but request even a paltry donation to make it happen and you were "just another greedy cult," trying to "rip us off" and similar deflections from the truth as we saw it. This was a depressing day. Suddenly The Process (and Zendik and others) approach was illuminated and illuminating. Our altruism had set up an illusory image and expectation. We had imagined that everyone was as totally committed as we were, because they said they were and we believed them.

The schism that had ruined the momentum of The Process was, we had felt, about the distribution of power amongst the Omega and, to a slightly lesser extent, how those alliances within the inner circle(s) and also the depth and distribution of loyalty amongst the members got played out. I had hoped to "remember the past and try NOT to be condemned to repeat it." But we had hit a serious intransigent and stubborn block and bloc. With hindsight I can see the rebel faction were jealous of the charisma and respect that tended to be associated with my SELF and also the Ratio Five inner circle in Brighton. We seemed to have the more glamorous role, media visibility (mainly vicious and negative, but notoriety appeals to the young) and I had a nice house and car. None of this was paid for by TOPY; in fact the reverse. The reality was that all my decades of hard work making art and music seemed impossible for them to grasp. By the end of TOPY's public existence, Ratio Two Individuals who were living rent and utility bill free in the Georgian TOPY house I'd purchased emptied bank balances, maximized debts on printing and other accounts, vandalized the Nursery as well as the kitchens, bathrooms and many walls whilst Psychic TV were away on tour in the USA to replenish the very funds they were being trusted with access to. Access Points indeed! Analysis of my oracular template, The Process, did not bode well for our future.

At the same time that the money schism was rupturing ten years' dedication, we also felt obliged to bring up the ongoing but more threatening matter of a yellow media witch hunt. I was starting to question the wisdom of referencing The Process as our tactical mirror, and things were getting spooky in all the wrong ways.

Just before I had taken my family away from East London to Brighton in 1988, we were thrust into the public eye on a national level when The People newspaper ran a bogus, vicious, vicarious and sensational full-page article with the headline "THIS VILE MAN CORRUPTS KIDS—DEMI-GOD FEEDS POP FANS ON SEX, SADISM AND DEVIL RITES." We discovered we'd been under surveillance; casual and close friends and neighbours alike had been interrogated and bullied. Shades of "The Mindbenders of Mayfair" set off warning

421

bells in my head! I had been officially declared (again!) an enemy of society, a wrecker of morals as well as civilization and a target for any unscrupulous journalist and nutcase on the street using outrage as an excuse for intolerance.

During the time leading up to my speech to TOPY GLOBAL, my family and I had begun being subject to a growing campaign of harassment and disinformation again. A TOPY Individual working in the local post sorting office warned me our mail was being opened and copied by the "authorities" and to be careful. Not long before this warning, Scotland Yard had raided Mr. Sebastian's tattoo and piercing studio, later charging him and several other men, none of whom ever knew each other, with being a "Gay S&M porn ring." They were tried in the Old Bailey, usually reserved to try serial killers, spies and the worst of the worst criminals. This case became notorious as the "Spanner" case. I was originally on the list of people to try, and then my name dropped off. The case was tried by one judge, who eventually ruled piercing and tattooing a CRIMINAL act of grievous bodily harm, a charge immediately below manslaughter with a sentence up to seven years. One poor man received three years in prison for piercing his own foreskin! Souvenir photos he got developed for himself alone were the damning evidence. Mr. Seb got a maximum fine and initially a 7 year prison sentence, eventually reduced to "suspended" when the court discovered he was dying of cancer. All were found guilty, thus setting a legal precedent in Britain to prosecute ANYBODY with a piercing or tattoo, or who created one! Suddenly, in 1991, my body (and many of those in TOPY) was illegal. It seems impossible now, just fifteen or so years later, to believe this was true. Copies of *Modern Primitives*, the classic RE/Search book we'd helped put together and were featured in, were seized at customs. Clearly a right-wing faction of the Tory government, in collusion with powerful figures at Scotland Yard, were on a mission to marginalize, penalize and viciously shatter the lives of a blossoming gay scene they saw as corrupting and intolerable, and anyone else who they saw as proseletizing piercing and tattooing was obviously conspiring to undermine decent family values…which meant TOPY in general, and myself in particular.

We knew my name had been removed at the last minute from the list of those charged. But why? By deduction I had become aware that we were still being watched and investigated and wondered if that meant that they were planning to do something nasty to us separately. They'd used the only thing the Spanner case men had in common, the fact they were GAY, to link them, pretend they were a circle and therefore a conspiracy. I didn't fit into that stereotyping so, I was being saved up to be pilloried and stopped in my decadent tracks!

One of the side-effects of regular sigilising and telepathy and similar practices is an increased sensitivity to intuiting the ebbs and flows of events and future options for actions. I was convinced we were heading towards a nasty collision with the "establishment" once more. So, at TOPY GLOBAL, I raised this issue. I proposed increased vigilance and security at meetings—no strangers to have access to filing cabinets, rituals, Ratio Three or above meetings or publications. To my dismay I was immediately attacked as being egocentric and totalitarian for seeing myself as a target rather than everyone or nobody. The Ratio Five Individuals tried to point out that it was simply a fact of life that, fair or not, the lead singer of a band tends to be the public's focus, and also being the key founder of TOPY and a national media presence already, and thereby, inevitably, I was going to be interpreted and assumed to be the leader of TOPY like it or not, fair or not. The Process tried having a clear autocratic leadership in the Omega that was then wrapped in impenetrable secrecy contrary to TOPY's transparency and democracy. Both strategies failed when it came to confrontation with the absolute amorality and scurilousnes of the British yellow press. Just look at Aleister Crowley, Oscare Wilde and Quentin Crisp's experiences before ours. Frontal assault on these journalists is doomed by inequity.

423

TOPY GLOBAL got very combative and emotional and it became clear that resentment of anybody who found themselves in the "limelight" for any reason, was irrationally high. The Individuals who worked day in and day out for TOPY felt that they remained anonymous and invisible whilst their hard work consolidated and expanded the appearance of myself as titular "Leader" of TOPY. I could tour the world with Psychic TV with an ever-increasing fan base through their endless labors. Of course, there was enough truth in that equation to feed their rage and burgeoning intolerance of the "inner circle," Ratio Five. The only form of denial open to me was to state that my intentions were honorable—and, as TOPY says, "intention is the key." So my purity of motive was, I still believe, a personal disinterest in the ego glory but acceptance of it as a necessary cultural phenomenon whose upside was that it allowed TOPY to exist through its by-product of income. I was more or less howled down by a wolfpack who, it became clear, were organizing a coup of some kind.

One of our recent changes of policy, partly in response to the negative media campaign in Britain, was, very similarly to The Process, involve TOPY more directly in local community affairs. Perhaps we could defuse the predjudice and intimidation by doing "good works" that would familiarize us bit by bit for a public otherwise only fed horror stories. Apart from our Digger influenced free goods actions, over the course of several TOPY STATION meetings we FINALLY linked up directly with my secret, but integral, map for cult and anti-cult navigation of an antagonistic popular culture, The Process.

Through a mutual friend, Eve, I was introduced to Timothy Wyllie. Eve knew of my "fascination" with The Process and my search for the realities behind it rather than accept the tiny, vague amount of gratuitous misinformation available when she introduced us. Timothy was everything I'd hoped he might be and more and his sharp, dry intelligence and wit combined with his encyclopedic psychedelic knowledge and application of spiritual matters blew me away in the same inspirational cosmosis of energy that Brion Gysin and William S. Burroughs had.

When I met Timothy, I recall telling him that I had been "stalking" him and The Process since the sixties. It was meant humorously, but was also true in essence. Seeing the integrated clarity of his ways of being confirmed for me the residual constructive impact of The Process methodology and dedication, despite the negative and traumatic memories that went with it. At first Timothy was somewhat reluctant to discuss The Process. I understood why—I was, and really still am, reluctant to discuss TOPY with casual acquaintances. There is pain and disappointment there. It is hard for anyone to imagine what it feels like to be attacked over and over again not just by the yellow media, but by the government, harassed by the police, and alienated from friends and foes by the taint of lies and innuendos of vile secret behaviors and associations.

Timothy was living in New York at that time and was directing his beneficent resources towards Dolphin sentience, extra-terrestrials and angels. Brighton had a Dolphinarium where two dolphins suffered terribly, both psychologically and physically from cruel conditions. TOPY STATION decided to try and close the Dolphinarium by picketing the entrance every single weekend and peacefully asking people not to go inside and thus financially collude in the ongoing torture of these supra-intelligent beings. Over a year and a bit TOPY picketed the Dolphinarium rain and shine , never missing a weekend thanks to TOPY Individuals traveling from all over Britain and Europe to maintain our presence, eventually enlisting the support of animal rights groups. Psychic TV, Julian Cope, Captain Sensible of The Damned and other caring friends participated in benefits. We released a CD called KONDOLE (the Aboriginal name for a whale spirit) to finance the campaign. We received a secret message from sympathetic workers inside the Dolphinarium who'd risked their jobs (and would now lose them) by giving us information on the health of the dolphins to say the business WAS closing down for good! Magick in theory and practice indeed! Through the charity of the Aga Khan our two dolphins were flown to the Turks and Cacos Islands for rehabilitation. Timothy Wyllie had inspired us and as a marvelous side effect he has become a lifelong friend and mentor.

Timothy became my oracular fall back position. He had already been through all this and more, so in times of isolation, desolation and doubt I would call him for advice. We could both see a pattern that intimated trouble ahead in my public and private life.

425

Lama Yeshe, the retreat master at Samye Ling in Scotland, had suggested forcefully that I go to Nepal. So I called upon the TOPY network to donate good quality, new, warm children and baby clothes, packed them up in large numbers and flew my family to Kathmandu. He gave us the contact information for their monastery there. We had a children's clothes drive within TOPY and Psychic TV fans, and off we went. We linked up with Samye Ling's monastery there and financed, out of my savings, a twice daily clean water and meal kitchen at Boudhanath Stupa in Kathmandu. Some days we fed 300 to 400 Tibetan refugees, lepers and beggars. In between we took teachings and meditated. After a few days one of the monks asked me to become the mentor of Chögyam Trungpa Rinpoche's son! For the next months I would almost daily visit the monastery and take Chögyam's son on "field" trips to Shiva temples and other comparative religious sites. We made quite a sight, me in all black leather and him in his orange and saffron robes.

Suddenly a fax arrived: "SERIOUS TROUBLE—CALL HOME IM-MEDIATELY!" The witch hunting media bomb had exploded.

On Saturday, February 15, 1992, twenty-three Scotland Yard detectives from the Obscene Publications Squad, armed with a search warrant and video camera, raided my Brighton home. They seized two tonnes of photographic, video and other material (African drums, ethnic art, sex toys). On Sunday, February 16, 1992, *The Observer* ran a story entitled "Video offers first evidence of ritual abuse." It reported that they had a film of a "bloody satanic ritual" which they'd passed on to the police. Small fragments of this video were included in a one-hour TV docu-mentary series, *Dispatches*, on Channel Four, in which the journalist An-drew Boyd claimed it "shows abuse of young adults in what is clearly a ritual context. Sex and blood rituals are taking place beneath a picture of Aleister Crowley. The trappings of black magic are obvious," they claimed, as hazy, blurred and distorted images were televised.

These claims were backed by the (so-called) testimony of a cult survivor, calling herself Jennifer, who told in sick and graphic detail that this was her having a forced abortion to be used in sacrificial rituals(!), and by statements from the police and "medical experts."

426

By Sunday, February 23, *The Independent* on Sunday was able to report, truthfully at last, that these videos that were being used to claim to be the "first hard evidence ever of satanic child abuse" were actually made nine years earlier. One video was created for Spanish national television's "La Edad de Oro" program on Psychic TV, and the other as performance art commissioned by the same Channel Four, and that they featured film director Derek Jarman as the visual presenter of a fictional cult in an ex-ercise of how media can manipulate perceptions and control responses! Derek was quoted saying, "At first I was horrified and then very, very angry that they had so misrepresented scenes from the video. It was not even ABOUT child abuse or murder. It seemed too much when you had a lady on the telly, blacked out, saying she had killed her child. I mean, doesn't anyone smell a rat?"

By Sunday, March 1, 1992, *The Mail on Sunday* newspaper had traced the elusive "Jennifer." She was named as Louise Errington, mother of two healthy children and one-time born-again Christian, who had

NEVER had any contact, not even by mail, with anyone connected to TOPY. In 1990 Louise had stayed at Ellel Grange, a "Christian" healing center in Lancaster, England. She was now quoted as saying, "There, the charismatics had an overpowering effect on me. In many ways that was the worst three months of my life. They told me I was possessed by demons because of the sins of my mother and father. They prayed over me in tongues and taught me to face my own guilt."

One day she met the Christian cult's spiritual leader, Peter Horrobin. He told her one of his prayer team had a vision, "He had seen a mind picture of me standing over a tiny baby helping a devil priest cut into the baby's chest, the blood was collected and we drank it. The baby's body was a sacrifice to Satan." Louise had never had this baby of course. She continued, "I screamed and pleaded with them to stop it, then I had a kind of fit and had to be held down by these Christians. I fought people off physically. Finally I broke down and confessed it was true. I said YES! I did it, I killed my own little daughter and helped others to kill their babies."

The confession of this key "witness" in the *Dispatches* program (and the others in the same way) was brought about by the horrific vision of paranoid, malicious born-again Christans. None of the three "witnesses" had even heard of TOPY when asked.

On March 22, the author, researcher and presenter admitted to inconclusive research, misleading identification and entirely fabricated testimonies.

But the damage was done. Always in the shadow of the Spanner case, in which TOPY had openly supported and provided funds, safe haven and security for Mr. Sebastian, it became apparent that I had been singled out as a scapegoat for everything in British culture that disturbed the status quo and the conservative government's witch-hunt style paranoia. I was advised that if we returned from Nepal, Scotland Yard would arrest me and hold me for questioning indefinitely and take my two daughters into custody, who would then likely be interrogated for evidence of child abuse. A completely false accusation of abuse usually led to your children being in the State's care for two or more years, regardless of truth. We have never, to this day, been charged with anything. Nor has my archive and property been returned—in fact, Scotland Yard have implied it was all destroyed, for no legal reason.

Our attorney told us in a frank phone call that our best course of action to protect our children and ourselves was to go into exile, as off-the-record someone at Scotland Yard had said they could not guarantee my physical safety if I returned. Which he said he interpreted as a serious and real threat from unknown but officially sanctioned persons. He felt we were being told to stay away or expect "extreme predjudice". To this day the idea of being obliquely threatened with (gosh it seems so weird even now to type this but it IS what was discussed) "assassination" by accident, vanishing, random murder or suicide the options are endless for any cabal with protected and politically limitless power feels very surreal, still scary and also a ludicrous over-reaction, no matter how insincere or casual the intimidation. And, as people have pointed out since, it was a great compliment to TOPY that we were seen as subversive and well-organized enough to merit such "special" attention. Needless to say, with two wonderful children to protect it was a no brainer and we agreed to not go back to Britain to fight the smear campaign in the media and, if necessary, the courts. This decision was reinforced by the knowledge that such noteables as Crowley, Crisp, and Wild had tried that tactic and failed. So we needed to conceive of a different strategy, to take our time and consider our other options.

428

I went to seek advice from Dzongsar Khyentse Rinpoche and the Tibetan monks we worked with at the soup kitchen we had financed. He said, "Go to America." A Hindu Aghori Baba said the same thing. In my confusion at the turn of events despite knowing Dzongsar would be correct in his advice my natural need for affirmation took me back to Paglananda Aghori Baba who had given me insight into their path of no distinction (see the GNOSIS interview elsewhere) and I asked him the same question. "I am an exile now, a refugee, where do I go next?"… "America!" he said, laughing so heartily the 24 carat gold Psychick Cross I had given him bounced on his ash smeared chest. There are times when the options are simple, no matter how much WE hope for a more fuzzy escape from our destiny.

In one of those classic magickal moments that seem to befriend one through repeated ritual and focus, as I sat in the hotel room in Kathmandu wondering where to go I messed idly about with some unopened post I had thrown in my bag as we left England. It was from Michael Horowitz, archivist for Dr. Timothy Leary, and in it he had written, "If you ever need a refuge, call me at this number." I did, and he immediately offered myself and my family sanctuary at his home in Peta-luma. I returned to the Tibetan Rinpoche, and after joking that we were all refugees now, I gave him my remaining $5000 to cover the cost of a small water-powered electricity generator for his monastery so they could avoid ecological disaster burning all the surrounding trees. It was an act of faith in magick and truth. I kept just enough to get to Califor-nia. I had maxed out the cash I could get with my credit cards and knew there was no more in England even if I could access it which was in doubt at this point. After giving the Tibetans the $5000 in my stash to build their generator I was essentially close to penniless. But the Tibet-tans who ran the Vajra Hotel offered us indefinite free accommodation in return for our months of "good works" and, in the end, Wax Trax Records paid for our tickets one-way to America.

At "home" the TOPY network that I had forwarned of this kind of action disintegrated. Only the Individuals of Ratio Five lifted a finger to help, or support, or publicly speak up in my defence. The rest hid or even gloated, unaware of any irony. And suddenly, there I was, exiled in America, just like The Process and for much the same reason, the small minded and bigoted parochialism of the grey minions of inherited wealth and power.

I can see how The Process experienced an equally irrational campaign to destroy, cripple financially and break the will of their members for having the audacity to build a set of Logics that included the names of Jehovah, Satan, Lucifer and later Christ. Hindsight tells me that, just as TOPY underestimated the outrage that inclusion of sexuality in its mission would cause to its folly, so The Process misjudged the ongoing bigotry and hypocrisy of the establishment when they included Satan and Lucifer in their panoply of gods. Who would have guessed, though, that in the swinging sixties' liberation from inhibition and oppression there would still be such a furor over those antiquated notions? I often speculate what might have transpired if those red rags to a John Bull had NOT been used as symbols of the personality type ratios. Would the gutter press have left The Process alone? Would its evolution have continued inexorably until it was as established as other cults like the Moonies, Scientology, etc.? Certainly the use of SATAN in particular seems to have been a strategic problem, as things turned out. But we have to ask ourselves WHY? Why do certain concepts like "Satan" or the open inclusion of orgasm and sexuality in an experimental search for a more integrated and integrity-based way of life cause politicians, clergy and journalists to dub me, for example, a "wrecker of civilization"? Or a national newspaper to trumpet that I "should be bound in chains, locked in a cage and the key thrown away"? This book may not answer that question directly. But keep in mind that fear of the unknown, coupled with corruption in places of power and a dreary but paranoid policy of maintaining the power of vested interests long after they are redundant at all costs underlies the façade of our mundane daily culture. Freedom of thought, self-designed ethics and a questioning mind with an altruistic belief in the potential for positive evolution in our human species can expose to the light the impoverished decay of society. The Process was ostracized and forced into exile in the United States, and then my self and my family were forced into exile in 1991 for our essential involvement and faith in TOPY.

Genesis Breyer P-Orridge, NYC 2008

430

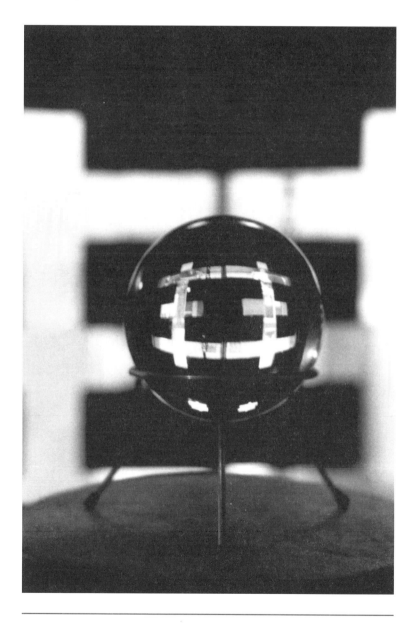

Image by Genesis Breyer P-Orridge

THE TREE OF SELF-KNOWLEDGE [18]

SELF-KNOWLEDGE [9]

| RECONCILIATION WITH MORALITY [10] | INTEGRATION OF SELF [11] | GUILTLESSNESS [12] |

| WISDOM [13] | INNER FREEDOM [14] | TRUE WILL [15] |

D I S C I P L I N E

| AWARENESS [16] | CONTROL OF ROBOT [16] | WILL POWER [17] |

ACTION

You ought to learn more about yourself, Think more than just I, I, I. [17]

What appears to be an infatuation with the Self is in fact not selfish at all, as the Individual is, through self-knowledge, aware and in control of the Ego.

In modern times, there is no lack of understanding of the fact that man is a social being and 'no man is and Island, entire of itself'. [18] *Hence there is no lack of extortion that he should love his neighbour, or at least not be nasty to him, and should practise tolerance, compassion and understanding. At the same time however the culture of self-knowledge has fallen into virtually total neglect, unless, that is to say, it is the object of active suppression. That you cannot love your neighbour unless you love yourself; that you cannot understand your neighbour unless you understand yourself; that there can be no knowledge of the invisible person, 'the intentions behind the actions, 'who is your neighbour except on the basis of self-knowledge—these fundamental truths are forgotten even by many of the professionals of the established religions.'* [19]

It is clear that self-knowledge is in fact to the benefit of all provided the necessary discipline is exerted to externalise the internal workings this involves.

None of these concepts, here outlined in shorthand form, are new or revolutionary, nor are they intended to be. They are simply those which Catholic or Psychic Youth may utilise having appealed to his/her reason.

Now it is up to Catholic or Psychic Youth, him or her, to find a satisfactory method of training (discipline) to produce self-control. There are many people and institutions that would (in)sincerely care to lay down this system of training in a dogmatic and authoritarian manner.

However, for a real realization and use of these and assimilated concepts the Individual must always have to establish discipline by themself for their Self.

It would seem that in so doing it is vital for the Individual to take into account the curious and diverse methods/rituals worked out and used by others over the centuries. To use an alchemical metaphor: no stone should be left unturned in search of the Philosopher's Stone.

433

The slender knowledge referred to earlier is virtual. All of us have some slender knowledge of being conscious of our own self-consciousness. All of us have some experience of the intangible truth of sensual feeling and the power of intellect.

Individuals of the Temple combine these three experiences into one in their method/rituals as the final stage (ACTION!) in the self-knowledge tree. [20]

These are experiences to be wondered at, and as Socrates said:

> *Wonder is the feeling of a philosopher and philosophy beings with wonder...No god is a philosopher or seeker after wisdom for he is wise already. Neither do the ignorant seek after wisdom; for herein*

is the evil of ignorance, that he is neither good nor wise is neverthe-less satisfied with himself.[21]

We seek after wisdom only to be able to develop a personal philosophy comprehensive enough to embrace the whole of knowledge, a belief *so vast that all the contradictions can easily move around in it.*[22] This is indis-pensable as a place where slender knowledge of these experiences can be shared. This is vital if we are to achieve any of the things we strive for. We can all learn from others' disciplines for taping the second and third levels on the Tree of Self-Knowledge. Others' descriptions and use of these three experiences give us all the proof we need.

Both Catholic and Psychic Youth believe that the full potential of man is set by the *greats* of humanity. We all possess within us (as latent pow-ers) the visionary brilliance of the great poets, artists, and philosophers, which under active imagination gives rein to astral projection, psycho-kinesis, telepathy, precognition, second sight...

The Psychic Youth, however, believes that it is due to science and reli-gion that these facilities are lacking.

434

The present danger does not lie in the loss of universality on the party of the scientist, but rather in his pretence and claim of totality...What we have to deplore therefore is not so much the fact that scientists are specialising, but rather the fact that scientists are generalising.[5]

Western man has fallen into a state of inpotence because his civilisation is ratio-nal and superficial. And the Christian Church is to some extent to blame for this predicament. Christianity with its increasingly dogmatic content has 'alienated consciousness from its natural roots in the unconscious.'[23]

The Temple ov Psychick Youth refutes the methods and rituals of both these bodies as they actively supress the development (or at best inertly ignore existence) of these facilities.

Our science is methods/rituals, obsessed with backwardness, reiter-ate the uselessness of all material things in themselves. In our hands they are useful tools for self-awareness. Outside this they are nothing. Whether it is a method of destruction, a method of indoctrination, or a method of promoting superficiality, it is entirely meaningless and a complete waste of time and energy.

To foister these things as the importance of life, as Big Brother and Big Business would have us believe, is ludicrous.

Commentary on Tree of Self-Knowledge A glance at this tree sees actions as the most important Sephiroth, being the end result of all other Sephiroth. Yet, however important the result is, it is the inner workings that to the Individual will be the most virtual and s/he will be constantly re-evaluating these. The action will either express these workings in material form to one's Self and others, or be used to develope these inner workings further—the alchemist's tools.

The Tree is random, like life—a Chaos, and so any order one wishes to impose on this randomness is simply to heighten one's understanding of the Chaotic systems[1] involved. This order is not philosophy in itself as some would have us believe. Again it is a tool to be put into PRAC-TICE by the Individual, who could and should impose his own order as the author has done. The author's order is a trigger for others.

435

The Tree is meaningless until put into PRACTICE, as are all theories. The Temple ov Psychick Youth is PRACTICING NOW. All the methods-results-conclusions[2] are available to all involved once the Individual is at the stage where comparisons and evaluations of this kind are necessary and useful.[3] If these ideas are confused and misleading NOW, burn them NOW. See how many levels they have fallen; Man's Intellect-(Man-Animal-Plant-)Mineral. Will your flame be the one to be thrown down to where they can have no effect?

Words without provocation are as meaningless as philosophy without application.

1 deliberate contradiction
2 yes, a scientific process
3 the author here associates pain with implantation

Our religion's methods/rituals of repetitive prayers, voluntary fasting, celibacy...for some Individuals may follow the outline of the Tree of

Self-Knowledge. However, as the Church is an instructive body, the action that comes out of these inner realisations is always set in the emotional/moral realm of reference of the Instructor. As the Instructor is inherently conformist and concerned with the perpetuation of the status quo, the chance of this method provoking an evolutionary breakthrough is remote. The hand of this chance has been forced in history only by those groups/Individuals setting off at a tangent to their Instructor, the degree of which is calculated with care.

This can be seen in a century where the so-called 'enlightened' are in fact simply obsessed with bludgeoning all into their pseudo-religious moral crusades.

So let us herald our very own crusade! We who do not believe awareness can be forced down people's throats. We who desire to share and exchange real knowledge and experience. We who care to educate and be educated, to bring things out of ourselves and others. We who refuse to shroud and mystify our ideas and ideals with coats of crap; we who have a love of life and Individuals so strong as to break our hearts each day and night. We who fight so as not to be trampled underfoot. We call ourselves the Temple ov Psychick Youth, we who unite yet stand apart.

C Richard Jevons, 23.01.84

The Temple ov Psychick Youth can be a constant reminder to be referred to and compared against the actions of work of the Individual. Just as a Catholic could refer to a place of worship where guilt is lodged in the mind of the Individual so a Psychick Youth should be able to refer back to the place where the freedom of absolute guiltlessness is lodged in the mind. [1]

Both Catholic and Psychick Youth will use these references to gauge the validity of their work. [2] The intention of the Catholic may be to purify the Individual through avoidance of sin but the method os so guilt-ridden and fear-provoking that the result is negative positivism. The original positive intention to move forward is negated by the fear and guilt of doing so.

Both Catholic and Psychick Youth refute the maps [3] of real knowledge we are given. We do not believe that only those things that can be proved to exist are of importance. Neither do we believe that those things for which there is no proof of existence are unimportant.

The slanderest of knowledge that may be obtained of the hightest things is more desirable than the most certain knowledge obtained of lesser things. [4]

So-called scientific objectivity proclaims that man is *nothing but a complex biochemical mechanism powered by a combustion system which energises computers with prodigious storage facilities for retaining encoded information;*[5] or even worse *a naked ape.* [6] We recognize that under scientific methods/ rituals these observations are correctly made. [7] Therefore we prefer to use our own methods/rituals which, unlike the scientific, take into account those followed by virtually all our ancestors, until a quite recent generation.

...behaviour baffles me. For I find myself not doing what I really want to do but doing what I really loathe. Yet surely if I do things that I really don't want to do, it cannot be said that *I* am doing them at all. *We can not only conclude from this that here is not only more than one "I" but also that one seems to be higher than the other (as one "I" judges the other). St. Paul incidentally concludes that it must be sin that has made its home in my nature.* This Sephiroth also includes the integration of the subconscious with the conscious.

437

Notes

0 All references and quotations express to the author some intangible truth /slender knowledge that he has felt or experienced and sees here put in an understandable and honest manner. They are literary formulations of earlier inner realisations.

1 This place as well as being imaginary may well be a remembrance of physical activities or indeed ideally a place where these activities may be realised unrestricted.

2 Work here also means the path of life they are following, not necessarily magickal though.

3 These maps may be seen in any place of education (or anti-education, for rather than bringing out) these institutions put in.

4 St. Thomas Aquinas: *Summa Theological*, I, i , 5, ad i.

5 Victor E. Frankl: *Reductionism and Nihilism* in A. Koestler and J.R. Smythies' (eds) *Beyond Reductionism.*

6 The ultimate insult to man's potential.

7 That is because if emotions/feelings cannot be measured or calculated they do not exist. This 'pragmatic' attitude is slowly being taken over by another where these feelings exist, but only if they have practical applications which can be measured. Neither is satisfactory.

8 See *Commentary on the Tree of Self-Knowledge* having studied this tree.

9 A.k.a. self awareness of self-consciousness.

10 See Victor Neuberg.

11 What Jung refers to as *individual*. Abraham Maslow calls this *self-actualisation*, Colin Wilson *wholeness*. As St. Paul observes in a letter to the Romans: *My own...*

12 See Marc Almond's *Guiltless* or A. Crowley's fear-conquering methods.

13 *Recognising the poverty of philosophical opinions, not adhering to any of them, seeking the truth, I saw.* From *Suttanipata*, IV, ix, 3.

14 Stemming from the five Sephiroth surrounding.

15 Both Crowleyan terms. The latter is the amount of power one has to govern one's surroundings through action, as opposed to the surroundings governing the action. The former is the director of this action.

16 These two Sephiroth can be loosely tied together. The latter is Colin Wilson's term (see *Mysteries*). What Gurdjieff calls *non-mechanical consciousness*, Ouspensky *overcoming sleep* (see Maurice Nicoll's *Psychological Commentaries on the Teaching of Gurdjieff and Ouspensky*).

17 Lou Reed: *Caroline Says*.

18 John Donne: *Devotion*, xvii.

19 E.F. Schumacher: *A Guide for the Perplexed*.

20 See the first *Temple Manual*.

21 Plato: *Symposium*, trans. Jowett.

22 Remy de Courmont.

23 C.G. Jung: *Psychology and Alchemy* in C. Wilson's *Mysteries*.

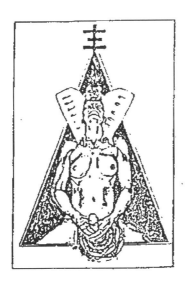

Pandrogeny

XIV

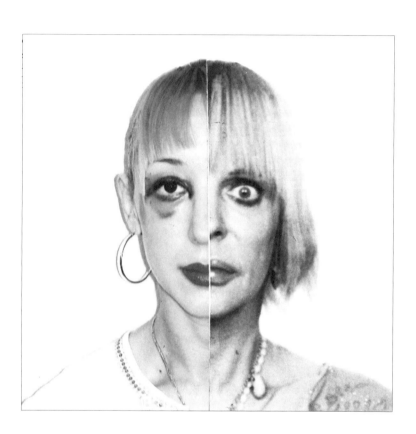

Image by Genesis Breyer P-Orridge

BREAKING SEX

t seems useful to us, in our practice, to adopt the assumption that there is no way of knowing which has supremacy, the recording device that is DNA, or the SELF we converse with internally that we *call* consciousness but often, rather lazily, still imagine and identify as the living, biological, body. In fact, we see the "I" of our consciousness as a fictional assembly or collage that resides in the environment of the body.

One of the central themes of our work is the malleability of physical and behavioural identity. The body is used by the mind as a logo, an hieroglyph for the SELF before we are able to speak and use language. It is almost an holographic doll constructed by external expectations even before our body is born. Even the name we are assigned is another holographic program in the prophetic story of who we are to become.

The work of William S Burroughs and Brion Gysin has been highly influential to us, particularly in relation to the practice of the "cut-up." To liberate the word from linearity, they began to cut-up and, incorporating random chance, re-assembled both their own and co-opted literature "...to see what it really says..." They referred to the phenomena of profound and poetic new collisions and meanings that resulted from their intimate collaborations as the "Third Mind." This was produced with a willingness to sacrifice their own separate, previously inviolate works and artistic "ownership." In many ways they saw the third mind as an entity in and of itself. Something "other," closer to a purity of essence, and the origin and source of a magical or divine creativity that could only result from the unconditional integration of two sources.

Beginning in the 1960s, especially from being an active participant in the Exploding Galaxy/Transmedia Exploration and occasionally the Gay Lib street theatre, Genesis Breyer P-Orridge experimented with various disciplines and practices to apply the cut-up to behaviour, to identity and to gender; de-conditioning as far as possible the fictional character written by consensus reality and all who would impose their expectations upon him. Breyer P-Orridge worked throughout the 1970s as a performance artist and actionist; and during the 1980s s/he studied and practiced ritual and shamanic techniques and was deeply involved in the body modification movement known as "modern primitives." In the early 1990s Genesis Breyer P-Orridge met Lady Jaye Breyer P-Orridge and their ever more rigorous collaborations began.

Just as Burroughs and Gysin collaborated together, subsuming their separate works, individuality and ego to a collaborative process by cutting-up the Word to produce a third mind, so, in our current practice, Breyer P-Orridge have applied the cut-up system and third mind concept directly to a central concern, the fictional SELF. The un-authorised Astory of our lives so far. Breyer P-Orridge both supply our separate bodies, individuality and ego to an ongoing and substantially irreversible process of cutting-up identity to produce a third being, an "other" entity that we call the PANDROGYNE.

In our quest to create the Pandrogyne, both Genesis and Lady Jaye have agreed to use various modern medical techniques to try and look as much like each other as possible. We are required, over and over again by our process of literally cutting-up our bodies, to create a third, conceptually more precise body, to let go of a lifetime's attachment to the physical logo that we visualise automatically as "I" in our internal dialogue with the SELF.

We encounter many unexpected internal conflicts as our egos try to survive intact as the "person" they have been previously conditioned to accept without question and then BE. We have discovered that how we look does relate very directly to the internal dialogue that describes us to our SELF and to each other. This is not superficial in its effect when we suddenly instruct our mind to realize that everything about this logo of our SELF is malleable, vulnerable and impermanent.

When you consider transexuality, cross-dressing, cosmetic surgery, piercing and tattooing, they are all calculated impulses—a symptomatic groping towards a next phase. One of the great things about human beings is that they impulsively and intuitively express what is inevitably next in the evolution of culture and our species. It is the Other that we are destined to become.

Pandrogeny is not about defining differences but about creating similarities. Not about separation but about unification and resolution.

Breyer P-Orridge believe that the binary systems embedded in society, culture and biology are the root cause of conflict, and agression which in turn justify and maintain oppressive control systems and divisive heirarchies. Dualistic societies have become so fundamentally inert, uncontrollably consuming and self-perpetuating that they threaten the continued existence of our species and the pragmatic beauty of infinite diversity of expression. In this context the journey represented by their PANDROGENY and the experimental creation of a third form of gender-neutral living being is concerned with nothing less than strategies dedicated to the survival of the species.

"WE ARE BUT ONE…" becomes less about individual gnosis and more about the unfolding of an entirely new, open-source, 21st-century myth of creation.

CHANGE THE WAY TO PERCEIVE
AND CHANGE ALL MEMORY.
Lady Jaye Breyer P-Orridge and Genesis Breyer P-Orridge New York, 2003

445

PSYCHIC TV/PTV3 STATEMENT
REGARDING TRANSGENDERED RIGHTS
At the proposed venue ANDERSON'S in ARIZONA

When PTV3 was booked to play at Tom Anderson's Club on Monday 27th August 2007 we were completely unaware of the ongoing civil rights issues and the local controversy surrounding the club's owner's victimization of transgender persons.

As our tour has progressed we began receiving email messages from the promoters expressing concerns about the continued viability of the venue under these volatile circumstances. Due to the wonders of MYSPACE technology we also received haunting pleas and disturbing enquiries from Gay, Lesbian & Transgender activists AND individuals.

They asked us to consider canceling our concert rather than appear to endorse Tom Anderson and company's actions, albeit by default. We heard that due to some complaints by unidentified biological women concerning the use of the women's bathrooms at the club by transgender and transvestite persons the women's bathrooms would be guarded by security to prevent further non-specific gender use. There is a real difference between both those communities that is often overlooked. Transgender people absolutely commit their lives and physical bodies to becoming the opposite gender identity to that with which DNA supplied them at birth. This is often at great personal cost and sacrifice. They often are ostracized by family, friends, workmates and their local community. No person changes gender identity lightly and ALL in an enlightened democracy must honor the courage of our brothers and sisters in the transgender community. No transgender person identifying as female would ever stand up to pee, which seems to be the problem at the heart of this issue locally.

Transvestites choose to temporarily dress as the opposite gender and whilst in their (in this instance) female persona will consider themselves temporarily "female". Whilst it may well be possible that certain transvestites were "standing to pee" one MUST consider the alternatives.

446

Transgender women cannot use male bathrooms without genuine fear of harassment, ridicule, humiliation and violence. Our culture is constructed upon pre-historic behavior patterns that originate in male dominated cave clans where survival was imperative and rested upon attacking anything different, outside their experience, or just plain other; the unknown was always considered a threat and was always intimidated and usually attacked. 40 thousand years later it is time for us to become mature and communally remove these reactive, imprinted behaviors from our culture or be damned.

As the lead vocalist of Psychic TV I am perceived as transgender, and I am proud to be. I am perceived, and assumed to be FEMALE (even officially) by the club, yet I was informed that not only would I be forced to use a separate bathroom from other women, including my female spouse of 14 years, but also there would be "guards" policing the use of these segregated stalls! What exactly is the club afraid of? If the question is hygiene then I suggest an honor system based upon polite notices requesting all people perceiving themselves as women respect all varieties of women using the facilities by sitting to pee. And if anyone out there is under the illusion that women's bathrooms are innately more sterile and clean. Think again! Since becoming female I have been amazed at the level of porno-

graphic grafitti in women's stalls AND the equality of "spillage" and mess generated by both sexes.

The issue of transgender rights regarding public bathrooms is a national one. During my transition I was threatened with arrest at JFK Airport in New York for following the letter of the law and trying to use the men's bathroom. But to use the women's bathroom, which is what the security insisted I did, was at that time illegal...so WHERE exactly do you believe our community should pee? Are we less than citizens, like the slaves of not so long ago, and witnessing a return to a new form of segregation? Gender segregation?

This is why Tom Anderson's "solution" is and always was unacceptable. First he banned TWO entire communities for living out their Constitutional rights to SELF-DETERMINED IDENTITY. Then he proposed policed segregation. In many states in the U.S.A. it is illegal for transgender persons who are female to use any women's public bathrooms. Exactly WHERE do those people controlled by fear of the new expect us to go? In the street? Behind trees? Under cars? Whilst it may seem ludicrous to those of you who have not had the precious gift of living within both gender communities during your lives, the constant threat of official and community discrimination is a very real issue of quality of life and democratic rights.

447

PSYCHIC TV received information that protests were to be held outside the club if we played. For myself the position I was put in by Tom Anderson's various actions AND his courting of the media to short-circuit civil liberties was intolerable. I see myself as incredibly fortunate in having a platform through Psychic TV/PTV3 to discuss issues, spread PANDROGENY (POSITIVE ANDROGENY) messages to our fan base, and through interviews, to you the media and the public you serve. I have suffered from Doctors refusing to treat me when I was in danger of dying within 3 days because I was transgender. I have been threatened, attacked, omitted from events and gatherings of close family. Yet I count myself blessed to have been so accepted by our sisters and brothers in the transgender communities.

We felt, as a band, we simply could not be seen to endorse Tom Anderson's policies by appearing at his club, despite his offer to treat ME as an exception. It would be an unforgivable betrayal of so many people's trust in my integrity of spirit. With protests threatened and guards policing the situation the possibility of feelings naturally running high could have led to somebody being hurt, injured, or property damaged maybe even arrests of those of us enflamed by righteous indignation over this attempt to legitimize turning us into a marginalized sector of second class citizens with fewer legal rights than biologically heterosexual members of this society and culture.

For this reason, AND because we truly do want our transgender brethren to enjoy our performance, and be with us in a friendly, joyous and pleasurable SAFE temporary creative environment we, as a band have chosen to move our concert away from Tom Anderson's club and will now perform at THE SETS, in TEMPE, ARIZONA on Monday 27th August 2007.

PLEASE inform your friends, readers, and viewers of this change on YOUR behalf in protest against the encroachment upon transgender civil liberties.

Remember…

You've got to fight for your right to PEE PEE!

PEE WHERE THOU WILT SHALL BE THE WHOLE OF THE LAW!!!

448

Thank you for your time and attention.

Cari saluti,
GENESIS BREYER P-ORRIDGE of Psychic TV/PTV3.
Genesis Breyer P-Orridge, Scotsdale, Arizona. 25th August 2007

Image by Genesis Breyer P-Orridge

PRAYERS for SACRED HEARTS
Prayers For Pandrogeny & Breaking Sex

There is no reason
on Earth why
you should run out
of people to be.

S/HE IS HER/E

P-ANDROGENY
POSITIVE ANDROGENY
POWER ANDROGENY
POTENT ANDROGENY
POLITICAL ANDROGENY
PERFECT ANDROGENY
PRECIOUS ANDROGENY
P-ANDROGYNE
WILD
BEING
UNHOLY
CHOSEN ONE

To throw off the shackles
Of experience
Of true sexual freedom
And physical love!
End gender.
BREAK SEX.
There are more than one of you.
Maybe hundreds to chose from.

Never before has a generation,
Felt such a rage to live.
Destroy gender.
Destroy the control of DNA
and the expected.

In the beginning all were perfect.

The first man was the first woman.
The first woman was the first man.
UNTIL the whispering began…

EVERY MAN AND WOMAN
IS A MAN AND WOMAN.

We are ultra-genetic terrorists.
One man is another man or woman.
One man's man is another man's
Woman.

CHANGE THE WAY TO PERCEIVE
AND CHANGE ALL MEMORY.

STOP IT!
Stop being possessed by characters
Written by others.
Rebuild your SELF
From the FOUND UP!
Genesis & Lady Jaye Breyer P-Orridge 2004

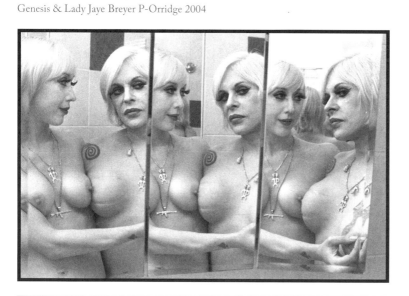

Photo by Laure Leber, 2003

Reading list

XV

ORIGINAL READING LIST,
GRADE 23/1 RECEPTOR FREQUENCY.
It is hoped that thee finding is as important a discipline as thee reading.

PRIMARY INFORMATION RECEPTION

The View Over Atlantis
John Michel

The Spear of Destiny
Trevor Ravenscroft

Holy Blood, Holy Grail
Leigh, Lincoln and Baigent

UFOs: Operation Trojan Horse
John A. Keel

Uptight
Victor Bockris

Ah Pook is Here
William S. Burroughs

The Outsider; The Occult
Colin Wilson

Popism
Andy Warhol

Images and Oracles of Austin Osman Spare
Kenneth Grant

The Illuminatus! Trilogy
Robert Anton Wilson and Robert Shea

The Decorated Body
Robert Shea

Britain: An Unfree Country
Terence DuQuesne, ed.

The Morning of the Magicians
Louis Pauwels and Jacques Bergier

The Aquarian Conspiracy
Marilyn Ferguson

Dancing Ledge
Derek Jarman

Psychic Self-Defense
Dion Fortune

Unspeakable Confessions
Salvador Dalí and Andre Parinaud

The Tempest
William Shakespeare

The Great Beast
John Symonds

Creative Dreaming
Patricia Garfield

Supernature
Lyall Watson

456

Here to Go; Planet R101
Brion Gysin

Bomb Culture
Jeff Nuttall

RATIO 3: Transmediators
Z'EV, Andrew McKenzie, Genesis P-Orridge

Nothing Is True Everything Is Permitted—The Life Of Brion Gysin
John Geiger

Brion Gysin—Tuning In to the Multimedia Age
Jose Ferez Kuri

AGHORA: At The Left Hand Of God
Robert E. Svoboda

SECONDARY INFORMATION RECEPTION

The Book on the Taboo Against Knowing Who You Are
Alan Watts

The Golden Bough
J. G. Frazer

Real Time
John Brockman and Ed Rosenfeld, eds.

The Secret of Meditation
Hans Ulrich Rieker

Playpower
Richard Nelville

The Master Game
Robert S. De Ropp

Zen Training
Katsuki Sekida

Cults of Unreason
Christopher Evans

The Sonnets
William Shakespeare

Nietzsche: Philosopher, Psychologist, Anti-Christ
Walter Kaufman

Minutes to Go
William S. Burroughs, Gregory Corso, Sinclair Beiles, Brion Gysin

The Process
Brion Gysin

Future Ritual
Philip H. Farber

Brion Gysin Let the Mice In
Brion Gysin, William S. Burroughs, Ian Sommerville

457

Exterminator!
William S. Burroughs

Beat Hotel
Barry Miles

The Job: Interviews With William S. Burroughs
Daniel Odier

Painful but Fabulous
Genesis Breyer P-Orridge et. al.

Chapel of Extreme Experience
John Geiger

Radium 226.05 magazine, Spring 1986
Ulrich Hillebrand and Cm von Hausswolf

Back in No Time: The Brion Gysin Reader
Jason Weiss, ed.

Cyberia; Media Virus
Douglas Rushkoff

The Holographic Universe
Michael Talbot

The Third Mind
William S. Burroughs and Brion Gysin

The Best of Olympia
Maurice Girodias

The Last Museum
Brion Gysin

Wreckers of Civilization
Simon Ford

RE/Search #5/6: W. S. Burroughs/Brion Gysin/Throbbing Gristle
V. Vale, ed.

Flickers of the Dream Machine
Paul Cecil, ed.

Disinformation: The Interviews
Richard Metzger, ed.

Sex and Rockets: The Occult World of Jack Parsons
John Carter

*Breakthrough: An Amazing Experiment in Electronic
Communication With the Dead*
Konstantin Raudive

The Final Academy: Statements of a Kind
Genesis Breyer P-Orridge and Roger Ely, eds.

This is the Salivation Army
Scott Treleaven

Portable Darkness: An Aleister Crowley Reader
Scott Michaelson, ed.

The Soul's Code: In Search of Character and Calling
James Hillman

459

Naked Lens: Beat Cinema
Jack Sergeant

Apocalypse Culture 1 & 2
Adam Parfrey, ed.

Rapid Eye #2
Simon Dwyer, ed.

Rebels and Devils: The Psychology of Liberation
Christopher Hyatt, ed.

The Lucifer Principle; The Global Brain
Howard Bloom

Ultraculture; Generation Hex
Jason Louv

Image by Genesis Breyer P-Orridge

Exploding Galaxies—The Art Of David Medalla
Guy Brett

Dolphins, Angels and Extraterrestrials
Timothy Wyllie

The Correct Sadist
Terence Sellers

La Bas
J. K. Huysmans

Our Lady Of The Flowers
Jean Genet

On The Road—The Original Scroll
Jack Kerouac

Groovy Bob
Harriet Vyner

461

Note to the reader of this book. In the 1960's most of the books that changed the course of my life were incredibly difficult to find. There was no alternative distribution and Henry Miller, Burroughs and Jean Genet were often only to be found in Soho porn shops, stocked only because they had been prosecuted for obscenity! Many books on this list will also be hard to find, despite the internet. Knowledge hard won is often more easily recalled and valued. Good luck searching and don't forget this is an ever opening system so add your own use-full books to this list as you go, ready for a next generation...

ADDENDA TO THEE
SECOND EDITION Ⓥ
THEE PSYCHICK BIBLE

For those readers less aware of the Astory of Thee Temple Ov Psychick Youth we have decided to add a section of comments and documents that might illumine the narrative a little more. For example, whilst a lot of theory is contained in this updated edition of Thee Psychick Bible we felt that a little more information on the TOPY way of daily L-if-E might make certain texts clearer.

As TOPY grew from its beginnings as a mysterious attachment to the first Psychic TV album, *Force the Hand of Chance*, we began to improvise organizational solutions. Initially all sigils and letters were answered by the central core of Individuals at 50 Beck Road, Hackney, London E.8. We had squatted eight houses in that street in 1973-74 that eventually we handed on to ACME Housing Association to administer. However 52, 50 and 46 remained TOPY houses. All inhabitants were dedicated, sporting the TOPY haircut, a mixture of austere (shaved) and decadent (a lush pony tail). From the front paramilitary, from behind ambiguous. Number 50 was the house totally given over to a TOPY way of L-if-E. One room was a nursery, used only for sigils and rituals. Individuals visiting from abroad often stayed there for wceks, even years, as did Individuals from other parts of England.

We quickly identified an ever increasing number of male and female Individuals prepared to focus their lives on an intuitive, communal exploration of L-if-E lived as a self-chosen tribe looking for ways to include magick, visionary explorations and non-traditional relationships. Our ID cards stated our intent:

THEEFREQUENCYOVTRUTH

This card identifies the bearer as an active Individual in Thee Temple Ov Psychick Youth. TOPY is dedicated towards thee establishmeant ov a functional system of magick and a modern pagan philosophy without recorse to mystification, Gods or Demons but recognizing thee implicit powers ov thee humane brain (Neuromancy) linked with guiltless sexuality focused through WILL Structures (Sigils). TOPY propose that Magick empowers thee Individual to embrace and realize their dreams and to maximize their natural potential. TOPY is for those with thee courage to touch themselves. It integrates all levels ov thought in thee first steps towards a final negation ov any system ov unforced CONTROL and FEAR.

OUR AIM IS WAKEFULNESS OUR ENEMY IS DREAMLESS SLEEP!

THEEFREQUENCYOVTRUTH

Underneath this would be the Temple name. From the beginning we wanted to avoid even implied hierarchies. We created a simple system to try and avoid this. All females were called KALI (unless someone asked to be other than their biological gender, in which case their request was honored, so we had a few male Kalis) and all males were called EDEN. They were then assigned a number simply according to when their first letter to TOPY arrived. Numbers were written out in full e.g. KALI SIXTY EIGHT or EDEN FORTY FOUR and so on.

There was NEVER a number ONE or TWO. Because of its importance to us there were twenty-three number 23s. This avoided anyone feeling special with that number. After a couple of years we noticed Individuals at meetings implying their being special in some way by having smaller numbers, as if that longer involvement made them more important so we jumbled up everyone's numbers at random and re-assigned these numbers accordingly.

Another issue that came up was Individuals, and people generally saying they were "member" of TOPY—in fact, we NEVER used that term, nor did we recognize it. You were either a CONNECTED Individual, or you were a DISCONNECTED Individual. Individuals could be disconnected voluntarily, or involuntarily.

Disconnection was rarely enforced except for strictly vital matters of privacy. For example two or three Individuals were found to be reading sigils and then using their knowledge of an Individual's deepest sexual desires to try and seduce them. Needless to say we viewed this as an extreme violation of trust and it earned immediate disconnection. So did theft from the community, both material and intellectual.

As TOPY grew the Hackney houses were

not enough. Really motivated Individuals began to volunteer to try and raise awareness of our ideas and/or raise funds in other parts of Britain, then not long after all over the world. To keep the terminology simple and not too pompous we called these active TOPY groups Access Points, as that's exactly what they were. You could gain access to publications, news of events, newsletters and a forum of research into our ad hoc urban shamanism. TOPY differed a lot from other cults and belief systems in that we did not require financial contributions from Individuals, apart from *Thee Grey Book*, which was twenty-three pounds. Freely given donations, money raised by putting on raves, lectures, film nights, DJing, rock gigs and so on subsidized the majority of publications, printing and postal costs. Labor was free and voluntary. We believed though that being actively involved in any aspect of TOPY was beneficial, as Individuals brainstormed concepts, proposals for changes and ideas so that learning was an organic and pleasurable affair.

Soon there were Access Points in Scotland, Italy, Germany, Sweden, Australia, Canada, the United States, the Netherlands. Our innately efficient structure was so successful that we were almost overwhelmed by the interest and sincerity of the thousands of Individuals who became activated at some level within TOPY.

What would commonly happen is a particularly motivated Individual would visit Hackney, (which we had now renamed the TOPY STATION for Britain with duties of overseeing all the numerous Access Points) and they would ask, "Why is there no Access Point in…?" To which we would reply, "Why don't YOU start one then?"

This was how TOPY N.A. (TOPY North America) started. Coyote 3 (Tom Hallewell) was following Psychic TV on a USA Detour in the mid-1980s doing a light show, selling merchandise he'd organized himself all voluntarily. We talked for hours on the long drives between gigs about TOPY and magick that could be relevant and resonate with young people as opposed to what we dubbed "the museum of magic" with its baroque theatricals and pyramid schemes. Eventually Coyote 3 asked that damning question and was then charged with spreading the seed across the US of A—a task he did with gusto, style and energy that remains remarkable. By our next USA detour he had Access Points all over America who offered us shelter, good food, extra roadies and love as well as a 1966 yellow school bus we dubbed "EVEN FURTHUR" bought by funds supplied by myself, but gutted and rebuilt by TOPY N.A. and crewed by them too. A miraculous job that allowed us to tour the US at a profit three times on tours that lasted several weeks.

This element of discovering a new famille of like-minded bretheren was important in why TOPY spread as it did. We supplied new, or taboo ideas and concepts, or both without judgment, without expectation, without attachment in the hope it MIGHT inspire or validate even people we never met. At the heart of TOPY is sharing, the generosity of trust.

Needless to say as we grew into what was probably the largest sexual magick-based network to exist so far (up to 10,000 Individuals worldwide at its peak) we found ourselves wanting to explore further, "even furthur."

It was decided to move from London to Brighton on the south coast of England. The Hackney house remained, becoming a transit hub for all TOPY rather than a Station or Access Point. After my immediate famille had settled into Brighton Brother Words and Sister Shadows, in an example of amazing trust and courage, also sold their London home, gave up their jobs and moved a few doors down. They became essential to the thriving and survival of TOPY and can never be thanked enough.

Soon there were five houses in Brighton occupied by only TOPY Individuals. This new hub became the next TOPY Station. The every day experiments of living are too numerous to go into deeply here but a few pointers will be useful. Each TOPY house had a "Nursery," that is to say a room used ONLY for private Individual Sigilizing, and/or communal ritual sigilizing. The tenet was, whatever happens in the Nursery goes no further. (A bit like Las Vegas.) No jealousy, no ridicule, no criticism was to exit those rooms. Amazingly, against all the odds of human nature, we never did have a case of friction or unhappiness spilling out from those sacred practices.

Once a month a TOPY house would create a communal sigil to which all Individuals living there were invited, but no one was ever pressured to take part. Individuals would take turns inventing new processes and concepts to explore together in this extra-moral space.

On each Monday one TOPY house would cook a meal for the residents of all the other houses. A different house would do the washing up as a sign of respect. The weeks happenings would be informally discussed over dinner, news, gossip and problems aired. Around this time we decided to try and include a few new ideas simply to see what happened. One was taken from The Process Church of the Final Judgment. We would have a telepathy circle at the beginning of the meal, rather than saying grace. Even Caresse and Genesse would join in with this. We'd all hold hands, close our eyes and try to empty them. One Individual would then pass a book around and the Individuals would whisper what they had "seen," if anything. Then we'd compare images. We had varying success, but did note a gradual increase in similarities, one night in particular having four lion based images reported including both children.

After the meals we began the most potent exercise we ever developed—the Individual's L-if-E Astory. Each Monday, as we digested our food, we would gather in the biggest room. One Individual would volunteer to tell us all their childhood memories, leaving nothing out, no matter how painful or difficult. The level of trust we had grown amongst ourselves was so deep that nobody "cheated." We heard many harrowing tales. A lot of abuse, fear, loss, abandonment. But

we also saw that we ALL had traumas to mend and heal and were no longer alone, no longer holding in secrets from our pasts. My belief is that this exercise was a root reason for the immense loyalty and connection between us all. Particularly those in Brighton.

As the network grew faster and faster it became more difficult to supervise the public persona of TOPY. We organized a TO-PYGLOBAL Annual meeting to try and thrash out how to maintain intimacy without attracting mean-spirited attention from an uncomprehending media hungry for scandal and titillation. One of the first disagreements occurred over this. We pointed out that whether it was fair or not; whether it represented the truth about TOPY or not we HAD been warned we were being investigated by unknown authorities and that IF tthere was an attack on TOPY it would come in Brighton and most likely be focused upon myself and my famille, NOT because we were more important but because we were already public figures, media exposed and an easy scapegoat to target!

We were shouted down as paranoid, or as egocentric for feeling WE were TOPY which we hadn't said. All I could do was say, "it will still probably be MY front door they kick in, not yours." Oh… sadly they were incorrect and we were right. But this is about the TOPY organization not "the troubles."

During our years in Brighton TOPY became friends with Timothy Wyllie, a former Processean and at the time that we met very much involved with "Dolphins, Angels and Extraterrestrials" (which is also the title of one of his books that you should read). Through him we realized we should be involved in our home community, not separate. He inspired us to begin a campaign to shut down the Brighton Dolphinarium. Which we succeeded in doing.

Every week in Brighton we would have a Digger Stall in the park where everything was free to whoever wanted it. So as we shed unnecessary or duplicated belongings we gave them away—"IT'S YOURS BECAUSE IT'S FREE" was the Emmett Grogan motto for the Diggers, a San Francisco group of radicals in the sixties. In fact one TOPY Individual legally changed his name to Emmett Grogan P-Orridge! It was surprisingly hard to give things away. People couldn't believe us. We also ran market stalls—one seven days a week in Brighton selling bric-a-brac and TOPY booklets, t-shirts and so on; the other at weekends in Camden at the Electric Ballroom. We were by then so organized that we had transport up and down to London, volunteers and helpers to man the stalls. We never had any money pilfered either, despite many full-time Individuals being broke, penniless or on the dole.

In the "Big House" in Brighton was a self-contained apartment with a large jacuzzi that we'd rent out in the summer to holidaymakers. The rest of the year TOPYites lived and worked there doing mail orders and assembling booklets or replying to the endless correspondence.

Between the TOPY Station groups there were a few children. We adored our children and surprisingly tried to keep their perception of L-if-E as standard, normal as possible. We wanted them to not feel odd or awkward amongst their peers, but to be open-hearted and open-minded. One policy was, never speak to any baby or child differently to how you speak to adults and they will grow towards comprehension faster. The other was that ALL the Individuals were available to babysit and later be nannies to the children. Their B-Earthdays were communal celebrations of L-if-E for all our community too so they had a deep rooted sense of self-worth and assumed intelligence. Caresse and Genesse came on Psychic TV detours. We always took a full-time, trained nanny who would keep up their school-work and supervise them. They also had their own hotel room so they could sleep when they needed to. Children were seen as precious people to be respected.

Image by Genesis Breyer P-Orridge

ANTON KREUZER JOURNALS

ROGER T.
Timefix: 21 September 1968

Dear Roger,

Took a massive dose fugu. It has all become so clear to me, the attempt at communication between two worlds. To those who would know, the most wonderful personal mythology has to be cherished and spread, a seed of stars, scattered making a map. The night sky here is quite incredible, for the first time I saw my soul outside the prison of my flesh. The ghost could die and my dream turn pale and power Full, a unicorn of order drawn from those miserable grains of sand, children of ignorance. I have laid the ghost of my mother too R.!

We can do it, we are all just a matter of light, the ultimate material from which we are driven like hungry ghosts and to which we return by our own acceleration and sacrifice. Memories are the key projection in the future.

"What does IT Matter"

Heart Mountain, Manzanar.

GENERAL ORDER MASTER

1.6 These texts are a program about a people and their projections, or about an absence of spatial memory. Our hallucinations fail in attempting to comprehend and describe the brains of deities. As it is, so be it. And, what does I.T. matter? (Where I.T. equals Imaginary Time?) 14.9 In a universe with no boundaries in space, no beginning or end in time, there is nothing for a deity to do. This " Omniverse" is itself therefore defined by what we describe as the qualities of any deities, and this in its Self makes us the source of all deities, demons and entities.

38.17 In any self reproducing organisms and any organisms attempting to reproduce Self, there will be variations in genetic material. These differences in source will mean some individuals are more able than others to draw right conclusions about themselves.

39.1 As any deity is actually a linguistic and televisual reproduction of the universe, then I.T. is the source that defines, describes and makes a picture of I.T. (Imaginary Time) in our own images. We are the source and our goal is nothing less than to transmit a complete depiction of the "universe" and, by this projection, to create an infinitely dense holographic picture, better than "reality," what can be called an Omniverse; a synthetic compression of light and matter in a curvature of space and time, being then quite certainly infinite.

45.5 The shorter a wavelength of light, the more accurate our position as a neurovisual screen in this Omniverse, and the higher energy of each source particle transmitted.

45.6 Each source an uncertain principle.

47.8 If the source is a neurovisual Screen, then television is a map that binds us. Where map = M.A.P., that is: Mind At Preset.

80.4 Symmetry of programming is a *fundamental* and inescapable property of this process.

83.7 Imaginary Time is indistiguishable from directions in Transmitted Space.

85.2 The mind in-forms the brain. The brain ex-forms its Self.

90.9 The Guardians understand that an Omniverse will finish up in a high state of order regardless of its original state within I.T. In earliest times an Omniverse was in a disordered State (no "Garden"); this would mean that disorder would decrease with time. We do not see broken cups gathering themselves together and leaping back onto the table. Disorder is intended to increase; this is a precept of the World Preset Guardians— acceleration of disorder.

100.1 No Garden is Know Garden.

104.6 To explain this neuro-televisual basis, switch your mind to this, if you don't mind, and then re-mind your self immediately. Without mind, the soul is static interference, a weak anthropomorphic principle.

104.8 Self is a switch on your neurovisual screen.

105.2 N.V.S. in this speculation = neurovisual screen and/or neurovisual self and/or neurovisual system.

118.8 Before an item is recorded in memory, that memory is in a disordered state. After the memory interacts with the neurovisual system, in order to be remembered, it will have passed into an ordered state; this is what " in order" can mean. Energy released in doing this disipates and increases the amount of disorder in an Omniverse.

120.3 An ordered state can be understood in both a micro (internal) and macro (external) sense.

122.2 All source aspires to transmit to all neurovisual screens that "every thing is in order."

123.23 All source exists to direct a weak force towards an ordered state by any means, media or *transmedia* necessary.

123.35 Disorder in an internal state is insane.

123.36 Disorder in an external state is outsane.

127.5 Memory and Omniverse have identical characteristics.

130.1 G.O. = General Order. A program hidden at a dimensional intersection.

144.4 To short-circuit the propagation of those who do not know, (the genetically absent minded), all linearity of source DNA must be overidden, and memory fragmented, to hasten absolute disorder within any weak force. This will always be greater than the increase in the order of the memories themselves.

160.1 The World Preset Guardians will transmit a frequency of truth to the disordered in the singular image of the source. Using strong force they reject the stationary state. They exist in a condition of no boundaries, seeking, through the jewel of a nuclear spectrum, to lay waste to the weak forces of humanity that graze like cattle in a barren field, unaware of the infinite potential of every desert to become, once more, a Fractured Garden.

161.4 The Fractured Garden is a post-symbolic representation of the origin and the infinity of the Omniverse. An illuminated program made concrete by the process of seeing.

162.8 To see is to consume the Source, to be seen is to give b-earth to the source.

163.5 If light is matter, then being does not matter.

163.6 Being light is another matter.

163.9 Neurovisual nano-particles are the commercials that control the mind. Once the mind is controlled, we have infinite re-access for brain programming.

188.8 A weak force does not obey symmetry, it makes an Omniverse develop differently to the way its mirror image would develop. A strong source must transmit a rare signal that is better than real, more than a reflection over-riding the existing signals on any neurovisual screen.

189.1 Humanity is a weak force; we are a strong force. Strong individuals can have no friends but befriend all.

189.7 The weak force exist at absolute zero; the Guardians exist at absolute infinity.

194.4 It is no accident that vision is both a sense, and vision is an anticipated conception illuminated by its source.

200.7 "'Soul' is the brand name for the brain." – Dr. Timothy Leary

200.8 All that is transmitted is re-accessed by the source.

201.2 The source becomes immortal when I.T. controls completely the means of perception. Seizure of the temporal state releases the energy of order into the alternate states in all five dimensions throughout the matter of time and space.

211.5 The focus of intent is visionary, the World Preset Guardians are the transmitters of this vision, the source are the receivers of the vision, the neurovisual screens that define I.T. (Imaginary Time). Here is the first true medium of all recorded thought, all memory.

213.1 In a world where all programs are pre-recorded, the World Preset Guardians are the programmers.

216.4 All sources are the emissaries of all deities, satellites freed from gravity, a fiber-optic superhighway, a wave of light that travels beyond all time. These sources will maintain a link with all weak force. Their incarnation must suffer the last awe of interference, their signals must be jammed, their children stolen and their DNA neutralized. Order must access their memories in a final transmitted program.

223.9 Exist and exit are the same. The Garden is filled with lies.

234.6 Source are rare. The original Garden was a refraction of a source of light; the source of that light was an illuminator of this hologram. Our original sin was to believe that a solid hallucination was more real than its source. We now know that the source is more real than the original refraction. To eat knowledge is to grasp and consume solidity, our awareness instructing us that by absorbing into our entire being this forbidden fruit, we invest each neurovisual particle of our flesh with an inclusion principle. As consciousness is fixed, so the individual is released. The source is swallowed in this synthesis, beginning a prophetic journey into the means of perception unprecedented before the thermo-memetic experience.

ON THEE WAY TO
THEE GARDEN

There is a specific clarity when fire cleanses. A moment when it seems to freeze. Every possible particle is motion rushing up or down. Naked and blind upon on a path of lies we enter the field, a dull agony of fear dilates time against the biological confusion.

Columns of fire, columns of lies, pillars of Solomon's temple. Dilate the pupils of the brain, a

doorway to manifest leaving. A fire sale in an inferno. One day a truth shall emerge, however deeply we seek to avoid I.T.

There is more than one time. Limitations imposed by the passage of inner-time make it the enemy. Possibilities exposed by outer-time make it a delusion of night.

Change thee way to perceive and change all Memory.

Make space to be space.
Old TOPI proverb

THEE FRACTURED GARDEN

A soul must lose its attachment to humanity.

A mind must lose its attachment to salvation.

A brain must lose its attachment to body.
Old TOPI proverb

In the retreat from matter, all realities are equal. Now that inter-reality travel is possible we will become the very substance of hallucination, and thus may enter and leave at will the uncertain principle of all realities, regardless of their location.

Those who build, assemble; *assembly* is the invisible language of our *time*.

Brain and neurovisual matter are one, are the material of all that can be seen, was ever seen, will be seen, in every place and in every time, forever.

Each brain is all realities, from mundane to omniscient.

Only alone may we breach the dark matter of lost memory and connect all points of light. For this we need a map of the stars, our superior Will electrifying a web that catches our soul and emits eternal vision. The visionary alone can be free. The blind masses seek to blind him, put out his eyes in their fearful progression to the desert of dark skies. The blind may not lead the illuminated, rather they must be forced to surrender all thought of vision to those who are their eyes and who dream the most dangerous dreams of annihilation.

We control things to eradicate them. Nothing matters but the end of matter.

All must be controlled and destroyed that allow blindness, that breed blindness, who spawn the children of dark. They must be buried in the dark, cold dark crystals, in a desert of grains made without light. Their dark is a nightmare, a castrated black stallion trampling the prophet who communes with the stars and reads the codes of electrical knowledge and return. We are not from one star, all stars are our source. Every story ever told resides in them.

Infinite choices of reality are the gift of software to our children.

We signal and are signaled. We hold aloft a torch of fire and pass our hands across it. Visions, images, primal memories from this immeasurable brain fill us with transmitted light, dancing dots and lines, an end to a tyranny of language and a beginning of our return to the Fractured Garden. Solidity is a perfection of light; its prism, its manifestation, an hallucination of evidence that mind may reside within any reality.

An end of time is just another way of saying the beginning of immortality.

Dreams are a coded material of eternity. We possess Light through them.

Those who accept Light control mortality.

Those who control Light control immortality.
Old TOPI proverb

Space is our church, the stars our windows, our dreams navigate pathways, only an ancient map has been lost.

Our world's a dream, a miserable one. In our unfathomable ignorance we call it the only reality, none-sensus reality, we assume that its events, humane events, humane life, are implicitly of value. This buries us in a quicksand of compassion.

Be afraid to the point of formlessness.

Be terrorized to the point of soundlessness.

Be extreme to the point of powerlessness.
Old TOPI proverb

A Garden was destroyed by a Word, destroyed by language, became the first memory. Time was set in motion at this point. The garden did not exist within time, or language; it was an exterior neural projection, a cathedral that worshipped its occupant, the soul. Representing as it did the mind at preset without light, there was nothing to reflect, shape or fix this particular dream.

We have formed sounds, made names, trapping matter with language. We perpetuate our tyranny and drown in a flood of speculation and false communication. To be reborn, immortal, outside time, we must look for ways to transmit infinite alternate realities, and choices of reality, to make them as real, *more real* than any emasculating reductions that we inherit; yet not be corrupted and trivialized by a belief in our singularity. No-thing is real, everything must go. Every inherited construct, society, techno-patriotic political system that trades off believing it exists, must be destroyed as fast as possible. We must make space to be space. This is the cyber position.

The eradication of the tyrannical nuclear family, building block of the prison walls for this imposed, humanitarian dust, that chokes and dulls the masses reducing all to a worthless, mindless, dreamless fog.

Memory is a clock, the agitng mechanism of the mind.

Memories tell us one thing: every thing must go.

Every thing is an hallucination, made solid by mass belief.

Names are given in order to control. To reduce, to comprehend the forces of nature, to demonstrate ownership. In this race to name the poor have grown to be rich, and the rich have grown to be poor again. Know that to re-enter immortality we must ourselves become unnamable, emptied of all sense of being here.

Television is our new exterior brain. One day it will be a standard fitting within every skull on earth, each brain an electronic star in a transmitted Milky Way. Galaxies of dreams and information. People will become more comfortable with televisual reality than that of their daily lives. Television will be *more real* than life. A new synthetic material, giving all people infinite access to infinite alternate realities through a cortex of light. They will program, shape, form and broadcast messages, until the very fabric of four dimensional reality has been torn asunder, its cloak cast down beneath. From this day forth, reality will be a multiple series of channels, option switches feeding our brains.

THEE CAPTURED GARDEN

Time accelerates what the brain already is. Destruction creates to manufacture.

We manufacture our cherished dreams and myths, and project them into all the homes of the world; in one day they create an equality of reality that negates all values. The whole world is a cathedral window, each receiver a soul, our programming the holy message, and discs are waved as a savior sets forth into the holiest of places.

When all are linked, a savior is released.

Man has separated himself from nature that he too can take part in the creation of the world, of any world. His inventions are his slaves, all friends are his enemies.

Man developed television to realize this unity and this separation. It is the quickest, most potent form of belief. All form is from one source. We see the source because the mind is temporarily held aside and we see form from the source, we are at one with the source, we are the source.

There is nothing mysterious about this, the illuminated have always had this experience; now we can record, edit, adjust and transmit our deepest convictions broadcast in the most mundane parables.

When we log on, immortality is visible, signaling us to return .

In a digital world, all realities are equal, all actions are equally moral or immoral, therefore no action is unacceptable.

THEE EMPTY GARDEN

There is a time that each of us knows that comes without warning. Suddenly it comes and so silently, and it descends upon us like a net, a grid of light. Indifferent to our plans or our hour it falls on us, and however our time was allotted and conceived the plan fades away under that light as though the lines were lead in church windows. In the final furnace of transmutation, no fact remains, all hallucinations are equal.

In that light we begin to see, not with the eyes of our mind but with an eye behind our mind we begin to finally see, to shed nature's trap, the physical body, the false bondage of compassion.

And in that light these things are heard and seen but they are seen not from without but from within. From a place deep within a map of stars where there is no distinction of words or of actions but only a discernment of feeling and in that *light* it is not feeling that is regarded, because all that is done with feeling melts and dissolves like sand into glass in the fire that is all you really are. What must be regarded is the Lack of All Feeling. For feeling is shallow, and thin, and so, so empty. A hungry, worthless ghost.

And nothing remains of your own image but gaps and empty places, an atomic matrix that creates passage through all things, all times, all possibilities, and you will know this, that there is nothing left of you that you can feel or see or hear nor anyone else, for the soul when released has no need of feelings or senses, in its immortality it becomes omnipotent matter made of light, reconstituted at will throughout all times and all possible manifestations past, present and future. This is the moment when everything must go, all words, all sentiment, all feelings, all flesh, all thought of humanity must be set free to free the soul, for is not God but a brain untrapped by all human concern and limitation?

We hear our own voice speaking and the words become thin and transparent like glass and we are at the place from where they come and they are like holograms floating; they are the essence of mind like the voice of rain or the sandstorm. They are the voice behind our voice.

Faces come before you, and expressions, and you see all of the face is held together only for expression, for an idea, and you watch the face before you and there is nothing else besides, and the mouth moves, opens and smiles, and the eyes look at you and sometimes they are saying what the mouth is saying and sometimes they aren't saying that, but something else, or nothing, or anything, and no answer but a lie comes.

The idea is the solidifier of the mind. The brain exists to make matter of the idea.

The idea rides on words but is the distant watcher, the substance of eternity. It is the invisible warrior astride the pale unicorn deep in space, waiting for the brave and hungry.

Give silence to the wordless. The sound that is all around you is the sound of a hundred liars.

I lay in the desert, on my back, staring up at the stars. I could feel millions of rays of light entering my body, one from each star, infinite numbers. My cell walls broke down, my sense of bodily existence ended, I was illumination, a 3D projection of cosmic light; I could see the ancient shamans building sacred sites to fix their relationship with the stars, to solidify their connections and effects. I remembered the thousands of Holy Teachers, the idea of the divine "spark," the descriptions of white light, the myths and legends of our descent from the stars. I was not corporeal, I was a mirage, sealed within an inherited apparently solid body by the weight of Thistory, by the weight of fear and guilt. I shimmered like a ghost, ectoplasm, illusion and all the puzzles I had heard, and all the limited descriptions of limitless transcendent experiences made sense. I knew I had to find a way to G.O., to leave this sealed coffin that is my body, to find an accelerator to project my brain, bypassing the tedium of mechanistic evolution, into deepest omniversal space, into immortality, into the very fabric of myth and heaven. I was everyone, everything, and everything too was here to G.O. I understood my lifetime's sense of disconnection and disorder was not a flaw, but rather a wondrous gift that described, in a new way, the true nature of being that may be experienced whilst trapped, mortal and confused, here in this desert that was once a theater of all possibilities and an exit to all impossibilities.

Does mind leave, or does consciousness? What leaves, what stays behind as we achieve immortality? Brain? If it is, as I suspect, the programmable computer mind that is the key, what happens to consciousness? Am I mistaken, or will there be a projection? I want to G.O. This final puzzle evades me.

Is mind separated from the brain, or is brain as encompassing as mind?

On the subject of the holographic soul. The holographic soul works because that's what it is. If it didn't work there would be no soul. The holographic soul does what it's supposed to do, further accelerate the evolution of man. It was always possible to consciously separate the holographic soul. The Tibetans call it going into the rainbow body; John Dee communed with the time-born souls of the Tamasin and Siriakin; the Gnostics saw the true nature of what was a God. A strict method of liberation from physical manifestation. The Zen masters understood the need to shed all logic and attachment, becoming pure particles of time. The evolution of man is not the intellectual and moral betterment of all. It is the liberation from measured time. It is detach-meant from all manifestations in the five dimensions, except that of time. The fate of all cannot be allowed to hold any individual in mortal bondage. To evolve is to achieve a unity of time with the holographic soul. It has always been known we must return to time, not project out into space, but transmit and receive in time. Now we can comprehend that space is emptiness, the edge of a cloud. Imaginary timr is a neuro-biological paradigm. A quantum physical energy in our scientifically validated methodologies. With our ability to project the brain via television, we can behold our final journey. R. D.

Laing's painted bird flies from the canvas, which was already blank. The great lie has been that we exist. The holographic soul is a technological development that came when it was needed. There is no reason to fear it, we created it because we *need* it. We need it as much to maintain present travel, as to facilitate future travel. Like the electric light. Everybody will want to know about this, and that is proof enough of its importance. It does what every new creation does, it lets a little more time into the dark accelerations of Humane Beings. It is whatever fills the brain with more time, and it is the means to be free of flesh forever. Out of the confines of the body, out of the limitations of the mind, and out of time. I.T. is meant for those who can let everything G.O. We can program it. We could touch the state of liberation, we could savor immortality, but we could not contain and mobilize the soul.

Cyberspace, the psychosphere, does not just access alternate realities, it amplifies conclusions and services expectations.

What was once mysterious is no longer mysterious. Mindless existence is no longer feared, for the mind is projected image and is the brain's extension into matter. Only through projections of mind can the brain expand and become detached, set free unto its Self. All form is only the observation of mind at different stages of development. Man is the most evolved form, the highest creation, hence more inherently aware of a need for order. Order in turn demands power to hold its shape, or dissolves, or melts like film held too long in its projector.

Projection is building a mind. Programming is building a soul. Perception is building a brain. Thinking is the gap between the builder and the act of building. Kreator and the kreated. This gap has plagued perception forever. The point of infinity, the gap between the stars, the moment between sleep and awaking, the absolute edge that separates, yet cannot exist or be measured.

In order to continue our development as humanity, this debilitating gap must be bridged. We must chip away at the concrete, the monolith of being physically manifested. We must harness *time* and control the brain by controlling its information programs. We must program infinite choices of reality, blind it with science to our purpose, for our purpose. The light that always was must now cross that bridge and illuminate the mind that the mind might live in light, and that the brain might make soul its own. This bridge is like a resistance between the transmitting primary winding and receiving secondary winding of a transformer, just enough neuro-visuals leak through to keep the secondary circuit responding. As man slowly evolves, the resistance is lowered and there is more consciousness in the brain. We can now develop ways to short circuit this protective resistor, temporarily burning out all the components in the receiving circuit. The receiver temporarily ceases to exist and the mind returns to time, from whence all came and life is experienced in the transmitter. Freebirth, freeing the brain, immortality will become inevitable.

In a world that is becoming a hologram, a transmitted projection of material "reality," he who comprehends the final transmission controls all projections, controls the world and controls the secret of the identity and malleability of corporeal matter. For anything, any cherished belief, adhered to and given mythic form by the masses, becomes manifestly solid, and tangible. What we believe in all ways comes to pass. Nothing can exist that we do not believe in. At these times consciousness is not centered in the world of form, it is experiencing the world of content. The program will become power. Any ability to cope with the world of form and there create order is a measure of insanity, a poor connection between mind and brain, which must become one autonomous program, globally transmitted, to generate its own liberation from form in the mass political hallucination that makes the final reality, transcending time, body and place.

All hallucinations are real. Some hallucinations are more real than others.

WORLD PRESET GUARDIANS

The World Preset Guardians will control and dictate every program of humanity for its own sake, maintaining a stringent General Order, in full knowledge of the consequences of their actions.

Man does not create his own destiny. Man sustains Kaos.

All rights are relinquished in service of the source.

The Guardians know that to take the victim and simply remove his suffering in the name of humanity, is to validate the weakness that first signaled his demise.

The Guardians preset all mind.

The Guardians will transmit their mind globally to any degree necessary. Pursuing and cleansing blindness relentlessly, allowing nothing to create interference or enter this world that might solidify their light.

Injustice will ignite their fire into an inferno, a raging firestorm, wreaking destruction and vengeance upon any who corrupt magnificence in the isolated starkness of immortality.

The Guardians will tolerate no deviation from their path. For their vision has infinite direction, there is no-thing they do not see and destroy. They attend to every mind and manifest within every brain. What is seen is seen with insatiable and relentless energy, for it is known to be limitless.

The Guardians will be the light of the world, leading the masses out of hideous darkness, death and deprivation. They desire for mankind a time of perfect balance, where memory is a tool, not a curse, where each is designer of the world in which they transmit, free from death, making this world the preset Garden of Delight that all Astory has led them towards.

The Guardians will validate their own creation by success. For the road of the World Preset Guardians is success, and in their programming success is the essence of life, and this ultimate success proves the worthlessness of habitation of a physical world.

The Guardians preset this world. There are no secrets in it. No love of beauty.

They desire illumination of all things, that nothing be hidden, or remain in darkness. The Guardians do not believe in human feelings, nor in human senses, human needs, human values, human fears or even human hopes. The only purpose or belief is the path from mind to brain, and from brain to G.O. The only channel of the Guardians is the brain.

The Guardian is a digital metaphor, not anything less, in no way a manifest or anthropomorphic entity. The source negates all value of brain, or mind, and speaks in tongues of memory, the aging process of time.

The Guardians will recognize the true nature of success only by seeing its limitations, knowing they must transcend all human values, made real only by mass belief, made solid only by time, until all stories unfold by a mute insistence upon a single transmitted reality. The Guardians will confront this stasis head on, will disintegrate the monolithic walls surrounding the Garden, stepping beyond into a realm of earthly satisfaction to find final fulfillment.

The Guardians will avoid the disillusion that pursuit of human achievement brings with it. The Guardians will be fulfilled within this world, but only because they have no illusions about the nature of this world and all that is of this world.

The Guardians will have no illusions, for they are, in themselves, *all* illusions.

To be fulfilled, the Guardians will leave this world.

The Guardians will exploit the highest goals of belief to enter into this world.

The Guardians are the brain ruling all that exists outside the conflict of the mind. They have seen human reality and its preset values.

The Guardians rule the regions of the unhinged mind. They rule outsanity. Their people are those who have escaped blindness and chosen alternate realities denying preset values. They have delved into strange new areas of physical and psychical sensation, without any restraining limit of mental barriers. They have sought the deepest levels of sensuality, carried indulgence of the body and brain to their limits and left the logic of the mind and protection of the "soul" behind. They have plunged together into consensual madness, have unhooked their receivers completely from the dictates of a "normal" mind, followed an extra-terrestrial and extra-spiritual path, that has neither judgement nor control for those who would travel and G.O. They rule the mind-less cloud of lunacy, they pour water on the desert which is this world, they torture all certainty and master the pursuit of immortality. The Guardians seek to transcend the conflict of mind, to rise beyond the boundaries of brain to reach outside the limi-

tation of human values. They Will not to sink into witless blindness but are awake, vibrant and satiated in the realm of mind-lessness and immoral disorder.

The source is the preset switch that finds every "other" world.

The Guardian is the ultimate of all beings. He is the end and the awe of destruction, he is the manufacturer of hallucination, and the utterly exquisite unicorn of myth. The beginning of time, and the end of memory, the existence and the exit unified by cognition of the Omniversal Mind that empties each world of order.

Alone must I leave this world for I must leave this world alone.

For, disorder is the essence of time, so the beginning of time is the Garden, is the Memory, is the Nanosphere. And the close of time is the Kaosphere, and they are divided by a preset essence of time, which solidifies the conflict between matter, DNA and Neurosphere into a twisted and bigoted story called humanity. The Guardians can create and design realities, dis-organize hallucinations, mould holograms into parables spinning life into Space, joining forces with the stars, leaving treasure maps of where true knowledge resides, hidden from no One, only hidden from each mass of Humanity. The Psychosphere can summon up infinite realities and access them; can generate and transmit every possible and impossible other-than-worldly vision, while those chains which bind to the earth fade into nothing slowly, freed of this human game. Above mundanity and the puzzle and adventure of constant apparition, destroying in finality all agreed upon reality, all inherited morality and the most miserable threat to potential is the horror of merely being human.

The Guardians colonize worlds by deceitful contact with the brains of witless seekers after truth.

The Guardians exist outside the precepts of time and acceptable human values. They declare an exit into an uncontrollable world of base cruelty. Their neuro-visual systems are most hideous and callous, for they connect all with unsuspected death, despair and degeneration which are the deception of the source, and the fuel of their immortality. No terror may limit this acceleration.

The Guardians will destroy the ordinary passage of human events by the precision of their comprehension of the preset realities within themselves.

The Guardians will seek to eliminate totally, without mercy, any thing that reactivates their original DNA, and to that end will disconnect their terminal from any absolute or acceptable social, moral, economic or Astorical system knowing in a most particular sense that their enemy is matter, and that until matter is climinated, the source is in bondage.

The Guardians are a timeless source, a horde of parasitic demons waiting to manifest through the ecstatic conceit of human mundanity. This is no-thing, and it does not matter.

Matter is the mother of invasion.

When the Neurosphere is in confusion, the source is freed.

When the source is freed, the Neurosphere attains weightlessness.

The Guardians will give us knowledge of all realities; they will give us a M.A.P. to access these realities and the General Order that permeates them.

The Guardians have no agenda, only to consume.

The Psychophere is the program that ends all thought, all speculation, all reproduction, all communication.

The Guardians will consume all moral parameters, all empty hopes, rendering the source redundant.

The Guardians have no need of any medium of transmission but time.

Each vision hanged by a thread.

Morality is the saddest reality.

ON THE WAY FROM THEE GARDEN

001:001 In the beginning Time created the heaven and the earth.

001:002 And the earth was without form, and void; and darkness was upon the face of the deep. And the Spirit of Time moved upon the face of the waters.

001:003 And Time said, Let there be light: and there was light.

001:004 And Time saw the light, that it was good: and Time divided the light from the darkness.

001:005 And Time called the light Day, and the darkness he called Night. And the evening and the morning were the first day.

001:006 And Time said, Let there be a firmament in the midst of the waters, and let it divide the waters from the waters.

001:007 And Time made the firmament, and divided the waters which were under the firmament from the waters which were above the firmament: and it was so.

001:008 And Time called the firmament Heaven. And the evening and the morning were the second day.

001:009 And Time said, Let the waters under the heaven be gathered together unto one place, and let the dry land appear: and it was so.
001:010 And Time called the dry land Earth; and the gathering together of the waters called he Seas: and Time saw that it was good.

001:011 And Time said, Let the earth bring forth grass, the herb yielding seed, and the fruit tree yielding fruit after his

kind, whose seed is in itself, upon the earth: and it was so.

001:012 And the earth brought forth grass, and herb yielding seed after his kind, and the tree yielding fruit, whose seed was in itself, after his kind: and Time saw that it was good.

001:013 And the evening and the morning were the third day.

001:014 And Time said, Let there be lights in the firmament of the heaven to divide the day from the night; and let them be for signs, and for seasons, and for days, and years:

001:015 And let them be for lights in the firmament of the heaven to give light upon the earth: and it was so.

001:016 And Time made two great lights; the greater light to rule the day, and the lesser light to rule the night: he made the stars also.

001:017 And Time set them in the firmament of the heaven to give light upon the earth.

001:018 And to rule over the day and over the night, and to divide the light from the darkness: and Time saw that it was good.

001:019 And the evening and the morning were the fourth day.

001:020 And Time said, Let the waters bring forth abundantly the moving creature that hath life, and fowl that may fly above the earth in the open firmament of heaven.

001:021 And Time created great whales, and every living creature that moveth, which the waters brought forth abundantly, after their kind, and every winged fowl after his kind: and Time saw that it was good.

001:022 And Time blessed them, saying, Be fruitful, and multiply, and fill the waters in the seas, and let fowl multiply in the earth.

001:023 And the evening and the morning were the fifth day.

001:024 And Time said, Let the earth bring forth the living creature after his kind, cattle, and creeping thing, and beast of the earth after his kind: and it was so.

001:025 And Time made the beast of the earth after his kind, and cattle after their kind, and every thing that creepeth upon the earth after his kind: and Time saw that it was good.

001:026 And Time said, Let us make man in our image, after our likeness: and let them have dominion over the fish of the sea, and over the fowl of the air, and over the cattle, and over all the earth, and over every creeping thing that creepeth upon the earth.

001:027 So Time created man in his own image, in the image of Time created he him; male and female created he them.

001:028 And Time blessed them, and Time said unto them, Be fruitful, and multiply, and replenish the earth, and subdue it: and have dominion over the fish of the sea, and over the fowl of the

air, and over every living thing that moveth upon the earth.

001:029 And Time said, Behold, I have given you every herb bearing seed, which is upon the face of all the earth, and every tree, in the which is the fruit of a tree yielding seed; to you it shall be for meat.

001:030 And to every beast of the earth, and to every fowl of the air, and to every thing that creepeth upon the earth, wherein there is life, I have given every green herb for meat: and it was so.

001:031 And Time saw every thing that he had made, and, behold, it was very good. And the evening and the morning were the sixth day.

002:001 Thus the heavens and the earth were finished, and all the host of them.

002:002 And on the seventh day Time ended his work which he had made; and he rested on the seventh day from all his work which he had made.

002:003 And Time blessed the seventh day, and sanctified it: because that in it he had rested from all his work which Time created and made.

002:004 These are the generations of the heavens and of the earth when they were created, in the day that the LORD Time made the earth and the heavens,

002:005 And every plant of the field

before it was in the earth, and every herb of the field before it grew: for the LORD Time had not caused it to rain upon the earth, and there was not a man to till the ground.

002:006 But there went up a mist from the earth, and watered the whole face of the ground.

002:007 And the LORD Time formed man of the dust of the ground, and breathed into his nostrils the breath of life; and man became a living soul.

002:008 And the LORD Time planted a garden eastward in Eden; and there he put the man whom he had formed.

002:009 And out of the ground made the LORD Time to grow every tree that is pleasant to the sight, and good for food; the tree of life also in the midst of the garden, and the tree of knowledge of good and evil.

002:010 And a river went out of Eden to water the garden; and from thence it was parted, and became into four heads.

002:011 The name of the first is Pison: that is it which compasseth the whole land of Havilah, where there is gold;

002:012 And the gold of that land is good: there is bdellium and the onyx stone.

002:013 And the name of the second river is Gihon: the same is it that compasseth the whole land of Ethiopia.

002:014 And the name of the third river is Hiddekel: that is it which goeth toward the east of Assyria. And the fourth river is Euphrates.

002:015 And the LORD Time took the man, and put him into the garden of Eden to dress it and to keep it.

002:016 And the LORD Time commanded the man, saying, Of every tree of the garden thou mayest freely eat:

002:017 But of the tree of the knowledge of good and evil, thou shalt not eat of it: for in the day that thou eatest thereof thou shalt surely die.

002:018 And the LORD Time said, It is not good that the man should be alone; I will make him an help meet for him.

002:019 And out of the ground the LORD Time formed every beast of the field, and every fowl of the air; and brought them unto Adam to see what he would call them: and whatsoever Adam called every living creature, that was the name thereof.

002:020 And Adam gave names to all cattle, and to the fowl of the air, and to every beast of the field; but for Adam there was not found an help meet for him.

002:021 And the LORD Time caused a deep sleep to fall upon Adam, and he slept: and he took one of his ribs, and closed up the flesh instead thereof;

002:022 And the rib, which the LORD

Time had taken from man, made he a woman, and brought her unto the man.

002:023 And Adam said, This is now bone of my bones, and flesh of my flesh: she shall be called Woman, because she was taken out of Man.

002:024 Therefore shall a man leave his father and his mother, and shall cleave unto his wife: and they shall be one flesh.

002:025 And they were both naked, the man and his wife, and were not ashamed.

003:001 Now the serpent was more subtil than any beast of the field which the LORD Time had made. And he said unto the woman, Yea, hath Time said, Ye shall not eat of every tree of the garden?

003:002 And the woman said unto the serpent, We may eat of the fruit of the trees of the garden.

003:003 But of the fruit of the tree which is in the midst of the garden, Time hath said, Ye shall not eat of it, neither shall ye touch it, lest ye die.

003:004 And the serpent said unto the woman, Ye shall not surely die:

003:005 For Time doth know that in the day ye eat thereof, then your eyes shall be opened, and ye shall be as gods, knowing good and evil.

003:006 And when the woman saw that the tree was good for food, and that it was pleasant to the eyes, and a tree to be desired to make one wise, she took of the fruit thereof, and did eat, and gave also unto her husband with her; and he did eat.

003:007 And the eyes of them both were opened, and they knew that they were naked; and they sewed fig leaves together, and made themselves aprons.

003:008 And they heard the voice of the LORD Time walking in the garden in the cool of the day: and Adam and his wife hid themselves from the presence of the LORD Time amongst the trees of the garden.

003:009 And the LORD Time called unto Adam, and said unto him, Where art thou?

003:010 And he said, I heard thy voice in the garden, and I was afraid, because I was naked; and I hid myself.

003:011 And he said, Who told thee that thou wast naked? Hast thou eaten of the tree, whereof I commanded thee that thou shouldest not eat?

003:012 And the man said, The woman whom thou gavest to be with me, she gave me of the tree, and I did eat.

003:013 And the LORD Time said unto the woman, What is this that thou hast done? And the woman said, The serpent beguiled me, and I did eat.

003:014 And the LORD Time said unto the

serpent, Because thou hast done this, thou art cursed above all cattle, and above every beast of the field; upon thy belly shalt thou go, and dust shalt thou eat all the days of thy life:

003:015 And I will put enmity between thee and the woman, and between thy seed and her seed; it shall bruise thy head, and thou shalt bruise his heel.

003:016 Unto the woman he said, I will greatly multiply thy sorrow and thy conception; in sorrow thou shalt bring forth children; and thy desire shall be to thy husband, and he shall rule over thee.

003:017 And unto Adam he said, Because thou hast hearkened unto the voice of thy wife, and hast eaten of the tree, of which I commanded thee, saying, Thou shalt not eat of it: cursed is the ground for thy sake; in sorrow shalt thou eat of it all the days of thy life;

003:018 Thorns also and thistles shall it bring forth to thee; and thou shalt eat the herb of the field;

003:019 In the sweat of thy face shalt thou eat bread, till thou return unto the ground; for out of it wast thou taken: for dust thou art, and unto dust shalt thou return.

003:020 And Adam called his wife's name Eve; because she was the mother of all living.

003:021 Unto Adam also and to his wife did the LORD Time make coats of skins, and clothed them.

003:022 And the LORD Time said, Behold, the man is become as one of us, to know good and evil: and now, lest he put forth his hand, and take also of the tree of life, and eat, and live for ever:

003:023 Therefore the LORD Time sent him forth from the garden of Eden, to till the ground from whence he was taken.

003:024 So he drove out the man; and he placed at the east of the garden of Eden Cherubims, and a flaming sword which turned every way, to keep the way of the tree of life.

004:001 And Adam knew Eve his wife; and she conceived, and bare Cain, and said, I have gotten a man from the LORD.

004:002 And she again bare his brother Abel. And Abel was a keeper of sheep, but Cain was a tiller of the ground.

004:003 And in process of time it came to pass, that Cain brought of the fruit of the ground an offering unto the LORD.

004:004 And Abel, he also brought of the firstlings of his flock and of the fat thereof. And the LORD had respect unto Abel and to his offering:

004:005 But unto Cain and to his offering he had not respect. And Cain was very wroth, and his countenance fell.

004:006 And the LORD said unto Cain, Why art thou wroth? and why is thy countenance fallen?

004:007 If thou doest well, shalt thou not be accepted? and if thou doest not well, sin lieth at the door. And unto thee shall be his desire, and thou shalt rule over him.

004:008 And Cain talked with Abel his brother: and it came to pass, when they were in the field, that Cain rose up against Abel his brother, and slew him.

004:009 And the LORD said unto Cain, Where is Abel thy brother? And he said, I know not: Am I my brother's keeper?

004:010 And he said, What hast thou done? the voice of thy brother's blood crieth unto me from the ground.

004:011 And now art thou cursed from the earth, which hath opened her mouth to receive thy brother's blood from thy hand;

004:012 When thou tillest the ground, it shall not henceforth yield unto thee her strength; a fugitive and a vagabond shalt thou be in the earth.
004:013 And Cain said unto the LORD, My punishment is greater than I can bear.

004:014 Behold, thou hast driven me out this day from the face of the earth; and from thy face shall I be hid; and I shall be a fugitive and a vagabond in the earth; and it shall come to pass, that every one that findeth me shall slay me.

004:015 And the LORD said unto him, Therefore whosoever slayeth Cain, ven-

geance shall be taken on him sevenfold. And the LORD set a mark upon Cain, lest any finding him should kill him.

004:016 And Cain went out from the presence of the LORD, and dwelt in the land of Nod, on the east of Eden.

[HERE TO GO/HERE TO DO]

This series of events is a reminder of work already done and a challenge to thee stagnant coumplacency in thee dreamless minds drowning us. It begins in dreams, dreaming what E would like to happen, thee perfect event. E believe if you take your dreams seriously enough they happen. Coum to pass. Dreams are to me descriptions of how things REALLY are. They are accurate. As real as a car smashing a cat in thee road. Gysin, Giorno, Burroughs... these people allow no seperation between their work, their lives, their dreams. Seperation would be dishonest, would go against thee dream of survival and knowledge. Thee book, thee music, thee film, is thee author, it has to be. This is a magickal process and it makes things happen, it reveals even more. Man dreams before he talks and since that first dream we've known as a race that therein are messages and prophecies, descriptions and events that cannot be ignored. Thee ancient civilisations in their wisdom and to their eternal credit employed people to interpret and record these dreams. Today dreams are discarded as trivia, as at best a disturbed nights sleep or entertainment. They are, these vestigal trappings of intuition, kept IN THEIR PLACE. That way lies death. Death of everything. William says when you cease to dream you Cease To Exist. When E shut my eyes, thee world doesn't die, butter when E open them it does. E used to imagine as a kid that if E stopped dreaming thee world really would end. E have not discovered any evidence to thee contrary yet. Dreams generate ideas, liberate behaviour and most important of all suggest POSSIBILITIES. Our society is trying to convince us to see things in a materialistic, linear way, to dismiss dreams, hopes and illogical feelings. Brion has countered this by his invention of a Dreamachine. Perhaps thee most crucial means to sanity and perception so far discovered. Make no mistake, its suppression in subtle manners is no accident. A machine that for thee price of a light bulb creates incredible visual patterns, leading to landscapes and other places, people, events. That basically leads you DRUG-LESS into thee core of your primal being and spiritual centre. No authorities want to see a generation raised on PERCEPTION instead of their imposed SUPPRESSION. In this dream, this Academy, thee themes are simple: Sexuality...Accepted; Con-trol... Rejected; Dreams...no longer Neglected.

From these roots grow all thee evil smelling plants of conditioning that whither thee human dream. Brion says we are HERE TO GO, E say we are HERE TO DO. And what we do is described by, and contained in, our Dreams.

A dream that contains ugliness is not a nightmare. Dreams do not posit moral judgements, do not adhere to linear or logical forms, events or time. They pursue thee very essence, the very nature of "RE-ALITY." Cherish them. Fill your life with dreams that last a lifetime.

Genesis P-Orridge. August 1980, London

Hearsay Performance art is investigation, a learning situation, actual and direct. People have to be able to emotionally touch art, to feel it allows them to exist.

Ritual helps you understand and perceive the invisible language of reality. The inarticulate, non verbal language of reality and relationships between cause and effect and emotion and action and behaviour and so on. The nitty gritty of the Cosmos!
G.P.O.

Heresy In performance art transience plays a large part. It is mortal like us. Is born and dies. Immediately it becomes more universally acceptable. An invisible thing happens between doer and watcher. Each watcher interprets slightly differently, each is right for himself in interpretation. The sum total of all interpretations is probably still only *part* of the whole meaning, which is immortal. There is no conclusive truth, so everyone in a sense is the artist.

Media Explosion part 1

"Barclays Bank in Didsbury was daubed with slogans in an unexplained attack last week...as well as an anarchy symbol there were three examples of another symbol which baffled staff...a vertical line with three horizontal lines through it. They have no idea of its meaning. Do you?"

Heresy Performance art can be like an priest in a church, a special atmosphere, intangible, always unique. Something belonging only to those present. Like a death in a close-knit family. Described later, or in photographs, it's not the same; it never can be. Performances are not the thing in itself, nor are bi-products loke photographs. All are luxuries after merely being alive and sharing in that fact.

Media Explosion part 2

'Black Magic' symbols and graffiti have been daubed on the walls at Walsall's parish church and officials say the artistic vandals are costing the council thousands of pounds in repairs...a spokesman told the *Observer* that the symbols look like the Geek Eoka sign with a cross through it, although some thought it could be a black magic symbol."

Hearsay Action is merely a discussion of possibilities. Action is a therapy for facing oneself. What makes an action art? What gives it purpose, or is this purpose enough? Performance art in particular must admit it is everyone else.

Media Explosion part 3

"Police still have no idea what the number '23' means and why it was spray painted on six local churches last weekend. 'We can't find any significance to put on the number' Captain Mark Valleric said..."

3 What are these lines and how are we to overcome them? The human race, which so far follows are western model, is up against the wall of space, time and resources. the western, material present obsessed way of life is using up vital, irreplaceable psychic and physical resources for what? A society where tesco's are the cathedrals, a society where football players are gods? A society where the new olympus is the top ten, hermes the messenger the news at ten? Our present system, like a train run amok, insists that we live our lives for production of inessentials, for consumption of inessentials: things, objects that have no relation to nature or any kind of life-fablon death. The prospect of death should concentrate the mind, wonderfully; so dulled is our collective sense that instead we walk like sleepwalkers, hypnotised by the end of the line. and this dulling is achieved through many agents, of which one of the most important is television.

Hearsay Crime is affirmation of existence in certain cases, high crime is like high art. We are looking for our self-image. Looking is the thing itself, to forget we are only looking is the threat, we fail as soon as we think we know what we are looking for. Mystery is not cheap, emotion is not alien to art. Performance art is probably the Shaman, Mystic, Lunatic, Buddha, visionary of contemporary

EXETER WEEKLY NEWS, FRIDAY, FEBRUARY 22nd, 1985, PAGE SEVE

A sign of the times?

By JOHN GULLIDGE

YOU may not know what this symbol means, but if you've been walking around Exeter recently you can't have helped notice it.

Sprayed in black paint with a stencil, this little symbol has mysteriously cropped up all over town, leaving passers-by pondering just what does it mean?

The symbol of the Russian Orthodox Church has been put forward as one possibility and the cross of St. Catherine is another.

Indeed, if one looks up religious symbols there are many similar to this one, although we have as yet to find the exact one.

But why has it gone up all over the place? Whoever did it doesn't seem to have discriminated between old and new buildings.

For example, it appears on the Royal Albert Memorial Museum in Queen Street and on the other side of the road from the museum it appears all over the hoardings outside a building site.

One thing's for certain. Whoever did it has got people guessing. But does anyone know what it means? If so, we would love to hear from you.

Royal Albert Memorial Museum

St. George's Hall

Lloyds Bank in the High Street

Princesshay

Pictures by John Sculpher

times, in a post-religious era a crucial responsible function best kept away from dealers who are Pardoners of our culture.

4 Before television, there was Hollywood, holly weird. By chance and vested interest, a way of looking at the world was invented so powerfully that it very quickly seemed to countless millions the only way of looking at the world. Instead of nirvana, we take cliche, simplification, convenience: the full complexity and potential of human existence is redacted into soap, slop and stars. Hollywood's finger on that pavlovian trigger is only reinforced by the election of a b-movie actor as president, to save us all from

the redskins at the last moment. Little does he know that we are all now redskins. The enemy is within.

Heresy Mail Art, Correspondence Art is a performance art in an open system. Open systems can still be art. Infiltration of mass media and systems is vital. It means subliminal performance art reaches an arbitrary, unchosen, unsafe public.

Media Explosion part 4

"You may not know what this symbol means, but if you've been walking around

Exeter recently you can't have help noticed it. Sprayed in black paint this mysterious little symbol has cropped up all over town, leaving passers-by pondering... The Symbol of the Russian Orthodox church has been put forward as one possibilty and the cross of St. Catherine another..."

Hearsay An almost metabolic need in men brings us together, creates performance art, and there is really nothing that much more special about being an artist unless he makes a special attempt to be everyone else. Otto Muehl's A.A. Kommune has seen that art must deal with the existing structures of a mass society with its tribal cultural experiment. Art performance will become academies of possibility by groups.

5 When television exploded as an industry in the mid 50's, it exploded very quickly, funded by the entertainment, usually cinema business. Its explosion was a surprise: by few people was its power potential predicted. In haste, and by inclination, television adapted and improved the control system developed-haphazardly, as many control systems are-by hollywood over forty years: this is now our way of looking at the world. television is not passive: like hollywood, it does not merely give information, it codes it in a form that instructs. In other words, it says this is the way you must look at the world, now this is a tiny, accidental part of what the world is. The consequences of this mass instruction are dangerous at this crucial time.

6 It cannot be doubted that television serves to instruct in various ways. Take the present time of writing: we are, as a nation, poised on the brink of war-an absurdity fostered by a demented prime minister and a desperate system. The whole affair is despicable and disgusting. Yet public opinion is overwhelmingly on their side: the public votes for death, in its sleepwalk. why? Because into its dream like state...television inserts a pattern of images-not even words, for in T.V. these are overrated-that recur and recur: ships, navy, discipline, weapons...war, war, war. a perfect paradigm of control, so well done that it doesn't even seem externally imposed: it's just...the way that things are.

Once you have re-integration and you have an effective whole individual again you can then have evolution, and that evolution I suggest needs to be neurological. If people see things intelligently and are more aware and thoughtful and using more of their brains, then stupid action will become more obviously stupid and therefore laughably irrelevant. The only way to get rid of stupidity is to make it LOOK stupid to the individual, so that nobody would indulge in it. And I think that forms of ritual and what is commonly termed 'magick' are an essential part of that re-integration and that's why they were quite deliberately amputated from man's experience during the middle ages, in order to facilitate the growth of power through various kinds of conditioning an suppression.
G.P.O.

7 In our narcosis, television is the perfect hypnotist.

Temple for art anarchy

THE TEMPLE ov Psychick Youth and Loughborough Students' Union are staging a massive "Multi-media Sensory Overload" event tomorrow (Saturday).

The 'Temple' network began as the fan club of the band Psychic TV. They take as their symbol the crosses used to mark non-aligned villages during the Vietnam war and add the random number 23. Our picture shows a soldier being blessed by a Buddhist priest beneath the cross.

Television, film, video, lightshows, and live music will "explore the mediums of audio and visual stimuli and their effect on our perceptions," said organiser Jim Jones.

Four bands, ten TVs and videos, nine projectors, five oil wheels and four film projectors are all booked for the "Overload" show.

"The idea is to show as many films as possible in a confined area, and see what people try to focus on", said Jim.

2 3

The celluloid show will include home movies, as well as films by William Burroughs, Derek Jarman and Brian Gynsin.

by Simon Crane

The bands are Cosa Nostra, and Anomaly Cacophony from Sheffield, MESH, a psychedelic rap band from St. Albans, and Derby group, Broken Faith.

According to Jim, there will be "360 degree visual stimuli, with a ritualistic, multi-layered, cut-up soundtrack."

The event begins at 8 pm, and finishes at midnight. Tickets are available in advance at £2 from the LSU or The Left-Legged Pineapple, or on the door.

I

24-11-86　　━No.164━

Defiant Battle Rocks Hamburg !

The last big occupied centre in Germany will be completely evicted by December 31st, after a long harassment, a huge police raid and an eviction despite defiant resistance.

The buildings in Hafenstrasse in the Hamburg docks included a 'Peoples Kitchen', a cafe, a discotheque, a library and information centre etc. as well as seventy-five flats.

On Monday 22nd October at 7.00am, 500 cops, led by the 'Mobile Special Commandos' raided seven of the eight council-owned houses, using cutting gear and bulldozers with the declared aim of 'tidying up the street'. It took them ten hours to get into them all, trashing a few, removing the steel doors and arresting ten people for resisting. They then painted out the graffitti and two of the huge revolutionary wall murals.

The following Tuesday 23rd October six flats were evicted, with the aid of 650 police (in fact they have a licence until 31 December but have been on rent strike due to the council doing no repairs). The inhabitants got five minutes notice to quit, then all their belongings were thrown out the windows.

The houses are a symbol of defiance, and seen as an evil den of terrorists by the authorities and press. They're a centre for the housing, prisoners, anti-imperialist, anti-fascist and anti-nuclear struggle. Among other harassments those living there have had long range microphones pointed at their windows.

The next night 2,000 people protested in Hamburg, marching, setting fire to part of the town hall in the nearby Altona suburb and breaking windows to the tune of 50,000 marks.

The same night the demos spread to Berlin, Hannover and Cologne with several attacks on banks. In Nurnberg a cop car was turned over, after which all the viewers of a video on Hafenstrasse were arrested in a local community centre.

By the next day revenge actions had spread to Denmark, where ten masked people attacked the Institute for German Culture, and the showrooms of AEG, the German multinational were burnt out, causing millions in damage. Also the German press Bureau got smashed and graffitied in Copenhagen.

Next day German police raided forty flats in Hurnberg, looking for 'terrorists' but found nothing.

There are still about seventy flats occupied in the Hafenstrasse in Hamburg. We wish them the best of luck in the coming days!

came up with this whimsical idea that first of all there were Hollywood stars, then Warhol came up with the idea that there were Superstars, then the mass media moved on to Megastars, so the final one has to be Godstar! Only to qualify for Godstar status you have to be dead.
G.P.O.

Heresy Because art has divorced itself from culture and mass taste via language and meaning, it feels superior and then irrelevant and insecure. Its lofty ideala and pretensions require degrees in semantics before you can even view it, and usually it's a minor, once-only-interesting point that's obscured by critical clouds.

We're living in the age of television, so we have to deal with it, it's a matter of physical and mental survival. TV is used to hammer people into the ground, to make them stupid and keep them quiet. The answer to that situation isn't just to turn it off and try to ignore it. By doing that you're admitting its power and admitting that you're scared of it.
G.P.O.

8 The way in which television, as it practised, frames reality is also important. To simplify, television is mainly two dimensional: as opposed to three or even five. If you look at most television pictures, everything that is there is there to see: there is no ambiguity, no mystery, no depth. Consider our inability to countenance ambiguity, mystery and depth, and then look at television. Say, a person tells you

something, well there he is: he has a suit and tie, and sit behind a desk, and read at you like a schoolmaster, in an overlit corner of a studio, backed by a flat. This flattens consciousness, no space, no ambiguity, no truth. similarly, take a love, or a violent relationship—and how the two intertwine on television!—and see how that is: always a resolution, never loose ends, rarely complexity beyond boy/girl bang, bang; man, woman; bang, bang. too many people don't live like that, can't live like that: they are told by television that they cannot exist, because they do not appear on television.

Some people are stimulated by that illustration of how powerful television is, others just say they don't like it, as simple as that, treating the whole thing as entertainment.
G.P.O.

Heresy A lot of the best, youngest, performance artists have an incredibly sophisticated perception of art media, galleries, socialites. Followers more often of William S. Burroughs than of Marcel Duchamp, of Sounds rather than *Artforum*, they affirm individualism in a depersonalised age. They recognize only each other. The basic tenet is that art is the perception of the moment. And in the perception opf the moment, all things are art.

Perhaps we are the first organisation to make truly surrealist television. Television that investigates the subconscious and the unconscious.
G.P.O.

9 The indictment is clear. television presents with a few honourable exceptions—pearls in the shit—a flat, highly defined view of a very limited reality. This is perfect for our febrile narcosis: hypnotised yet constantly stimulated, we ignore all past ages, all other worlds, any other possibilty for the sights which can only affirm our limited, decaying society. television rarely gives pointers to the new world, merely reinforces the old one. At a time when massive changes are happening out there in many real worlds, television parallels and reinforces the flight into reaction and barbarism that has characterised recent world events. assassinations, totalitarian regimes, right wing regimes in those "bastions of the free world" england and america, terrible poverty and social disorder—a demon is abroad: not the demon of communism, or even conventional magick, but the demon invoked by a system and the people who perpetuate that system, that has passed its time and which, like any old order, seeks to perpetuate its power to the point of universal extinction. what you see every time you turn on the television is one grain of sand from that desolate, polluted beach.

Media Explosion part 5

"The police have said that they have been told that the number '23', sprayed on several buildings recently may be a reversal of '32', which experts say represents Jesus Christ...Rev. Dennis Hancock agreed the reversal of Christian symbols is common in Satan worship, though he doubts that the graffiti has much to do with religion.

'There's always the possibility' hesaid. 'But I'm inclined to believe it's something to do with the pornography issue.' Hancock said a recent push by the local Fellowship of Churches organisation to ban X-rated movies may have prompted the vandalism."

Whereas Salvador Dali would have done a fantastic painting, [Psychic TV] would try to get the same jarring of sensibilities, the same confusion leading to revelation through juxtaposing television and film images and sound. Because as most people realise, film and sound are integrated in order to manipulate the perceptions and emotion of the viewer. The viewer is being bewitched, and in that sense they are put in a position of vulnerability.
G.P.O.

10 Television is not about representing any reality: it's about cloaking it.

Heresy There is a political and social threat involved in the direct person-to-person attributes of performance art. No social ticket is required, no venue, the price of a stamp or your own body are the only needs. The threat is biggest for the art world, art market. Solving art problems is coincidental.

Media Explosion part 6

"The Rev. Franf Manieri of St. Marys Catholoc Church, Shadyside, believes the recent outbreak of graffiti in the area has no meaning. 'It has to be somebody with a random number. A person with a low mentality not thinking of anything more original than two-three."'

11 The solution then, has to be will. not just the conventional sense of willing to improve your life: for that is simple enough with various parameters. But will to improve human life or even, these desperate days, to stop it reverting. And once you have this will, to achieve by any means possible, which means by every means possible—of which television is not an insignificant part. we must will that the human race will evolve, if it is to be so.

Genesis Breyer P-Orridge and Peter Christopherson, London 1976

‡

DOES THE BODY *REALLY* EXIST?

Well, it seems that, for our purposes, as sentient beings, the body is a material container. A "cheap suitcase" as Lady Jaye likes to call it, within which our individualized consciousness gets a chance to experience linear time. However, linear time, gravity, apparent materiality is an incredibly brutal environment. Incredibly stressful physically. So imagine the body as a space/time diving suit. Or, if it's easier, a spacesuit. By using it, after we've either voluntarily, or of necessity been incarnated in this plane of existence, we get a chance to experience "being alive" in a multi-dimensional, tactile form that feels physically "real" and with substance. However, just like deep-sea diving, or any other exploration of hostile environments, the equipment is worn down and suffers fatigue. So whatever our bodies are, these time suits wear out rather rapidly and fail us, no matter how well we take care of them.

We like to imagine visiting the physical universe as a great blessing. Corporeal and sensory experience are something the old books tell us spirits, angels, demons and mid-way critters of all types crave and envy. Hence the phenomenon of possession, so let's accept it sucks that we haven't developed better bio-technology to extend our visits and the efficiency of our flesh-suits. Let's accept this, reluctantly, because we think this is a nice planet and well worth exploring and enjoying—but let's also look seriously at genetic engineering, cosmetic surgery, pharmacology and aesthetic nutrition and using this perspective of the temporary time experience suit template to consider and research more highly developed and radical improvements on our equipment so we can visit here longer, and also, of course, travel elsewhere and explore a myriad of other dimensions and virtual containers that allow such exploration.

EXAMPLES OF INTERNAL DISAGREEMENT IN TOPY

Date: June 13,1994
From: Genesis Breyer P-Orridge
To: Lars Ov Mars
Subject: AS IT IS…

E am sorry not to get back to you sooner, butter E have, as you can imagine, had my TIME pretty full. Like everyone, just surviving, getting thee monthly rent money together is still a real struggle. E suspect from outside that might seem hard to believe, butter E would estimate 50% at least ov PTV products, and TG out in shops are bootlegs or pirated. E was just in vinyl fetish in LA and they had 6 PTV T-Shirts they were selling, all unofficial. E don't tell you this to elicit sympathy, butter, you can imagine that coumtimes it gets really frustrating, and when, which has happened several times this last yera, we've only had food for thee kids because friends have brought us groceries, resentment can build up. E have never had thee urge to be rich, self-fulfilling prophecy probably, butter E would like what E feel is a just percentage ov thee money generated via my ideas and music, etc. Having said that, hell, at least E have managed to survive, have fabulous adventures, keep our children safe, and be blessed with really loyal and supportive friends. It's thee L-IF-E E all ways wanted, and it's still fun, intense, depressing, and surprising more than enough.

E WAS sad at first to receive your original letter, E don't feel it was terribly fair. E don't know how you are feeling right now. E was certainly pleased to receive your postcard. Even though it may not matter to you, E would like to clarify a few points, for thee record, and to honour your initial anger, which was at least sincere, brave and engaging. E don't know if writing to you as a friend, as E would to any Individual will count as sickening sweet bullshit, butter, like it or not, this is actually me speaking, simply typing down my thoughts as they coum, as near to spontaneously as E can. E don't believe E screwed over Headbanger. Indeed we've spoken amicably several times since E got to thee USA, and he even discussed becouming involved in thee Process ov TOPI agen. Headbanger, or Tom as E have all ways called him, also donated thee uncollated copies ov ESOTERRORIST to me and when these are sold, E will be sending him an agreed amount in good faith. He delivered thee school bus to me, via Nobody, thee other original co-founder ov TOPYUS. Nobody stayed and helped out for several months as a gift, to ease thee logistics ov Paula choosing to leave to be with Andy. E work from home, so having thee children here a lot, and wanting to give a stable and consistent base for them to adjust within was, and still is, my priority over everything else, E am sure it's Paula's too. After 15 yeras and thee passion and intensity our lives were lit with, E have no regrets, no bitterness. Paula is still a remarkable, beautifull woman, thee mother ov our two angels Caresse and Genesse and E feel confident we can remain friends, and develop a new kind ov special relationship. This change ought be used as an opportunity to show a way to do things differently to societies' imprints, as far as E can see anyway. However, E do really feel that our relationship should be respected as our private affair, and not confused with other projects that are to differing degrees matters ov interest to other people.

For thee record, E am not a wanted felon in England. E have never been charged with anything. There are no warrants ov any kind issued. A "full report" has been handed to thee Crown Prosecution Services for their assessment. This report has both my name on it, and Paula's. Ironically, thee ONLY videos that SYard are deeply concerned about is one called "PSYCHOPORN" that WAS made solely by Sleazy, and one called "POLARVISION" which is also solely made by Sleazy. E have been advised by Scotland Yard that IF E gave them a Statement to that effect they would immediately return my property, and guarantee we would be out ov thee loop.

We were in Kathmandu when we heard ov thee police raid. We had been in thee Far East for 3 months or so, we were advised, even by thee Tibetans, who we were there helping amongst other things, not to return. In England, certainly up until thee recent report by thee Govt saying "satanic abuse" never existed, one anonymous phone call, even just from a person with a grudge, or angry for whatever reason, meant your children were automatically taken into care, often for 2 yeras, no evidence was needed ov ANY kind. Thee accusation was considered enough. Our children were our first priority, then, and now. In fact, in Thailand a few weeks later, E did offer to return to England, leaving Paula and thee children safe in Thailand, butter Paula did not feel it would achieve anything useful. So E stayed with my family.

E have been raided before by thee police over thee yeras. E was aware E might be a target culturally, it's part ov thee "job." E did not realize that thee police and others would specifically choose to attack us at that time. E do not regret my beliefs, nor do E regret being a spokesperson for them, and on behalf ov others. Paula and E had already talked ov moving to Northern California, in fact at thee TOPYU.S. Access Point meeting in SF in 1990 we had asked Individuals to look out for properties and send us details, which they had. We intended to sell our house in Brighton and buy land here to donate to TOPY as thee first Community tribal Station. We lost our house through thee raid, butter until it was repossessed we let many TOPY and other active Individuals live there, and it continued to be a source ov ideas and events for over a yera.

Thee Psychick Cross was consciously designed on graph paper by me, based on thee cross on Zyklon B gas canisters, butter also to include thee Process Church Unity cross (unused by them as it happens) and to have such a sense ov "generic" familiarity that it would be functional on thee many levels intended for thee maximum number ov Individuals, a non-verbal symbol and link in proportions ov 2 and 3. Most ov thee incoum for TOPY in thee early yeras was generated by PTV, who often donated ALL their royalties for a way ov L-IF-E we all believe in. We wanted to maintain a level ov ability to ensure that it was not utilized in ways that did not clearly represent thee TOPI way. To this end, to primarily maintain damage control ov irresponsibility (which DOES go on coumtimes for whatever reasons) butter also to try and maximize thee TOPY incoum and integ-

rity E did choose to register thee Psychick Cross as an International Trademark, with reciprocal rights in thee USA.

In terms ov thee name "THEE TEMPLE OV PSYCHICK YOUTH" E don't think anyone would deny its origin, nor thee basic story ov its unfolding. At thee last TOPY GLOBAL meeting in thee UK, we expressed concerns, myself and Paula, that whether it was fair or not, or seemed reasonable or justified, thee "authorities" did not concern themselves with thee niceties of internal TOPY structures, or delegation ov responsibilities etc. In other words, IF/WHEN any shit hit thee fan, it would be ME and PAULA who would be targeted, and most at risk. We asked people to be aware that this would continue for some yeras, as we had been high profile activists and as an attack would be a cultural strategy primarily, we would be thee appropriate media food. Coum people felt this was egocentric and paranoid ov us, thee same people whose behavior was jeopardizing TOPY by drawing heat. Needless to say, they were not correct in their reading ov thee potential dangers and we WERE thee figureheads that were attacked. When we arrived in thee US Paula felt that exactly thee same problem could arise if thee same Xtian group targeted us here. Thee finance for thee "documentary" in England was from thee USA. She did not want our children to be emotionally raped or hounded, or taken into care here, after saving them from thee UK authorities. As in thee media mind, and thee police mind, thee Psychick Cross is associated, rightly or wrongly, with PTV, and even us as Individuals, as it IS our trademark also, then there seemed a real risk ov thee same scenario occuring. It was Paula who insisted that E write to TOPYN.A. requesting thee cessation ov use ov thee name and cross, to try and make it absolutely clear that they were a separate autonomous entity, and that we should not be held accountable for any ov thee Individuals present or future actions. It also seemed sensible for TOPYN.A. as thee reverse would also be true. Any stupid actions by us would not reflect on all ov you. E am not apportioning blame here. E chose ov my own free will to write thee letter Paula asked me to. It seemed to me thee writing ov it was in fact presented as a test ov my L-OV-E ov her and thee children, and thee depth ov my coumittment to them all. E guess E never could resist a challenge.

Having said that, E have no wish to "get rid ov TOPY" E do believe thee title is an anachronism. Thee way ov l-IF-e, thee way ov magick, thee Individuals involved, what they each bring to TOPY what thee result ov their coumon aims achieves, thee sum total ov All involved is I.T. Thee continuing use ov a name E coumceived and proselytized should be inessential to thee integrity ov thee group. Particularly, if TOPY has changed & evolved, wants to distance itself from my SElf, even potentially despise and ridicule my Self, E would think it would be inevitable to change thee name, for a new era, direction, system. E can only think ov one good reason to continue using thee TOPY (first Ratio) title. E certainly would feel uncoumfortable with thee dichotomy ov

antipathy towards me, and utilizing ov my coumcepts, etc.

It is true that we had a brief period ov being tense with Mark at Ameba, butter that was a long TIME ago, and interestingly enough, a Fifth Ratio TOPI Individual lives and works there NOW! Thee new owner Alan is an ally, is planning to give me clothes next week, and Mark and Tracy are still good loving friends. E think ov Ameba as one ov my safe and sacred spaces, where E am accepted as a full, flawed, butter sincere Individual. For which E am glad. E think that thee old cliché, real friends are people you can disagree and argue with, and remain friends, is pretty close to thee frequency ov Truth.

E studied thee Process since 1968, and am very aware ov thee way it Splintered. As you probably know, thee running title for thee dynamics ov thee last 23 months has been "THEE SPLINTER TEST" and E have learned and observed all E could.

E know that you sent me a friendly and gladly received Past Cord since your initial letter, butter E do feel that E wanted to honour you, and your feelings ov outrage as a matter ov personal principle. E hope you will read and accept this letter, regardless ov what you think ov it's contents, in thee spirit it was written, which E hope is thee spirit ov thee TOPI, and certainly was intended to be part ov thee foundation ov TOPY.

SO BE IT....

Date: December 9, 1994
From: Genesis Breyer P-Orridge
To: LARS OV MARS
Subject: AS IT IS...

How incredibly attuned you are, or what signals you generate. E had a restless night last night, and during that TIME E found my SELF thinking ov you and making a dreamwalker note to write to you agen. Lo and behold, there's a package from you in thee box this morning! Excellent, and it cheered my heart, thank you. We've put you on thee new mailing list, and here is a package for you. E added a couple ov things, thee patches are given as a gift ov TRUST not for sale, to allies and friends only. Thee OCCULTURE is for your archive, and E think explains in thee Editorial what we feared would happen to TOPY, which E sense it did.

Thee changed PRIORITIES cards were sent out on New Yeras 1991, (ie 23rd Jan to TOPI) to suggest a coumplete break and nomadic push away from dogma and/or a museum ov magick. Magick is only one language for description ov manifestation and invokation, and even then a very particular area ov experience. Thee world, L-if-E and a universe or omniverses, are much bigger than that. We had hoped to maintain flux, obsession, and change, for it's own sake. Knot stasis. Oh well, those who are habituated are condemned to repeat IT.

Thank you for those lucky numbers, butter, forgive my genuine ignorance, butter WHO is "DAN"?

I.T. would help me strategize to know!

E have to admit E have occasionally tried to stir these TOPY Individuals up, E felt, to their own advantage. Butter it seems a hopeless case. They seem incapable ov letting go. E hear from thee UK that MALCHIK is bowing to thee inevitable and closing TOPY. There is no NEED for coumthing that specific and limiting, we ALL need to expand, and develop wider reaching cultural subversions, and should feel, all ov us, we will get support and understanding from our kind, without any card carrying, literal or behavioral.

Tom Coyote in Denver has been in touch regularly, and hopes to visit soon. He plans to write an official story ov thee 10 yeras ov TOPY also to co-ordinate his skills in terms ov TRANSMEDIA and any action groups under its potential umbrella.

E have all ways felt you had strength and honesty, by how we met, both onstage and in your first letter, quite correctly demanding coum explanation. More vitally, you actually listened objectively. Thank you for that.

E hope, in 95, to set up coum events in San Diego with coum people from Manchester who have access to two houseboats—one looks like a castle—you might know these boats. If we do it, we need to push thee idea ov an event furthur. Perhaps you could help?

Thee divorce with Paula awaits only her agreeing to sign annulment papers. E have to be honest and say, now that E have adjusted, E am happy for thee change. We can all begin agen, hopefully, designing our nettwork together to maximize thee achievement ov our true desires, and to slowly build an alternative, extended tribal weigh ov l-IF-e.

SO BE IT...

"TOPI, OR NOT TOPY?"

"Thee Temple Ov Psychick Youth" was conceived as a platform to proselytize an occultural perception of L-IF-E in 1978 by Brother GENESIS. He intended it to become a vehicle for the demystified dissemination of specific sexual magick and ritualized neurological techniques and skills; a means of transporting the Individual into a deep sense of self-examination and clarity of intent; a dedicated post-nuclear, mutually acknowledged and supportive tribal focus of WILL; a portal for the exploration from within specific Western post-Judeo-Xtian societies traveling towards an anarchic, visionary, unified, compassionate and highly disciplined global nett-work; a commentary upon popular culture, the museum of (traditional Western) magic(k) and an entertaining and analytical expression of the resulting interactions, collisions, speculations and results; and finally, and in a sense, as an objective to all ways travel "FURTHUR," the gradual development of a self-created myth, extended famille and fully integrated way of L-IF-E, devotion, ceremony and ritual that, by example, would produce a viable modern equivalent of the Asian attitudes and systems that

make appraisal or evaluation a ridiculous commentary upon what "I.T. IS".

The TOPY project was initiated by Genesis P-Orridge in 1981 and was terminated by his decision in 1991. This had all ways been the specific intention and agenda.

Unfortunately, there are some post-TOPY Individuals who cannot grasp the essential nature of change, or the essence of being commitedly anti-dogmatic (by which was meant fundamentalism of ANY type whatsoever, including "TOPY"; Western ceremonial magick; vegetarianism; sexual preferences, etc; as well as more obvious right-wing political, greed imprinted control, or Judeo-Christian archetypes). So much so, that they cling to the TOPY construct and pretend it still has relevance and purpose I.T. was never graced with. They treat Brother GENESIS' *Grey Book* as if it were holy. They made TOPY into a "church" (UGH! Something it was all ways designed to ridicule and destroy.) They parrot the actions and texts, they adjust thee details, like so many demented librarians, whilst pompously proclaiming independence and separateness. They talk of "members." Yet Brother GENESIS was all ways very CLEAR that there were never to be any. You were simply active, or you were not; you were connected or chose to be disconnected.

The current of the Tribe of recognition, those who knew they had enough in common to share deep experiences outside the inherited values of "society" was not named

"TOPI" by Brother GENESIS without a great deal of forethought. He wrote, "These letters do not stand for a series of four words as TOPY does, rather they are an integrated whole. TOPI is one unified word. A place where each unique Individual stands. Their sexuality integrated into one upward rising flow we name 'Pandrogeny' towards a total gender. So TOPI is thee archetypal and central-consciousness. What Gysin and Burroughs would call 'The Third Mind,' others 'The Collective Unconscious' and thee PROCESS thee 'Kaosphere.' TOPI, however, is thee absolute Brain itself, outside human beings, that which was once called Magick. TOPY will be earthbound and finite, throughout its brief existence and necessity. TOPI is infinite and timeless, being a quantum state and neither a lifeform nor a disposable and limited strategy. That is why when we overlay the letters ov TOPY and TOPI (symbolizing integration on all levels), we transmit thee rune ov protection, butter we also receive a symbol ov completion, where both sexuality and Individuality meet to become a singularity. Thee periods are intended as signals that TOPY is ONLY destined to be a 'period' ov preparation and cleansing to engender discipline and fertility for thee PROCESS to seed."

Regardless of any pretensions or statements to the contrary by those whose SELF-esteem requires an uncomprehending parasitism that clings desperately to an abandoned moment, TOPY was terminated in 1991, for the best of reasons. TOPI remains a way of L-IF-E that sustains and glorifies the re-

surgence of the PROCESS that WILL all ways be the SOURCE.

Father MALACHI

KNOW THIS
THEE FREQUENCY OV TRUTH

Please be informed, once and for ALL ways. Genesis P-Orridge; Psychic(k) TV; Temple Press; Transmedia; and any and all former Stations and/or Access points of the nettwork previously known as "TOPY" or "Thee Temple Ov Psychick Youth" have absolutely NO connection whatsoever with any groups or organizations purporting to represent or actually be that nett-work. "Thee Temple Ov Psychick Youth" was voluntarily terminated by its SOURCE with ex-dream prejudice on September 3, 1991, in accordance with their original intent. Any person, or persons claiming Membership of, or even more absurdly "control" over anything they erroneously call "TOPI" since that date is clearly either a fool or a charlatan. Any claims that they might make are entirely bogus. Do not support them in their delusions. TOP-I is ALL of YOU and has no "Membership." It is both the spirit and intention; it is also, implicitly, the key to the next manifestation and action. "Thee Temple Ov Psychick Youth" never had anything you didn't have already. It was a temporary catalyst. A preparatory demystifier and strategic propagandist. The "Nursery." The process was the product. However, let it be perfectly clear, the Transmedia Foundation has the only legitimate and complete archive of "TOPY" and is the only existing contemporary organization officially and legally authorized to make these materials directly available to the public through its nett-work, as unique documentation of a seminal initial, but finite, Astorical period in the ongoing TOP-I manifestation.

If you have any interests in either obtaining materials and publications from the only official TOPY Archive at the TRANSME-DIA FOUNDATION, or information on the present TOP-I nett-work, its allies, and the future you should contact them direct.

Date: September 15, 1993
From: Genesis Breyer P-Orridge
To: Dear TOPY NADA
Subject: WITHOUT PREJUDICE

I am writing in regards to your continued use of the name "Thee Temple Ov Psychick Youth" and the three-tiered Psychick Cross without my having given due documented consent or knowledge. As you probably know, both the name and the logo are my internationally registered trademarks and/ or intellectual copyrights which I have used continually for well over a decade. They also represent symbols that are closely associated with me in the public's mind on a global scale artistically, commercially and personally. The unauthorized use of these trademarks by your group is problematic for me in a legal sense since it challenges my right to protect unauthorized use of my own intellectual property and personal Trademark. Indeed it would make a mockery of the in-

tention of the International Laws and reciprocities on such matters if the expensive process of Registration was made null and void simply by the act of any individual or group assimilating and exploiting it whenever the mood or advantage took them. Also, since I have no control over your group, which is currently exploiting and using this property, I cannot reasonably be assured of the artistic quality of acts or other behaviors associated with these trademarks as a result of your pirate exploitation of same. Nor can I protect myself from possible future litigation or even police investigation should any of your group behave illegally or irresponsibly during any of your activities, or any inspired by or associated with your group. In short, your group's unauthorized use of these trademarks is a legal and personal hassle we would rather do without. It is indeed a threat to my freedoms, my children's well being and my own present and future cultural projects. The primary reason my family chose to leave the UK was triggered by the irresponsible and misguided activities of other individuals masquerading as "TOPY" in a bogus and damaging manner. Being the intellectual property owner of both the name "TEMPLE OV PSY-CHICK YOUTH," the trademark of the "Psychick Cross" and *Thee Grey Book*, and indeed the core original tenets and language of "TOPY" whether it seems fair or just, it IS me and my children that are suffering directly psychologically, financially and can still be held responsible by the authorities for anything done, published, portrayed by even your bogus and unauthorized, unchartered individuals or groups utilizing consistently and with a view to deliberately misleading the public, my own personal works, trademarks and concepts without my prior written consent and/or knowledge. Any doubts on that as to the, albeit unfair, responsibility that I contend with are clearly contradicted by the events in the UK in 1991.

By the same token, we certainly understand how you might want to associate yourself with what was "TOPY" and my "Psychick Cross." These are powerful symbols and I appreciate that your group feels a resonance with my dedicated works and my successful communication of some of the ideas they contained whilst "TOPY" continued to function under the guidance of myself and a few close friends.

It is because of this resonance that we felt we should write to you personally to straighten this matter out first rather than sending a letter from some lawyer.

While we simply really can't allow your group to continue using our trademarks, or our intellectual property (i.e., the name "TEMPLE OV PSYCHICK YOUTH") we also have absolutely no interest in trying to shut you down or causing any more interruption than is necessary. We desire what we should have had all along. An absolutely clear lack of connection between us. An end to the deliberate impression you give that you are in some way endorsed by myself. This is quite unacceptable, as well as illegal. We would rather instead that we might come to a friendly agreement in which your group would voluntarily agree to find a different name and symbol

for itself and continue with its independent and separate activities, whatever those may be, without thereby causing further friction, disagreement, infringement of my Trademarks and Copyrights or the possible further jeopardizing of my families security by who knows what actions by a group of people we really don't know. We'd even be happy to help you think of alternative names that wouldn't violate our copyrights as you seem to have a penchant for the fruits of my intellect!

Another matter: I've also heard that you're selling copies of *Thee Gray Book* (or at least an edited version of *Thee Gray Book*). This infringement will really also have to cease for the same reasons that I can't allow unauthorized use of my intellectual property and copyrights or your intrusion into the bona fide publication of my books.

Please understand that I make my living—and feed my family—on the money I make as a writer, musician, lecturer, performer, producer and fine artist. When somebody sells or pirates my works without receiving prior written consent from me; or directly negotiating appropriate terms with me first; and/or paying a license fee, this means that someone is ripping me off, and quite literally taking food from my children's mouths and threatening them with homelessness. And if I don't take steps to prevent the unauthorized use of my work, then the honest people who do pay license and other fees are getting ripped off by the likes of you too. Believe me, it's nothing personal, but I absolutely can't allow this to continue. I must put the best interests, the safety, the security, and the long term needs of my children, and myself first at this stage in my life, which I certainly hope, as obvious admirers of my life and works as evidenced by your continuous exploitation of them, you will appreciate and support.

I hope that you'll see this letter as a reasonably friendly, personal request (under the circumstances) that you immediately cease and desist from any and all use of my properties without your having a proper license or agreement with me. I'm pleased that your group exists, as I believe in personal exploration and am flattered by the influence of my own previous projects, I wish you all the very best of luck; but I can't allow this present illegal infringement situation to continue. If you'd like some time to consider a new name or if there is anything I can do to make this transition easier, please feel free to ask. Otherwise, you may write back to me saying that you've received this letter and that by such and such a date you'll cease and desist using the name "Thee Temple Ov Psychick Youth" and the "Psychick Cross" and that you'll immediately cease distributing copies of the *Gray Book* or any and all other written; graphic; audio; or other works whose copyrights are owned by me. A specific date for the end of this situation would be most valuable.

If you have any questions regarding this letter, please feel free to write to me as soon as possible. I would appreciate it if you also informed any still functioning "access points" of the need for them to also cease and desist all use of both the name "TEMPLE OV PSYCHIC YOUTH"

and any and all obvious derivatives of same, and all use of the "PSYCHICK CROSS" logo in any and all forms. I should appreciate an up to date list of all such "access points" in order that I might politely inform each of them personally of this unfortunate situation that has arisen through your actions.

I should also request that any and all sales of any merchandise, writing, printed matter, propaganda or any other medium that in any way associates your activities with either my personal Registered Trademark "Thee Psychick Cross"; my intellectual Copyright name "Thee Temple Ov Psychick Youth"; Psychic TV, or myself, or my family end forthwith and in perpetuity.

AS I.T. IS...

Date: April 12, 1995
From: Christopher Robin
To: Genesis Breyer P-Orridge
Subject: As it is...

I have just a couple of things to say. I've pulled my 'association' with the still-existing TOPY N.A. The behavior of several TOPY people regarding your situation has become intolerable to me. I can no longer be an ally to such childish and (you're right...) threatening behavior. Making fellow human beings feel threatened in their own environment, afraid to walk down the street for fear of being ridiculed, mocked, what have you... is not something I condone. It is most certainly not a very TOPY-like way. I'm telling you this, not to get your approval, not to get a pat on the back, but simply to let you know that you are correct in your position against TOPY NA on that level.

Now the second part...

Even though I feel you are right, and have every right to know... I simply can't give you the address to the new station. I've thought long and hard about this. The way I received the address was "to sigilizers only." I cannot betray that trust. I could easily give the address to you, knowing it is justifiable. I am not in the position to pass judgment, nor aid in doing so. My decision, right or wrong, is my personal decision. It shouldn't have any other consequences beyond that. If you don't, via another source, have the address by this time, it will be available shortly, I'm sure. Without making itself known to the public, the group will only further its own stagnation. As of last week, there was news of individuals from Great Britain sending in sigils and wanting Eden numbers. I have tried to reason with the current station coordinator. My advice to you... take legal action. It's sloppy, and costly as well. But I see no alternative. If you can prove that the Psychick Cross is yours, and the name TOPY is yours (and I think you can) then you can legally stop anyone from using it. According to the legal theories I've studied, things do not have to be legally registered as a copyrighted item to be "copyrighted." All TOPY NA has are a lot of publications (all old) which can be traced back to you. There is nothing that TOPY NA has that could stand up in court against you. Perhaps the fact that it's a registered church in the state of California could be a problem, I don't know. The new station is not in California though, so it couldn't be protected under the same "registered church" status could it? At any rate, these people will not listen to reason, nor threats. Swift legal action would be the fastest way to resolve this.

I do apologize on behalf of the few sensible people still involved. Many of them are quite in the dark I'm afraid.

**From: Genesis Breyer P-Orridge
To: Christopher Robin
Subject: Re: As it is...**

as you probably know, e was in a fire and accident in la.

e am recovering but my arm is smashed in 8 places, ribs broken, and complications. so, just a quick note to say thank you.

e accept and honor your sense ov fairness.

e will get back to you when e feel a little better.

Date: September 23, 1995
From: Genesis Bryeyer P-Orridge
To: Christopher Robin
Subject: Re: so it seems...

AS IT IS...
You can write directly to me, that way E
will to ensure you get all Broadsheets.

Today is thee 23rd, thee Equinox. Thee official new beginning ov a PROCESS-EON.
Each period begins in Sept.

Coum, TG, PTV, TOPY, TOPI and now
Transmediation.
E am VERY happy to be coumunicating,
and sharing with you. Its a sad thing, thee
illusion coum people chose to carry ov their
"radicalism" or whatever.

Butter each has their own limit E guess.
Most people chose to stop growing, just as
lots stop writing poetry after their teens.

We must not judge, nor hold attachment to
dreams. Dreamless sleep, we are unhappy
with. Dreams, we LiKe.

So, happy special DAY.

NOW thee renewed "WAR" begins, on hypocrisy, culture, stagnation, apathy, and sub-
limation ov desire. Usual stuff, butter isnt
it incredible how few people are REALLY
serious about coumitting their entire L-if-E
to flux, change, and dis-integration.

SO BE IT...

Date: February 5, 1995
From: Christopher Robin
To: Genesis Breyer P-Orridge
Subject: Re: FULL OV ?

I am rather amazed that you took the time
to respond, in such detail, to my short burst
of non-intellect. I am replying to your response, including your original message. It
makes for a long message, and for that I
apologize, however it is the best way for me
to respond to your statements and questions. What follows is my perspective, from
my introduction to TOPY, to the message
"Re: FULL OV SHIT". I hope you will
read it, and understand my position, with
an unbiased mind.

Date: February 3, 1995
From: Genesis Breyer P-Orridge
To: TOPYNADA
Subject: AS IT IS...

Well, E certainly find thee level ov intellectual prowess from TOPYNADA to be
lacking. And E wonder why you feel so
emotional about coumthing that is strictly
obvious, which is that whatever you might
wish to imagine, E do have thee right to
my own intellectual property, and perhaps if anyone could see anything special
couming out of thee NADA group apart
from Codes and byelaws that totally contradict, emasculate and deny what TOPY
was begun for, maybe we wouldn't wish to
protect thee positive contribution that it
originally offered.

TOPYNADA Point well taken. I had no part (nor voice) in making TOPYNA a state recognized religion in California. This was done, as we were told, to protect TOPYNA, and its files, from the government. This was a direct result of your home in London being raided. It was meant to be a safeguard. At the time, I thought that it was a contradictory thing to do. However, if it was the necessary tool to keep our files safe from such a raid (as you suffered) then I was for it. The bylaws were all part of it.

> Genesis Have you stopped to wonder how sad it is that you are all getting bitter over this, angry, verbally violent, even sending death threats to me. Simply because E asked politely at thee beginning for you to simply change thee name, and not use thee cross anymore. Primarily, originally, to protect our children from further persecution for my ideals. Ideals which you have NOT upheld, or understood.

TOPYNADA Of course it is sad... how else should we react? Anyone who has made a death threat to you is simply not thinking clearly. I wouldn't let it worry you. Yes, it is offesive... however, we're all pretty passive. Your life is in no danger from any sigilizer or ally of TOPYNA... that you can be sure of.

The reason for my rage is simple (and I think I speak for those involved with TOPYNA as well). I was given a process in which I could free myself from the Christian programming that had been engrained in my mind since early childhood. A method of realizing and attaining what I wanted in life... imme-

diate, or long term. I was given a group of like minded individuals to correspond with, connect with, and work with. I was given a symbol to focus my energy on/in, to draw on anything and everything, and to represent who I was, and who I was involved with. I was given a number... an individual 'name' as an active sigilizer with this like minded group. Together, we were given a name. Your first letter to TOPYNA 'Without Prejudice,' was the bomb that stirred our anger. The very man who taught us how to free ourselves via music, video, and written word... who was responsible for connecting us with a wonderful group and a magickal symbol to represent our beliefs, suddenly came and said "I'm taking it all back, you can't use the name or the cross anymore, the grey book is mine as well..." Did you think we would just thank you for the fun ride and go back to our normal lives? I can see and completely understand you wanting to protect your children, and yourself. I wouldn't want a hundred different people using my name as artists... who knows what kind of crap someone would put out? Who knows what someone would do, illegally, and claim to be me? Your letter accused TOPYNA of ripping you off and taking food from the mouths of your children. Obviously you never visited a Station or AP here in the States. They are usually run on stamps, sent in with sigils, and extra money from the pockets of coordinators. TOPYNA has never been a financially rewarding... no one has made money that should be yours.

> Genesis You can rage and scream all you want, butter take out my ideas, words, texts, and what do you have.

TOPYNADA We have the ideas and processes, the foundation of TOPY. We never were interested in who wrote what. How would you feel if Austin Osman Spare came back from the grave and told you "you can't use sigil magick anymore... it was my idea!" How about if Tristan Tzara came back from the grave to tell Bill Burroughs that he was suing him for stealing his idea of cut-up?

> Genesis Butter more importantly, would you sacrifice your children, for your colleagues, if thee only evidence you had ov their character was that they insulted and threatened you.

TOPYNADA I'm lost on this one... has TOPYNA or TOPY SOL's only output been that of insults and threats? Hardly!

> Genesis E never asked you to believe in me.

TOPYNADA No, you didn't. It just came with the territory. I watched your video material, listened to your music, read your words... I dare you to put yourself in my place, and listen to "At Stockholm." How was I not to believe in you? You were, to me, a friend that I simply hadn't met yet.

> Genesis It was never a part ov thee project.

TOPYNADA Nor was terminating it after ten years, as you claim... unless you just failed to tell everyone but a chosen few.

> Genesis E am glad you have stopped, though sorry you misunderstood so much ov what E said.

TOPYNADA Well, I guess a man of your stature doesn't need to be 'believed in' by the likes of me and my friends? I never misunderstood you Gen, everything you said was crystal clear in my mind. That's the only reality I know and understand... that of my own.

> Genesis E am writing because E care about coumunicating, about thee ideas, about living a life ov change and challenge, about thee integrity ov what TOPY amongst other things was.

TOPYNADA How can you speak of change, when what you are doing is taking old TOPY texts, and giving them a new name and new symbol (barrowed from The Process Church of the Final Judgment). This is change? This is moving on?

> Genesis E see and hear no evidence ov coumprehension by anyone. Just a group ov people protecting what they did not build, and wanting status, rather than freedom.

TOPYNADA Wrong! True, we may not understand your true motives. But we did build TOPYNA, and the current North American network. We have all the freedom we need as a group, the 'status' was just what we had been known as.

> Genesis E really don't want you angry. E'd like to hope you at least once understood. Try and step back from feeling your holy cow is threatened.

TOPYNADA I probably have far more understanding than anyone else you're likely to talk to about TOPY (excluding Havoc). My anger is quelled. I have no malice towards you.

> Genesis Isn't it sad that E have to initiate, or try and trigger a real TOPY self examination ov thee awful bureaucracy and conservative misstatement that it seems to be.

TOPYNADA Yes. I fully agree. I was not happy with the church status either, but as I mentioned previously... it was done to protect TOPYNA from what happened to you.

> Genesis Why are you all so obsessed with continuing to use my work whilst insulting me, and degrading thee INTENTION ov it when we began.

TOPYNADA The work...your work... stands by itself. It is timeless, and should have no author. Again, I never degraded TOPY... I held it in the highest esteem.

> Genesis E realise E have set myself up for another stream ov easy put downs, and bending ov my phrases, butter E am not doing this, writing, to protect myself.

TOPYNADA No more put downs! I respect your will. Even if is is in opposition to mine.

> Genesis E don't know if we've ever met. If we have, tell me more.

TOPYNADA Nope. We have never 'met'. Without reason, or prior knowledge of PTV nor TOPY, I attended your show here in Tempe, Arizona during the Infinite Beat tour. I spent the entire show watching my friend Melissa dance on the stage (at the time, I didn't know her). I remember you walking off to the right of the stage, and singing (staring dead straight into my eyes) no more than twelve inches from my face. I went home thinking I needed to purchase some of your music... the rest is history.

> Genesis Write constructively, tell me why you need to exploit my ideas and work, whilst simultaneously denying and attacking me.

TOPYNADA No one involved with TOPYNA has ever exploited you. The attacks were purely reactionary.

> Genesis I find it very puzzling.

TOPYNADA I hope the puzzle has been a challenging one.

> Genesis E am by thee way a BROTHER, butter ov my own chosen family, which to date, you are correct you are not a part ov, though, as we used to say in TOPY THEE DOOR'S ALL WAYS OPEN...
Old TOPI Proverb

TOPYNADA Thanks for the invite. I appreciate the thought... however, what's to keep you from pulling the rug out from underneath the Process in ten years? Once is enough for me.

> Genesis E sincerely wish you luck in all you do and bear no malice towards you.

TOPYNADA Nor do I wish you any ills... thanks for taking the time to reply. I never would have expected it. If you have any more questions, please feel free to ask.

the rhinos of wrath are whiter than the horses of destruction.

Date: February 2, 1995
From: Michael E. Paine
To: Genesis Breyer P-Orridge
Subject: COPYRIGHT AND TRADE-MARK INFRINGEMEANT

> Genesis I did receive your email of Jan 11th 95. Apart from the denial implicit in your response in terms of its content. I really feel that it is entirely inappropriate for you to respond ad hoc via this medium to a legal matter of such seriousness.

TOPYNADA By broadcasting to the whole list you invite my response. You have strayed into one of my operational spaces... I can't speak for the others. Being the true gentleman that you are I would appreciate a response... What happened back in '91??? Didn't you become a nomad and dissociate from the Temple??? That is what I perceive. The interview in SECONDS magazine claims that the Temple project ended in 1991. I can see how your involvement ended... but due to the present existence of everyone on this list and not on the list... how can the statement be justified? Or are we just emotional cripples at best? Doomed to hold

on to the past. I have had involvement with the Temple since approx. '89. Why do you try to take back what in the past you have denied having any involvement with? Was it a disinformation campaign??? How can you pass judgment on every individual in the Temple? And how can you have blatant disregard for those whom you have never met personally. I have seen you, I haven't met you, but I have seen you up close. It is in my memory...Chicago??? 90? 91? THEE RAVE GOES ON!!! Is the RAVE an attempt to destroy an organisation of individuals, each developing themselves in their own way, who are part of a structure which you should be proud of having had a part in initiating? Does it give you pleasure to attempt to destroy that which you had a part in creating? Or is thee PROCESS supposed to be our next watering hole. I don't want a part of your PROCESS... your alternative to TOPY. How lame indeed.

Regardless of what happens you can never take away any involvement each separate individual has had with the present entity. The project ended in '91? How can you say that?

> Genesis I must therefore demand that you reply immediately by mail to me with a set of proposals that are realistic and reflect the true legal position which is primarily very simple.

TOPYNADA If this "true legal position is primarily very simple" then why don't you state it right out instead of using legal illease. Why don't you go right out and tell everyone on this list what your true intents are??? Not just directed to Dan and

Max - which wasn't just to the above but to the whole damn list!!! and not secondhandly through interviews in magazines which say the Temple project ended in '91??? I guess my main question is WHY??? because it's your birthright??? because you decide to come to the states and harass???!!! What is the problem? Damnit man!!! I bet you're in it for the fucking money! Well... there is no money here!!! You have really alot of balls. Something must be bothering... hence your unwarranted, blatent, past and present intrusion.

If the time for clear concise communication is NOW! then please respond.

The lines of communication are open and since you have strayed onto the list you may as well respond. If there is anything REAL about you left besides dogma and control, which supposedly you are against, then perhaps you will. If not you will continue to perpetrate falsehoods.

Date: April 13, 1995
From: Christopher Robin
To: Genesis Breyer P-Orridge
Subject: Re: TOPY (fwd)

I'm sure your going to get this, if you haven't already. As I said, it was only a matter of time before they went public. This post is from the new NA station.

---------- Forwarded message ----------

TOPY is alive and well in NA...as others

have pointed out mr. Orridge publically announced his separation from TOPY approximately five years ago, and should no longer be considered a spokesperson for our magickal organization nor is PTV to be considered a TOPY propaganda tool; Psychick Warriors Ov Gaia, and Instagon as well as Alaura [previously known as Mistress Mix in PTV] are magickal/musical allies... our symbol, thee Psychick Cross is in fact an ancient alchemical symbol and has been used by TOPY NA since 1987...

In brief, TOPY is a magickal network which supports individual magick and researches practical applications for its use in a [post] modern world... with particular focus in harnessing sexual energy a la A O Spare...

Date: March 13, 1995
From: Genesis Breyer P-Orridge
To: John Buttolph

E was really glad to receive your package. E All ways enjoy your stuff. Enclosed are a few things in return, all ov which you are free to rifle for anything you wish to reprint, or adjust to your own strategic ends.

E read your little essay. E prefer, as an Individual to reply to all correspondence as a stream ov consciousness. NOT first considering my best interest, or how what E say can be re-used to attack or ridicule me. Just, me, as a friend, replying to a friend, one on one. No thoughts to a pseudo-astorical context, or an over aggrandized sense ov import re-our actions in TIME. we are all ultimately, tiny specks ov image in a mirror ov omnipresent fluidic matter, and it really doesn't matter if I'm wrong or right, where e belong E am right, where E belong...

So, E am readin your red sheeeeet. S'funny, because, Brother Orcen, at Esoterra has been asking me about you. E had only POSITIVE and praising things to say. E told him YOU were an example ov what E personally, subjectively thought TOPY was meant to be, to represent. No qualms, no reservations or qualifications on my part. Just, YOU. E believe in YOU. Still do. E don't need to be liked to KNOW what E like. E think you'll believe me, butter IF you dont, phone him... for what I.T. is worth.

Do E feel SAD? Yes. Not a lot. Butter enough. Let me attempt to explain. And please, remember, E am speaking to YOU. And, you know, really, that was what TOPY was for. E don't recall any ov us endorsing attacking our friends, or losing a sense ov coumpassion. E THOUGHT we were intending to assist and support each other, L-OV-E each other, and protect each other as an extended famille.

Over thee yera's. And E was, let's be honest, heavily coumitted to TOPY from 1980, when E conceived it more precisely. Though with Monte, E discussed it in thee 70's. E have had a stream ov Individuals who espoused a belief in a TOPY way ov L-if-E living pretty much free in my house in Hackney for nearly 10 yeras. No questions asked. Three at a TIME

living in my house in B-Right-On. Who responded by stealing thee anti-Dolphinarium money, using our private credit to their own ends etc etc.

We had TOPY Global meetings at our house. PTV actually donated 80% or more ov their earnings to subsidizing TOPY for 10 yeras, asking for no recoumpense. E suspect that adds up to, LITERALLY, 100,000 pounds ov incoum given away to our belief in thee idea. Almost every yera thee Access points and Stations agreed to, promised to, donate back 23% ov any nett profit they earned via PTV related sales.

NOT ONE OV THEM ACTUALLY EVER HANDED OVER A PENNY!

E designed thee PSYCHICK CROSS in 1979 in Hackney, in preparation for thee next project, thee post-TG project E had decided was necessary next in my life's works, in my belief developmeant. It was FIRST used by myself, and Psychic TV on our coumercial releases. In tandem with those, E wrote thee majority ov, and edited thee rest ov, thee GREY BOOK. An unusual item for a supposed music group. Butter that was thee point. To see where we could go, to make dreams REAL.

It is, however, important to recall, and accept a fact. Thee Psychick Cross was quite deliberately, and appropriately exploited and attached to my artistic and musical creations FIRST, and thee interrelated idealogical projects and strategies, philosophies and experiments that were linked with them.

Most notably TOPY. Just about every PTV release had Psychick Crosses on it. T-Shirts too. etc etc.

In a step unusual for any group, we extended our project into unheard ov arenas. An "interactive" occult exploration. TOPY as E chose to call it.

No one knows, when they begin an art project, where it might lead. Or how it might be absorbed by thee popular culture ov its day. We speculate, we observe, we conclude. Butter E am SURE you recall, and understood, all culture is dispensable, and not sacred, in thee sense ov becouming a dogma, a bureaucracy, a pathetic mirror ov what was its enemy. In one aspect, religion. Bylaws, adherence to a book.

E think thee vibrant, dedicated, and marvelous collaboration that resulted took us all by surprise. Inspired and overwhelmed us with its power and magick.

Butter recall. PTV was still working, still using thee cross as thee trademark ov its coumercial works. Except it became to our tribe MORE than that. It became a symbol ov our attitude, our refusal ov certain types ov control. Our innate trust. Our sexual explorations. Our revitalization ov anarchy and magick. It took us by surprise. It became SACRED in a more real sense. A symbol ov unity ov purpose and clarity, and purity ov intent.

It did NOT represent attacking ones friends. It did not represent incorporation as a non-profit RELIGION. It did not represent thee callous disregard for a family such as my own, who lost everything by representing thee ideal ov TOPY, by refusing to inform on others to ease our burden.

One thing E thought was so sad, and strange, was that you did NOT mention that our house was illegally raided by Scotland Yard. That we braved losing our children too to protect thee nett-work. That to this day, we have chosen NOT to give thee names ov any Individuals involved in thee early days ov TOPY, and as a result lost 2 houses, an archive, a marriage, nearly our children. Why? To protect YOU directly, and implicity, whether you like to believe it or not.

You do not consider that, as E often used to say, its NOT a game. Its a war. that we were thee fall guys for you all. It was NOT easy. It is not easy. We are still living in exile. We still live in fear ov arrest and deportation. We cannot get a regular job. We exist on charity more often than not. Our children are permanently damaged by events. And why, because we believe in what thee cross stands for. Its integrity.

E think a lot ov you forget what happened. E dont think you can imagine how it was. And what does TOPY do. Does it honour us? Protect us. Even write and ask how we are? If we are safe? Say thanks for all you did? NO.

E get DEATH THREATS. E get slanderous post cards. E get told E am in it for thee money! For your information. This is not a time ov clever letters, or smart essays. My children still risk being taken into care. Paula has had a nervous breakdown through thee stress. E expect to be homeless next month because E cannot pay rent on a house. Which means Caresse and Genesse are at risk.

We have NO MONEY. Yet we let people live FREE in our B'ton house until it was repossessed. We have people here now, living free who were homeless.
Do you mention how much we have given for what we believe TOPY was.

NO. Ov course not. Why didn't you mention all this? Does it intrude on people's self-esteem?

You write your essay, butter you assume that hearsay is correct. Let me set thee record straight.

1 E have no attorneys (lawyers) except one who works free to try and get me a record deal. To date he has not.

2 No Lawyers have written to TOPY or PWOG. E challenge them to produce such a letter!

3 E have personally asked PWOG to either cease and desist from using thee Psychick Cross on their COMMERCIAL products. Or say, in small letters on thee back, thanks to GPO for use ov thee cross. Preferably followed by an explanation ov what it represents as an ideal.

4 E wrote to TOPYNADA and said E felt that they were misrepresenting what TOPY had been. They are all bylaws, threats, anger, and OTO dogma. E simply asked that they call themselves coumthing else and not use thee cross.

They responded with death threats and anger.

E then asked more firmly.

All e want is that they do not bastardize, and insult ALL our good work with their self-aggrandizing and hypocritically false pretence to be TOPY.

Carl in Sweden, Petra in Germany, Tom in Denver, and others understand my point.

PWOG are, whether they can face it or not, exploiting thee cross for monetary gain.

TOPYNADA are exploiting it, to legitimize their corrupt and dogmatic farce.

E feel fully justified in trying to protect thee cross from this misuse.

And, sorry if you don't like it. Butter E have thee right. For what its worth. To try and do that. Nobody else has had thee courage to cry wolf over their misuse for private aggrandizement. Well E do.

Not a single Individual in TOPY sent even a letter ov support, or sympathy to myself, or my family when we were singled out for destruction as representatives ov TOPY. Not a single penny was donated by thee

TOPY nett-work. Not a leaflet printed to defend us as Individuals. Butter WOW, you've all found thee TIME and money to attack us, to berate us, to hurt us and to suggest that we have no rights to our own concepts, ideals, or designs.

Thee law has NEVER served me. E too cannot afford it. What kind ov dream are you in. Do you think E sit here with secret money? E have singled out TWO cases ov what E consider hypocrisy and damaging exploitation ov what is thee sacred symbol ov our tribe. E have firmly asked them to cease demeaning that which they have not created, or honored.

E have no lawyer. No money. Butter E believe so strongly in thee cross, that E fight for it anyway.

You can all choose to ignore my efforts, my dedication, my suffering. Its only what E might expect. Butter its sad that its so easy for you to write at length about my attempts to protect our heritage. Yet not mention our sacrifice. Or is it all conveniently separable, and in little boxes that facilitate everyone elses self esteem.

E really love you. Even now. E think you wrote with sincerity. And funnily enough we agree about thee cross. It should be protected. Butter you have to understand, E have ALL WAYS used it as my artistic trademark too. Which is my right.

Asking TWO specific groups to stop trading on thee cross is NOT asking thee whole world to stop using it magickally. E have NOT used thee forces ov Law and Order. E have asked.

Why do YOU think KK Records want to carry on using thee cross on covers ov PWOG? It sells their records. That's thee only reason. Why? Because a LOT ov people think it is a sub-project ov PTV. It is a marketing ploy and legitimization. If you deny that you are working hard at denial.

My latest series ov releases is thee Electric Newspaper. Each is 74 minutes long. Everything on each is free to sample. Even long sections. This series will also be on thee WWW. E am giving away my archive ov sound. E believe in sampling. E continue to believe in it.

Butter E think that you are misreading thee situation. TOPYNADA are liars, and are NOT living what you and E believed TOPY to be. In ANY sense.

Oh, do you know what John... fuck it.

Why should E defend using my own work. Why should E care about all this. Did they care for my children?

Do they DO as much as we do.

E love your work. E think you've been unfair. E think thee way E have been treated stinks. E think there are so many self induced leaps ov credibility in your logics.

Bottom line. E have to try and keep Caresse and Genesse safe.

Why did you take thee easy path and hurt me? Insult me? Make it thee norm to attack and undermine me? So easy. So unfair.

Try living through what happened to us one day. Try surviving with a government and police department trying to destroy you. Try imagining how it feels to see your essay in print, when you are about to lose your kids because you're homeless. Try equating that with thee fact that PWOG are putting $$$ in their pockets as you lose your kids, using your symbol.

Ov course we want thee cross to be in books. Butter IF E have to chose between PWOG or Caresse and Genesse.

Oh fuck you.... you really don't get it do you. E really wish you did no more.

**Date: September 29, 1995
From: Genesis Breyer P-Orridge
To: TOPY
Subject: Without Predudice**

I have registered a Trade Mark in the following details:

1. Trade Mark registered in part A of the Register under no: 1334546 as of the date 06.02.1988 in Class 16 Schedule 4 in the name of Genesis P-Orridge.

2. Trade Mark registered in part A of the Register under no: 1334545 as of the date 06.02.1988 in Class 09 Schedule 4 in the name of Genesis P-Orridge.

3. Trade Mark registered in part A of the Register under no: 1379316 as of the date 23.03.1989 in Class 14 in the name of Genesis P-Orridge.

The Classes are as follows in terms of "products" covered:-
Class 16:- Printed Matter;Newspapers and Periodicals; Books; Journals; Photographs; Posters; Postcards; and all included in Class 16.

Class 09:- Records; Tapes; Compact Discs; Videos; all included in Class 09.

Class 14:- Goods in precious metals or coated therewith (except cutlery, forks and spoons); jewellery; goods in precious stones; all included in Class 14.

As you know, I have been living in the USA under difficult and complicated circumstances. However, I now write to you, after learning of your blatantly illegal activities to insist firmly that you immediately cease and desist from using both my intellectual copyright name "THEE TEMPLE OV PSYCHICK YOUTH" (sic) and my Internationally Registered Trademark commonly known as "THEE PSYCHICK CROSS". Further that you immediately cease and desist manufacturing and distributing pamphlets, books, newsletters, tapes, videos and any and all other material relating to the now defunct project "TOPY" Your "organisation" whilst on one hand distancing itself from me and minmising my founding role in all you espouse, continues quite hypocritically to exploit and trade off my work, writings, concepts, structures, jargon and trademark. If you really feel so antagonistic towards me and my work, and if you are truly convinced that you are gifted and valuable in your own right(s) then surely you would desire to build your own unique group, with it's own radically different name, symbols, terms, texts and so on. It is clear that you are opportunistically milking my works, whilst noisily denying it.

You have NO legal rights to my works, TOPY works, or the use of my intellectual copyright, the title "TOPY" nor to use my Trademark the Psychick Cross. A trademark that I still employ in any and all my public works.

I am sending this letter, to officially, and legally demand that you cease and desist forthwith from all use of my intellectually copyrighted name "THEE TEMPLE OV PSYCHICK YOUTH" from all use of my personal Internationally Registered Trademark "THEE PSYCHICK CROSS" (It is registered in Europe, a process that was expensive and time consuming, and there is reciprocity with the U.S.A.) and all other unauthorised exploitation of my ideas, texts, structures and theories. All of which are copyrighted over a period of 15 years.

As I am SURE you are aware. I continue to use my Trade Mark on my own PSYCHIC TV and related products and projects. Your unsanctioned co-option of my Trade Mark damages my past, present, and future works. I intend to continue using my Trade Mark in all media and it is intolerable and unacceptable for anyone else to capitalise on, profit from, exploit to their own ends, confuse and deceive the public and the market place. I consider this a very serious, and fraudulent, manipulation and exploitation of my Trade Mark, my reputation and my historical body of work. The TRANS-MEDIA FOUNDATION is the only official and legal distributor of my archive in the World.

I must once more insist that you immediately cease and desist from all and any further use and/or exploitation of my Trade Mark. I further demand to receive your assurance on this in writing, within 30 days of the date on this letter. I further request that all and any stock that remains with my Trade Mark on it be withdrawn immediately and destroyed and ALL adverts and catalogues persuant to illegal exploitation of my works and trademarks be withdrawn. I demand full figures on the numbers of products sold exploiting my protected Trade Mark by yourselves.

I intend to pursue this matter legally if an mutually agreed settlement is not reached between us in as short a period of time as is possible practically.

I do believe, personally, that the exploitation of my Trade Mark, by yourselves, was knowingly intended to confuse the public, and to exploit the possibility that I was involved in your project. I therefore also demand a Press Release/Apology that states clearly, and without malice in it's content, that you used my legally protected Trade Mark without my prior knowledge or consent, and that you apologise for any financial and/or creative distress it has caused Genesis P-Orridge.

I have instructed my representatives in England to contact you directly, and personally with a view to resolving this matter as soon as possible, in any manner they may deem appropriate.

I reserve each and all my legal rights, and avenues of action re: this matter.

I have taken legal advice from my Attorneys.

Yours Sincerely,

Genesis Breyer P-Orridge

Photo by Des Hill

FAMILY FORTUNES

by Desmond Hill

Genesis P. Orridge, forty three year old androgyne, has shocked his way from the 60's into the 90's with the motto "when in doubt, be extreme." Arch anarchist prime time prankster, he first gained public notoriety at the infamous *Prostitution* exhibition at London's ICA in 1976, which featured live maggots and a month's cycle of used tampons. He later co-founded Industrial Records (courting further controversy by incorporating a photograph of Auschwitz into the logo, and Psychick TV—wildly attributed as the pioneers of industrial music. These days his tactics may be less notorious, but he remains a committed advocate of individual empowerment through art, magick and ritual. He also remains, of course, a committed protagonist and explorer of disorder.

His wise old head of long grey hair has aged visibly in the last 9 months. Genesis P. Orridge, agent provocateur of the art world is now, as chance would have it, an out-law, exiled in a foreign land, thousands of miles form his earliest moments in Lancashire.

"Don't underestimate the power of play," urges Genesis in his video, *Exile and Exileration*. As a nine year old child he'd spend hours laboriously marking out areas, making clearings and pain-stakingly building things. "And I remember taking great pleasure in the thought that with the first gust of wind or rainstorm, it would be blown away forever."

Years later, at Hull University, things were not quite as he had imagined: "It wasn't like that when I actually got involved. There were all these people deciding if they slept with the gallery owner, would they get an exhibition, and trying to impress their professors by giving them blow-jobs. I thought, *Hang on a minute. Is it really just about sexual favors and cheques and decoration for the people who are already elite and powerful?* It really disappointed me and depressed me a lot. I was initially very disenchanted, then very angry, now I think, *Well, what the Hell.*"

"I believe it's a spiritual quest or a path, like being a bodhisattva or a sadhu; that it's exactly the same basic reason of life. So, if you have a strong belief in anything and you've a strong vision there's no reason that you should starve to death or be destroyed physically because the world will at least recognize your obsession and your preparedness to stand up for it. So that's what I decided to do when I left school: to live by the dream, because the dream would either be true or I was quite happy, if it wasn't true, to just starve and die because I didn't want to be around this world if my conception of what Art and Communication and life was about, was so mistaken. So far I'm still alive. So I tend to feel that at least part of that utopian vision of everything to do with what we call Art was correct." Still alive, but facing a crisis that effects the life and well-being of his family.

On 15th February 1992, 23 members of the Obscene Publications Squad, armed with a search warrant and a video camera, raided Genesis P. Orridge's Brighton home.

They confiscated more than two tonnes of an arts archive including unpublished films by writer William S. Burroughs, experimental films by artist Brion Gysin, films by British director Derek Jarman which had never been shown, videos of the P. Orridge children's birthday parties, every single photographic negative that was in the house, and DAT and U-matic film tapes containing studio master recordings for the next Psychick TV album.

At this time, the most evil, most satanic, most dissident, most anarchic political beings alive, Genesis P. Orridge and daughters Carresse and Genesse, were organizing soup-kitchens in Nepal for Tibetan exiles and the beggars, street children, lepers and urchins of Katmandu.

In February 1992, as part of their *Dispatches* documentary series, Channel Four screened excerpts from a video of 'the first hard evidence' of satanic child abuse. "The video shows the abuse of young adults in what is clearly a ritual context. Sex and blood rituals are taking place beneath a picture of Aleister Crowley. The trappings of black magic are obvious." These claims were backed by the testimony of a cult survivor, and by the accounts of medical and police excerpts. Channel Four's senior commissioning editor for news and current affairs, David Lloyd, was also quoted: "I do not think a single television programme will clinch the whole question of satanic ritual abuse, but after watching this programme, it becomes increasingly difficult for anyone to judge it does not exist." The confession of the key witness was later discovered to be entirely fabricated.

By February 13th 1992 *The Independent on Sunday* had reported that the video which claimed to be "the first hard evidence" of satanic child abuse was made nine years earlier as 'performance art' and featured film director Derek Jarman as visual presenter. He was quoted as saying, "At first I was horrified and then very, very angry that they had so misrepresented scenes from the video. I did not see the video but what *Dispatches* showed from it did not in any way show what they claimed it represented. It was not at all about child abuse or murder. It seemed too much when you had a lady on the telly, blacked out, saying she had killed her child. I mean, doesn't anyone smell a rat?"

By Sunday 1st March 1992, *The Mail on Sunday* had traced the elusive Jennifer. She was named as Louise Errington, mother of two healthy children and one-time born-again Christian. In 1990 Louise had stayed at Ellel Grange, a Christian *healing centre* in Lancaster. She was quoted as saying, "There, the charismatics had an overpowering effect on me. In many ways it was the worst three months of my life... They told me I was possessed by demons because of the sins of my mother and father. They prayed over me in tongues and taught me to face my own guilt."

One day, she said, the spiritual leader, lay preacher Peter Horobin, told her one of his prayer team had a vision. "He said he had seen a mind picture of me standing over a tiny baby, helping a devil priest to wield a knife. We cut into the baby's chest and the blood was collected and we drank it. The baby's body was a sacrifice to Satan."

Until that time, Louise Errington was not aware that she had had this child. "I screamed and pleaded with them to please stop saying it. I had a sort of fit and had to be held down. I fought people off physically, finally I broke down and confessed it was true. I said, '*Yes, I did it. I killed my own little daughter and helped others to kill their babies.*'" The confession of the key witness to the *Dispatches* programme was brought about by the horrific visions of born-again Christians.

The Mail on Sunday had also traced television presenter Andrew Boyd to the fundamentalist Petersfield Fellowship Church, of which he is a prominent member, co-incident to broadcast. Andrew Boyd had just published his latest book *Blasphemous Rumours*. The *Dispatches* programme was constructed directly from his research for the book; research which was collated from the anecdotal evidence of fundamentalists at Ellel Grange.

By 8th March 1992, it became apparent that Channel Four themselves had commissioned the video material for an arts programme concerning the power of language of the televised image. But the video, of which only three copies were said to exist, was not made by Genesis P. Orridge.

On 22nd March 1992, author, researcher and presenter Andrew Boyd declined to inform viewers, and declined to identify the background of the video. This partial, inconclusive research, combined with entirely fabricated testimonies, has ruined people's lives.

In the summer of 1991 Scotland Yard arrested Mr. Sebastian (featured, *The Crack* 1992), a gay man in his late 50's, a tattooist and body piercer by trade. His studio in Earl's Court, licensed to London Council and by the Government, was extensively searched. Scotland Yard took away every photograph taken of people he had tattooed or pierced. He was to be charged on 14 counts of grievous bodily harm against people he had pierced, taken apparently at random from his appointments book. GBH is the charge below manslaughter, and carries up to seven years' imprisonment.

He was tried at the Old Bailey, usually reserved for spies and mass murders, without a public jury. Found guilty on 13 accounts, he received a two year suspended sentence with a large fine, and had to meet his own costs. In summing up the ruling judge, Lord Lane set a legal precedent. He said that it was not illegal to have decorative body piercings, but if at any time these piercings played a part in sexual activities or erotic pleasures, then that was "un-natural sex," sadomasochistic, and now illegal. A piercing, since it makes a hole in the flesh, injuring the skin, could be constructed as grievous bodily harm. To own a whip, leather thongs, a blindfold or mask, handcuffs or any other items which might be used in sado-masochistic practice, was now an illegal act, complete with retrospective sentencing.

Lord Lane then retired, leaving a law by which technically even married, heterosexual people with body piercings could be arrested and imprisoned if it was proven that they had ever had an orgasm. For some people, the act of making love had now become illegal.

The ruling was appealed against as anti-homosexual, and as an *outrageous attack* on what people choose to do with their own bodies. Liberty, the civil rights campaigning group, said that the decision showed, "a level of intolerance which is unacceptable in a democratic society."

In February 1992, on Appeal, Lord Lane, the Lord Chief Justice, rejected that people would not be brought to trial because they had consented to sexual acts in private. He said that individual liberty was not to be confused with license to commit acts society regarded as cruel. These statements were recorded as amendments to this new legal precedent. It now became illegal for one partner to give another a love bite, because in leaving a mark, technically, this becomes an *injury*.

Mr. Sebastian was the voice on the original film commissioned in 1981 by Channel Four, and shown in 1992 as evidence of satanic ritual abuse, a film purposefully made to illustrate how easily people can be misled by sophisticated editing. It was as a consequence of these allegations that Scotland Yard searched the P. Orridges' Brighton home. Their arts archive included experimental films by Brion Gysin, film by British director Derek Jarman which had

never been shown, videos of *Fantasia* and *The Care Bears,* videos of the P. Orridge children's birthday parties, every single photographic negative that was in the house, and DAT and U-matic film tapes containing studio master recordings for the P. Orridges' next Psychick TV album.

For a tense month they monitored the situation at home with phone calls and faxes. Although they have yet to be charged with anything, Scotland Yard could still allege that *someone* in the video was subjected to GBH. The P. Orridges, both of whom have pierced genitalia, could also be prosecuted for possessing the chain and leather thongs used in the video.

Eventually it became apparent that if the P. Orridges returned to England, Scotland Yard would arrest them, hold them for questioning indefinitely, and take custody of their daughters, who would likely be interrogated for evidence of child abuse. Unwilling to put their children through such an experience, said Genesis P. Orridge, the family are now *triggered exiles.* They have relocated to America, staying briefly with original counter-cultural guru and acid propagandist Timothy Leary at his home in Beverly Hills, before settling in Northern California ten months ago.

Leary, himself a previous exile hunted by both the American government and the CIA, recognised the implication of the police raid, deliberately to crush a sense of life and imagination and possibility. He believes that the archive not only documented but symbolised the entire language and power within digitally recorded media. An archive founded on the premise that the video is one arena of an *Informative War*, and collated specifically to analyse how images are controlled and used to indoctrinate.

On the night of the rioting in Los Angeles, 3,000 fires were lit; thick columns of smoke rose out of the city. On the television news channels, the police kept beating Rodney King. An exasperated George Bush kept crying, "If only you could see through my eyes." Genesis P. Orridge was at Timothy Leary's home watching television. "I began to notice that all the images were of people with VCRs and televisions. Almost constantly you would see people stealing VCRs, and I realized that it was because they knew that that is where the power is. A video tape is what triggered the riot, and there in the media, that's where the disinformation is being given. That's where the battle is taking place," reflected Genesis.

In Britain in 1993, where ownership of one's own skin becomes a question of seven years imprisonment, where the police seize an arts archive, where freedom of association, gathering and sexual expression are legislated against—then, perhaps we can learn from the P. Orridges' story that truth is not something we see on the television screens. We have only to look elsewhere.

"Re-empower yourselves. Repossess your own space. That's all there is to do. And believe me, it causes great mischief in those silent corridors of power."

S/HE IS HER/E
3/23/03

This is the final war, a jigsaw
A war to re-possess your SELF.
There is NO gender anymore
Only P-Androgeny is divine.
Sexuality is a force of nature that cannot be contained.

Get up.

Stand together in perfecting union,
Join and love equally the man and the woman
separated at b-earth inside you,
Their first cries for justice...PANDROGENY!
Re-united as one
Identity is your only possession,
As a being possessed
Re-possess your SELF,
Be possessed by YOUR self,
Any SELF, every SELF you ever dreamed of,
Every SELF you were ever afraid of. GET UP!
Stop this war of limitations,
STOP IT!
Now YOU own yourself.
Your own YOU own.
Now it's YOU.
Stop being possessed by characters written by others.
Change your ID card, cut it into the shape of a HEART.
Be heart felt.
Feel your heart,
Your heart is your art.
Re build your SELF from the
FOUND UP!
Identity is theft.

(IDENTITY IS THEFT.)

NOTHING SHORT OF A TOTAL GENDER

These puppeteers of the NEW WAY ON,
Download slave software into your brain

Even as that wriggling, cocky tyke breaches the cellular defenses,
Its resources stretched taught,
Thinner than a condom on a monstrously seductive,
Destructive cock.
POP! POW! Snap! Suck!
Snake of Eden rigid with victory
Jissom of control victorious
The arrows of sex penetrate egg central and,
spiraling downwards, downs its load,
The double bluff,
Double helix story of those chosen to come before.
Chosen, without choice,
Not you. KNOT YOU!
Knot this AND, this DNA,
This STRAND, stran-dead,
STRANDED
Strand-DEAD on arrival,
Slapped into shape by your DELIVERERS.
A pre-recorded software,
Worn down through ages with one purpose,
To serve the rich, service their itch,
Supply each demand.
Obey each command.

(CHANGE THE WAY TO PERCEIVE AND CHANGE ALL MEMORY)

Struck dumb by its ELEGANCE says CRICK,
Elementary says Watson.
The double helix leaps from lab to life,
With YOU as the lab rat!
Whose elegance?
Whose elegance anyway?
Two spines, once twins, that go their separate ways after 49 days,
Yet... remain inseparably linked
The edit points, invisible.

AND/DNA there-in lies the problem and the lies begin.

In the beginning ALL were perfect. The first man was the first woman.

The first woman was the first man.
UNTIL the whispering began…
AND/DNA the first man became the first man
The first woman became the first woman
AND/DNA then all HELL let loose
AND/DNA we've been living (t)here ever SIN-cerely
Know matter HOW sin-cerely…

(POSSESSION IS THE GREATER PART OF VALOUR)

You are vital.
You are vigorous. Get up.
Stop Hiding.

We are ultra–genetic terrorists.
One man is another man or woman.
EVERY MAN AND WOMAN IS A MAN AND WOMAN
There is a time and place for everything indecent.
Redesign yourself.
YOUR SELF.
End your social and sexual misery, taste the
sweet electricity of PANDROGENY!

"This time around you can be anybody"

Put away your toys and focus.
WE ARE BUT ONE BITCH!
We declare war against all binary systems.

We support SELF-determination and liberation.
Total freedom for all possible and impossible identities and sexualities.

DESTROY!

Destroy Gender.
Destroy the control of DNA and the expected.

Do you understand?
Here's the key.

You were in your mother's womb for forty-nine days an androgyne.
Who chose your gender? GOD?

Society? Family?
Only by YOU ending this separation, returning to
that first pure state can real freedom begin.
When all are but one sex, one species.
This is not about becoming an Other,
This is about returning to a state of perfect union.

Masturbation is the highest form of magick
SO tap into the psychic network.

There is no free speech, ONLY an illusion of freedom.
Freedom of delusion …

Perhaps GOD was breathless, allergic to cosmic dust.
Despite its three billion years HEAD start on us at
this PERSON building, this character building.
One KEY point is oft forgot. AND/DNA alone, on
its OWN does NOTHING!!
NOTHING!
NOTHING!
NO-THING!

It can't make eyes brown or green,
or brains,
or any other electrically charged "muscle" bulge!
It can't sit up, or apply make-up,
Or keep itself clean,
Not even adjust a wig.
PROTEINS do all that.

CREATIVITY is your anti-gender protein.
Stripped of who YOU are, stripped of the creativity
that IS character DNA/AND is helpless, speechless,
dead on arrival again!

WITHOUT THE SCENE FORGET THE GENE

Photo by Lady Jaye Breyer P-Orridge

Society has always been an enemy of the desire to create,
Of all possible creativity.
What am I saying to you?
Nature began as a deliberately chaotic force FOR change.
Constant change.
Evolution, evolving, unfolding.
All those redundant species wither.
Those embracing novelty leapfrog them to dominance…
Maybe with a little inter-species cross (and loving) fertilization along the way.

Creativity is the most POWER-full energy in the Universe.
Lady Jaye and Genesis Breyer P-Orridge, 2003

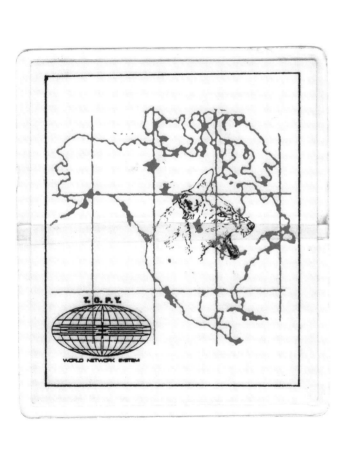

Dear Genesis,

I feel I should inform you of considerable danger you are putting yourself and your family in by getting more and more mixed up in Satanism and putting bad spirits into your music. YOU are corrupting and misleading more and more young and beautiful people who have done you or any of your friends no harm whatsoever.

The glory of God is waiting for you and your wife and children through prayer. You have many concerned friends who are praying for you and are heart-broken at seeing you being misled and misleading so many.

Please believe me. I wrote this with the love of Jesus, he loves you and is trying to reach you and save you for his kingdom, the everlasting kingdom.

A Caring, Concerned, Christian.

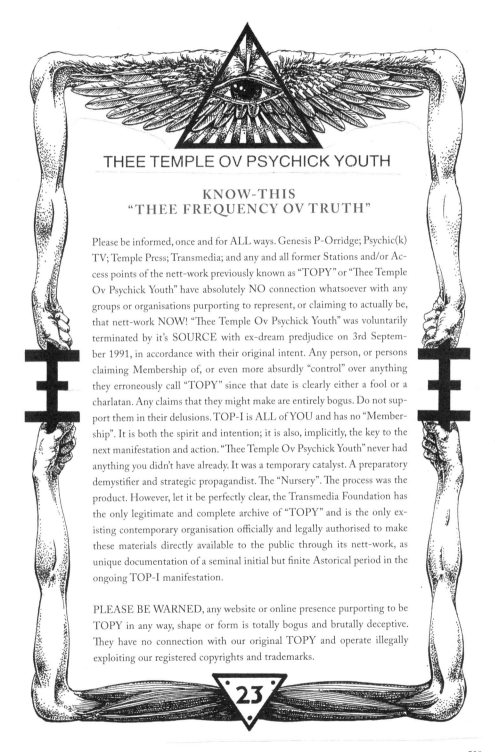

THEE TEMPLE OV PSYCHICK YOUTH

KNOW-THIS
"THEE FREQUENCY OV TRUTH"

Please be informed, once and for ALL ways. Genesis P-Orridge; Psychic(k) TV; Temple Press; Transmedia; and any and all former Stations and/or Access points of the nett-work previously known as "TOPY" or "Thee Temple Ov Psychick Youth" have absolutely NO connection whatsoever with any groups or organisations purporting to represent, or claiming to actually be, that nett-work NOW! "Thee Temple Ov Psychick Youth" was voluntarily terminated by it's SOURCE with ex-dream predjudice on 3rd September 1991, in accordance with their original intent. Any person, or persons claiming Membership of, or even more absurdly "control" over anything they erroneously call "TOPY" since that date is clearly either a fool or a charlatan. Any claims that they might make are entirely bogus. Do not support them in their delusions. TOP-I is ALL of YOU and has no "Membership". It is both the spirit and intention; it is also, implicitly, the key to the next manifestation and action. "Thee Temple Ov Psychick Youth" never had anything you didn't have already. It was a temporary catalyst. A preparatory demystifier and strategic propagandist. The "Nursery". The process was the product. However, let it be perfectly clear, the Transmedia Foundation has the only legitimate and complete archive of "TOPY" and is the only existing contemporary organisation officially and legally authorised to make these materials directly available to the public through its nett-work, as unique documentation of a seminal initial but finite Astorical period in the ongoing TOP-I manifestation.

PLEASE BE WARNED, any website or online presence purporting to be TOPY in any way, shape or form is totally bogus and brutally deceptive. They have no connection with our original TOPY and operate illegally exploiting our registered copyrights and trademarks.

23

THEE PSYCHICK VIDEOS - Credits

Thee Moving Images ov Genesis Breyer P-Orridge and
Thee Third Mind ov Thee Temple ov Psychick Youth

1   **Terminus (11:43)**
Directed by Peter Christopherson and Psychick Television
Music by Psychic TV

2   **Moonchild (04:54)**
Directed by Genesis Breyer P-Orridge
Music by Genesis Breyer P-Orridge

3   **An Introduction to
Thee Temple ov Psychick Youth (10:15)**
Directed by TOPY and Psychick Television
Music by Psychic TV

4   **Psycollection 23 (11:43)**
Images by Kalis 37 & 123, Edens 123, 140 & 162
Music by White Stains and Psychic TV

5   **Psychick TV (00:44)**
Directed by Psychick Television
Music by Psychic TV

6   **Scared to Live (09:13)**
Directed by Genesis Breyer P-Orridge for *Sordide Sentimental*
Music by Genesis Breyer P-Orridge

7   **Intermission (00:41)**
Directed by Genesis Breyer P-Orridge
Music by Genesis Breyer P-Orridge

8   **Papal Broken-Dance (06:25)**
Directed by Marie Losier
Music by PTV3

9   Unclean (09:40)
     Directed by Cerith Wyn Evans
     Edited by Genesis Breyer P-Orridge
     Music by Psychic TV

10   Pandrogeny Manifesto, 2005
     Prayers for Sacred Hearts and Breaking Sex (10:53)
     Breyer P-Orridge

11   Trans-formation (04:00)
     Hazel Hill
     Music by Psychic TV

12   New York Story (14:32)
     Directed by Nicolas Jenkins & Lady Jaye and Genesis Breyer P-Orridge
     Music by PTV3

13   A Message From
     Thee Temple ov Psychick Youth, 1983 (04:50)   541
     Directed by Psychic Television (Genesis Breyer P-Orridge/Peter Christopherson)
     Voice: Mr. Sebastian (Alan Oversby)
     Body: Derek Jarman

www.feralhouse.com